John Alexander McClung, Henry Waller

Sketches of Western Adventure

John Alexander McClung, Henry Waller

Sketches of Western Adventure

ISBN/EAN: 9783337340742

Printed in Europe, USA, Canada, Australia, Japan

Cover: Foto ©Thomas Meinert / pixelio.de

More available books at **www.hansebooks.com**

SKETCHES

OF

WESTERN ADVENTURE:

CONTAINING AN

ACCOUNT OF THE MOST INTERESTING INCIDENTS
CONNECTED WITH THE SETTLEMENT OF
THE WEST, FROM 1755 TO 1794;
WITH AN APPENDIX.

BY JOHN A. M'CLUNG.

—ALSO—

ADDITIONAL SKETCHES OF ADVENTURE,

COMPILED BY THE PUBLISHERS,

—AND—

A BIOGRAPHY OF JOHN A. M'CLUNG,

BY HENRY WALLER.

COVINGTON, KY.:
PUBLISHED BY RICHARD H. COLLINS & CO.
1872.

ILLUSTRATIONS.

Portrait of Rev. John A. M'Clung, D.D..............Frontispiece.
Boone and Findley's First View of Kentucky......... Page 46
Capture of Boone and Callaway's Daughters............... " 53
Patterson's Escape from the Battle of the Blue Licks... " 78
Simon Kenton saving the Life of Daniel Boone......... " 86
John Slover hiding in the Grass from Indians........... " 147
A Bear assists Downing to Escape from an Indian...... " 189
Mrs. Merril's Defense against a Midnight Attack........ " 197
Messhawa rescues two Boys from Chickatommo......... " 226
Indian Woman revealing the Conspiracy of Pontiac...... " 328
Fearful Leap of Major Samuel McColloch................ " 368

ELECTROTYPED AT THE
FRANKLIN TYPE FOUNDRY,
CINCINNATI.

Entered according to Act of Congress, in the year 1872, by
RICHARD H. COLLINS & CO.,
In the Office of the Librarian of Congress, at Washington, D. C.

PREFACE.

IN these "latter days," when a rage for book making pervades all ages, sexes, and conditions, it is scarcely necessary to offer the usual hackneyed apology, for what is modestly called "a trespass upon the patience of the public!" Should the book prove entertaining, and in some degree useful, no apology will be necessary—if otherwise, none will be received. I shall content myself with referring distinctly to the sources from which the materials for this work have been derived, in order to give an opportunity of ascertaining its authenticity.

For the correctness with which the adventures of BOONE, SMITH, and JOHNSTON are detailed, I refer the reader to the printed narratives of each of those gentlemen. In the life of Boone are many particulars relating to the siege of Bryant's Station and the battle of the Blue Licks which are not to be found in Boone's narrative. For some of these I am indebted to Mr. Marshall; but most of them have been taken from a series of "Notes," which appeared, about 1830, in the Kentucky *Gazette*, and which were carefully taken down from the verbal communications of individuals who were actively engaged in those scenes.

For the striking incidents attending the expedition of CRAWFORD, I am indebted to the printed narrative of KNIGHT and SLOVER, published immediately after their return to Virginia, when the affair was fresh in the recollection of hundreds, and any misstatement would instantly have been corrected. KENTON'S adventures are taken from a manuscript account dictated by the pioneer himself, and now in the possession of Mr. John D. Taylor, of Washington, Ky. The adventures of JOHONNET are from a printed account by himself, which appeared in 1791, immediately after the defeat of St. Clair; and those of KENNAN, from his own account—which the author, in common with many others, has heard repeatedly from his own lips. For the rest I refer the reader generally to Metcalf's collection, Mr. Withers' "Border Wars," and the "Notes on Kentucky," already mentioned.

A small portion of the minor details have been gathered from personal conversation with the individuals concerned. I might have given a host of anecdotes, partaking strongly of the marvelous, and some of them really worthy of being inserted, could I have been satisfied of their *truth!* But I have chosen to confine myself to those given upon unquestionable authority; and can conscientiously affirm, that I have admitted nothing which I myself, at the time, did not believe to be true.

J. A. McC.

PUBLISHERS' PREFACE TO THE EDITION OF 1872.

The foregoing is the material portion of the Author's Preface to the *original* edition of these "Sketches of Western Adventure"—first published in 1832, by our father, Judge LEWIS COLLINS, then editor of the Maysville (Ky.) *Eagle;* at whose instance the Sketches were written by the most gifted friend of his boyhood. Daniel Boone had been a resident of Maysville only a few years before Mr. C. settled there, and his relatives still lived there. Simon Kenton, William Kennan, James Ward, Charles Ward, Maj. Hugh McGary, Thomas Marshall, and a few other heroes of the within "Adventures," were acquaintances or personal friends of both the Author and the Publisher—some of them as early as 1806-13. They had every facility that existed, at that day, to verify, and were thoroughly assured of, the accuracy of these sketches.

Inquiries in the neighborhood where the brothers lived, developed that it was Andrew, and not Adam Poe, who had the terrible adventure with Big Foot. We have changed the name accordingly. Recent examination of documents and correspondence of which the Author had no knowledge, has satisfied the present Publishers of several slight inaccuracies, and of one error in criticism of public conduct; and these have been corrected. The work is more than ever deserving the rank it took in 1832 as authentic history. Many editions, and many thousand copies, were subsequently published, but none since 1860-1.

The subjoined biographical sketch of the Author, Rev. JOHN A. McCLUNG, D.D., is from the pen of his life-long friend, HENRY WALLER, Esq., one of the ablest members of the Chicago bar for seventeen years past, and, for nearly twenty years prior, of the Maysville bar, an honored representative of Mason county in the Kentucky Legislature, a president of the Maysville and Lexington Railroad, etc. It is a beautiful, rich, and thrilling tribute—as just as it is elegant—to one of the noblest and most gifted of Kentuckians—who was, in succession, minister, author, lawyer, statesman, and again minister of the Gospel; a model in them all, and always the highest type of a Christian gentleman.

The "Additional Sketches," beginning with page 335, we have compiled from the most authentic sources. They are of the same thrilling character as those which gave the work a standard reputation forty years ago.

RICHARD H. COLLINS,
VAL. P. COLLINS.

Covington, Ky., January 1, 1872.

BIOGRAPHY OF THE AUTHOR.

JOHN ALEXANDER McCLUNG was born near the town of Washington, in the county of Mason, State of Kentucky, on the 25th day of September, 1804. His father, Judge William McClung, a native of Virginia, of Scotch extraction, was distinguished in the early history of his adopted State for his legal ability and judicial purity and firmness. On the 25th of May, 1793, he had married Miss Susan Marshall, a daughter of Col. Thomas Marshall, and sister of Chief Justice Marshall, of Virginia. She was a lady of rare intellectual powers, brilliancy of conversation, sweetness of disposition and elevated piety.

Judge McClung died when John was a little boy, and he was thus left to the care and training of a gifted and devoted mother. During their lives they were rarely separated; and for many years and to the close of her life she resided in the family of her son, who was most tenderly attached to her. She reached the great age of 84 years, and died in Maysville, Ky., on the 5th of November, 1858.

In early boyhood, John exhibited unusual eagerness for knowledge and a passionate fondness for books. He not only acquired easily and rapidly, but digested and retained what he read to a remarkable extent. So soon as he was sufficiently advanced, his mother sent him to the celebrated Academy at Buck Pond, in Woodford County, Ky., under the supervision of his uncle, Dr. Louis Marshall. There he had the advantage of being instructed by Mr. William R. Thompson, a Scotch gentleman of the highest attainments in classical learning, who was not only a most critical scholar, of pure and pious character, but a rigid disciplinarian, with a rare faculty of imparting his knowledge, and of winning the attachment of his pupils. The great mind of Dr. Marshall produced, also, a powerful impression upon the students, by opening up wide fields of knowledge, acquainting them with new modes of analysis and thought, and stimulating to a generous emulation. And there was a larger number of highly-gifted and ambitious youths in the Academy, at that period, than at any other similar institution in the West, as has been abundantly shown by their distinguished records in after life.

It was in the midst of such influences, that young McClung may be said to have commenced his career as a student. He was retiring in his nature, quiet, unobtrusive, meditative in his habits, and select in his companionships; and noted, even at that early day, for his long, solitary walks. His application to his studies was close and indefatigable; and he soon was regarded as one of the most thorough and accurate scholars in that bright circle of young intellects.

In the spring of 1820, a revival of religion occurred at the Pisgah Presbyterian meeting-house, which brought within its influence some of the most promising boys in the Academy—young McClung in the number. Shortly after, a malignant fever prevailed amongst the students, resulting fatally in many cases. He suffered a severe attack, but after a long, hard struggle, his strong constitution triumphed, and he was partially restored to health. But he never recovered from the fearful effects of heavy doses of calomel which were administered to him, according to the medical practice of that day. Thus, when he left the school, his mind was already richly furnished for one so young, his constitution was permanently impaired, and he had dedicated his life to his Savior.

In his 18th year, he was enrolled as a student in the Theological Seminary at Princeton. His application to his studies was so intense, that his frail health yielded to the strain, and he was forced to return to Kentucky in 1824. There, as his health revived, he continued his Theological studies.

He was married, on the 25th of November, 1825, to Miss Eliza Johnston, of Washington, Ky., a daughter of Dr. John Johnston, formerly of Connecticut, and a sister of Hon. Josiah Stoddard Johnston, afterward Senator from Louisiana, and of Gen. Albert Sidney Johnston. She was one of the gentlest, purest, most unselfish of women, refined and elevated by a deep and fervent piety.

In 1828, he was licensed by the Ebenezer Presbytery to preach the Gospel. At this period of his life his reputation for scholarship was very high. His reading, independent of his Theological studies, had been very extensive in all the great departments of classical and modern thought. He was a critical scholar in Latin, Greek, and Hebrew, and could quote largely and with fluency from the originals of the leading authors. So it was in history, philosophy, poetry, and belles-lettres generally. The most gifted and eloquent of all his fellow-students stated, in conversation, years afterward, that McClung was superior to all whom he had ever known, in the exactness and scope of his studies, and the clearness and power with which he grasped and held all that he read; that every page was, as it were, *printed on his brain*, as he could not only state substantially the contents of a book, but quote the language by page and line.

The first efforts of the young preacher produced a great sensation in Kentucky. His thought was original, his diction ornate, his manner dignified and impressive; he was bold, logical, eloquent, enthusiastic, and promised soon to rank with the most brilliant and powerful orators of the pulpit. During the brief period of two or three years, he preached in various sections of the State, and crowded assemblies greeted him wherever he went. But on the very threshold of this opening future of high promise and wide usefulness, in the midst of popular commendations and rapidly-rising reputation, he paused; his faith wavered; the eloquent lips were silent. His convictions of the truth of Scripture had become disturbed, and he was too conscientious to preach what he doubted in his heart. He promptly stated his condition to Presbytery, and asked to be relieved. In the discussion which ensued, a motion was made to go to the extent of expulsion. The Rev. John Todd, a noble and venerable soldier of the cross, rose and said: "Brethren, I hope no such action will be taken. Brother McClung is honest; he is a seeker after truth, but under a cloud; give him time; relieve him as he asks; do nothing more. The light will again dawn upon him, and *he will surely return*." Thus it was settled.

This was in 1831. In 1832, at the instance of his life-long friend, Lewis Collins, Esq., editor of the Maysville Eagle, he wrote the "*Sketches of Western Adventure.*" They were published in book-form by Mr. Collins, became very popular, and passed through many editions. These sketches were dashed off rapidly, but are vivid, graphic, and truthful delineations of wild pioneer life, and the fierce struggles of border war. They are faithful pictures of the primeval forests of the West, of the savage chiefs and tribes that roamed them, and of the heroic, indomitable adventurers who conquered both.

In 1830, through the celebrated publishing house of Carey & Lea, Philadelphia, he had published a work of fiction, entitled "Camden"—a tale of the South during the revolutionary period—of singular interest and power, in which he gave a description of the battle of Camden that is a very master-piece of military narration.

He had, indeed, a passionate admiration of military exploits, and was gifted in comprehending and accurately describing them. He was not satisfied, as men ordinarily are, with a general conception of a battle. He looked closely into details; he studied the topography of the field of operations, until he became familiar with all its military features; he examined into the numbers, material, and condition of the opposing forces; the qualifications of leaders and subalterns; the strategy and maneuvers preceding and during the battle; the positions of the various corps, divisions, and regiments, and the particular part in the struggle performed by each; the swaying tides of the fight, the advance and retreat, the turning point, the decisive charge, and all the causes conspiring to the grand result. He gathered these details from all sources accessible—history, biography, official reports of commanding and inferior officers, and contemporary correspondence—and, after thorough collation and scrutiny of these, he formed his own conclusions as to the contest and its consequences.

It was after this fashion he had studied history, ancient and modern, civil as well as military, in all its amplitude. Upon such vast acquisitions he had brought to bear his rare powers of generalization, and so traced causes and results in their continuous flow from the earliest to the latest periods, and so arranged and connected the great facts of history, that the origin, migration, and intermingling of races, the rise, progress, and decay of nations, with their deep teachings of philosophy, lay in his memory in one connected and consistent outline.

Shortly after retiring from the ministry, he determined to undertake the study of the law. At the May term, 1835, he was admitted to the bar of the Mason Circuit Court, and immediately entered upon the practice. He had formed a partnership with Harrison Taylor, Esq., a gentleman of legal ability and great worth, who was associated with him so long as he practiced law, and who has continued a prosperous professional career to the present time, besides being for four years Speaker of the House of Representatives of Kentucky, and filling other offices of high honor in the State. On the day of his admission, Mr. McClung argued, before the Court, a question involving the construction of a statute and a difficult point in pleading. His argument was brief, clear, and cogent; and although the subject had been considered very doubtful, it was felt, when he concluded, that a demonstration had been made. The decision was promptly rendered in his favor. From that time he took position in the front rank of his profession, and, during a practice of fifteen years duration, was regarded as one of the leading lawyers and ablest advocates in the State.

As a speaker before courts and juries, he was never monotonous or tedious, rarely elaborate, always earnest and effective. There was nothing desultory in his efforts. His statement, in opening, was concise, and the order and logic of his argument wonderfully lucid. In cases in which he had not the conviction that his client was in the right, McClung was rarely up to the standard of his own powers. The consciousness of advocating a cause unjust, seemed to sap his strength, and blunt the edge of his intellect. He was not a master in the tricks or chicanery of the profession; nor could he tolerate insincerity, sophistry, or subterfuge. He was a cautious, conscientious counselor, frank always in his opinions given to clients, and never advising litigation unless based on a just claim. This course had the effect of generally placing him in the advocacy of the right. And so clear and sharply-defined was his character for integrity and truth, so deep in the popular heart was the conviction of his unswerving fidelity to principle, that he won, nay, he commanded as a tribute, the confidence alike of clients, juries, and judges. Hence, when he appeared in a cause which he believed to be just, and threw himself into it with all the earnestness of his convictions, the weight of his character and the full power of his massive logic, warmed and flashing with the fires of his eloquence, he was well-nigh irresistible, and success almost assured.

He was not ambitious in the ordinary sense, and cared nothing for place or power. Practically, he ignored all the arts by which men, who seek preferment, wield the populace to their purposes and profit. He never descended to the low plane on which schemers and demagogues plot and struggle, nor did he attempt to influence men by motives indirect, secret, or sinister. But he took a lively interest frequently both in Federal and State politics, and exercised, for many years, a wide political influence in the State in favor of conservative principles. Especially, in the heated contests succeeding the election of Mr. Van Buren and the financial collapse of 1837, he took an active part, and frequently and with great effect addressed large gatherings of the people. At the solicitation of many friends, he consented and was elected to represent his native county in 1837, and took his seat in the Legislature in the winter of that year.

South Carolina had conceived a sectional scheme, by which she proposed to run a railroad from Charleston, through the States of North Carolina and Tennessee, to Louisville, in Kentucky, and at the same time and in conjunction therewith to establish a mammoth bank, with its head-office in Charleston, and branches in the other States. It was brought forward in the Kentucky Legislature, at the session of 1837, and defeated, Mr. McClung opposing it. He was re-elected, and took his seat at the session of 1838. Great efforts had been made in the canvass of that year to secure for the project able friends in the Legislature, and every possible appeal directed to Southern sympathies and pride, as well as to sectional interests and State aggrandizement. The success was very encouraging, and, upon the assembling of the Legislature, it was believed by its friends that the charter for road and bank would surely pass. Under far more favorable auspices than in 1837, its passage was formidably urged by a body of able, zealous, and eloquent men, with the distinguished Commissioner, Col. Memminger, of South Carolina, as its chief advocate. The public interest had become intense, influential men had congregated from all quarters of the country, and the capital was filled with the intellect and fashion and beauty of the State. Every appliance had been enlisted and used to insure a triumph. The debate had progressed for several days; the friends of the measure were already flushed with the anticipations of victory; the opposition was firm, stern, and uncompromising. It was at this point that Mr. McClung, with erect and manly form, took the floor.

In opening, he alluded to the advantages which the friends of the bill contended would result, and said:

"At a first glance they are imposing. The grandeur of the object intended to be accomplished—the total revolution in the trade, commerce, and political associations of Kentucky, which would result from its completion—strikes the mind of the statesman with an emotion bordering on awe, and for a time deprives him of the power of examining the subject with that calm scrutiny which a project so novel and vast imperiously demands of a

Kentucky statesman. But this scrutiny, Mr. Chairman, it is our duty to give. Let the romantic dreamer of the closet unbridle his fancy, if he please, and overlooking all obstacles suggested by reason and experience, let him career at will among the clouds, sunbeams, and golden vapors of romance and fiction—ours is a more homely and more severe duty."

He then took up, in their order, the four positions on which the friends of the measure rested its claims, compared them with the provisions of the bill, and examined the whole subject in a searching and powerful analysis. He showed himself master of the great questions of banking, commerce, and political economy, and exposed the fallacy of the assumption that the bank was needed or fitted to stimulate and regulate commerce, or to correct and lower the exchanges, or that it could build the road, or that the road could be built without heavy taxation. In commenting upon the claim of Carolina to control the operations of the vast scheme, with lofty and swelling form and flashing eyes, he exclaimed:

"Sir, the money-power of a nation is the crown and scepter of sovereignty. It is the eagle-plume in the cap, the brightest jewel of the diadem. Strike it out, yield it into the hands of a foreign government, and the sovereignty of that nation is gone. The same tremendous power which the mother bank of the United States possessed over the branches established in the States, this bill now proposes to give, not to the Union of all the States, not to Congress, where we are represented and have a voice potential and proportioned to our political strength, but to a junto of nullifiers in the city of Charleston. Sir, if it was with reluctance that Kentucky yielded this power to a bank controlled by the General Government, of which she is a part and where her voice is heard, how much more reluctantly should she yield her neck to the yoke of haughty Carolina, in whose councils she has no voice, whose principles are at war with ours, whose designs are treasonable to this fair and noble Union, who is fettered to the chariot-wheels of John C. Calhoun, wheeling as he wheels, and obeying his every nod, beck, and signal. Strike out that section, sir, so degrading to Kentucky, or war to the knife is the cry of its opponents. But, sir, they do not choose to have it stricken out. Money-power, commercial sovereignty, is what that haughty State wants, and she had rather lose her bank than lose that section that places the bit in our mouths and the reins in her hands. I have myself explained to her Commissioner how hateful that section was to our feelings, how revolting to our pride; and have told him that the bank might pass, if it was stricken out. But no! *aut Cæsar, aut nihil!* She must queen it over four States, or she does not want the bank. She herself is too proud to submit to a United States bank. The power is too great. But she is perfectly willing to wield that power herself with which she is afraid to trust the General Government. She wants a Sub-treasury at New York!

but a Southern confederated bank at Charleston, embracing four States, with the Charleston junto holding the reins, curbing the four horses in her chariot, and holding them to the track as suits her purposes. What are those purposes, sir? Do they bode peace to the Union, harmony to this beautiful confederacy of sister States? Has she abandoned her wild dream of nullification and dismemberment? Oh, yes, says her Commissioner; she has abandoned all those wild visions; she loves this Union; she has no dark designs of dismemberment. She does not wish, by her commercial bank, to league together four States against a National Bank and a National Union, and to bind them to her chariot-wheels by fetters of silver, against the coming trouble which she is daily fomenting on the floor of Congress, and daily striving to accelerate by the harsh and inflammatory course of her representatives in Congress! There is no design, sir—none in the world! Then, gentlemen, strike out that section! 'Out with that damned spot,' which puts a yoke upon the neck of Kentucky, and the reins in the hands of South Carolina. Sir, we are proud of our native State. She stands upon a level with any other State. She is true to this Union, to the last of her steel and the last of her breath. She has proved it, sir, in times of blood and danger. Where is the battle-field within her reach where her war-cry has not been heard, and where her rifles have not sounded? Upon the land and upon the water, upon the beechen flats of the Thames, and the cypress savannahs of the Mississippi, her sons have offered their breasts to the foe, and poured out their hearts' blood as freely as the flask gives its wine to the revel. When the blue waters of Erie blushed red with the life-current of our seamen, Kentucky was there. When the cypress plains of New Orleans pealed to the earthquake shout of victory, Kentucky was there."

Discomfiture and dismay in the enemy's ranks succeeded the flush and hope of triumph, as position after position was carried. Unpausing and still onward, with the precision of a serried host and the measured tread of massed battalions in column of attack, his great argument moved steadily and surely upon the remaining strongholds. The charge was irresistible. A gallant effort was made to rally the shattered forces, and a splendid passage of arms between Memminger and Thomas F. Marshall formally closed the conflict; but all was unavailing. The blow delivered by McClung was mortal; there was no recovery. The power of the South was broken; the scheme was crushed, and Kentucky safe.

The impression of this noble effort throughout the State was very great; and had he been ambitious, he could easily have reached high honors from a grateful and admiring people. But he declined all solicitations, and never afterward returned to public life. It was entirely unsuited to his habits, to his tastes, and to the inclinations and temper of his mind. Besides, his health was infirm, and he could illy endure the excitements and harrassments of political strife. Accordingly, he quietly resumed his profession, and met the demands of a laborious practice until the close of 1849.

On the 20th of January, 1848, by special invitation, he delivered, in Frankfort, an address before the Kentucky Colonization Society. It was very able, and has been greatly commended. He undertook to show that slavery, in the Northern Slave States, at least, was not a permanent but merely a temporary institution, which was slowly receding South, and would certainly disappear; that this recession did not rid those States of the black population, but left them encumbered with free blacks; and lastly, that this society would not only relieve those States of that encumbrance, but would, in all probability, become the agent for regenerating the African continent, and converting it into the seat of great civilized and Christian nations.

The first two great propositions he demonstrated rigidly by a comprehensive and exhaustive examination of the census returns, from 1790 to 1840, for the States of Rhode Island, Connecticut, Pennsylvania, New York, New Jersey, Delaware, Maryland, District of Columbia, Virginia, North Carolina, Kentucky, and Missouri. He claimed that a great law was in operation, and closed this branch of his address in these words:

"There are in the natural as in the moral world great and slow movements, both of recessson and advance, often continued through centuries of change, which arrest the eye of the naturalist and philosopher, the final result of which is confidently predicted long before it is clearly unfolded to the busy masses of mankind. No naturalist hesitates with absolute certainty to declare that the buffalo, the beaver, and the Indian races, are drawing near the close of their career, and destined, in a few brief years, to disappear forever. Their recession, from east to west, commenced nearly three centuries ago, when the bark of the Pilgrims first grated upon the Plymouth sands. The fated race of the Anglo-Saxon came over the blue waters from the distant east, and from that moment the death-knell of the indigenous tribes has wrung mournfully in the ear of the world. No human power, not the combined armies and navies of Christendom, no paper protests, or legislative enactments, can arrest the melancholy march of the Indian race to their ocean-grave in the far west. . . . No less distinct, although of far later origin, is the recession of the Spanish and the advance of the Anglo-Saxon race from north to south. . . . For good or for evil, for weal or woe, the Anglo-Saxon race advances, westward and southward, with a haughty step which no barrier can arrest; and the Indian and Mexican retreat before him, perishing as they recede. Not less distinctly marked, but with a step more noiseless and slow, is that great combined moral and physical recession which I have endeavored to illustrate. There is a steadiness along a vastly extended line, a slow, sullen, massive regularity, which suggests the idea of vast power, and fixed and immutable purpose. It hears no remonstrance, it respects no prejudice, it regards no boundary, it pauses for no obstacle. Day and night, summer and winter, with a step that never tires, yet which never seems to move, it still moves on, through granite and steel, to its final destiny. What is that destiny, and where is the home which nature has provided for this slow and sable wanderer?"

Then, after rapidly sketching the condition of the free blacks in the Northern Slave States, he continues:

"There is upon the western coast of Africa a vast tract of fertile territory, capable of furnishing subsistence to fifty millions of men. Here is the cradle of the negro race. Here he was originally planted by the Creator, and from this coast he was torn by violence more than three hundred years ago. Nature has given to the negro a constitution adapted to its burning sun and deadly night-dew; but the white man sickens and dies where the negro thrives and prospers. The great Author of nature, who has created such an infinite variety of plants and animals, has generally assigned to each a local habitation, adapted to its nature, from which, if left to itself, it will rarely wander. The natural habitation of the negro is under the African tropical sun."

He then gives a brief history of the establishment and growth of Liberia; and as the discussion of the last of his three propositions is so masterly, and looks to the solution of a great problem, which is still before the American people, and has become, from the accelerating influences of the past ten years, far more threatening in its aspect and vastly exaggerated in its proportions, a few additional extracts will doubtless be pardoned, and regarded not out of place in this brief memoir of a truly great man:

"The little colony," he continues, "maintains democratic institutions in peace and security; and without a standing army, without tumult or disorder, preserves a prodigious ascendancy among the surrounding tribes, who regard her with admiration and wonder. There is not an old-established government in Europe, at this day, which would dare to imitate her example. No doubt her growth has been slow, but it is easy to show that the slowness of her growth was absolutely necessary to her future greatness, and is the surest evidence which man can derive that she is destined to be a light to the African world, and a home to the emancipated slave of America. . . . Democratic institutions are, of all others, the most difficult to maintain, and no nation has ever yet successfully maintained them, save by a long previous training, upon a small scale at first, and gradually enlarging its bounds, as by practice it becomes skillful in the art of governing.

"Such was the growth of the American Republic. The nucleus of American greatness, the embryo of that colossal power, whose shadow is thrown darkly over the future of the old world, was the little pilgrim church, which the Mayflower bore over the wintry ocean, and left to the mercy of Heaven, upon the cold and rocky shore of Plymouth. The stern morality, the mature yet ardent taste for religious freedom, was the solid foundation, upon which, slowly and gradually, a vast superstructure has been raised. . . . Liberia, beginning like New England, upon a small scale, with a well-selected material, slowly and gradually increasing, has already passed the critical period of infancy, and will soon become capable of bearing large accessions from our black population, without anarchy or confusion. . . .

"He who expects that an age of miracles will return, that the operation of second causes will be dispensed with, and that time will cease to be an element in the advancement of human affairs, may regret that the growth of Liberia has been slow and gradual. But the enlightened and steady friend of the African race will not be discouraged by a circumstance which he regards as a happy omen of future grandeur and renown. All that is great, and permanent, and salutary on earth, is slow in its development. The bird, the insect, the flower, that rushes earliest to maturity, is ever the first to perish and decay. Of all the animals which inhabit our earth, the infancy of man is the longest, the most helpless and the most painful; yet he alone, of all the busy throng, is destined to triumph over death, and survive even the wreck of the planet he inhabits.

"Of all the pageants which have dazzled the earth, the Empire of Napoleon was the most splendid. Like the enchanted palace of the Arabian tale, it sprung up to maturity in a night, and so massive were its proportions, so gigantic seemed its strength, that the profound and far-reaching sagacity of even Pitt and McIntosh was at fault, and predicted for it a duration commensurate with the iron materials of which it seemed composed. But scarcely were the predictions recorded, when the mighty mass crumbled in ruins, and in less than twelve months scarce a wreck remained.

"Not so the vast fabric of Roman greatness. From a little association of shepherds and herdsmen, upon the banks of a trifling stream, it gradually and slowly rose, through long centuries of continued growth, to the empire of the world. Where are now the enemies that grappled with her green youth, or triumphed over her declining years? Carthage and Macedon, Goths and Vandals, Parthians and Huns, have long passed away. Religions, languages, empires, all have perished, but the eternal city still lifts her gray head above the wreck of dead empires.

"Liberia grows slowly, but she consolidates her strength, and becomes familiarized with self-government. . . . As religious oppression in the old world caused a constant stream of emigration to the infant colonies of New England—as that emigration has slowly increased during the last two hundred years, until now it has swelled to a roaring flood—so the uneasy and degraded condition of the free blacks in this country, contrasted with the brilliant prospect which unites them to Liberia, together with the continued and increasing operation of the great movement I have endeavored to illustrate, will cause the tide of emigration to set toward the African shore at last, with a force which even the most sanguine can now scarcely imagine. All the great causes now in operation are surely destined to continue and to grow in power. The root and foundation of the whole, the life and soul of the mighty movement, is the public opinion of the Christian and civilized world. . . .

"If that opinion is onward and not backward, then shall the long night of African barbarism come to a close, and the starry flag of her great republic shall yet flout the blue skies of the tropical world. Time, the mighty workman, the great philosopher, the builder of truth, and the destroyer of error, time alone is necessary to disclose to a wondering world the incredible tale of African greatness. . . . Let democratic freedom and geographical position exert but one-half the influence upon her that they have shown in the Anglo-Saxon race, and her flag will cover the ocean and ransack every sea with the rich produce of her tropical climate. Let the Protestant religion have one-half the influence with them which it has exercised over the more favored races, and the interior of Africa will sparkle in the light of the Christian faith, and the active hum of civilized industry will awaken the echoes of her long-slumbering mountains. . . .

"There is a general tendency to *compensation* in all things, an equalizing adjustment of the balance of good or evil, traces of which are clearly apparent in the history of the world. Power and civilization, greatness and renown, have never been permanent in races or localities, climates or colors. Within the short period of authentic history, the scepter of civilization and power has been successively wielded by many different races, from all of whom, in turn, it has been wrested by another race. It has alternately occupied and abandoned many regions of the earth, which have successively passed through the extremes of power and degradation, of refinement and barbarism. Assyria and Egypt at one time monopolized the power, the arts, and the science of the world. They have long been sunk in barbarism and degradation. The freedom, the eloquence, the renown of Greece, once held the world in admiration and fear; but for long centuries she has been the slave of barbarism, and as barbarous as her oppressors. Italy has alternately been the seat of freedom and slavery, power and weakness, enlightenment and superstition. Within the last four hundred years, Spain has passed through the extremes of freedom and renown, slavery and disgrace. Even the cheerless deserts of Arabia have not been always deserted, and the darkness of the middle ages was lightened up by the science, civilization, and greatness of her Saracen Caliphs.

"Almost every other race has had its day of light, however deep the darkness which has followed. But the lot of the negro has as yet been an unmingled heritage of woe. That beautiful system of *compensation* which pervades the work of the Creator, by which any apparent injustice or defect in one gift to his creatures is atoned for and compensated in some other way, is finely illustrated by Paley, and is too familiar to be dwelt upon by me. And if the African negro is not the only one of his creatures to whom the rule does not apply, we would suppose it natural, that at some time and in some way, the long-delayed hour of compensation would arrive. What a splendid illustration of the rule will be given, if the negro race shall finally be exalted by the same hand which laid them low! if arts and civilization, wealth and renown, life and immortality, shall be bestowed upon their country by the Anglo-Saxon, in return for the dark atrocity of the slave-trade, and the long bondage of the deadly rice-swamp!"

The emancipation of the colored race, which, in 1848, seemed the slow work of great philosophic causes, peacefully reaching a consummation through the lapse of many years, was suddenly accomplished, it is true, in the violent convulsions of civil war. Constitutional amendments and legislative enactments have conferred citizenship, suffrage, and civil equality upon the blacks. But, in spite of all efforts, philanthropic or partisan, to elevate them to an equality with the white race, the problem still is, can the two races and colors commingle, or co-exist in civil and social equality on the same soil? Can the *fiat* of nature, which would seem to protest against it, be reversed, or the mark which the God of Order has fixed, so significant of separation, if not of inequality, be obliterated?

If not, the question so sharply stated by Mr. McClung still recurs: "*What is the destiny and where is the home which nature has provided for this slow and sable wanderer?*" And may not the answer given, with such power of philosophic deduction and prophetic forecast, be the true solution? "The natural habitation of the negro is under the African tropical sun;" under the influence of urgent social laws, "the tendency of the free blacks to Liberia will become general and irresistible," and by force of freedom and religion, "the interior of Africa will sparkle in the light of Christian faith, and the hum of civilized industry will awaken the echoes of her long-slumbering mountains."

During all the years of his estrangement from the church, and his laborious service in high secular employments, Mr. McClung never ceased to feel an interest in religion, or failed to show it reverence. When, in 1831, he withdrew from the ministry, he did not, at once, abandon his investigation of the points on which his mind had hesitated. He was left, as he himself said, in a wretched state of anxiety, apprehension, and doubt. To relieve the suspense, he sought diligently, for years, to reach the conviction that the Scriptures were untrue, and to anchor himself on infidelity. He searched for information at every accessible source, and gathered from all quarters, and read with eager interest, the works of skeptics and infidels the world over. But he was unsatisfied; he could draw from them neither conviction nor consolation; he could find no rock on which to rest. The secret was, he did not seek to deceive or delude himself; he had no heart for error, no patience with sophistry; he was honest; he sought truth; he loved light. Long afterward, he declared emphatically he never was, and he found he could not be, an infidel; but he was in deep darkness, and his soul was oppressed with gloom.

In the year 1848, he listened to a sermon of Rev. Dr. Grundy, in Maysville, upon one of the points of difficulty which had originally disturbed his faith. Something that fell from the preacher arrested his attention, and he determined to take up again the whole subject and carefully revise his opinions. He was induced to this by the hope that his long experience at the bar, and the severe training he had undergone, might enable his mind, under a fresh impulse, and by better processes, to reach the light at last. He knew well that, where fundamental truth was involved, his mind was averse to taking any thing on mere trust, and imperiously demanded demonstration. Not that he was incapable of conceiving or accepting truth in the high regions of the supernatural and the mysterious, for his mind often turned with real delight to the mystic and the spiritual. But he had been unable to answer the subtle argument of Gibbon, in his celebrated chapters on the Secondary Causes for the rapid growth of Christianity; and in his examination of the sacred writings, he had been shaken as to the authenticity and accuracy of the record, and its integrity and consistency as a great body of inspired truth.

Under these conditions, he undertook to review his early studies, and to reconstruct, if possible, his early faith. Fortunately, he met with a rare work—a reply to Gibbon's chapters on the Secondary Causes, by an old but very able Scotch common law judge, Sir David Dalrymple. The analysis of Gibbon's arguments, and the exposure of his false quotations and statements, are exhaustive and complete. So far as Gibbon's sophistries were concerned, the perusal of this book was a great enjoyment and relief to Mr. McClung; and his study of the Scriptures became now unremitting and intense. Day after day, night after night, till late hours—sometimes throughout the night—

did this earnest man, this giant student, bend his energies to the examination and close collation and comparison of all the books of the Old and New Testaments, in the original and in translation. It was done conscientiously certainly, and no doubt prayerfully.

After many months of unceasing application to this great and solemn labor, the clouds were rolled away, the darkness disappeared, the Divine Word was vindicated, the weary mind had found its anchor and its rock, and the Sun of Righteousness, with healing on his wings, beamed upon his heart.

His convictions seemed to have been very profound, and were undisturbed to the close of his life. In describing the character and course of his investigations, and the elaborate process through which he had gone, he stated to a friend, as a sample of the foundations he had reached for his intellectual faith, that in the Book of Acts, alone, he had found upward of sixty instances of minute and undoubtedly undesigned coincidences verifying the accuracy of the narrative; very few of which had ever been noticed by any of the numerous commentators he had read.

On the night of the 23d of February, 1849, in the midst of a series of protracted meetings in the Presbyterian Church, in Maysville, he rose from his seat, went forward, and offered himself for admission to membership. The narrative then given of his experiences, his difficulties, his sufferings, his life-battle, including his avowed belief in the genuineness of his conversion in boyhood, and terminating with a triumphant testimony to the truth of the *whole Bible* as the Word of God, is said to have been most simple, touching, and soul-subduing. The surrender of this strong man to his Savior was child-like and complete. The prophecy of his old friend, Mr. Todd, that *he would surely return,* was accomplished. And it is believed that it is not going too far to say that the return of *such a wanderer*—so greatly endowed, so richly accomplished, so flattered and tempted in the secular walks, so severe in his scrutiny, so rigid in his demand for demonstration, so unsparing in his researches, so reliant on his mental strength and moral consistency, and so entirely honest and sincere—was regarded throughout the wide circle of his admirers and friends, and by the whole Christian community, as one of the most marked, signal, and convincing testimonies to God's blessed truth that has occurred amongst men in modern times.

He scarcely hesitated as to his future life. Although in the midst of a prosperous professional career, upon the proceeds of which his family were mainly dependent for support; although past the meridian of life, and suffering greatly from the infirmities of a weakened constitution and waning strength, he cast aside these and all other considerations, and counted all as loss for the Cross of Christ. "I do not think," says a daughter, "it was ever understood how completely my father sacrificed his own and his children's worldly prospects by abandoning the practice of law for the ministry. Not that he considered it a sacrifice; but still it was; and so was the emancipation of his slaves."

To recruit his shattered health, in preparation for his new work, he passed a few months, during the winter of 1849-50, at the water-cure establishment in Brattleboro, Vermont. He returned much improved, and with spirits renovated and buoyant. Under a licensure, in 1850, and an ordination, in 1851, from the Presbytery of Ebenezer, he resumed the long-abandoned labors of his young life, his early love. Here are some passages from the pen of the same gifted daughter, beautifully descriptive of his student habits during his ministerial life:

"He threw himself, heart and soul, into his ministerial work. His reading, which had always taken the widest range of history, science, poetry, and fiction, was thenceforth mainly confined to the Scriptures, and every work of any celebrity written for their exposition. He quickly gathered about him all the best authors on these and kindred subjects; but he was particularly devoted to the German commentators. But first, last, and above all, he studied the Scriptures in the original. Even our servants, who could not read, knew his Hebrew Bible and Greek Testament; and it was amusing to see with what gravity and promptness they would select them from a pile of miscellaneous books when called for. . . . He indeed 'searched the Scriptures;' and as a burning glass collects the faint and scattered rays of the sun into one intense and brilliant flame, so he gathered from 'Moses and the Prophets' the dim foreshadowings of the Sun of Righteousness; and through the medium of his vivid and powerful intellect, poured such a flood of light upon the sacred page that the simplest and most unlearned of his hearers might read the dark sayings and understand the hidden things of God. Yet he was equally instructive and delightful when he chose some theme from the Gospel or the Epistles. It is a matter of deep regret that these sermons, so pure, so strong, so rich, so spiritual, should live only in the memory of those who heard them, and there only in faint and shadowy outline. But my father never wrote out a sermon, as I have often heard him say to those who, on various occasions, sought them for publication. He always composed with a pen in his hand and a half-sheet of paper before him, on which he would occasionally write a word, or make some mark significant only to himself; but he generally left this scrap on his desk, and used no notes in the pulpit. I have often possessed myself of these bits of manuscript afterward, but the few cabalistic words and signs suggested almost nothing to my mind. . . . He had a number of little notebooks, one of which he had always beside him as he read, and in which he made copious entries, but in the same fragmentary style, which, while perfectly intelligible and satisfactory to himself, was hopelessly confusing to any other mind. . . . But in the midst of these notes, Hebrew, Greek, and English—scarcely more intelligible to me—my father had penned brief, fervent sentences, evidently the spontaneous overflow of deep, devotional feeling; and at the beginning of each little volume, in a few solemn words, he consecrated himself anew to the service of the Lord Jesus, signing his name in full, as if it were a covenant between his soul and God; and doubtless he so regarded it."

The following synopsis of his labors, from 1851 to 1857, was given by Judge Lewis Collins, in a notice published in 1859:

"During the summer and fall of 1851, he occupied the pulpit of Rev. Dr. W. L. Breckinridge, at Louisville, in the absence of that gentleman in Europe. In the fall of 1851, he was called to the pastoral care of the First Presbyterian Church of Indianapolis. He preached with great acceptability to that congregation, which was devotedly attached to him, for between four and five years. During that time he was elected, by a unanimous vote of the Board of Trustees, President of South Hanover College, Indiana, which office he was induced to accept—but, at the earnest entreaty of his church, afterward resigned. He was subsequently called to the Central Church of Cincinnati, vacated by the removal of Dr. Rice to St. Louis, which he declined. About the close of the year 1855, he was compelled, by failing health, to resign the pastoral charge of the Indianapolis Church. Near the close of his pastorate in that church, he was invited to take charge of the large and flourishing Presbyterian Church at Augusta, Georgia—and, in the hope of restoring his health in a

Southern climate, he accepted the invitation. He preached to that people for a few months, but, upon his return home to remove his family South, his health was again prostrated, and he was compelled, in consequence, to relinquish the charge.

"During his ministry of nine years, he received invitations to various other pulpits, among them that of the large Presbyterian Church at New Orleans, to which Dr. Scott, of San Francisco, for many years ministered, and of which Dr. Palmer, of South Carolina, is now pastor.

"Upon leaving his beloved flock at Indianapolis, he removed, with his family, to St. Paul, where his only son, J. W. McClung, Esq., had a short time previously located. During his residence there of some twelve or fifteen months, the cold, dry, and bracing air of the North so far restored his physical energies that he again ventured to preach, and supplied, occasionally, the pulpits of his ministerial brethren in St. Paul."

Another writer said of him: "With the zeal and almost with the eloquence of one of the old apostles, he began his ministry. In Louisville, no church could contain the crowds that flocked to hear him, and so warm and devoted were his admirers that they wished to build him a church. To this he would not consent. In Cincinnati the same results followed."

The able editor of *The Presbyterian*, of Philadelphia, in 1859, thus speaks of him in the General Assembly:

"On the only occasion on which *Dr. McClung was ever a member of the General Assembly, he made an impression by a brief but most telling speech, which can not be forgotten by those who were present. It was on a subject which had already occupied much time, of which the Assembly was heartily weary, and in regard to which an hour had been fixed for taking the vote. When the appointed hour came, Dr. McClung, who was personally unknown to most of the members, rose and asked to be heard; but there was a manifest determination to listen to no further discussion. He plead for but ten minutes, which was at length very reluctantly granted. He had no sooner begun his speech than the attention of the Assembly was riveted; they were evidently captivated by his remarkable combination of logic, humor, eloquence, and courtesy. They saw that a new star had arisen in our ecclesiastical firmament. When his ten

---

*He had received the degree of Doctor of Divinity a short time previous to this.

minutes expired, he was about to yield the floor, but the Moderator told him to go on, that the Assembly was evidently very much pleased to hear him. When he concluded, the vote was taken on his proposition, and carried by a vast majority, although the decision was thought by many to be in direct collision with a previous action on the same subject. This was the first and last time that eloquent voice was heard in the General Assembly. Like a brilliant meteor, he shot athwart the skies, and then appeared no more."

Dr. Robert J. Breckinridge, in alluding to this effort, said he had never witnessed such an effect, in so short a time, upon such a body of men, in all his experience. The grave members were spell-bound during its delivery, and so fascinated by his downright sincerity and earnestness, his unusual powers of argument and oratory, and the sparkling playfulness of his wit, that he believed they were ready, when he concluded, to do any thing he wished them to do. They certainly reversed their previous action; and the Doctor thought they did wrong.

In the spring of 1857, the Maysville pulpit having become vacant, and it being understood that his health had improved, the desire that Mr. McClung should be called became very strong. A private letter was addressed to him by a friend, to which, on the 1st of April, 1857, he replied: "I have no hesitation in saying, that it would give me pleasure to return to my old haunts and mingle in friendly intercourse with my old friends. I have long been severed from my native State, and although much of my time has been pleasantly spent, among warm and attached friends, yet every thing around is foreign to my early habits of thought and association, and I would willingly return should Providence open the way. If the Maysville Church should *heartily and without dissension* call me, I will certainly accept the call, if I live and enjoy my present ability to labor."

He was unanimously called, and on the first Sabbath in June undertook his charge and preached his first sermon. Once more he was with a people who had known him from his birth, watched with pride the bright dawn of his opening powers, sustained and sympathized with him in his labors and trials, and witnessed with exultant joy the triumphs of his manhood. He had come now to renew the associations and friendships, and warm once more into life the memories of other times; to minister to the spiritual interests of this beloved people, and, in their midst, to offer up his last testimonies to the truth. Never did the simplicity and purity of his life appear so conspicuous and attractive. He sought, at once, to know personally every member of his congregation, to perform in all fidelity the double duty of preacher and pastor, and to watch over his whole flock as a loving shepherd.

Those who had known him before only in his public life, and been accustomed to regard his habits as exclusive and retiring, were surprised and touched to see the great student and thinker throw off his seclusion, and surrender himself with genuine enjoyment to the little incidents, the delicate duties and sweet amenities of pastoral, social, every-day life. But the fountain of genial companionship, of kindness and tenderness, was in his heart; and they who knew his inner life were not surprised. See what a charming picture his daughter has drawn of her father's home-habits:

"He was always domestic in his tastes, and from my earliest recollection did much of his office-work at home, frequently receiving his clients in the family sitting-room, where he also elected to do his reading and writing, apparently undisturbed by the constant ebb and flow of a large and busy household. We used to play under the very table where he sat at work, taking his books of reference to build doll-houses. But he was generally oblivious of the giggling and whispering which accompanied our quietest amusements, and only noticed our presence to bestow an occasional caress, or a little 'baby-talk,' of which he possessed an endless and charming variety. Even when we were no longer children, he often used the old fondling phrases, and called us by our pet names. Sometimes, at dusk, he would throw aside book and pen, and challenge us to a game of romps; in summer would run races on the grass, or, tying us securely in the swing with a large silk handkerchief, would toss us into the branches of the old willow.

"But though always tender and indulgent, and often condescending to become our play-fellow, he had a certain dignity and reserve which checked familiarity, unless invited by himself. We stood in wholesome awe of his displeasure, and though he never punished us in any way, children and servants obeyed his lightest word.

"My father was very familiar with the poets, and many a snatch from Scott, Byron, Burns, and Moore, I knew by heart, long before I read them, from hearing him repeat them as he paced the floor at twilight. When I afterward read the Waverly novels, many portions were quite familiar to me; for instance, Wamba's song:

> "'Anna Marie, love, up with the sun—
> Anna Marie, love, morn is begun!
> Flowers are waking, love, birds singing free—
> Up with the sun, then, love, Anna Marie!'

"You know my sister's name is Anna Maria. Morning by morning, my father chanted this in our ears to waken us. He was fond of singing, had a sweet, mellow voice, and would often burst out in sudden song as he sat at work, or walked to and fro in the room, as was his life-long custom."

Under his ministry at Maysville, a deep interest was awakened and continued, and the church blessed by large accessions and increased spirituality. So great was the impression he made, that the ministers of other denominations frequently dispensed with their evening services, in order that they and their congregations might have the opportunity of listening to his discourses.

So conscious was he of the fullness of his knowledge, and so devoted to the Master's service, that he delighted in the exposition of the Scriptures, in familiar conversation in private interviews and the social circle, as well as in the pulpit. Although this was his life-theme, the subject of his constant meditations, and although ever ready to minister to the hungry and thirsty, he was never obtrusive; always judicious and discriminating as to persons and occasions, his conversations were so seasonable and so full of information and interest, that few ever listened who did not regret when he ceased to speak. But he was no controversionalist; he had no taste for polemics in religion. He did not conceive that his appointed work lay in this field, and was careful never to attack the opinions or offend the feelings of those who differed with him as to doctrines. He was, indeed, very tolerant as to differences in doctrine and church-government within the limits of recognized evangelical belief, and co-operated with ministers of other denominations heartily, as brothers in Christ and co-laborers in the same vineyard. Hence his relations with them were kind and warm, and he was enabled to wield a wonderful influence in the promotion of harmony and the general interests of the church. Although entirely clear and firm in his opinions, and although he occasionally discussed the great distinctive doctrines of his church, and presented them as a comprehensive body of divine truth, he was not a *doctrinal* preacher.

He was a great teacher of the Scriptures, an expositor of the Bible.
The memory of his own mental difficulties and long resistance to the truth, led him, no doubt, to feel that the first thing to be accomplished was to lay, broadly and deeply in the mind, the firm conviction that the Bible was inspired and certainly true. Hence, he was oftentimes at great pains to explain the history, composition, authenticity, and preservation of the various books of the Old and New Testaments, and the links, apparent and secret, which bound them together as the inspired word. Hence, he dwelt with so much interest and emphasis upon the types and symbols and oriental imagery of the Bible, with which he was so familiar; and which, under his teaching, resolved so many obscurities of the sacred record, brought out so many hidden harmonies, and threw such broad lights upon the spiritual significance and beautiful consistency of the whole. Hence, he turned so frequently to the prophecies of the Old Testament, which had run their course, and proved, from the concurring testimony of history, sacred and profane, how certain and wonderful had been the fulfillment. In this connection, he discussed, in their natural and logical relations, as well as in the light of an overruling Providence, the dealings of God with his chosen people and the Gentile nations, to show how all had proceeded to a consummation which prophecy had foretold. Especially did he point to the chastisement and dispersion of the Jews, under which they have suffered for so many centuries and are still suffering, in perfect accordance with a prophecy uttered and recorded certainly thousands of years ago, as a demonstration of the inspiration of the Bible, unanswerable and overwhelming. He loved to trace the earliest intimations of mercy to man as they glimmer, in the twilight of time, through sacrifice, and symbol, and type; and to gather up and mold into symmetry and shape the fragmentary portraitures of a Savior, by seer, and psalmist, and prophet, as they come darkly down, scattered along generations and centuries, to the manger and the cross.

He often unfolded the parables and dwelt on the teachings of our Lord, in their wide and minute application to all the inner and outer experiences of life, to show that they indeed disclosed the only true wisdom. And, sometimes, in the midst of a great passage, when pressing the claims of the gospel upon the immediate attention of his hearers, and urging them, upon the infallible truth of its precious promises, to dedicate their whole lives to the Savior's service—his long arms would be suddenly folded on his breast, his form drawn up to its full height, and, with look and manner intensely earnest, he would cry out, in thrilling tones, "Will you listen to me! will you remember!"

He was totally free from the formal mannerism which frequently mars pulpit delivery. He had spoken too often to juries and popular assemblages, not to know that the direct look, the natural bearing, the familiar illustration, the free, energetic, emotional delivery, as the extemporaneous thought pressed to its conclusions, was the only way to arrest and hold the attention, sway the feelings, and command the convictions of his audience.

At this period he seemed to feel very deeply the necessity laid upon him to do quickly what he had to do in his Master's service. His devotion was unsparing, and his physical system so frail, that his health, in spite of his heroic efforts to maintain it, gradually declined. A touching incident, illustrative of his entire dedication to his work, occurred in the early part of 1859. He had been absent a few days, on hard service, and returned on Saturday night, much exhausted. At the morning services succeeding, in reading the 19th chapter of Job, it was observed that he was very feeble, and rested on the pulpit for support. As he proceeded, his voice became scarcely audible, and his head gradually drooped. In the midst of the 21st verse—"Have pity upon me, have pity upon me, oh ye, my friends; for the hand of God hath touched me"—his articulation ceased, his head sank; he had fainted. He was promptly surrounded by his friends, who caught him before he fell, and laid him on the floor of the pulpit. Restoratives were applied, and he slowly became conscious. His physician said he should be carried home as soon as his strength permitted. McClung shook his head. It was urged that his life would be endangered, if he persisted in the services. But he could not be influenced. "*I must preach the gospel!*" he said; and he did preach to that awed and sympathizing congregation a noble discourse on that chapter of Job.

His mournful end was now near at hand. The great light was soon to be extinguished. On Wednesday, the 3d of August, of that year, he left Maysville, on an excursion for the benefit of his health. Passing through Cincinnati and Cleveland, he stopped, on Friday, at the village of Tonawanda, about nine miles from Niagara Falls, intending to spend the Sabbath there. But finding that there was no Presbyterian Church in the town, it is supposed that on Saturday, the 6th, he walked over to the steamboat-landing, at Schlosser, on the Niagara, and, after arriving there, went into the river to bathe. It had been his habit, for years, to take long walks and bathe in cold water, daily. His clothes were found on the dock, where he had prepared for bathing; and he was never seen afterwards in life. Being very weak, he may have been suddenly chilled and cramped, or borne out too far by a strong current, and so carried over the Falls. His body was found in an eddy on the American side, near the mouth of the river, four days after, and interred in the Niagara Fort burying-ground. Subsequently his remains were removed to Kentucky, and funeral services performed in his church, in Maysville, by the Rev. Messrs. Worrall, Coons, and Scudder, of the Presbyterian Church; Rev. Mr. Nash, of the Episcopal, and Rev. Mr. Bayless, of the Methodist Church. A very able sermon was preached by Mr. Worrall, before one of the largest audiences ever assembled in the city, from part of the 17th verse and 48th chapter of Jeremiah, "How is the strong staff broken, and the beautiful rod!" After the ceremonies were concluded, a long and sorrowing procession followed, and consigned his body to its last resting-place, in his native county, near the city, on the banks of the Ohio.

He left a wife, one son, and three daughters, to mourn him. Mrs. McClung survived only till the 28th December, 1860, when she died at St. Paul, Minnesota.

The shock of such a death was fearful throughout the community, and there was mourning in the land. A great and good man had fallen in Israel. A dispensation, so sudden and severe, was felt to be mysterious indeed. In his 55th year, in the maturity of his powers, and of his wide usefulness, he had been stricken down, by an accident, in an hour, far from family, and home, and friends, and gathered to his rest. Yet he had lived long enough to reach eminent distinction as student, scholar, lawyer, statesman, and divine, and to do a great work for his fellow-men.

In person he was tall, and of striking presence. His carriage was not graceful, though free; for he had the angular motions of a student, walking erectly and rapidly, with a long, swinging stride, and an independent, oftentimes abstracted air. His forehead was broad, prominent, and massive, with heavy brows arching widely over his deep, dark-brown, expressive eyes; mouth large, chin square and firm; and his whole face full of mental power, earnestness, and resolution.

In no aspect was he an ordinary man. Nature and education had fitted him for high trusts, and worthily did he fill them. His career in the law displayed, in clearest light, a master quality of his being—the spirit of justice. His sense of truth and right was so absolute, and his courage so superior to intimidation, that he recognized and guarded, with highest courtesy, the rights of others. A firm will and unbending purpose gave him weighty influence with his associates, and a rigid control over himself. Penetrating insight into human motive, and large powers of observation and generalization, rendered his views of life philosophic, and his opinions of public men and measures sagacious and sound.

Although he wandered long and far from the sublime way to which he was early called, twenty years of secular life succeeding exhibited such high qualities of head and heart, so elevated him to conspicuous position among men, and commanded their confidence, that his return to his sacred office, in the providence of God, signalized far more strikingly his testimony to truth, and may have wrought out more of good to man and glory to God, than would have resulted from an unbroken ministry. And that very experience no doubt operated to the elevation of his spiritual life, and to a more devoted and blessed consecration to his Master's cause.

SKETCHES

OF

WESTERN ADVENTURE.

CHAPTER I.

THE English settlements in North America, until late in the eighteenth century, were confined to the country lying east of the Alleghany Mountains. Even the most adventurous traders from Virginia and Pennsylvania rarely penetrated beyond the head waters of the Ohio River; and the spot where Pittsburgh now stands was, for a long time, an extreme frontier point, where the white fur-traders and the western Indians were accustomed to meet and exchange their commodities. All beyond was an unexplored wilderness, which was known only as occupying certain degrees of latitude and longitude upon the map. Shortly before the old French war of 1755, this spot was occupied by the French and a fort erected, which, in honor of their commander, was called Du Quesne.

The possession of this fortress was keenly debated during the earlier years of the war, and was soon rendered memorable by the disastrous expedition of Braddock and Grant. Omitting a regular detail of these events—which have been often related—we shall commence our desultory history with a detail of the adventures of Col. JAMES SMITH, who subsequently removed to Kentucky, and for many years was a resident

(13)

of Bourbon County. He was the first Anglo-American who penetrated into the interior of the Western country—at least the first who has given us an account of his adventures; and in a succession of sketches, like the present, designed to commemorate individual rather than national exertions, he is justly entitled to the distinction which we give him. If we mistake not, his adventures will be found particularly interesting, as affording more ample specimens of savage manners and character, than almost any other account now in existence.

In the spring of the year 1755, James Smith, then a youth of eighteen, accompanied a party of three hundred men from the frontiers of Pennsylvania, who advanced in front of Braddock's army for the purpose of opening a road over the mountains. When within a few miles of the Bedford Springs, he was sent back to the rear to hasten the progress of some wagons loaded with provisions and stores for the use of the road cutters. Having delivered his orders, he was returning, in company with another young man, when they were suddenly fired upon by a party of three Indians, from a cedar thicket which skirted the road. Smith's companion was killed on the spot; and although he himself was unhurt, yet his horse was so much frightened by the flash and report of the guns as to become totally unmanageable, and, after a few plunges, threw him with violence to the ground. Before he could recover his feet, the Indians sprung upon him, and, overpowering his resistance, secured him as a prisoner.

One of them demanded, in broken English, whether "more white men were coming up;" and upon his answering in the negative, he was seized by each arm and compelled to run with great rapidity over the mountain until night, when the small party encamped and cooked their supper. An equal share of their scanty stock of provisions was given to the prisoner; and in other respects, although strictly guarded, he was treated with great kindness. On the evening of the next day, after a rapid walk of fifty miles through cedar thickets and over very rocky ground, they reached the western side of the Laurel Mountain, and beheld at a little distance the smoke of an Indian encampment. His captors now fired their guns and raised the *scalp halloo!* This is a long yell for every scalp that has been taken, followed by a rapid succession of shrill, quick, piercing shrieks, somewhat resembling laughter in its most excited tones. They were answered from the Indian camp below by a discharge of rifles and a long whoop, followed by shrill cries of joy; and all thronged out to meet the party. Smith expected instant death at their hands, as they crowded around him; but to his surprise, no one offered him any violence. They belonged to another tribe, and entertained the party in their camp with great hospitality, respecting the prisoner as the property of their guests.

On the following morning Smith's captors continued their march, and on the evening of the next day arrived at Fort Du Quesne, now Pittsburgh. When within half a mile of the fort, they again raised the scalp halloo, and fired their guns as before. Instantly the whole garrison was in commotion. The cannon were fired, the drums were beaten, and French and Indians ran out in great numbers to meet the party and partake of their triumph. Smith was again surrounded by a multitude of savages, painted in various colors, and shouting with delight; but their demeanor was by no means as pacific as that of the last party he had encountered. They rapidly formed in two long lines, and, brandishing their hatchets, ramrods, switches, etc., called aloud upon him to run the gauntlet.

Never having heard of this Indian ceremony before, he stood amazed for some time, not knowing what to do; but one of his captors explained to him that he was to run between the two lines, and receive a blow from each Indian as he passed, concluding his explanation by exhorting him to "run his best," as the faster he run the sooner the affair would be over. This truth was very plain, and young Smith entered upon his race with great spirit. He was switched very handsomely along the lines for about three-fourths of the distance, the stripes only acting as a spur to greater exertions; and he had almost reached the opposite extremity of the line, when a tall chief struck him a furious blow with a club upon the back of the head, and instantly felled him to the ground. Recovering himself in a moment, he sprung to his feet and started forward again, when a handful of sand was thrown in his eyes, which, in addition to the great pain, completely blinded him. He still attempted to grope his way through, but was again knocked down and beaten with merciless severity. He soon became insensible under such barbarous treatment, and recollected nothing more until he found himself in the hospital of the fort, under the hands of a French surgeon, beaten to a jelly, and unable to move a limb. Here he was quickly visited by one of his captors—the same who had given him such good advice when about to commence his race.

He now inquired, with some interest, if he felt "very sore." Young Smith replied that he had been bruised almost to death, and asked what he had done to merit such barbarity. The Indian replied that he had done nothing, but that it was the customary greeting of the Indians to their prisoners; that it was something like the English "How d'ye do?" and that now all ceremony would be laid aside and he would be treated with kindness. Smith inquired if they had any news of General Braddock. The Indian replied that their scouts saw him every day from the mountains; that he was advancing in close columns through the woods (this he indicated by placing a number of red sticks parallel to each other, and pressed closely together); and that the Indians would be able to shoot them down "like pigeons."

Smith rapidly recovered, and was soon able to walk upon the battlements of the fort, with the aid of a stick. While engaged in this exercise, on the morning of the ninth of July, he observed an unusual bustle in the fort. The Indians stood in crowds at the great gate, armed and painted. Many barrels of powder, ball, flints, etc., were brought out to them, from which each warrior helped himself to such articles as he required. They were soon joined by a small detachment of French regulars, when the whole party marched off together. He had a full view of them as they passed, and was confident that they could not exceed four hundred men. He soon learned that it was detached against Braddock, who was now within a few miles of the fort; but from their great inferiority in numbers, he regarded their destruction as certain, and looked joyfully to the arrival of Braddock in the evening as the hour which was to deliver him from the power of the Indians. In the afternoon, however, an Indian runner arrived with far different intelligence. The battle had not yet ended when he left the field, but he announced that the English had been surrrounded, and were shot down in heaps by an invisible enemy; that instead of flying at once, or rushing upon their concealed foe, they appeared completely bewildered, huddled together in the center of the ring, and that before sundown there would not be a man of them alive.

This intelligence fell like a thunderbolt upon Smith, who now saw himself irretrievably in the power of the savages, and could look forward to nothing but torture or endless captivity. He waited anxiously for further intelligence, still hoping that the fortune of the day might change. But about sunset, he heard at a distance the well-known scalp halloo, followed by wild, quick, joyful shrieks, and accompanied by long-continued firing. This too surely announced the fate of the day. About dusk the party returned to the fort, driving before them twelve British regulars, stripped naked, and with their faces painted black! an evidence that the unhappy wretches were devoted to death.

Next came the Indians, displaying their bloody scalps—of which they had immense numbers—and dressed in the scarlet coats, sashes, and military hats of the officers and soldiers. Behind all came a train of baggage horses, laden with piles of scalps, canteens, and all the accouterments of British soldiers. The savages appeared frantic with joy, and when Smith beheld them entering the fort dancing, yelling, brandishing their red tomahawks, and waving their scalps in the air, while the great guns of the fort replied to the incessant discharge of rifles without, he says that it looked as if h—ll had given a holiday and turned loose its inhabitants upon the upper world.

The most melancholy spectacle was the band of prisoners. They appeared dejected and anxious. Poor fellows! They had but a few months before left London, at the command of their superiors, and we may easily imagine their feelings at the strange and dreadful spectacle around them. The yells of delight and congratulation were scarcely over when those of vengeance began. The devoted prisoners—British regulars—were led out from the fort to the banks of the Alleghany, and to the eternal disgrace of the French commandant, were there burnt to death, one after another, with the most awful tortures.

Smith stood upon the battlements and witnessed the shocking spectacle. The prisoner was tied to a stake, with his hands raised above his head, stripped naked, and surrounded by Indians. They would touch him with red-hot irons, and stick his body full of pine splinters and set them on fire, drowning the shrieks of the victim in the yells of delight with which they danced around him. His companions in the meantime stood in a group near the stake, and had a foretaste of what was in reserve for each of them. As fast as one prisoner died under his tortures, another filled his place, until the whole perished. All this took place so near the fort that every scream of the victims must have rung in the ears of the French commandant.

Two or three days after this shocking spectacle, most of the Indian tribes dispersed and returned to their homes, as is usual with them after a great and decisive battle. Young Smith was demanded of the French by the tribe to whom he belonged, and was immediately surrendered into their hands.

The party embarked in canoes, and ascended the Alleghany River as far as a small Indian town about forty miles above Fort Du Quesne. There they abandoned their canoes, and, striking into the woods, traveled in a western direction, until they arrived at a considerable Indian town in what is now the State of Ohio. This village was called Tullihas, and was situated upon the western branch of the Muskingum. During the whole of this period, Smith suffered much anxiety from the uncertainty of his future fate; but at this town all doubt was removed. On the morning of his arrival, the principal members of the tribe gathered around him, and one old man, with deep gravity, began to pluck out his hair by the roots, while the others looked on in silence, smoking their pipes with great deliberation.

Smith did not understand the design of this singular ceremony, but submitted very patiently to the man's labors, who performed the operation of "picking" him with great dexterity, dipping his fingers in ashes occasionally, in order to take a better hold. In a very few moments Smith's head was bald, with the exception of a single long tuft upon the center of his crown, called the "scalp-lock." This was carefully plaited in such a manner as to stand upright, and was ornamented with several silver brooches. His ears and nose were then bored with equal gravity, and ornamented with ear-rings and nose-jewels. He was then ordered to strip; which being done, his naked body was painted in various fantastic colors, and a breech-cloth fastened around his loins. A belt of wampum was then fastened around his neck, and silver bands around his right arm.

To all this Smith submitted with much anxiety, being totally ignorant of their customs, and dreading lest, like the British prisoners, he had been stripped and painted for the stake. His alarm was increased, when an old chief arose, took him by the arm, and leading him out into the open air, gave three shrill whoops, and was instantly surrounded by every inhabitant of the village, warriors, women, and children. The chief then addressed the crowd in a long speech, still holding Smith by the hand. When he had ceased speaking, he led Smith forward, and delivered him into the hands of three young Indian girls, who, grappling him without ceremony, towed him off to the river which ran at the foot of the hill, dragged him in the water up to his breast, and all three suddenly clapping their hands upon his head, attempted to put him under. Utterly desperate at the idea of being drowned by these young ladies, Smith made a manful resistance; the squaws persevered; and a prodigious splashing of the water took place, amidst loud peals of laughter from the shore.

At length, one of the squaws became alarmed at the furious struggles of the young white man, and cried out earnestly several times, "No hurt you! no hurt you!" Upon this agreeable intelligence, Smith's resistance ceased, and these gentle creatures plunged him under the water, and scrubbed him from head to foot with equal zeal and perseverance. As soon as they were satisfied, they led him ashore and presented him to the chief, shivering with cold, and dripping with water. The Indians then dressed him in a ruffled shirt, leggins, and moccasins, variously ornamented, seated him upon a bearskin, and gave him a pipe, tomahawk, tobacco, pouch, flint, and steel. The chiefs then took their seats by his side, and smoked for several minutes in deep silence, when the eldest delivered a speech, through an interpreter, in the following words: "My son, you are now one of us. Hereafter, you have nothing to fear. By an ancient custom, you have been adopted in the room of a brave man, who has fallen; and every drop of white blood has been washed from your veins. We are now your brothers, and are bound by our law to love you, to defend you, and to avenge your injuries, as much as if you were born in our tribe."

He was then introduced to the members of the family into which he had been adopted, and was received by the whole of them with great demonstrations of regard. In the evening, he received an invitation to a great feast; and was there presented with a wooden bowl and spoon, and directed to fill the former from a huge kettle of boiled corn and hashed venison. The evening concluded with a war dance, and on the next morning the warriors of the tribe assembled, and leaving one or two hunters, to provide for their families in their absence, the rest marched off for the frontiers of Virginia. In leaving the village, the warriors observed the most profound silence, with the exception of their leader, who sung the traveling song, as it is called; and when some distance off, they discharged their rifles slowly, and in regular succession, beginning in front, and ending with the rear. As soon as the warriors had left them, Smith was invited to a dance, in which the Indian boys and young unmarried squaws assembled, and entertained themselves for several hours together. They formed in two lines facing each other, at the distance of about twenty feet. One of the young men held a gourd in his hand, filled with pebbles, or beads, which he rattled in such a manner as to produce music, and all the dancers, singing in concert with their leader, moved forward in a line until the parties met; then retired, and repeated the same exercise for hours, without the least variation.

Young Smith was merely a spectator in this scene, and his chief entertainment arose from observing the occasional symptoms of gallantry and coquetry which diversified the monotony of the dance. Heads were often bent close together as the two lines met, and soft whispers, ogling-glances, and an occasional gentle tap on the cheek, convinced Smith, that Indians are not so insensible to the charms of their squaws as has been represented. An Indian courtship is somewhat different from ours. With them, all the coyness, reserve, and pretty delays, are confined to the gentlemen. The young squaws are bold, forward, and by no means delicate in urging their passion; and a particularly handsome or promising young hunter is often reduced to desperate extremities, to escape the toils of these female Lotharios. Smith was uniformly treated with the greatest kindness, and was for some time particularly distressed by the pressing invitations to eat, which he received from all quarters.

With the Indians, it is uniformly the custom to invite every visitor to eat, as soon as he enters the wigwam; and if he refuses, they are much offended, regarding it as an evidence of hostility to them, and contempt for their housekeeping. Smith, ignorant of this circumstance, was sometimes pressed to eat twenty times in a day, and observing their dark and suspicious glances when he declined their hospitality, he endeavored at length to satisfy them at the risk of stuffing himself to death. Making it a point to eat with all who invited him, he soon found himself in great favor, and in the course of a week after his adoption an old chief honored him with an invitation to hunt with him. Smith readily consented. At the distance of a few miles from the village, they discovered a number of buffalo tracks. The old Indian regarded them attentively, and followed them with great caution, stopping frequently to listen, and rolling his eyes keenly in every direction. Smith, surprised at this singular conduct, asked him why he did not push on more rapidly, and endeavor to get a shot. "Hush!" said the Indian, shaking his head, "may be buffalo—may be Catawba!"

Having at length satisfied himself that they were really buffalo, he pushed on more rapidly, and on the way, assigned his reasons for his hesitation. He said that the Catawbas had long been at war with his tribe, and were the most cunning and wicked nation in the world. That, a few years ago, they had secretly approached his camp in the night, and sent out a few of their spies, mounted upon buffalo hoofs, who walked round their camp, and then returned to the main body. That, in the morning, he and his warriors, perceiving their tracks, supposed a herd of buffalo to be ahead of them, and moved on rapidly in pursuit. That they soon fell into the ambuscade, were fired on by the Catawbas, and many of them killed. The Catawbas, however, quickly gave way, and were pursued by his young men with great eagerness. But they had taken the precaution to stick a number of slender reeds in the grass, sharpened like a pen, and dipped in rattlesnake's poison, that, so as his young men pursued them eagerly, most of them were artificially snake-bitten, and lamed. That the Catawbas then turned upon them, overpowered them, and took the scalps of all who had been lamed by the reeds. The old man concluded by shaking his head, and declaring that "Catawba was a very bad Indian; a perfect devil for mischief."

Smith, however, was so unfortunate a few days afterward, as to fall into discredit with these simple people. He had been directed to go out and kill some venison for the squaws and children, who had suffered for several days, during the absence of the greater part of the warriors. As this was the first time that he had been intrusted with so weighty a commission alone, he determined to signalize his hunt by an unusual display of skill and enterprise. He, therefore, struck out boldly into the woods, and at a few miles distance, falling upon a fresh buffalo trail, he pushed on for several miles with great eagerness. Despairing, however, of overtaking them, as the evening came on he began to retrace his steps, and as he had taken a considerable circuit, he determined to cut across the hills, and reach the village by a shorter way. He soon became inextricably involved in the mazes of the forest, and at dark found himself completely bewildered. He fired his gun repeatedly, in hopes of being heard, but his signal was unanswered, and he wandered through the woods the whole night, totally unable to find his way home.

Early in the morning, the Indians, probably suspecting him for desertion, started out in pursuit of him, but observing the zigzag manner in which the young woodsman had marched, they soon became satisfied of the truth, and their anger was changed to laughter and contempt. Smith's rifle was taken from him, and a bow and arrow (the weapons of a boy) were placed in his hands; and although he was treated with undiminished kindness by all, yet it was evident that it was mingled with compassion and contempt for his ignorance of the woods. He was now placed under the particular care of Tontileaugo, his adopted brother, and a renowned hunter and warrior. With the aid of his directions, he soon learned all the mysteries of hunting. He trapped beaver, killed deer, bear, and buffalo with great readiness, and, in the course of the winter, rose considerably in reputation. The warriors were still absent, and the women and children depended on them entirely for subsistence.

Sometimes they were three days without food; particularly, when the snow became hard, and the noise which they made in walking on the crust frightened the deer, so that they could not come within gunshot. Their only resource, then, was to hunt bear trees; that is, for large hollow trees in which bears lay concealed during the winter. The hole is generally from thirty to fifty feet from the ground, and they are often compelled to climb up and apply fire, in order to drive Bruin out, who obstinately maintains his ground until nearly stifled with smoke, and then, sneezing and snuffling, and growling, he shows himself at the mouth of his hole, for a little fresh air. The hunter stations himself below, and fires upon him as soon as he appears. Toward spring, the warriors generally return, and game is then killed in abundance.

We shall here pause in our narrative, to mention some traits of Indian character and manners, which, perhaps, will be interesting to many of our readers, who have not had opportunities of informing themselves on the subject. The lives of the men are passed in alternate action of the most violent kind, and indolence the most excessive. Nothing but the pressing call of hunger will rouse them to much exertion.

In the months of August and September, when roasting-ears are abundant, they abandon themselves to laziness, dancing, and gaming, and can rarely be roused, even to hunt, so long as their corn-fields will furnish them food. During these months they are generally seen lying down in idle contemplation, dancing with their squaws, playing at foot-ball, or engaged in a game resembling dice, of which they are immoderately fond. War and hunting are their only serious occupations, and all the drudgery of life devolves upon the squaws. Smith gave high offense to the warriors by taking a hoe into his hands, and working with the squaws for half an hour, at a time when they were engaged in planting corn. They reprimanded him with some severity for his industry, observing, that it was degrading to a warrior to be engaged in labor like a squaw; and for the future he must learn to demean himself more loftily, always remembering that he was a member of a warlike tribe, and a noble family.

They are remarkably hospitable, always offering to a stranger the best that they have. If a warrior, upon entering a strange wigwam, is not immediately invited to eat, he considers himself deeply affronted, although he may have just risen from a meal at home. It is not enough on these occasions that ordinary food, such as venison or hominy, is offered. It is thought rude and churlish, not to set before their guest their greatest delicacies, such as sugar, bear's oil, honey, and, if they have it, rum. If there is no food of any kind in the house, which is often the case, the fact is instantly mentioned, and is at once accepted as a sufficient apology. Smith was so unfortunate as to incur some reproach upon this subject also. While he and his adopted brother, Tontileaugo, were encamped in the woods, hunting, there came a hunter of the Wyandott tribe, who entered their camp, faint and hungry, having had no success in hunting, and, consequently, having fasted for several days.

Tontileaugo was absent at the time, but Smith received the visitor with great hospitality (as he thought), and gave him an abundant meal of hominy and venison. Shortly after the Wyandott's departure, his brother, Tontileaugo, returned, and Smith informed him of the visit of the stranger, and of his hospitable reception. Tontileaugo listened with gravity, and replied: "And I suppose, of course, you brought up some of the sugar and bear's oil, which was left below in the canoe?" "No," replied Smith, "I never thought of it; it was at too great a distance." "Well, brother," replied Tontileaugo, "you have behaved just like a Dutchman! I can excuse it in you for this time, as you are young, and have been brought up among the white people; but you must learn to behave like a warrior, and never be caught in such *little* actions! Great actions, alone, can ever make a great man!"

Their power of sustaining long-continued fatigue is very extraordinary. Even their squaws will travel as fast as an ordinary horse, and pack an incredible quantity of baggage upon their backs. In the spring of 1756, a great quantity of game had been killed, at a considerable distance from the village; and all the inhabitants, including squaws and boys, turned out to bring it home. Smith was loaded with a large piece of buffalo, which, after packing two or three miles, he found too heavy for him, and was compelled to throw it down. One of the squaws laughed heartily, and coming up, relieved him of a large part of it, adding it to her own pack, which before was equal to Smith's. This, he says, stimulated him to greater exertion than the severest punishment would have done.

Their warriors, for a short distance, are not swifter than the whites, but are capable of sustaining the exercise for an incredible length of time. An Indian warrior can run for twelve or fourteen hours without refreshment; and after a hasty meal, and very brief repose, appears completely refreshed, and ready for a second course. Smith found it more difficult to compete with them in this respect, than in any other. For although he ran with great swiftness for a few miles, he could not continue such violent exertion for a whole day. While he and his brother, Tontileaugo, were encamped at a distance from the others, they were much distressed from having to pack their meat from such a distance, and as three horses were constantly grazing near them (for there was grass under the snow), Tontileaugo proposed that they should run them down, and catch them, it having been found impossible to take them in any other way.

Smith, having but little relish for the undertaking, urged the impossibility of success. But Tontileaugo replied that he had frequently run down bear, deer, elk, and buffalo, and believed that, in the course of a day and night, he could run down any four-footed animal, except the wolf. Smith observed, that, although deer were swifter than horses for a short distance, yet, that a horse could run much longer than either the elk or buffalo, and that he was confident that they would tire themselves to no purpose. The other insisted upon making the experiment, at any rate; and at daylight, on a cold day in February, and on a hard snow several inches deep, the race began. The two hunters stripped themselves to their moccasins, and started at full speed. The horses were in very high order, and very wild, but contented themselves with running in a circle of six or seven miles circumference, and would not entirely abandon their usual grazing ground.

At ten o'clock, Smith had dropped considerably astern, and before eleven, Tontileaugo and the horses were out of sight; the Indian keeping close at their heels, and allowing them no time for rest. Smith, naked as he was, and glowing with exercise, threw himself upon the hard snow; and having cooled himself in this manner, he remained stationary until three o'clock in the evening, when the horses again came in view, their flanks smoking like a seething kettle, and Tontileaugo close behind them, running with undiminished speed. Smith being now perfectly fresh, struck in ahead of Tontileaugo, and compelled the horses to quicken their speed, while his Indian brother, from behind, encouraged him to do his utmost, after shouting "Chako! chokoa-nough!" (pull away! pull away, my boy!)

Had Tontileaugo thought of resting, and committed the chase to Smith alone, for some hours, and then in his turn relieved him, they might have succeeded; but neglecting this plan, they both continued the chase until dark, when, perceiving that the horses ran still with great vigor, they despaired of success, and returned to the camp, having tasted nothing since morning, and one of them at least having run nearly one hundred miles. Tontileaugo was somewhat crest-fallen at the result of the race, and grumbled not a little at their long wind; but Smith assured him that they had attempted an impossibility, and he became reconciled to their defeat.

Their discipline with regard to their children is not remarkably strict. Whipping is rare with them, and is considered the most disgraceful of all punishments. Ducking in cold water is the ordinary punishment of misbehavior; and as might be expected, their children are more obedient in winter than in summer. Smith, during his first winter's residence among them, was an eye-witness to a circumstance, which we shall relate as a lively example of Indian manners. His brother, Tontileaugo, was married to a Wyandott squaw, who had had several children by a former husband. One of these children offended his step-father in some way, who, in requital, gave him the "strappado," with a whip made of buffalo hide.

The discipline was quite moderate, but the lad shouted very loudly, and soon brought out his Wyandott mother. She instantly took her child's part with great animation. It was in vain that the husband explained the offense, and urged the moderation with which he had inflicted the punishment. All would not do. "The child," she said, "was no slave, to be beaten and scourged with a whip. His father had been a warrior, and a Wyandott, and his child was entitled to honorable usage. If he had offended his step-father, there was cold water enough to be had; let him be ducked until he would be brought to reason, and she would not utter a word of complaint; but a 'buffalo tug' was no weapon with which the son of a warrior ought to be struck: his father's spirit was frowning in the skies at the degradation of his child."

Tontileaugo listened with great calmness to this indignant remonstrance; and, having lit his pipe, strolled off, in order to give his squaw an opportunity of becoming cool. The offense, however, had been of too serious a nature, and his squaw, shortly after his departure, caught a horse, and, taking her children with her, rode off to the Wyandott village, about forty miles distant. In the afternoon, Tontileaugo returned to his wigwam, and found no one there but Smith, an old man, and a boy. He appeared much troubled at his squaw's refractory conduct, uttered some deep interjections, but finally did as most husbands are compelled to do—followed her to make his peace.

They are remarkably superstitious, and hold their "conjurers" in great veneration. These dignitaries are generally old and decrepid. On the borders of Lake Erie, one evening, a squaw came running into camp, where Smith, Tontileaugo, and a few others were reposing, after a long day's journey, and alarmed them with the information, that two strange Indians, armed with rifles, were standing upon the opposite shore of a small creek, and appeared to be reconnoitering the camp. It was supposed they were Johnston Mohawks, and that they would shortly be attacked. Instantly the women and children were sent into the woods, and the warriors retired from the light of the fires, taking their stations silently in the dark, and awaiting the enemy's approach.

Manetohcoa, their old conjurer, alone remained by the fire, regardless of the danger, and busily employed in his necromantic art. To assist him in his labors, he had dyed feathers, the shoulder-blade of a wild cat, and a large quantity of leaf tobacco. Thus accoutered, he conjured away, with great industry, in the light of the fire, and exposed to the most imminent danger in case of an attack, as he was very lame, totally deaf, and miserably rheumatic. After a few minutes' anxious expectation, old Manetohcoa called aloud upon his friends to return to the fire, assuring them that there was no danger. They instantly obeyed with the utmost confidence, and their squaws and children were recalled, as if no further danger was to be apprehended. Upon coming up, they found old Manetohcoa enveloped in tobacco smoke, and holding the bone of the wild cat in his hand, upon which his eyes were fixed with great earnestness.

He told them, after having burnt his feathers, fumigated himself with the tobacco, heated his blade bone, and pronounced his charm, that he expected to see a multitude of Mohawks arise upon the surface of the bone; but, to his surprise, he saw only the figures of two wolves! He assured them that the woman had mistaken the wolves for Mohawks, and that no enemy was near them. The Indians instantly composed themselves to rest, relying confidently upon the truth of the old man's assertions. In the morning, to Smith's astonishment, the tracks of two wolves were seen at the spot where the squaw's account had placed the Mohawks. The Indians expressed no surprise at this extraordinary confirmation of the old man's skill in divination; but Smith's infidelity was powerfully shaken! Admitting the truth of the facts (and from Colonel Smith's high reputation for piety and integrity, we presume they can not be questioned), it must be acknowledged either an extraordinary instance of sagacity, or else we must class it among those numerous fortunate circumstances which occasionally have staggered the faith of much more learned men than Colonel Smith. Johnston's superstition is well known; and Smith's doubts may at least be pardoned.

Their military principles are few and simple, but remarkable for sagacity, and singularly adapted to the character of the warfare in which they are generally engaged. Caution, perhaps, rather than boldness, is the leading feature of their system. To destroy their enemy at the least possible risk to themselves, is their great object. They are by no means, as has been sometimes supposed, destitute of discipline. Their maneuvers are few, but in performing them they are peculiarly alert, ready, and intelligent. In forming a line, in protecting their flanks by bodies arranged *en potence*, or in forming a large hollow square for the purpose of making head against a superior force, they are inferior to no troops in the world. Each movement is indicated by a loud whoop, of peculiar intonation, from their leader, and is irregularly but rapidly obeyed. The result is order, although during the progress of the movement the utmost apparent confusion prevails.

Nothing astonished them more than the pertinacity with which Braddock adhered to European tactics, in the celebrated battle on the banks of the Monongahela. They often assured Smith that the Long Knives were fools; that they could neither fight nor run away, but drew themselves up in close order, and stood still, as if to give their enemies the best possible opportunity of shooting them down at their leisure. Grant's masquerade before the walls of Fort Du Quesne also gave them much perplexity. A venerable Caughnewaughga chief, who had, in his youth, been a renowned warrior and counselor, and who excelled all his contemporaries in sagacity and benevolence, frequently told Smith that Grant's conduct was to him totally inexplicable.

This general formed the advance of General Forbes in 1777. He marched with great secrecy and celerity through the woods, and appeared upon the hill above Du Quesne in the night. There he encamped, and, by way of bravado, caused the drums to beat and the bagpipes to play, as if to inform the enemy of his arrival. At daylight he was surrounded by Indians, who, creeping up under cover of bushes, gullies, etc., nearly annihilated his army without any sensible loss to themselves. The old chief observed, "that as the great art of war consisted in ambushing and surprising your enemy, and preventing yourself from being surprised, that Grant had acted like a skillful warrior in coming secretly upon them; but that his subsequent conduct in giving the alarm to his enemy, instead of falling upon him with the bayonet, was very extraordinary; that he could only account for it by supposing that Grant, like too many other warriors, was fond of rum, and had become drunk about daylight."

They have the most sovereign contempt for all book learning! Smith was occasionally in the habit of reading a few elementary English books which he had procured from traders, and lost credit among them by his fondness for study.

Nothing, with them, can atone for a practical ignorance of the woods. We have seen, that, for losing himself, Smith was degraded from the rank of a warrior and reduced to that of a boy. Two years afterward he regained his rank, and was presented with a rifle, as a reward for an exhibition of hardihood and presence of mind. In company with the old chief, to whom we have just referred, and several other Indians, he was engaged in hunting. A deep snow was upon the ground, and the weather was tempestuous. On their way home, a number of raccoon tracks were seen in the snow, and Smith was directed to follow them and observe where they treed. He did so, but they led him off to a much greater distance than was supposed, and the hunters were several miles ahead of him when he attempted to rejoin them.

At first their tracks were very plain in the snow, and although night approached, and the camp was distant, Smith felt no anxiety. But about dusk his situation became critical. The weather became suddenly much colder, the wind blew a perfect hurricane, and whirlwinds of snow blinded his eyes and filled up the tracks of his companions. He had with him neither a gun, flint, nor steel; no shelter but a blanket, and no weapon but a tomahawk. He plodded on for several hours, ignorant of his route, stumbling over logs, and chilled with cold, until the snow became so deep as seriously to impede his progress, and the flakes fell so thick as to render it impossible to see where he was going. He shouted aloud for help, but no answer was returned, and, as the storm every instant became more outrageous, he began to think that his hour had come.

Providentially, in stumbling on through the snow, he came to a large sycamore with a considerable opening on the windward side. He hastily crept in, and found the hollow sufficiently large to accommodate him for the night, if the weather side could be closed so as to exclude the snow and wind, which was beating against it with great violence. He instantly went to work with his tomahawk and cut a number of sticks, which he placed upright against the hole, and piled brush against it in great quantities, leaving a space open for himself to creep in. He then broke up a decayed log, and, cutting it into small pieces, pushed them, one by one, into the hollow of the tree, and lastly crept in himself. With these pieces he stopped up the remaining holes of his den, until not a chink was left to admit the light. The snow, drifting in large quantities, was soon banked up against his defenses, and completely sheltered him from the storm, which still continued to rage with undiminished fury. He then danced violently in the center of his den for two hours, until he was sufficiently warmed, and, wrapping himself in his blanket, he slept soundly until morning.

He awoke in utter darkness, and, groping about, he

found his door and attempted to push it away, but the snow had drifted against it in such quantities that it resisted his utmost efforts. His hair now began to bristle, and he feared that he had, with great ingenuity, contrived to bury himself alive. He laid down again for several hours, meditating upon what he should do, and whether he should not attempt to cut through the tree with his tomahawk; but at length he made one more desperate effort to push away the door, and succeeded in moving it several inches, when a great bank of snow fell in upon him from above, convincing him at once of the immense quantity which had fallen. He at length burrowed his way into the upper air, and found it broad daylight, and the weather calm and mild. The snow lay nearly four feet deep; but he was now enabled to see his way clearly, and, by examining the barks of the trees, was enabled to return to camp.

He was received with loud shouts of joy and congratulation, but not a single question was asked until he had dispatched a hearty meal of venison, hominy, and sugar.

The old chief, Tecaughnetanego, whom we have already mentioned, then presented him with his own pipe, and they all remained silent until Smith had smoked. When they saw him completely refreshed, the venerable chief addressed him in a mild and affectionate manner (for Smith at that time was a mere boy with them), and desired to hear a particular account of the manner in which he had passed the night. Not a word was spoken until Smith concluded his story, and then he was greeted on all sides with shouts of approbation.

Tecaughnetanego arose and addressed him in a short speech, in which his courage, hardihood, and presence of mind, were highly commended. He was exhorted to go on as he had begun, and assured that one day he would make a very great man; that all his brothers rejoiced in his safety, as much as they had lamented his supposed death; that they were preparing snowshoes to go in search of him when he appeared; but, as he had been brought up effeminately among the whites, they never expected to see him alive. In conclusion, he was promoted from the rank of a boy to that of a warrior, and assured that, when they sold skins in the spring, at Detroit, they would purchase for him a new rifle. And they faithfully observed their promise.

They are extravagantly fond of rum; but drinking does not with them, as with the whites, form a part of the regular business of life. They occasionally indulge in a wild and frantic revel, which sometimes lasts several days, and then return to their ordinary habits. They can not husband their liquor, for the sake of prolonging the pleasure of toping. It is used with the most reckless profusion while it lasts, and all drink to beastly intoxication. Their squaws are as fond of liquor as the warriors, and share in all their excesses.

After the party to which Smith belonged had sold their beaver skins, and provided themselves with ammunition and blankets, all their surplus cash was expended in rum, which was bought by the keg. They then held a council, in which a few strong-bodied hunters were selected to remain sober, and protect the rest during the revel, for which they were preparing. Smith was courteously invited to get drunk, but upon his refusal, he was told that he must then join the sober party, and assist in keeping order. This, as he quickly found, was an extremely dangerous office; but before engaging in the serious business of drinking, the warriors carefully removed their tomahawks and knives, and took every precaution against bloodshed. A shocking scene then commenced. Rum was swallowed in immense quantities, and their wild passions were stimulated to frenzy! Smith and the sober party, were exposed to the most imminent peril, and were compelled to risk their lives every moment. Much injury was done, but no lives were lost.

In the Ottawa camp, where the same infernal orgies were celebrated, the result was more tragical. Several warriors were killed on the spot, and a number more wounded. So long as they had money, the revel was kept up day and night, but when their funds were exhausted, they gathered up their dead and wounded, and, with dejected countenances, returned to the wilderness. All had some cause of lamentation. The blanket of one had been burnt, and he had no money to buy another; the fine clothes of another had been torn from his back; some had been maimed; and all had improvidently wasted their money.

The religion of the Indians, although defaced by superstition, and intermingled with many rites and notions which, *to us*, appear absurd, contains, nevertheless, a distinct acknowledgment of the existence of a Supreme Being, and a future state. The various tribes are represented by Dr. Robertson as polytheists; and Mr. Hume considers polytheism as inseparably attendant upon the savage state. It appears, however, that the Western Indians approached more nearly to simple deism than most savage nations with whom we have been heretofore acquainted. One Great Spirit is universally worshiped throughout the West; although different tribes give him different names. In the immense prairies of the West, he is generally termed the Wahcondah, or master of life. With the Indians of the lakes, he was generally termed Manito, which, we believe, means simply "The Spirit." In the language of Smith's tribe he was known by the title of "Owaneeyo," or the possessor of all things.

Human sacrifices are very common among the tribes living west of the Mississippi; but I have seen no evidence of such a custom among those of the North-west.

Tecaughnetanego, the veteran chief whom we have already mentioned, was esteemed the wisest and most venerable of his own nation; and his religious opinions, perhaps, may be regarded as a very favorable sample of Indian theology. We shall take the liberty of detailing several conversations of this old chief, particularly upon religious subjects, which to us were the most interesting passages of Smith's diary; growing, as they did, out of a situation which required the exercise of some philosophy and reliance upon Providence. We have already adverted to the precarious nature of the Indian supplies of food, dependent, as they are, upon the woods for their meat, and liable to frequent failures from the state of the weather, and other circumstances over which they have no control.

It so happened that Smith, together with Tontileaugo and the old chief, Tecaughnetanego, were encamped at a great distance from the rest of the tribe, and during the early part of the winter they were very successful in hunting, and were abundantly supplied with all necessaries. Upon the breach between Tontileaugo and his wife, however, Smith and the old chief were left in the woods, with no other company than that of Nungany, a little son of the latter, not more than ten years old. Tecaughnetanego, notwithstanding his age (which exceeded sixty), was still a skillful hunter, and capable of great exertion when in good health; but, unfortunately, was subject to dreadful attacks of rheumatism, during which, in addition to the most excruciating pain, he was incapable of moving his limbs, or helping himself in any way. Smith was but a young hunter, and Nungany totally useless except as a cook; but while Tecaughnetanego retained the use of his limbs, notwithstanding the loss of Tontileaugo, they killed game very abundantly.

About the middle of January, however, the weather became excessively cold, and the old chief was stretched upon the floor of his wigwam, totally unable to move. The whole care of the family now devolved upon Smith, and his exertions were not wanting. But from his youth and inexperience, he was unable to provide as plentifully as Tontileaugo had done, and they were reduced to very short allowance. The old chief, notwithstanding the excruciating pain which he daily suffered, always strove to entertain Smith, at night, with agreeable conversation, and instructed him carefully and repeatedly in the art of hunting. At length the snow became hard and crusty, and the noise of Smith's footsteps frightened the deer, so that, with the utmost caution he could use, he was unable to get within gunshot. The family, in consequence, were upon the eve of starvation.

One evening Smith entered the hut, faint and weary, after a hunt of two days, during which he had eaten nothing. Tecaughnetanego had fasted for the same length of time, and both had been upon short allowance for a week. Smith came in very moodily, and laying aside his gun and powder-horn, sat down by the fire in silence. Tecaughnetanego inquired mildly and calmly, what success he had had. Smith answered that they must starve, as the deer were so wild that he could not get within gunshot, and it was too far to go to any Indian settlement for food. The old man remained silent for a moment, and then, in the same mild tone, asked him if he was hungry? Smith replied, that the keen appetite seemed gone, but that he felt sick and dizzy, and scarcely able to walk. "I have made Nungany hunt up some food for you, brother," said the old man kindly, and bade him produce it. This food was nothing more than the bones of a fox and wild-cat, which had been thrown into the woods a few days before, and which the buzzards had already picked almost bare.

Nungany had collected and boiled them, until the sinews were stripped of the flesh, intending them for himself and father, both of whom were nearly famished; but the old man had put them away for Smith, in case he should again return without food. Smith quickly threw himself upon this savory soup, and swallowed spoonful after spoonful with the voracity of a wolf. Tecaughnetanego waited patiently until he had finished his meal, which continued until the last spoonful had been swallowed, and then handing him his own pipe, invited him to smoke. Little Nungany, in the meantime, removed the kettle, after looking in vain for some remnant of the feast for his own supper. He had watched every mouthful which Smith swallowed with eager longing, but in perfect silence, and finding that, for the third night, he must remain supperless, he sat down quietly at his father's feet, and was soon asleep.

Tecaughnetanego, as soon as Smith had smoked, asked him if he felt refreshed; and upon receiving an animated assurance in the affirmative, he addressed him mildly as follows: "I saw, my brother, when you first came in, that you had been unfortunate in hunting, and were ready to despair. I should have spoken at the time, what I am now about to say, but I have always observed that hungry people are not in a temper to listen to reason. You are now refreshed, and can listen patiently to the words of your elder brother. I was once young like you, but am now old. I have seen sixty snows fall, and have often been in a worse condition, from want of food, than we now are; yet I have always been supplied, and that, too, at the very time when I was ready to despair. Brother: you have been brought up among the whites, and have not had the same opportunities of seeing how wonderfully Owaneeyo provides food for his children in the woods! He sometimes lets them be in great want, to teach them that they are dependent upon him, and to remind them of their own weakness; but he never permits them absolutely to perish. Rest assured that your brother is telling you no lie; but be satisfied that he will do as I have told you. Go now; sleep soundly; rise early in the morning and go out to hunt; be strong and diligent; do your best, and trust to Owaneeyo for the rest."

When we recollect that this admirable speech came from a wild Indian, totally uninstructed, and untaught to restrain his passions; that, at the very time, he was suffering the most excruciating pain, both from disease and hunger; that he had denied himself a morsel of food, in order to bestow it upon Smith; and, lastly, that from the state of the snow and Smith's inexperience, he had no human prospect of relief; it is no exaggeration to say, that a more striking example of wisdom, mildness, and magnanimity, was never exhibited.

Smith was powerfully struck by the old man's reasoning; and still more affected by the patience and firmness with which he sustained himself, under the complicated suffering with which he was visited. In the morning, at daylight, he seized his gun, and commenced the duties of the day with great spirit. He saw a great many deer, but the crashing of the crust alarmed them as heretofore; and after hunting until noon without success, he began to suspect that Tecaughnetanego must have been mistaken, and that they were certainly destined to starve. His hunger seemed rather whetted than allayed by his sumptuous repast upon wild-cat bones, the evening before, and now became so ravenous as to divest him of all reason, and he determined to run back to Pennsylvania. True, the intervening country was crowded with hostile Indians, but the edge of the tomahawk was not keener than that of hunger; and a sharp and quick death infinitely preferable to the slow and torturing ravages of starvation.

Having hastily adopted this desperate resolution, he quickened his pace, and moved off steadily in the direction of Pennsylvania. He had not gone more than seven or eight miles, before he heard the lowing of buffalo in front, and in a few minutes, came in view of a noble heard, marching leisurely ahead of him. He ran with great rapidity in such a direction as to head them, and concealing himself in a thicket, awaited their approach. They passed leisurely within a few yards of him, so that he had an opportunity of selecting a fat heifer, which he killed at the first fire. He quickly struck fire from his flint—and cutting a few slices from the fleshiest part, he laid it upon the coals, but could not wait until it was done. After gorging himself with raw beef, which (with the exception of the wild-cat bones of the preceding night) he thought the most delicious food he had ever tasted, he began to be tenderly concerned for the old man and little boy, whom he had left in a famishing condition at the wigwam.

His conscience reproached him for leaving them to perish; and he instantly loaded himself heavily with the fattest and fleshiest pieces, and having secured the rest from the wolves, returned to their camp, with as much expedition as he could exert. It was late at night when he entered the wigwam. Tecaughnetanego received him with the same mild equanimity which had heretofore distinguished him, and thanked him very affectionately for the exertions which he had used, while the eyes of the famished boy were fastened upon the beef as if he would devour it raw. His father ordered him to hang on the kettle and cook some beef for them all; but Smith declared that he himself would cook for the old man, while Nungany broiled some meat upon the coals for himself. The boy looked eagerly at his father for his consent, and receiving a nod in reply, he sprung upon the meat as a kite would pounce upon a pullet, and unable to wait for the slow operation of the fire, began to eat it raw.

Smith, in the meantime, had cut several very thin slices and placed them in the kettle to boil; but supposing Tecaughnetanego as impatient as himself, he was about to take it off the fire after a very few minutes, when the old man, in a tone as calm and quiet as if he had not fasted for three whole days, desired him to "let it be done enough." At the same time he ordered Nungany, who was still eating like a shark, to take no more at present, but to sit down, and after a few minutes he might sup a little broth. The old man then reminded Smith of their conversation the night before; and of the striking truth with which his assurance of Owaneeyo's goodness had been accomplished. At length he desired Smith to give him the beef, observing that it had been boiled enough; and, as if he had reserved all his vigor for that moment, he assaulted it with a keenness and perseverance which showed that the gifts of Owaneeyo were not thrown away.

In the morning, Tecaughnetanego requested Smith to return to the spot where he had killed the buffalo, and bring in the rest of it to camp. He accordingly took down his rifle and entered the wood, intending to hunt on the road. At the distance of a few miles from camp, he saw a large elm, which had been much scratched, and perceiving a hole in it at the distance of forty feet from the ground, he supposed that a bear had selected it for his winter-quarters, and instantly determined to rouse him from his slumbers. With his tomahawk, he cut down a sapling which grew near the tree, in such a manner as to lodge it against the den. He then cut a long pole, and tied a few bunches of rotten wood to the end of it. Taking it then in his hand, he climbed the sapling, until he reached the mouth of the den, and setting fire to the rotten wood, put it into the hollow as far as he could reach. He soon had the gratification of hearing poor Bruin sneeze and cough, as if in great trouble; and rapidly sliding down the sapling, he seized his gun at the moment the bear showed himself. He instantly shot him, and having loaded himself with the hind-quarters, he marched back in high spirits to the wigwam. They were now well provided for a week; and in a few days the snow thawed so much as to enable him to kill deer; so that, during the rest of the winter, they fared sumptuously.

Early in April, Tecaughnetanego's rheumatism had abated so much as to permit him to walk, upon which, they all three built a bark canoe, and descended the Ollentangy, until the water became so shallow as to endanger their frail bark among the rocks. A council was then held, in which Tecaughnetanego proposed to go ashore, and pray for rain to raise the creek or river so as to enable them to continue their journey. Smith readily consented, and they accordingly disembarked, drawing their canoe ashore after them. Here the old Indian built a "sweating house," in order to purify himself, before engaging in his religious duties.

He stuck a number of semicircular hoops in the ground, and laid a blanket over them. He then heated a number of large stones, and placed them under the blanket, and finally crawled in himself, with a kettle of water in his hand, directing Smith to draw down the blanket after him, so as almost entirely to exclude the external air. He then poured the water upon the hot stones, and began to sing aloud with great energy, the steam rising from the blanket like a heavy mist. In this hot place he continued for fifteen minutes, singing the whole time, and then came out dripping with perspiration from head to foot. As soon as he had taken breath, he began to burn tobacco, throwing it into the fire by handfuls, at the same time repeating the following words in a tone of deep and solemn earnestness:

"O Great Owaneeyo! I thank thee that I have regained the use of my legs once more; that I am now able to walk about and kill turkeys, without feeling exquisite pain. Oh! ho! ho! ho! Grant that my knees and ankles may be right well, that I may be able not only to walk, but to run and to jump logs, as I did last fall! Oh! ho! ho! ho! Grant that, upon this voyage we may frequently kill bears as they may be crossing the Sandusky and Scioto! Oh! ho! ho! ho! Grant that we may also kill a few turkeys to stew with our bear's meat! Oh! ho! ho! ho! Grant that rain may come to raise the Ollentangy a few feet, that we may cross in safety down to Scioto, without splitting our canoe upon the rocks! And now, O Great Owaneeyo! thou knowest how fond I am of tobacco, and though I do not know when I shall get any more, yet you see that I have freely given up all that I have for a burnt-offering; therefore, I expect that thou wilt be merciful and hear all my petitions; and I, thy servant, will thank thee, and love thee for all thy gifts."

Smith held the chief in great veneration, and has observed, that he never in his life listened to a man who reasoned more clearly and powerfully upon such subjects as came before him; and he heard the first part of his prayer with great respect and due gravity; but when the attention of Owaneeyo was called to the tobacco, which his votary bestowed upon him so liberally, his muscles gave way, and in spite of his efforts to restrain himself, he burst into a low and half stifled laugh. Ridicule is at all times formidable, but particularly so in a moment of enthusiasm and sincere devotion. Tecaughnetanego was deeply and seriously offended, and rebuked his young companion in the following words:

"Brother, I have somewhat to say to you! When you were reading your books in our village, you know I would not let the boys plague you, or laugh at you, although we all thought it a foolish and idle occupation in a warrior. I respected your feelings *then;* but just now I saw you laughing at me!

Brother, I do not believe that you look upon praying as a silly custom, for you sometimes pray yourself. Perhaps you think my mode of praying foolish, but if so, would it not be more friendly to reason with me, and instruct me, than to sit on that log and laugh at an old man?"

Smith apologized with great earnestness, declaring that he respected and loved him sincerely, but that when he saw him throw the last of his tobacco into the fire, and recollected how fond he was of it, he could not help smiling a little, although for the future he would never have reason to complain of him on that account. The old man, without saying a word, handed him his pipe as a token of friendship, although it was filled only with willow bark; and the little difference was soon forgotten.

Smith then explained to him the outlines of the Christian religion, and dwelt particularly upon the doctrine of reconciliation through the atonement of Christ. Tecaughnetanego listened with patience and gravity until his companion had ended his remarks, and then calmly observed, that "it *might be so!*" He even acknowledged, "that it did not appear so absurd as the doctrine of the Romish priests, which he had heard at Detroit, but declared that he was too old *now* to change his religion; that he should, therefore, continue to worship God after the manner of his fathers; and if it was not consistent with the honor of the Great Spirit to accept of him in *that way*, then he hoped that he would receive him upon such terms as were acceptable to him; that it was his earnest and sincere desire to worship the Great Spirit, and obey his wishes, and he hoped that Owaneeyo would overlook such faults as arose from ignorance and weakness, not willful neglect." To a speech of this kind, the sentiments of which find an echo in almost every breast, Smith could make no reply. Here, therefore, the subject ended.

A few days afterward, there came a fine rain, and the Ollentangy was soon sufficiently deep to admit of their passage in safety, and after reaching the Sandusky they killed four bears and a great many wild turkeys. Tecaughnetanego gravely assured Smith, that this was a clear and direct answer to his prayer, and inferred from it, that his religion could not be as unacceptable to Owaneeyo as Smith supposed. Perhaps it would be difficult to disprove the first part of the old Indian's observation; the last is more questionable.

We have already gleaned all the most interesting parts of Smith's narrative, for the long details of huntings, trappings, and migrations, without particular object or incident, would scarcely be interesting to the reader. We have endeavored to select such circumstances, as woul l give the general reader a lively idea of the habits and opinions of the Western Indians, without burdening our narrative with too much detail. As most, if not all, the subsequent adventures, will have a close connection with Indian life, it was thought proper to commence with a narrative which should throw some light upon that subject. It is only necessary, further, to observe, that in the summer of 1759, and in the fourth year of his captivity, or rather, adoption, Smith, accompanied by Tecaughnetanego and Nungany, sailed in a bark canoe down the St. Lawrence, as far as Montreal.

Here he privately left his Indian companions, and went on board a French transport, which he had heard was about to sail, with a number of English prisoners on board, intended to be exchanged. After having been detained some time in Montreal, in consequence of the English fleet being below, he was at length exchanged and returned to his native country. His family and sweetheart received him with great joy; but to his inexpressible mortification, the latter had been married only a few days before his arrival. His subsequent adventures, although novel and interesting, do not properly come within the range of our present subject. We refer the reader, who may desire to know more, to Colonel Smith's own narrative, which has recently been reprinted.

CHAPTER II.

THE adventures which, in order of time, should come next, are those of the celebrated DANIEL BOONE; for of Findley—said to be the first white man who ever visited Kentucky—nothing is known but the simple fact that he *did* visit it, first alone, and afterward in company with Boone. It is much to be regretted that the materials for a sketch of Boone are so scanty. He has left us a brief account of his adventures, but they are rather such as one would require for the composition of an epitaph than of a biography. The leading incidents are mentioned in a general way; and there are some gaudy and ambitious sketches of *scenery* which swell the bulk of the piece without either pleasing the imagination or gratifying the curiosity. It would seem that the brief notes of the plain old woodsman had been committed to some young sciolist in literature, who thought that flashy description could atone for barrenness of incident.

A general summary of remarkable events neither excites nor gratifies curiosity like a minute detail of *all the circumstances* connected with them. This trait, so essential to the interest of narratives, and of which perhaps the most splendid example in existence has been given in Mr. Cooper's "Last of the Mohicans," is deplorably wanting in most of the materials to which we have had access. A novelist may fill up the blank from his own imagination; but a writer who professes to adhere to truth is fettered down to the record before him. If, therefore, in the following details, we should be found guilty of the unpardonable sin of dullness, we hope that at least a portion of the blame will fall upon the scantiness of the materials.

from the fierce conflicts which generally followed these casual rencounters, the country had been known among them by the name of "*the dark and bloody ground!*" The two adventurers soon learned the additional danger to which they were exposed. While roving carelessly from canebrake to canebrake, and admiring the rank growth of vegetation, and the variety of timber which marked the fertility of the soil, they were suddenly alarmed by the appearance of a party of Indians, who, springing from their place of concealment, rushed upon them with a rapidity which rendered escape impossible.

They were almost instantly seized, disarmed, and made prisoners. Their feelings may be readily imagined. They were in the hands of an enemy who knew no alternative between adoption and torture; and the numbers and fleetness of their captors rendered escape by open means impossible, while their jealous vigilance seemed equally fatal to any secret attempt. Boone, however, was possessed of a temper admirably adapted to the circumstances in which he was placed. Of a cold and saturnine, rather than an ardent disposition, he was never either so much elevated by good fortune or depressed by bad as to lose for an instant the full possession of all his faculties. He saw that immediate escape was impossible; but he encouraged his companion, and constrained himself to accompany the Indians in all their excursions with so calm and contented an air that their vigilance insensibly began to relax.

On the seventh evening of their captivity, they encamped in a thick canebrake, and, having built a large fire, lay down to rest. The party whose duty it was to watch were weary and negligent, and about midnight, Boone, who had not closed an eye, ascertained from the deep breathing all around him that the whole party, including Stuart, was in a deep sleep. Gently and gradually extricating himself from the Indians who lay around him, he walked cautiously to the spot where Stuart lay, and, having succeeded in awakening him without alarming the rest, he briefly informed him of his determination, and exhorted him to arise, make no noise, and follow him. Stuart, although ignorant of the design, and suddenly roused from sleep, fortunately obeyed with equal silence and celerity, and within a few minutes they were beyond hearing.

Rapidly traversing the forest, by the light of the stars and the barks of the trees, they ascertained the direction in which the camp lay; but upon reaching it on the next day, to their great grief they found it plundered and deserted, with nothing remaining to show the fate of their companions: and even to the day of his death Boone knew not whether they had been killed or taken, or had voluntarily abandoned their cabin and returned. Here, in a few days, they were accidentally joined by Boone's brother and another man, who had followed them from Carolina and fortunately stumbled upon their camp. This accidental meeting in the bosom of a vast wilderness gave great relief to the two brothers, although their joy was soon overcast.

Boone and Stuart, in a second excursion, were again pursued by savages, and Stuart was shot and scalped, while Boone fortunately escaped. As usual, he has not mentioned particulars, but barely stated the event. Within a few days they sustained another calamity, if possible, still more distressing—their only remaining companion was benighted in a hunting excursion, and while encamped in the woods alone, was attacked and devoured by the wolves.

The two brothers were thus left in the wilderness alone, separated by several hundred miles from home, surrounded by hostile Indians, and destitute of every thing but their rifles. After having had such melancholy experience of the dangers to which they were exposed, we would naturally suppose that their fortitude would have given way, and that they would instantly have returned to the settlements. But the most remarkable feature in Boone's character was a calm and cold equanimity, which rarely rose to enthusiasm and never sunk to despondence.

His courage undervalued the danger to which he was exposed; and his presence of mind, which never forsook him, enabled him, on all occasions, to take the best means of avoiding it. The wilderness, with all its dangers and privations, had a charm for him which is scarcely conceivable by one brought up in a city; and he determined to remain alone, while his brother returned to Carolina for an additional supply of ammunition, as their original supply was nearly exhausted. His situation we should now suppose in the highest degree gloomy and dispiriting. The dangers which attended his brother on his return were nearly equal to his own; and each had left a wife and children, which Boone acknowledged cost him many an anxious thought.

But the wild and solitary grandeur of the country around him, where not a tree had been cut nor a house erected, was to him an inexhaustible source of admiration and delight; and he says himself, that some of the most rapturous moments of his life were spent in those lonely rambles. The utmost caution was necessary to avoid the savages, and scarcely less to escape the ravenous hunger of the wolves that prowled nightly around him in immense numbers. He was compelled frequently to shift his lodging, and by undoubted signs saw that the Indians had repeatedly visited his hut during his absence. He sometimes lay in canebrakes, without fire, and heard the yells of the Indians around him. Fortunately, however, he never encountered them.

On the twenty-seventh of July, 1770, his brother returned with a supply of ammunition; and, with a hardihood which appears almost incredible, they ranged through the country in every direction, and without injury, until March, 1771. They then returned to North Carolina, where Daniel rejoined his family, after an absence of three years, during nearly the whole of which time he had never tasted bread or salt, nor seen the face of a single white man, with the exception of his brother and the two friends who had been killed. He here determined to sell his farm and remove with his family to the wilderness of Kentucky—an astonishing instance of hardihood, and we should even say indifference to his family, if it were not that his character has uniformly been represented as mild and humane, as it was bold and fearless.

Accordingly, on the twenty-fifth of September, 1771,

having disposed of all the property which he could not take with him, he took leave of his friends and commenced his journey to the west. A number of milch cows, and horses laden with a few necessary household utensils, formed the whole of his baggage. His wife and children were mounted on horseback and accompanied him, every one regarding them as devoted to destruction. In Powell's Valley they were joined by five more families and forty men well armed. Encouraged by this accession of strength, they advanced with additional confidence, but had soon a severe warning of the further dangers which awaited them. When near Cumberland Mountain, their rear was suddenly attacked with great fury by a scouting party of Indians and thrown into considerable confusion.

The party, however, soon rallied, and being accustomed to Indian warfare, returned the fire with such spirit and effect that the Indians were repulsed with slaughter. Their own loss, however, had been severe. Six men were killed upon the spot and one wounded. Among the killed was Boone's eldest son, to the unspeakable affliction of his family. The disorder and grief occasioned by this rough reception seems to have afflicted the emigrants deeply, as they instantly retraced their steps to the settlements on Clinch River, forty miles from the scene of action. Here they remained until June, 1774, probably at the request of the women, who must have been greatly alarmed at the prospect of plunging more deeply into a country upon the skirts of which they had witnessed so keen and bloody a conflict.

At this time, Boone, at the request of Governor Dunmore, of Virginia, conducted a number of surveyors to the falls of Ohio, a distance of eight hundred miles. Of the incidents of this journey we have no record whatever. After his return he was engaged under Dunmore, until 1775, in several affairs with the Indians; and, at the solicitation of some gentlemen of North Carolina, he attended at a treaty with the Cherokees for the purpose of purchasing the lands south of Kentucky River. With his usual brevity, Boone has omitted to inform us of the particulars of this conference, or of the peculiar character of the business upon which he was sent. By the aid of Mr. Marshall's valuable history, however, we are enabled to supply this silence, at least with regard to the latter circumstance.

It seems that the Cherokees, living within the chartered limits of the State of North Carolina, claimed all the land south of the Kentucky as far as Tennessee River. That Colonel Richard Henderson and some other gentlemen, animated by the glowing description of the fertility of the soil which Boone and his brother had given upon their return, determined to purchase the whole of this immense tract from the Cherokees, and employed Boone as their agent. The Cherokees gladly parted with an empty title for a solid, though moderate, recompense; and Henderson and his friends instantly prepared to take possession, relying upon the validity of their deed from the Indians. Unfortunately, however, for the success of these speculators, Kentucky lay within the limits of Virginia, according to the old charter of King James, and that State accordingly claimed for herself solely the privilege of purchasing the Indian title to lands lying within her own limits.

She lost no time, therefore, in pronouncing the treaty of Henderson null and void, as it regarded *his own title;* although, by rather an exceptional process of reasoning, they determined that it was obligatory upon the Indians, so far as regarded the extinction of *their* title. Whether or not the reasoning was good, I can not pretend to say; but, supported as it was by a powerful State, it was *made good*, and Henderson's golden dreams completely vanished. He and his associates, however, received a liberal grant of land lying on Green River as a compensation for the expense and danger which they had incurred in prosecuting their settlement.

It was under the auspices of Henderson that Boone's next visit to Kentucky was made. Leaving his family on Clinch River, he set out, at the head of a few men, to mark out a road for the pack horses or wagons of Henderson's party. This laborious and dangerous duty he executed with his usual patient fortitude, until he came within fifteen miles of the spot where Boonesborough afterward was built. Here, on the twenty-second of March, his small party was attacked by the Indians and suffered a loss of four men killed and wounded. The Indians, although repulsed with loss in this affair, renewed the attack with equal fury on the next day, and killed and woulded five more of his party. On the first of April, the survivors began to build a small fort on the Kentucky River, afterward called Boonesborough; and on the fourth they were again attacked by the Indians and lost another man. Notwithstanding the harassing attacks to which they were constantly exposed (for the Indians seemed enraged to madness at the prospect of their building houses on their hunting-ground), the work was prosecuted with indefatigable diligence, and on the fourteenth was completed.

Boone instantly returned to Clinch River for his family, determined to bring them with him at every risk. This was done as soon as the journey could be performed, and Mrs. Boone and her daughters were the first white women who stood upon the banks of the Kentucky River, as Boone himself had been the first white man who ever built a cabin upon the borders of the State. The first house, however, which ever stood in the *interior* of Kentucky, was erected at Harrodsburgh, in the year 1774, by James Harrod, who conducted to this place a party of hunters from the banks of the Monongahela. This place was, therefore, a few months older than Boonesborough. Both soon became distinguished, as the only places in which hunters and surveyors could find security from the fury of the Indians.

Within a few weeks after the arrival of Mrs. Boone and her daughters, the infant colony was reinforced by three more families, at the head of which were Mrs. McGary, Mrs. Hogan, and Mrs. Denton. Boonesborough, however, was the central object of Indian hostilities, and scarcely had his family become domesticated in their new possession, when they were suddenly attacked by a party of Indians, and lost one of their garrison. This was on the twenty-fourth of December, 1775.

Capture of Boone and Callaway's Daughters. [See page 58.]

In the following July, however, a much more alarming incident occurred. One of his daughters, in company with a Miss Calloway, were amusing themselves in the immediate neighborhood of the fort, when a party of Indians suddenly rushed out of a canebrake, and, intercepting their return, took them prisoners. The screams of the terrified girls quickly alarmed the family. The small garrison was dispersed in their usual occupations; but Boone hastily collected a small party of eight men, and pursued the enemy. So much time, however, had been lost, that the Indians had got several miles the start of them. The pursuit was urged through the night with great keenness, by woodsmen capable of following a trail at all times, and on the following day they came up with them.

The attack was so sudden and furious, that the Indians were driven from their ground before they had leisure to tomahawk their prisoners, and the girls were recovered without having sustained any other injury than excessive fright and fatigue. Nothing but a barren outline of this interesting occurrence has been given. We know nothing of the conduct of the Indians to their captives, or of the situation of the young ladies during the short engagement, and can not venture to fill up the outline from imagination. The Indians lost two men, while Boone's party was uninjured.

From this time until the fifteenth of April, 1777, the garrison was incessantly harassed by flying parties of Indians. While plowing their corn, they were waylaid and shot; while hunting, they were chased and fired upon; and sometimes a solitary Indian would creep up near the fort, in the night, and fire upon the first of the garrison who appeared in the morning. They were in a constant state of anxiety and alarm, and the most ordinary duties could only be performed at the risk of their lives.

On the fifteenth of April, the enemy appeared in large numbers, hoping to crush the infant settlement at a single blow. Boonesborough, Logan's Fort, and Harrodsburgh, were attacked at one and the same time. But, destitute as they were of artillery, scaling ladders, and all the proper means of reducing fortified places, they could only distress the men, alarm the women, and destroy the corn and cattle. Boonesborough sustained some loss, as did the other stations, but the enemy being more exposed, suffered so severely as to retire with precipitation.

No rest, however, was given to the unhappy garrison. On the fourth of July following, they were again attacked by two hundred warriors, and again repulsed the enemy with loss. The Indians retreated; but a few days afterward fell upon Logan's Station with great fury, having sent detachments to alarm the other stations, so as to prevent the appearance of reinforcements to Logan's. In this last attempt, they displayed great obstinacy, and as the garrison consisted only of fifteen men, they were reduced to extremity. Not a moment could be allowed for sleep. Burning arrows were shot upon the roofs of the houses, and the Indians often pressed boldly up to the gates, and attempted to hew them down with their tomahawks. Fortunately, at this critical time, Colonel Bowman arrived from Virginia with one hundred men, well armed, and the savages precipitately withdrew, leaving the garrison almost exhausted with fatigue, and reduced to twelve men.

A brief period of repose now followed, in which the settlers endeavored to repair the damages done to their farms. But a period of heavy trial to Boone and his family was approaching. In January, 1778, accompanied by thirty men, Boone went to the Blue Licks to make salt for the different stations; and on the seventh of February following, while out hunting, he fell in with one hundred and two Indian warriors, on their march to attack Boonesborough. He instantly fled, but being upwards of fifty years old, was unable to contend with the fleet young men who pursued him, and was a second time taken prisoner. As usual, he was treated with kindness until his final fate was determined, and was led back to the Licks, where his men were still encamped. Here his whole party, to the number of twenty-seven, surrendered themselves, upon promise of life and good treatment, both of which conditions were faithfully observed.

Had the Indians prosecuted their enterprise, they might perhaps, by showing their prisoners, and threatening to put them to the torture, have operated so far upon the sympathies of the garrisons, as to have obtained considerable results. But nothing of the kind was attempted. They had already been unexpectedly successful; and it is their custom, after good or bad fortune, immediately to return home and enjoy their triumph, or lament their ill success. Boone and his party were conducted to the old town of Chillicothe, where they remained until the following March. No journal was written during this period, by either Boone or his party. We are only informed that his mild and patient equanimity wrought powerfully upon the Indians; that he was adopted into a family, and uniformly treated with the utmost affection. One fact is given us, which shows his acute observation, and knowledge of mankind. At the various shooting matches to which he was invited, he took care not to beat them *too* often. He knew that no feeling is more painful than that of inferiority, and that the most effectual way of keeping them in a good humor with *him*, was to keep them in a good humor with themselves. He, therefore, only shot well enough to make it an honor to beat him, and found himself a universal favorite.

It is much to be regretted, that some of our wits and egotists, of both sexes, could not borrow a little of the sagacity of Boone, and recollect, that when they engross the attention of the company, and endeavor most to shine, that instead of being agreeable, in nine cases out of ten they are only *bores*.

On the tenth of March, 1778, Boone was conducted to Detroit, when Governor Hamilton himself, offered £100 for his ransom; but so strong was the affection of the Indians for their prisoner, that it was positively refused. Several English gentlemen, touched with sympathy for his misfortunes, made pressing offers of money and other articles, but Boone steadily refused to receive benefits which he could never return. The offer was honorable to them, and the refusal was dictated by rather too refined a spirit of independence. Boone's anxiety, on account of his wife and children, was incessant, and the more intolerable, as he dared not excite the suspicion of the Indians by any indication of a wish to rejoin them.

Upon his return from Detroit, he observed that one hundred and fifty warriors of various tribes had assembled, painted and equipped, for an expedition against Boonesborough. His anxiety at this sight became ungovernable, and he determined, at every risk, to effect his escape. During the whole of this agitating period, however, he permitted no symptoms of anxiety to escape him. He hunted and shot with them, as usual, until the morning of the sixteenth of June, when, taking an early start, he left Chillicothe, and directed his route to Boonesborough. The distance exceeded one hundred and sixty miles, but he performed it in four days, during which he ate only one meal. He appeared before the garrison like one risen from the dead.

His wife, supposing him killed, had transported herself, children, and property to her father's house, in North Carolina; his men, suspecting no danger, were dispersed in their ordinary avocations, and the works had been permitted to go to waste. Not a moment was to be lost. The garrison worked day and night upon the fortifications. New gates, new flanks, and double bastions were soon completed. The cattle and horses were brought into the fort, ammunition prepared, and every thing made ready for the approach of the enemy within ten days after his arrival. At this time one of his companions in captivity arrived from Chillicothe, and announced that his escape had determined the Indians to delay the invasion for three weeks.

During this interval it was ascertained that numerous spies were traversing the woods and hovering around the station, doubtless for the purpose of observing and reporting the condition of the garrison. Their report could not have been favorable. The alarm had spread very generally, and all were upon the alert. The attack was delayed so long that Boone began to suspect that they had been discouraged by the report of the spies; and he determined to invade them. Selecting nineteen men from his garrison, he put himself at their head, and marched with equal silence and celerity against the town of Paint Creek, on the Scioto. He arrived, without discovery, within four miles of the town, and there encountered a party of thirty warriors on their march to unite with the grand army in the expedition against Boonesborough.

Instantly attacking them with great spirit, he compelled them to give way with some loss, and without any injury to himself. He then halted and sent two spies in advance to ascertain the condition of the village. In a few hours they returned with the intelligence that the town was evacuated. He instantly concluded that the grand army was upon its march against Boonesborough, whose situation, as well as his own, was exceedingly critical. Retracing his steps, he marched, day and night, hoping still to elude the enemy and reach Boonesborough before them. He soon fell in with their trail, and, making a circuit to avoid them, he passed their army on the sixth day of their march, and on the seventh reached Boonesborough.

On the eighth the enemy appeared in great force. There were nearly five hundred Indian warriors, armed and painted in their usual manner, and, what was still more formidable, they were conducted by Canadian officers, well skilled in the usages of modern warfare. As soon as they were arrayed in front of the fort, the British colors were displayed, and an officer, with a flag, was sent to demand the surrender of the fort, with a promise of quarter and good treatment in case of compliance, and threatening "the hatchet" in case of a storm. Boone requested two days for consideration, which, in defiance of all experience and common sense, was granted. This interval, as usual, was employed in preparation for an obstinate resistance. The cattle were brought into the fort, the horses secured, and all things made ready against the commencement of hostilities.

Boone then assembled the garrison, and represented to them the condition in which they stood. They had not now to deal with Indians alone, but with British officers, skilled in the art of attacking fortified places, sufficiently numerous to *direct*, but too few to *restrain* their savage allies. If they surrendered, their lives might, and probably would be saved; but they would suffer much inconvenience, and *must* lose all their property. If they resisted and were overcome, the life of every man, woman, and child would be sacrificed. The hour was now come in which they were to determine what was to be done. If they were inclined to surrender, he would announce it to the officer; if they were resolved to maintain the fort, he would share their fate, whether in life or death. He had scarcely finished, when every man arose and, in a firm tone, announced his determination to defend the fort to the last.

Boone then appeared at the gate of the fortress and communicated to Captain Duquesne the resolution of his men. Disappointment and chagrin were strongly painted upon the face of the Canadian at this answer; but, endeavoring to disguise his feelings, he declared that Governor Hamilton had ordered him not to injure the men if it could be avoided, and that if nine of the principal inhabitants of the fort would come out into the plain and treat with them, they would instantly depart without further hostility. The insidious nature of this proposal was evident, for they could converse very well from where they then stood, and going out would only place the officers of the fort at the mercy of the savages, not to mention the absurdity of supposing that this army of warriors would "*treat*," but upon such terms as pleased them, and no terms were likely to do so short of a total abandonment of the country.

Notwithstanding these obvious objections, the word "treat" sounded so pleasantly in the ears of the besieged, that they agreed at once to the proposal; and Boone himself, attended by eight of his men, went out and mingled with the savages, who crowded around them in great numbers, and with countenances of deep anxiety. The treaty then commenced, and was soon concluded. What the terms were, we are not informed, nor is it a matter of the least importance, as the whole was a stupid and shallow artifice. This was soon made manifest. Duquesne, after many, very many pretty periods about the "*bienfaisance et humanité*" which should accompany the warfare of civilized beings, at length informed Boone, that it was a custom with the Indians, upon the conclusion of a treaty with the whites, for two warriors to take hold of the hand of each white man.

Boone thought this rather a singular custom, but there was no time to dispute about etiquette, particularly, as he could not be more in their power than he already was; so he signified his willingness to conform to the Indian mode of cementing friendship. Instantly, two warriors approached each white man, with the word "brother" upon their lips, but a very different expression in their eyes, and grappling him with violence, attempted to bear him off. They probably (unless totally infatuated) expected such a consummation, and all at the same moment sprung from their enemies and ran to the fort under a heavy fire, which fortunately only wounded one man.

We look here in vain for the prudence and sagacity which usually distinguished Boone. Indeed, there seems to have been a contest between him and Duquesne, as to which should display the greater quantum of shallowness. The plot itself was unworthy of a child, and the execution beneath contempt. For after all this treachery, to permit his prisoner to escape from the very midst of his warriors, who certainly might have thrown themselves between Boone and the fort, argues a poverty or timidity, on the part of Duquesne, truly despicable.

The attack instantly commenced by a heavy fire against the picketing, and was returned with fatal accuracy by the garrison. The Indians quickly sheltered themselves, and the action became more cautious and deliberate. Finding but little effect from the fire of his men, Duquesne next resorted to a more formidable mode of attack. The fort stood on the south bank of the river, within sixty yards of the water. Commencing under the bank, where their operations were concealed from the garrison, they attempted to push a mine into the fort. Their object, however, was fortunately discovered by the quantity of fresh earth which they were compelled to throw into the river, and by which the water became muddy for some distance below. Boone, who had regained his usual sagacity, instantly cut a trench within the fort in such a manner as to intersect the line of their approach, and thus frustrated their design.

The enemy exhausted all their ordinary artifices of Indian warfare, but were steadily repulsed in every effort. Finding their numbers daily thinned by the deliberate but fatal fire of the garrison, and seeing no prospect of final success, they broke up on the ninth day of the siege, and returned home. The loss of the garrison, was two men killed and four wounded. On the part of the savages, thirty-seven were killed and many wounded, who, as usual, were all carried off. This was the last siege sustained by Boonesborough. The country had increased so rapidly in numbers, and so many other stations lay between Boonesborough and the Ohio, that the savages could not reach it without leaving enemies in the rear.

In the autumn of this year, Boone returned to North Carolina for his wife and family, who, as already observed, had supposed him dead, and returned to her father. There is a hint in Mr. Marshall's history, that the family affairs, which detained him in North Carolina, were of an unpleasant character, but no explanation is given.

In the summer of 1780, he returned to Kentucky with his family, and settled at Boonesborough. Here he continued busily engaged upon his farm until the sixth of October, when, accompanied by his brother, he went to the Lower Blue Licks, for the purpose of providing himself with salt. This spot seemed fatal to Boone. Here he had once been taken prisoner by the Indians; and here he was destined, within two years, to lose his youngest son, and to witness the slaughter of many of his dearest friends. His present visit was not free from calamity. Upon their return, they were encountered by a party of Indians, and his brother, who had accompanied him faithfully through many years of toil and danger, was killed and scalped before his eyes.

Unable either to prevent or avenge his death, Boone was compelled to fly, and by his superior knowledge of the country contrived to elude his pursuers. They followed his trail, however, by the scent of a dog, that pressed him closely, and prevented his concealing himself. This was one of the most critical moments of his life, but his usual coolness and fortitude enabled him to meet it. He halted until the dog, baying loudly upon his trail, came within gunshot, when he deliberately turned and shot him dead. The thickness of the woods, and the approach of darkness, then enabled him to effect his escape.

During the following year, Boonesborough enjoyed uninterrupted tranquillity. The country had become comparatively thickly settled, and was studded with fortresses in every direction. Fresh emigrants with their families were constantly arriving; and many young unmarried women (who had heretofore been extremely scarce) had ventured to risk themselves in Kentucky. They could not have selected a spot where their merit was more properly appreciated, and were disposed of very rapidly to the young hunters, most of whom had hitherto, from necessity, remained bachelors. Thriving settlements had been pushed beyond the Kentucky River, and a number of houses had been built where Lexington now stands.

The year 1781 passed away in perfect tranquillity, and, judging from appearances, nothing was more distant, than the terrible struggle which awaited them. But during the whole of this year, the Indians were meditating a desperate effort to crush the settlements at a single blow. They had become seriously alarmed at the tide of emigration which rolled over the country, and threatened to convert their favorite hunting ground into one vast cluster of villages. The game had already been much dispersed, the settlers, originally weak, and scattered over the south side of the Kentucky River, had now become numerous, and were rapidly extending to the Ohio. One vigorous and united effort might still crush their enemies, and regain for themselves the undisputed possession of the western forests.

A few renegade white men were mingled with them, and inflamed their wild passions, by dwelling upon the injuries which they had ever sustained at the hands of the whites, and of the necessity for instant and vigorous exertion, or of an eternal surrender of every hope either of redress or vengeance. Among these, the most remarkable was *Simon Girty*. Runners were dispatched to most of the north-western tribes, and all were exhorted to lay aside private jealousy, and unite in a common cause against these white intruders. In the meantime, the settlers were busily employed in opening farms, marrying and giving in marriage, totally ignorant of the storm which was gathering upon the Lakes.

In the spring of 1782, after a long interval of repose, they were harassed by small parties, who preceded the main body, as the pattering and irregular drops of rain are the precursors of the approaching storm. In the month of May, a party of twenty-five Wyandotts secretly approached Estill's Station, and committed shocking outrages in its vicinity. Entering a cabin which stood apart from the rest, they seized a woman and her two daughters, who, having been violated with circumstances of savage barbarity, were tomahawked and scalped. Their bodies, yet warm and bleeding, were found upon the floor of the cabin. The neighborhood was instantly alarmed. Captain Estill speedily collected a body of twenty-five men, and pursued their trail with great rapidity. He came up with them on Hinkston Fork of Licking, immediately after they had crossed it, and a most severe and desperate conflict ensued.

The Indians, at first, appeared daunted and began to fly, but their chief, who was badly wounded by the first fire, was heard in a loud voice, ordering them to stand and return the fire, which was instantly obeyed. The creek ran between the two parties, and prevented a charge on either side, without the certainty of great loss. The parties, therefore, consisting of precisely the same number, formed an irregular line, within fifty yards of each other, and sheltering themselves behind trees or logs, they fired with deliberation, as an object presented itself. The only maneuver which the nature of the ground permitted, was to extend their lines in such a manner as to uncover the flank of the enemy, and even this was extremely dangerous, as every motion exposed them to a close and deadly fire.

The action, therefore, was chiefly stationary, neither party advancing or retreating, and every individual acting for himself. It had already lasted more than an hour, without advantage on either side, or any prospect of its termination. Captain Estill had lost one-third of his men, and had inflicted about an equal loss upon his enemies, who still boldly maintained their ground, and returned his fire with equal spirit. To have persevered in the Indian mode of fighting, would have exposed his party to certain death, one by one, unless all the Indians should be killed first, who, however, had at least an equal chance with himself. Even victory, bought at such a price, would have afforded but a melancholy triumph; yet it was impossible to retreat or advance without exposing his men to the greatest danger.

After coolly revolving these reflections in his mind, and observing that the enemy exhibited no symptoms of discouragement, Captain Estill determined to detach a party of six men, under Lieutenant Miller, with orders to cross the creek above, and take the Indians in flank, while he maintained his ground, ready to co-operate, as circumstances might require. But he had to deal with an enemy equally bold and sagacious. The Indian chief was quickly aware of the division of the force opposed to him, from the slackening of the fire in front; and readily conjecturing his object, he determined to frustrate it by crossing the creek with his whole force, and overwhelming Estill, now weakened by the absence of Miller.

The maneuver was bold and masterly, and was executed with determined courage. Throwing themselves into the water, they fell upon Estill with the tomahawk, and drove him before them with slaughter. Miller's party retreated with precipitation, and even lie under the reproach of deserting their friends, and absconding, instead of occupying the designated ground. Others contradict this statement, and affirm that Miller punctually executed his orders, crossed the creek, and falling in with the enemy, was compelled to retire with loss. We think it probable, that the Indians rushed upon Estill, as above mentioned, and having defeated him, recrossed the creek and attacked Miller, thus cutting up their enemy in detail.

Estill's party finding themselves furiously charged, and receiving no assistance from Miller, who was probably at that time on the other side of the creek, in the execution of his orders, would naturally consider themselves deserted; and when a clamor of that kind is once raised against a man (particularly in a defeat), the voice of reason can no longer be heard. Some scapegoat is always necessary. The broken remains of the detachment returned to the station, and filled the country with consternation and alarm, greatly disproportioned to the extent of the loss. The brave Estill, with eight of his men, had fallen, and four more were wounded, more than half of their original number.

This, notwithstanding the smallness of the numbers, is a very remarkable action, and, perhaps. more honorable to the Indians than any other one on record. The numbers, the arms, the courage, and the position of the parties, were equal. Both were composed of good marksmen, and skillful woodsmen. There was no surprise, no panic, nor any particular accident, according to the most probable account, which decided the action. A delicate maneuver on the part of Estill gave an advantage, which was promptly seized by the Indian chief, and a bold and masterly movement decided the fate of the day. The great battles of Austerlitz and Wagram exhibit the same error on the part of one commander, and the same decisive and successful step on the part of the other.

The Arch-Duke Charles extended his line to take the French in flank, and thereby weakened his center, which was instantly broken by a rapid charge of the whole French army. No movement seems more delicate and dangerous than that of Estill, and the first great check which Bonaparte received (that of Eylau) was chiefly occasioned by weakening his front in order to assail the enemy in rear. It requires, however, great boldness and promptitude in the opposite leader, to take advantage of it. A cautious and wary leader will be apt to let the golden opportunity pass away, until the detachment has reached his flank, and it is then too late. The English military critics censure our Washington for hesitation of this kind at Brandywine. They say, that when the detachment of Cornwallis was absent on its march to take the Americans in flank, Washington should have crossed with his whole force, and have fallen upon Kniphausen. Lee says, that such a maneuver was contemplated, but was prevented by false intelligence.

The news of Estill's disaster was quickly succeeded by another, scarcely less startling to the alarmed settlers. Captain Holder, at the head of seventeen men, pursued a party of Indians who had taken two boys from the neighborhood of Hoy's Station. He overtook them after a rapid pursuit, and in the severe action which ensued, was repulsed with the loss of more than half his party. The tide of success seemed completely turned in favor of the Indians. They traversed the woods in every direction, sometimes singly, sometimes in small parties, and kept the settlers in constant alarm.

At length, early in August, the grand effort was made. The allied Indian army, composed of detachments from nearly all the North-western tribes, and amounting to nearly six hundred men, commenced their march from Chillicothe, under the command of their respective chiefs, aided and influenced by Girty, McKee, and other renegade white men. With a secrecy and celerity peculiar to themselves, they advanced through the woods without giving the slightest indications of their approach; and on the night of the fourteenth of August, they appeared before Bryant's Station, as suddenly as if they had risen from the earth, and surrounding it on all sides, calmly awaited the approach of daylight, holding themselves in readiness to rush in upon the inhabitants the moment that the gates were opened in the morning. The supreme influence of fortune in war was never more strikingly displayed.

The garrison had determined to march at daylight on the following morning, to the assistance of Hoy's Station, from which a messenger had arrived the evening before, with the intelligence of Holder's defeat. Had the Indians arrived only a few hours later, they would have found the fort occupied only by old men, women and children, who could not have resisted their attack for a moment. As it was, they found the garrison assembled and under arms, most of them busily engaged throughout the whole night in preparing for an early march on the following morning. The Indians could distinctly hear the bustle of preparation, and see lights glancing from block-houses and cabins during the night, which must have led them to suspect that their approach had been discovered. All continued tranquil during the night, and Girty silently concerted the plan of attack.

The fort, consisting of about forty cabins placed in parallel lines, stands upon a gentle rise on the southern bank of the Elkhorn, a few paces to the right of the road from Maysville to Lexington. The garrison was supplied with water from a spring at some distance from the fort on its north-western side; a great error, common to most of the stations, which, in a close and long-continued siege, must have suffered dreadfully for want of water.

The great body of Indians placed themselves in ambush within half rifle shot of the spring, while one hundred select men were placed near the spot where the road now runs after passing the creek, with orders to open a brisk fire and show themselves to the garrison on that side, for the purpose of drawing them out, while the main body held themselves in readiness to rush upon the opposite gate of the fort, hew it down with their tomahawks, and force their way into the midst of the cabins. At dawn of day, the garrison paraded under arms, and were preparing to open their gates and march off as already mentioned, when they were alarmed by a furious discharge of rifles, accompanied with yells and screams, which struck terror to the hearts of the women and children, and startled even the men.

All ran hastily to the picketing, and beheld a small party of Indians, exposed to open view, firing, yelling, and making the most furious gestures. The appearance was so singular, and so different from their usual manner of fighting, that some of the more wary and experienced of the garrison instantly pronounced it a decoy party, and restrained the young men from sallying out and attacking them, as some of them were strongly disposed to do. The opposite side of the fort was instantly manned, and several breaches in the picketing rapidly repaired. Their greatest distress arose from the prospect of suffering for water. The more experienced of the garrison felt satisfied that a powerful party was in ambuscade near the spring, but at the same time they supposed that the Indians would not unmask themselves until the firing upon the opposite side of the fort was returned with such warmth, as to induce the belief that the feint had succeeded.

Acting upon this impression, and yielding to the urgent necessity of the case, they summoned all the women, without exception, and explaining to them the circumstances in which they were placed, and the improbability that any injury would be offered them, until the firing had been returned from the opposite side of the fort, they urged them to go in a body to the spring, and each to bring up a bucket full of water. Some of the ladies, as was natural, had no relish for the undertaking, and asked why the men could not bring water as well as themselves? observing that *they* were not bullet-proof, and that the Indians made no distinction between male and female scalps!

To this it was answered, that women were in the habit of bringing water every morning to the fort, and that if the Indians saw them engaged as usual, it would induce them to believe that their ambuscade was undiscovered, and that they would not unmask themselves for the sake of firing at a few women, when they hoped, by remaining concealed a few moments longer, to obtain complete possession of the fort. That if *men* should go down to the spring, the Indians would immediately suspect that something was wrong, would despair of succeeding by ambuscade, and would instantly rush upon them, follow them into the fort, or shoot them down at the spring. The decision was soon over.

A few of the boldest declared their readiness to brave the danger, and the younger and more timid rallying in the rear of these veterans, they all marched down in a body to the spring, within point-blank shot of more than five hundred Indian warriors! Some of the girls could not help betraying symptoms of terror, but the married women, in general, moved with a steadiness and composure which completely deceived the Indians. Not a shot was fired. The party were permitted to fill their buckets, one after another, without interruption, and although their steps became quicker and quicker, on their return, and, when near the gate of the fort, degenerated into a rather unmilitary celerity, attended with some little crowding in passing the gate, yet not more than one-fifth of the water was spilled, and the eyes of the youngest had not dilated to more than double their ordinary size.

Being now amply supplied with water, they sent out thirteen young men to attack the decoy party, with orders to fire with great rapidity and make as much noise as possible, but not to pursue the enemy too far, while the rest of the garrison took post on the opposite side of the fort, cocked their guns, and stood in readiness to receive the ambuscade as soon as it was unmasked. The firing of the light parties on the Lexington road was soon heard, and quickly became sharp and serious, gradually becoming more distant from the fort. Instantly Girty sprung up at the head of his five hundred warriors, and rushed rapidly upon the western gate, ready to force his way over the undefended palisades. Into this immense mass of dusky bodies the garrison poured several rapid volleys of rifle balls, with destructive effect. Their consternation may be imagined. With wild cries they dispersed on the right and left, and in two minutes not an Indian was to be seen. At the same time, the party who had sallied out on the Lexington road came running into the fort at the opposite gate, in high spirits, and laughing heartily at the success of their maneuver.

A regular attack, in the usual manner, then commenced, without much effect on either side, until two o'clock in the afternoon, when a new scene presented itself. Upon the first appearance of the Indians in the morning, two of the garrison, Tomlinson and Bell, had been mounted upon fleet horses, and sent at full speed to Lexington, announcing the arrival of the Indians and demanding reinforcements. Upon their arrival, a little after sunrise, they found the town occupied only by women and children and a few old men, the rest having marched, at the intelligence of Holder's defeat, to the general rendezvous at Hoy's Station. The two couriers instantly followed at a gallop, and overtaking them on the road, informed them of the danger to which Lexington was exposed during their absence.

The whole party, amounting to sixteen horsemen and more than double that number on foot, with some additional volunteers from Boone's Station, instantly countermarched, and repaired with all possible expedition to Bryant's Station. They were entirely ignorant of the overwhelming numbers opposed to them, or they would have proceeded with more caution. Tomlinson had only informed them that the station was surrounded, being himself ignorant of the numbers of the enemy. By great exertions, horse and foot appeared before Bryant's at two in the afternoon, and pressed forward with precipitate gallantry to throw themselves into the fort. The Indians, however, had been aware of the departure of the two couriers, who had, in fact, broken through their line in order to give the alarm, and, expecting the arrival of reinforcements, had taken measures to meet them.

To the left of the long and narrow lane, where the Maysville and Lexington road now runs, there were more than one hundred acres of green standing corn. The usual road from Lexington to Bryant's ran parallel to the fence of this field, and only a few feet distant from it. On the opposite side of the road was a thick wood. Here more than three hundred Indians lay in ambush, within pistol shot of the road, awaiting the approach of the party. The horsemen came in view at a time when the firing had ceased and every thing was quiet. Seeing no enemy, and hearing no noise, they entered the lane at a gallop, and were instantly saluted with a shower of rifle balls from each side, at the distance of ten paces.

At the first shot the whole party set spurs to their horses, and rode at full speed through a rolling fire from either side, which continued for several hundred yards, but, owing partly to the furious rate at which they rode, partly to the clouds of dust raised by the horses' feet, they all entered the fort unhurt. The men on foot were less fortunate. They were advancing through the cornfield, and might have reached the fort in safety but for their eagerness to succor their friends. Without reflecting that, from the weight and extent of the fire, the enemy must have been ten times their number, they ran up, with inconsiderate courage, to the spot where the firing was heard, and there found themselves cut off from the fort and within pistol shot of more than three hundred savages.

Fortunately, the Indian guns had just been discharged, and they had not yet had leisure to reload. At the sight of this brave body of footmen, however, they raised a hideous yell, and rushed upon them, tomahawk in hand. Nothing but the high corn and their loaded rifles could have saved them from destruction. The Indians were cautious in rushing upon a loaded rifle with only a tomahawk, and, when they halted to load their pieces, the Kentuckians ran with great rapidity, turning and dodging through the corn in every direction. Some entered the wood and escaped through the thickets of cane, some were shot down in the corn-field, others maintained a running fight, halting occasionally behind trees and keeping the enemy at bay with their rifles; for, of all men, the Indians are generally the most cautious in exposing themselves to danger. A stout, active young fellow, was so hard pressed by Girty and several savages, that he was compelled to discharge his rifle (however unwilling, having no time to reload it), and Girty fell.

It happened, however, that a piece of thick sole-leather was in his shot-pouch at the time, which received the ball and preserved his life, although the force of the blow felled him to the ground. The savages halted upon his fall, and the young man escaped. Although the skirmish and the race lasted for more than an hour, during which the corn-field presented a scene of turmoil and bustle which can scarcely be conceived, yet very few lives were lost. Only six of the white men were killed and wounded, and probably still fewer of the enemy, as the whites never fired until absolutely necessary, but reserved their loads as a check upon the enemy. Had the Indians pursued them to Lexington, they might have possessed themselves of it without resistance, as there was no force there to oppose them; but, after following the fugitives for a few hundred yards, they returned to the hopeless siege of the fort.

It was now near sunset, and the fire on both sides had slackened. The Indians had become discouraged. Their loss in the morning had been heavy, and the country was evidently arming and would soon be upon them. They had made no impression upon the fort, and without artillery could hope to make none. The chiefs spoke of raising the siege and decamping, but Girty determined, since his arms had been unavailing, to try the efficacy of negotiation. Near one of the bastions there was a large stump, to which he crept on his hands and knees, and from which he hailed the garrison.

He highly commended their courage, but assured them that further resistance would be madness, as he had six hundred warriors with him, and was in hourly expectation of reinforcements with artillery, which would instantly blow their cabins into the air; that if the fort was taken by storm, as it certainly would be when their cannon arrived, it would be impossible for him to save their lives, but, if they surrendered at once, he gave them his honor that not a hair of their heads should be injured. He told them his name, inquired whether they knew him, and assured them that they might safely trust to his honor.

The garrison listened in silence to his speech, and many of them looked very blank at the mention of the artillery, as the Indians had, on one occasion, brought cannon with them and destroyed two stations. But a young man by the name of Reynolds, highly distinguished for courage, energy, and a frolicsome gayety of temper, perceiving the effect of Girty's speech, took upon himself to reply to it.

To Girty's inquiry, "Whether the garrison knew him?" Reynolds replied, "That he was very well known; that he himself had a worthless dog, to which he had given the name of 'Simon Girty,' in consequence of his striking resemblance to the man of that name; that if he had either artillery or reinforcements, he might bring them up and be d——d; that if either himself, or any of the naked rascals with him, found their way into the fort, they would disdain to use their guns against them, but would drive them out again with switches, of which they had collected a great number for that purpose alone; and finally, he declared, that *they* also expected reinforcements; that the whole country was marching to their assistance; and that if Girty and his gang of murderers remained twenty-four hours longer before the fort, their scalps would be found drying in the sun upon the roofs of their cabins."

Girty took great offense at the tone and language of the young Kentuckian, and retired with an expression of sorrow for the inevitable destruction which awaited them on the following morning. He quickly rejoined the chiefs; and instant preparations were made for raising the siege. The night passed away in uninterrupted tranquillity, and at daylight in the morning the Indian camp was found deserted. Fires were still burning brightly, and several pieces of meat were left upon their roasting sticks, from which it was inferred that they had retreated a short time before daylight.

Early in the day, reinforcements began to drop in, and by noon, one hundred and sixty-seven men were assembled at Bryant's Station. Colonel Daniel Boone, accompanied by his youngest son, headed a strong party from Boonesborough; Trigg brought up the force from the neighborhood of Harrodsburgh, and Todd commanded the militia around Lexington. Nearly a third of the whole number assembled, was composed of commissioned officers, who hurried from a distance to the scene of hostilities, and for the time took their station in the ranks. Of those under the rank of colonel, the most conspicuous were Majors Harland, McBride, McGary, and Levi Todd, and Captains Bulger and Gordon. Of the six last-named officers, all fell in the subsequent battle, except Todd and McGary. Todd and Trigg, as senior colonels, took the command, although their authority seems to have been in a great measure nominal. That, however, was of less consequence, as a sense of common danger is often more binding than the strictest discipline.

A tumultuous consultation, in which every one seems to have had a voice, terminated in a unanimous resolution to pursue the enemy without delay. It was well known that General Logan had collected a strong force in Lincoln, and would join them at farthest in twenty-four hours. It was distinctly understood that the enemy was at least double, and, according to Girty's account, more than treble their own numbers. It was seen that their trail was broad and obvious, and that even some indications of a tardiness and willingness to be pursued, had been observed by their scouts, who had been sent out to reconnoiter, and from which it might reasonably be inferred that they would halt on the way, at least march so leisurely as to permit them to wait for the aid of Logan. Yet so keen was the ardor of officer and soldier, that all these obvious reasons were overlooked, and in the afternoon of the eighteenth of August, the line of march was taken up, and the pursuit urged with that precipitate courage which has so often been fatal to Kentuckians. Most of the officers and many of the privates were mounted.

The Indians had followed the buffalo trace, and as if to render their trail still more evident, they had chopped many of the trees on each side of the road with their hatchets. These strong indications of tardiness made some impression upon the cool and calculating mind of Boone; but it was too late to advise retreat. They encamped that night in the woods, and on the following day reached the fatal boundary of their pursuit. At the Lower Blue Licks, for the first time since the pursuit commenced, they came within view of an enemy. As the miscellaneous crowd of horse and foot reached the southern bank of the Licking, they saw a number of Indians ascending the rocky ridge on the other side.

They halted upon the appearance of the Kentuckians, gazed at them for a few moments in silence, and then calmly and leisurely disappeared over the top of the hill. A halt immediately ensued. A dozen or twenty officers met in front of the ranks, and entered into consultation. The wild and lonely aspect of the country around them, their distance from any point of support, with the certainty of their being in the presence of a superior enemy, seems to have inspired a portion of seriousness, bordering upon awe. All eyes were now turned upon Boone, and Colonel Todd asked his opinion as to what should be done. The veteran woodsman, with his usual unmoved gravity, replied:

"That their situation was critical and delicate; that the force opposed to them was undoubtedly numerous and ready for battle, as might readily be seen from the leisurely retreat of the few Indians who had appeared upon the crest of the hill; that he was well acquainted with the ground in the neighborhood of the Lick, and was apprehensive that an ambuscade was formed at the distance of a mile in advance, where two ravines, one upon each side of the ridge, ran in such a manner that a concealed enemy might assail them at once both in front and flank, before they were apprised of the danger.

"It would be proper, therefore, to do one of two things. Either to await the arrival of Logan, who was now undoubtedly on his march to join them, or if it was determined to attack without delay, that one-half of their number should march up the river, which there bends in an elliptical form, cross at the rapids and fall upon the rear of the enemy, while the other division attacked in front. At any rate, he strongly urged the necessity of reconnoitering the ground carefully before the main body crossed the river."

Such was the counsel of Boone. And, although no measure could have been much more disastrous than that which was adopted, yet it may be doubted if any thing short of an immediate retreat upon Logan, could have saved this gallant body of men from the fate which they encountered. If they divided their force, the enemy, as in Estill's case, might have overwhelmed them in detail; if they remained where they were, without advancing, the enemy would certainly have attacked them, probably in the night, and with a certainty of success. They had committed a great error at first, in not waiting for Logan, and nothing short of a retreat, which would have been considered disgraceful, could now repair it.

Boone was heard in silence and with deep attention. Some wished to adopt the first plan; others preferred the second; and the discussion threatened to be drawn out to some length, when the boiling ardor of McGary, who could never endure the presence of an enemy without instant battle, stimulated him to an act, which had nearly proved destructive to his country. He suddenly interrupted the consultation with a loud whoop, resembling the war-cry of the Indians, spurred his horse into the stream, waved his hat over his head, and shouted aloud: "Let all who are not cowards follow me!" The words and the action together, produced an electrical effect. The mounted men dashed tumultuously into the river, each striving to be foremost. The footmen were mingled with them in one rolling and irregular mass.

No order was given and none observed. They struggled through a deep ford as well as they could, McGary still leading the van, closely followed by Majors Harland and McBride. With the same rapidity they ascended the ridge, which, by the trampling of buffalo foragers, had been stripped bare of all vegetation, with the exception of a few dwarfish cedars, and which was rendered still more desolate in appearance by the multitude of rocks, blackened by the sun, which were spread over its surface. Upon reaching the top of the ridge, they followed the buffalo trace with the same precipitate ardor; Todd and Trigg in the rear; McGary, Harland, McBride, and Boone in front. No scouts were sent in advance, none explored either flank; officers and soldiers seemed alike demented by the contagious example of a single man, and all struggled forward, horse and foot, as if to outstrip each other in the advance.

Suddenly, the van halted. They had reached the spot mentioned by Boone, where the two ravines head, on each side of the ridge. Here a body of Indians presented themselves, and attacked the van. McGary's party instantly returned the fire, but under great disadvantage. They were upon a bare and open ridge; the Indians in a bushy ravine. The center and rear, ignorant of the ground, hurried up to the assistance of the van, but were soon stopped by a terrible fire from the ravine which flanked them. They found themselves inclosed as if in the wings of a net, destitute of proper shelter, while the enemy were in a great measure covered from their fire. Still, however, they maintained their ground. The action became warm and bloody. The parties gradually closed, the Indians emerged from the ravine, and the fire became mutually destructive. The officers suffered dreadfully. Todd and Trigg, in the rear; Harland, McBride, and young Boone, in front, were already killed.

The Indians gradually extended their line, to turn the right of the Kentuckians, and cut off their retreat.

This was quickly perceived by the weight of the fire from that quarter, and the rear instantly fell back in disorder, and attempted to rush through their only opening to the river. The motion quickly communicated itself to the van, and a hurried retreat became general. The Indians instantly sprung forward in pursuit, and falling upon them with their tomahawks, made a cruel slaughter. From the battle-ground to the river, the spectacle was terrible. The horsemen generally escaped, but the foot, particularly the van, which had advanced farthest within the wings of the net, were almost totally destroyed. Colonel Boone, after witnessing the death of his son and many of his dearest friends, found himself almost entirely surrounded at the very commencement of the retreat.

Several hundred Indians were between him and the ford, to which the great mass of the fugitives were bending their flight, and to which the attention of the savages was principally directed. Being intimately acquainted with the ground, he, together with a few friends, dashed into the ravine which the Indians had occupied, but which most of them had now left to join in the pursuit. After sustaining one or two heavy fires, and baffling one or two small parties, who pursued him for a short distance, he crossed the river below the ford, by swimming, and entering the wood at a point where there was no pursuit, returned by a circuitous route to Bryant's Station. In the meantime, the great mass of the victors and vanquished crowded the bank of the ford.

The slaughter was great in the river. The ford was crowded with horsemen and foot and Indians, all mingled together. Some were compelled to seek a passage above by swimming; some, who could not swim, were overtaken and killed at the edge of the water. A man by the name of Netherland, who had formerly been strongly suspected of cowardice, here displayed a coolness and presence of mind, equally noble and unexpected. Being finely mounted, he had outstripped the great mass of fugitives, and crossed the river in safety. A dozen or twenty horsemen accompanied him, and having placed the river between them and the enemy, showed a disposition to continue their flight, without regard to the safety of their friends who were on foot, and still struggling with the current.

Netherland instantly checked his horse, and in a loud voice called upon his companions to halt, fire upon the Indians, and save those who were still in the stream. The party instantly obeyed; and facing about, poured a close and fatal discharge of rifles upon the foremost of the pursuers. The enemy instantly fell back from the opposite bank, and gave time for the harassed and miserable footmen to cross in safety. The check, however, was but momentary. Indians were seen crossing in great numbers above and below, and the flight again became general. Most of the foot left the great buffalo track, and plunging into the thickets, escaped by a circuitous route to Bryant's Station.

But little loss was sustained after crossing the river, though the pursuit was urged keenly for twenty miles.

.om the battle-ground to the ford, the loss was very heavy; and at that stage of the retreat, there occurred a rare and striking instance of magnanimity, which it would be criminal to omit. The reader could not have forgotten Aaron Reynolds, who replied with such rough but ready humor to the pompous summons of Girty, at the siege of Bryant's. This young man, after bearing his share in the action with distinguished gallantry, was galloping with several other horsemen in order to reach the ford. The great body of fugitives had preceded them, and their situation was in the highest degree critical and dangerous.

About half way between the battle-ground and the river, the party overtook Captain Patterson, on foot, exhausted by the rapidity of the flight, and, in consequence of former wounds received from the Indians, so infirm as to be unable to keep up with the main body of the men on foot. The Indians were close behind him, and his fate seemed inevitable. Reynolds, upon coming up with this brave officer, instantly sprung from his horse, aided Patterson to mount into the saddle, and continued his own flight on foot. Being remarkably active and vigorous, he contrived to elude his pursuers,

Capt. Patterson's Escape from the Battle of the Blue Licks. [See page 78.]

and turning off from the main road, plunged into the river near the spot where Boone had crossed, and swam in safety to the opposite side. Unfortunately, he wore a pair of buckskin breeches, which had become so heavy and full of water as to prevent his exerting himself with his usual activity; and while sitting down for the purpose of pulling them off, he was overtaken by a party of Indians, and made prisoner.

A prisoner is rarely put to death by the Indians, unless wounded or infirm, until they return to their own country; and then his fate is decided in solemn council. Young Reynolds, therefore, was treated kindly, and compelled to accompany his captors in the pursuit. A small party of Kentuckians soon attracted their attention; and e was left in charge of three Indians, who, eager in pursuit, in turn committed him to the charge of one of their number while they followed their companions. Reynolds and his guard jogged along very leisurely; the former totally unarmed; the latter, with a tomahawk and rifle in his hands. At length the Indian stopped to tie his moccasin, when Reynolds instantly sprung upon him, knocked him down with his fist, and quickly disappeared in the thicket which surrounded them. For this act of generosity, Captain Patterson afterward made him a present of two hundred acres of first-rate land.

Late in the evening of the same day, most of the survivors arrived at Bryant's Station. The melancholy intelligence spread rapidly throughout the country, and the whole land was covered with mourning. Sixty men had been killed in the battle and flight, and seven had been taken prisoners, part of whom were afterward put to death by the Indians, as was said, to make their loss even. This account, however, appears very improbable. It is almost incredible that the Indians should have suffered an equal loss. Their superiority of numbers, their advantage of position (being in a great measure sheltered, while the Kentuckians, particularly the horsemen, were much exposed), the extreme brevity of the battle, and the acknowledged bloodiness of the pursuit, all tend to contradict the report that the Indian loss exceeded ours.

We have no doubt that some of the prisoners were murdered after arriving at their towns, but can not believe that the reason assigned for so ordinary a piece of barbarity was the true one. Still, the execution done by the Kentuckians, while the battle lasted, seems to have been considerable, although far inferior to the loss which they themselves sustained. Todd and Trigg were a severe loss to their families, and to the country generally. They were men of a rank in life superior to the ordinary class of settlers, and generally esteemed for courage, probity, and intelligence. The death of Major Harland was deeply and universally regretted. A keen courage, united to a temper the most amiable, and an integrity the most incorruptible, had rendered him extremely popular in the country.

Together with his friend, McBride, he accompanied McGary in the van, and both fell in the commencement of the action. McGary, notwithstanding the extreme exposure of his station, as leader of the van, and consequently most deeply involved in the ranks of the enemy, escaped without the slightest injury. This gentlemen will ever be remembered, as associated with the disaster of which he was the immediate, although not the original cause. He has always been represented as a man of fiery and daring courage, strongly tinctured with ferocity, and unsoftened by any of the humane and gentle qualities which awaken affection. In the hour of battle, his presence was invaluable; but in civil life, the ferocity of his temper rendered him an unpleasant companion.

Several years after the battle of the Blue Licks, a gentleman of Kentucky, since dead, fell in company with McGary at one of the circuit courts, and the conversation soon turned upon the battle. McGary frankly acknowledged that he, himself, was the immediate cause of the loss of blood on that day, and, with great heat and energy, assigned his reasons for urging on the battle. He said that, in the hurried council which was held at Bryant's on the eighteenth, he had strenuously urged Todd and Trigg to halt for twenty-four hours, assuring them, that with the aid of Logan they would be able to follow them even to Chillicothe, if necessary, and that their numbers, *then*, were too weak to encounter them alone. He offered, he said, to pledge his head, that the Indians would not return with such precipitation as was supposed, but would afford ample time to collect more force, and give them battle with a prospect of success.

He added, that Colonel Todd scouted his arguments, and declared "that if a single day was lost, the Indians would never be overtaken, but would cross the Ohio and disperse; that now was the time to strike them, while they were in a body; that to talk of their numbers was nonsense—the more the merrier; that for his part he was determined to pursue without a moment's delay, and did not doubt that there were brave men enough on the ground, to enable him to attack them with effect." McGary declared "that he felt somewhat nettled at the manner in which his advice had been received. That he thought Todd and Trigg jealous of Logan, who, as senior colonel, would be entitled to the command upon his arrival; and that, in their eagerness to have the honor of the victory to themselves, they were rashly throwing themselves into a condition, which would endanger the safety of the country."

"However, sir," continued he, with an air of unamiable triumph, "when I saw the gentlemen so keen for a fight, I gave way, and joined in the pursuit as willingly as any; but when we came in sight of the enemy, and the gentlemen began to talk of 'numbers,' 'position,' 'Logan,' and 'waiting,' I burst into a passion, d——d them for a set of cowards, who could not be wise, until they were scared into it, and swore that since they had come so far for a fight, they *should fight*, or I would disgrace them forever! That when I spoke of waiting for Logan on the day before, they had scouted the idea, and hinted something about 'courage'—that now it would be shown who had courage, or who were d——d cowards, that could talk big when the enemy was at a distance, but turned pale when danger was near. I then dashed into the river, and called upon all who were not cowards to follow!" The gentleman upon whose authority this is given, added that, even then, McGary spoke with bitterness of the deceased colonels, and swore that they had received just what they deserved, and that he for one was glad of it.

That the charge of McGary, in its full extent, was unjust, there can be no doubt; at the same time, it is in accordance with the known principles of human nature, to suppose that the natural ardor of the officers, both young men, should be stimulated by the hope of gaining a victory, the honor of which would be given them as commanders. The number of the Indians was not distinctly known, and if their retreat had been ordinarily precipitate, they would certainly have crossed the Ohio before Logan could have joined. But, leaving all the facts to speak for themselves, we will proceed with our narrative.

On the very day in which this rash and unfortunate battle was fought, Colonel Logan arrived at Bryant's Station, at the head of no less than four hundred and fifty men. He here learned that the little army had marched on the preceding day, without waiting for so strong, and necessary a reinforcement. Fearful of some such disaster as had actually occurred, he urged his march with the utmost diligence, still hoping to overtake them before they could cross the Ohio; but, within a few miles of the fort, he encountered the foremost of the fugitives, whose jaded horses, and harassed looks, announced but too plainly the event of the battle.

As usual with men after a defeat, they magnified the number of the enemy and the slaughter of their comrades. None knew the actual extent of their loss. They could only be certain of their own escape, and could give no account of their companions. Fresh stragglers constantly came up, with the same mournful intelligence; so that Logan, after some hesitation, determined to return to Bryant's until all the survivors should come up. In the course of the evening, both horse and foot were re-assembled at Bryant's, and the loss was distinctly ascertained. Although sufficiently severe, it was less than Logan had at first apprehended, and having obtained all the information which could be collected, as to the strength and probable destination of the enemy, he determined to continue his march to the battle-ground, with the hope that success would embolden the enemy, and induce them to remain until his arrival.

On the second day he reached the field. The enemy were gone, but the bodies of the Kentuckians still lay unburied, on the spot where they had fallen. Immense flocks of buzzards were soaring over the battle-ground, and the bodies of the dead had become so much swollen and disfigured, that it was impossible to recognize the features of the most particular friends. Many corpses were floating near the shore of the northern bank, already putrid from the action of the sun, and partially eaten by fishes. The whole were carefully collected by order of Colonel Logan, and interred as decently as the nature of the soil would permit. Being satisfied that the Indians were by this time far beyond his reach, he then retraced his steps to Bryant's Station and dismissed his men.

As soon as intelligence of the battle of the Blue Licks reached Colonel George Rogers Clark, who then resided at the Falls of Ohio, he determined to set on foot an expedition against the Indian towns for the purpose both of avenging the loss of the battle, and rousing the spirit of the country, which had begun to sink into the deepest dejection. He proposed that one thousand men should be raised from all parts of Kentucky, and should rendezvous at Cincinnati, under the command of their respective officers, where he engaged to meet them at the head of a part of the Illinois regiment, then under his command, together with one brass field-piece, which was regarded by the Indians with superstitious terror. The offer was embraced with great alacrity; and instant measures were taken for the collection of a sufficient number of volunteers.

The whole force of the interior was assembled under the command of Colonel Logan, and descending the Licking in boats, prepared for the purpose, arrived safely at the designated point of union, where they were joined by Clark with the volunteers and regular detachment from below. No provision was made for the subsistence of the troops, and the sudden concentration of one thousand men and horses upon a single point, rendered it extremely difficult to procure the necessary supplies. The woods abounded in game; but the rapidity and secrecy of their march, which was absolutely essential to the success of the expedition, did not allow them to disperse in search of it. They suffered greatly, therefore, from hunger as well as fatigue; but all being accustomed to privations of every kind, they prosecuted their march with unabated rapidity, and appeared within a mile of one of their largest villages, without encountering a single Indian.

Here, unfortunately, a straggler fell in with them, and instantly fled to the village, uttering the alarm whoop repeatedly in the shrillest and most startling tones. The troops pressed forward with great dispatch, and entering their town, found it totally deserted. The houses had evidently been abandoned only a few minutes before their arrival. Fires were burning, meat was upon the roasting-sticks, and corn was still boiling in their kettles. The provisions were a most acceptable treat to the Kentuckians, who were well-nigh famished, but the escape of their enemies excited deep and universal chagrin.

After refreshing themselves, they engaged in the serious business of destroying the property of the tribes with unrelenting severity. Their villages were burnt, their corn cut up, and their whole country laid waste. During the whole of this severe, but necessary occupation, scarcely an Indian was to be seen. The alarm had spread universally, and every village was found deserted. Occasionally, a solitary Indian would crawl up within gunshot, and deliver his fire; and once a small party mounted upon superb horses, rode up with great audacity, within musket-shot, and took a leisurely survey of the whole army, but upon seeing a detachment preparing to attack them, they galloped off with a rapidity which baffled pursuit.

Boone accompanied this expedition, but, as usual,

has omitted every thing which relates to himself. Here the brief memoir of Boone closes. It does not appear that he was afterward engaged in any public expedition, or solitary adventure. He continued a highly respectable citizen of Kentucky for several years, until the country became too thickly settled for *his* taste. As refinement of manners advanced, and the general standard of intelligence became elevated by the constant arrival of families of rank and influence, the rough old woodsman found himself entirely out of his element. He could neither read nor write; the all-engaging subject of politics, which soon began to agitate the country with great violence, was to him as a sealed book, or an unknown language; and for several years he wandered among the living group, which thronged the court-yard or the churches, like a venerable relic of other days. He was among them, but not of them! He pined in secret for the wild and lonely forests of the west—for the immense prairie, trodden only by the buffalo or the elk; and became eager to exchange the listless languor and security of a village for the healthful exercises of the chase, or the more thrilling excitement of savage warfare.

In 1792, he dictated his brief and rather dry memoirs to some young gentleman who could write, and who has garnished it with a few flourishes of rhetoric, which passed off upon the old woodsman as a precious morsel of eloquence. He was never more gratified than when he could sit and hear it read to him by some one, who was willing, at so small an expense, to gratify the harmless vanity of the kind-hearted old pioneer. He would listen with great earnestness, and occasionally rub his hands, smile, and ejaculate, "All true! every word true!—not a lie in it!" He shortly afterward left Kentucky and removed to Missouri. Hunting was his daily amusement, and almost his only occupation.

Until the day of his death (and he lived to an unusually advanced age), he was in the habit of remaining for days at a time in the forest, at a distance from the abodes of men, armed with a rifle, hatchet, knife, and having flints and steel to enable him to kindle a fire and broil the wild game upon which he depended for subsistence. When too old to walk through the woods, as was his custom when young, he would ride to a lick, and there lay in ambush all day for the sake of getting a shot at the herds of deer that were accustomed to visit the spot for the sake of the salt. We have heard that he died in the woods while laying in ambush near a lick, but have not at present the means of ascertaining, with certainty, the manner of his death.

He has left behind him a name strongly written in the annals of Kentucky; and a reputation for calm courage, softened by humanity, conducted by prudence, and embellished by a singular modesty of deportment. His person was rough, robust, and indicating strength rather than activity; his manner was cold, grave, and taciturn; his countenance, homely but kind; his conversation, unadorned, unobtrusive, and touching only upon the "needful." He never spoke of himself, unless particularly questioned; but the written account of his life was the Delilah of his imagination. The idea of "seeing his name in print," completely overcame the cold philosophy of his general manner, and he seemed to think it a masterpiece of composition.

The following incident is gathered from "Collins' Kentucky," page 385:

One morning, in 1777, several men in the fields near Boonesborough were attacked by Indians, and ran toward the fort. One was overtaken and tomahawked within seventy yards of the fort, and while being scalped, Simon Kenton shot the warrior dead. Daniel Boone, with thirteen men, hastened to help his friends, but they were intercepted by a large body of Indians, who got between them and the fort. At the first fire from the Indians, seven whites were wounded, among them the gallant Boone. An Indian sprang upon him with uplifted tomahawk; but Kenton, quick as a tiger, sprang toward the Indian, discharged his gun into his breast, snatched up the body of his noble leader and bore it safely into the fort. When the gate was closed securely against the Indians, Boone sent for Kenton: "Well, Simon," said the grateful old pioneer, "you have behaved yourself like a man to-day—indeed, you are a fine fellow." Boone was a remarkably silent man, and this was great praise from him.

Simon Kenton saving the life of Daniel Boone. [See page 86.]

CHAPTER III.

SIMON KENTON was born in Fauquier County, Virginia, on the fifteenth of May, 1755, the ever-memorable year of Braddock's defeat. Of his early years nothing is known. His parents were poor, and, until the age of sixteen, his days seem to have passed away in the obscure and laborious drudgery of a farm. He was never taught to read or write; and to this early negligence, or inability on the part of his parents, is the poverty and desolation of his old age in a great measure to be attributed. At the age of sixteen, by an unfortunate adventure, he was launched into life with no other fortune than a stout heart and a robust set of limbs. It seems that, young as he was, his heart had become entangled in the snares of a young coquette in the neighborhood, who was grievously perplexed by the necessity of choosing *one* husband out of *many* lovers.

Young Kenton and a robust farmer by the name of Leitchman seem to have been the most favored suitors, and the young lady not being able to decide upon their respective merits, they took the matter into their own hands; and, in consequence of foul play on the part of Leitchman's friends, young Kenton was beaten with great severity. He submitted to his fate for the time in silence, but internally vowed that, as soon as he had obtained his full growth he would take ample vengeance upon his rival for the disgrace which he had sustained at his hands. He waited patiently until the following spring, when, finding himself six feet high, and full of health and action, he determined to delay the hour of retribution no longer.

. He accordingly walked over to Leitchman's house one

morning, and finding him busily engaged in carrying shingles from the woods to his own house, he stopped him, told him his object, and desired him to adjourn to a spot more convenient for the purpose. Leitchman, confident in his superior age and strength, was not backward in testifying his willingness to indulge him in so amiable a pastime, and, having reached a solitary spot in the woods, they both stripped and prepared for the encounter. The battle was fought with all the fury which mutual hate, jealousy, and herculean power on both sides could supply; and after a severe round, in which considerable damage was done and received, Kenton was brought to the ground.

Leitchman (as usual in Virginia) sprung upon him without the least scruple, and added the most bitter taunts to the kicks with which he saluted him from his head to his heels, reminding him of his former defeat, and rubbing salt into the raw wounds of jealousy by triumphant allusions to his own superiority both in love and war. During these active operations on the part of Leitchman, Kenton lay perfectly still, eyeing attentively a small bush which grew near them. It instantly occurred to him that if he could wind Leitchman's hair (which was remarkably long) around this bush, he would be able to return those kicks which were now bestowed upon him in such profusion. The difficulty was, to get his antagonist near enough.

This he at length effected in the good old Virginia style, viz: by biting him *en arriere*, and compelling him, by short springs, to approach the bush, much as a bullock is goaded on to approach the fatal ring, where all his struggles are useless. When near enough, Kenton suddenly exerted himself violently, and succeeded in wrapping the long hair of his rival around the sapling. He then sprung to his feet and inflicted a terrible revenge for all his past injuries. In a few seconds, Leitchman was gasping apparently in the agonies of death. Kenton instantly fled, without even returning for an additional supply of clothing, and directed his steps westward.

During the first day of his journey he traveled in

much agitation. He supposed that Leitchman was dead, and that the hue and cry would instantly be raised after himself as the murderer. The constant apprehension of a gallows lent wings to his flight, and he scarcely allowed himself a moment for refreshment until he had reached the neighborhood of the Warm Springs, where the settlements were thin, and the immediate danger of pursuit was over. Here he fortunately fell in with an exile from the State of New Jersey, of the name of Johnson, who was traveling westward on foot, and driving a single pack-horse, laden with a few necessaries, before him. They soon became acquainted, related their adventures to each other, and agreed to travel together.

They plunged boldly into the wilderness of the Alleghany Mountains, and subsisting upon wild game and a small quantity of flour which Johnson had brought with him, they made no halt until they arrived at a small settlement on Cheat River, one of the prongs of the Monongahela. Here the two friends separated, and Kenton (who had assumed the name of Butler), attached himself to a small company, headed by John Mahon and Jacob Greathouse, who had united for the purpose of exploring the country. They quickly built a large canoe, and descended the river as far as the Province's settlement. There Kenton became acquainted with two young adventurers, Yager and Strader, the former of whom had been taken by the Indians when a child, and had spent many years in their village.

He informed Kenton that there was a country below, which the Indians called Kan-tuck-ee, which was a perfect Elysium; that the ground was not only the richest, and the vegetation the most luxuriant in the world, but that the immense herds of buffalo and elk, which ranged at large through its forests, would appear incredible to one who had never witnessed such a spectacle. He added, that it was entirely uninhabited, and was open to all who chose to hunt there; that he himself had often accompanied the Indians in their grand hunting parties through the country, and was confident that he could conduct him to the same ground, if he was willing to venture.

Kenton eagerly closed with the proposal, and announced his readiness to accompany him immediately. A canoe was speedily procured, and the three young men committed themselves to the waters of the Ohio, in search of the enchanted hunting-ground, which Yager had visited in his youth, while a captive among the Indians. Yager had no idea of its exact distance from Province's settlement. He recollected only that he had crossed the Ohio in order to reach it, and declared that, by sailing down the river for a few days, they would come to the spot where the Indians were accustomed to cross, and assured Kenton that there would be no difficulty in recognizing it, that its appearance was different from all the rest of the world, etc.

Fired by Yager's glowing description of its beauty, and eager to reach this new El Dorado of the West, the young men rowed hard for several days, confidently expecting that every bend of the river would usher them into the land of promise. No such country, however, appeared; and at length Kenton and Strader became rather skeptical as to its existence at all. They rallied Yager freely upon the subject, who still declared positively that they would soon witness the confirmation of all that he had said. After descending, however, as low as the spot where Manchester now stands, and seeing nothing which resembled Yager's country, they held a council, in which it was determined to return, and survey the country more carefully; Yager still insisting that they must have passed it in the night. They accordingly retraced their steps, and successively explored the land about Salt Lick, Little and Big Sandy, and Guyandotte. At length, being totally wearied out in searching for what had no existence, they turned their attention entirely to hunting and trapping, and spent nearly two years upon the Great Kenawha, in this agreeable and profitable occupation. They obtained clothing in exchange for their furs from the traders of Fort Pitt, and the forest supplied them abundantly with wild game for food.

In March, 1773, while reposing in their tent, after the labors of the day, they were suddenly attacked by a party of Indians. Strader was killed at the first fire, and Kenton and Yager with difficulty effected their escape; being compelled to abandon their guns, blankets, and provisions, and commit themselves to the wilderness, without the means of sheltering themselves from the cold, procuring a morsel of food, or even kindling a fire. They were far removed from any white settlement, and had no other prospect than that of perishing by famine, or falling a sacrifice to the fury of such Indians as might chance to meet them. Reflecting, however, that it was never too late for men to be utterly lost, they determined to strike through the woods for the Ohio River, and take such fortune as it should please heaven to bestow.

Directing their route by the barks of trees, they pressed forward in a straight direction for the Ohio, and during the two first days allayed the piercing pangs of hunger by chewing such roots as they could find on their way. On the third day their strength began to fail, and the keen appetite which, at first, had constantly tortured them, was succeeded by a nausea, accompanied with dizziness and a sinking of the heart, bordering on despair. On the fourth day, they often threw themselves upon the ground, determined to await the approach of death; and as often were stimulated by the instinctive love of life to arise and resume their journey. On the fifth, they were completely exhausted, and were able only to crawl at intervals. In this manner they traveled about a mile during the day, and succeeded, by sunset, in reaching the banks of the Ohio. Here, to their inexpressible joy, they encountered a party of traders, from whom they obtained a comfortable supply of provisions.

The traders were so much startled at the idea of being exposed to perils, such as those which Kenton and Yager had just escaped, that they lost no time in removing from such a dangerous vicinity, and instantly returned to the mouth of the Little Kenawha, where they met with Dr. Briscoe at the head of another exploring party. From him, Kenton obtained a rifle and some ammunition, with which he again plunged alone into the forest, and hunted with success until the summer of 1773 was far advanced. Returning, then, to the Little Kenawha, he found a party of fourteen men under the direction of Dr. Wood and Hancock Lee, who were descending the Ohio with the view of joining Captain Bullitt, who was supposed to be at the mouth of the Scioto, with a large party.

Kenton instantly joined them, and descended the river in canoes as far as the Three Islands, landing frequently and examining the country on each side of the river. At the Three Islands they were alarmed by the approach of a large party of Indians, by whom they were compelled to abandon their canoes and strike diagonally through the wilderness for Greenbriar County, Va. They suffered much during this journey from fatigue and famine, and were compelled at one time (notwithstanding the danger of their situation) to halt for fourteen days and wait upon Dr. Wood, who had unfortunately been bitten by a copperhead snake, and rendered incapable of moving for that length of time. Upon reaching the settlements the party separated.

Kenton, not wishing to venture to Virginia (having heard nothing of Leitchman's recovery), built a canoe on the banks of the Monongahela, and returning to the mouth of the Great Kenawha, hunted with success until the spring of 1774, when a war broke out between the Indian tribes and the colonies, occasioned, in a great measure, by the murder of the celebrated chief Logan's family, by Captain Cresap. Kenton was not in the great battle near the mouth of the Kenawha, but acted as a spy throughout the whole of the campaign, in the course of which he traversed the country around Fort Pitt, and a large portion of the present State of Ohio.

When Dunmore's forces were disbanded, Kenton, in company with two others, determined on making a second effort to discover the rich lands bordering on the Ohio, of which Yager had spoken. Having built a canoe, and provided themselves abundantly with ammunition, they descended the river as far as the mouth of Big Bone Creek, upon which the celebrated Lick of that name is situated. They there disembarked, and explored the country for several days; but not finding the land equal to their expectations, they re-ascended the river as far as the mouth of Cabin Creek, a few miles above Maysville.

From this point, they set out with a determination to examine the country carefully, until they could find land answering, in some degree, to Yager's description. In a short time, they reached the neighborhood of May's Lick, and for the first time were struck with the uncommon beauty of the country and fertility of the soil. Here they fell in with the great buffalo trace, which, in a few hours, brought them to the Lower Blue Lick. The flats upon each side of the river were crowded with immense herds of buffalo, that had come down from the interior for the sake of the salt; and a number of elk were seen upon the bare ridges which surrounded the springs. Their great object was now achieved. They had discovered a country far more rich than any which they had yet beheld, and where the game seemed as abundant as the grass of the plain.

After remaining a few days at the Lick, and killing an immense number of deer and buffalo, they crossed the Licking, and passed through the present counties of Scott, Fayette, Woodford, Clarke, Montgomery, and Bath; when, falling in with another buffalo trace, it conducted them to the Upper Blue Lick, where they again beheld elk and buffalo in immense numbers. Highly gratified at the success of their expedition, they quickly returned to their canoe, and ascended the river as far as Green Bottom, where they had left their skins, some ammunition, and a few hoes, which they had procured at Kenawha with the view of cultivating the rich ground which they expected to find.

Returning as quickly as possible, they built a cabin on the spot where the town of Washington now stands, and having cleared an acre of ground in the center of a large canebrake, they planted it with Indian corn. Strolling about the country in various directions, they one day fell in with two white men near the Lower Blue Lick, who had lost their guns, blankets, and ammunition, and were much distressed for provisions and the means of extricating themselves from the wilderness. They informed them that their names were Fitzpatrick and Hendricks; that, in descending the Ohio, their canoe had been overset by a sudden squall, and that they were compelled to swim ashore, without being able to save any thing from the wreck; that they had wandered thus far through the woods, in the effort to penetrate through the country to the settlements above, but must infallibly perish unless they could be furnished with guns and ammunition.

Kenton informed them of the small settlement which he had opened at Washington, and invited them to join him and share such fortune as Providence might bestow. Hendricks consented to remain; but Fitzpatrick, being heartily sick of the woods, insisted upon returning to the Monongahela. Kenton and his two friends accompanied Fitzpatrick to "the point," as it was then called, being the spot where Maysville now stands, and, having given him a gun, etc., assisted him in crossing the river, and took leave of him on the other side.

In the meantime, Hendricks had been left at the Blue Lick, without a gun, but with a good supply of provisions, until the party could return from the river. As soon as Fitzpatrick had gone, Kenton and his two friends hastened to return to the Lick, not doubting for a moment that they would find Hendricks in camp as they had left him. Upon arriving at the point where the tent had stood, however, they were alarmed at finding it deserted, with evident marks of violence around it. Several bullet-holes were to be seen in the poles of which it was constructed, and various articles belonging to Hendricks were tossed about in too negligent a manner to warrant the belief that it had been done by him.

At a little distance from the camp, in a low ravine, they observed a thick smoke, as if from a fire just beginning to burn. They did not doubt for a moment that Hendricks had fallen into the hands of the Indians, and, believing that a party of them were then assembled around the fire which was about to be kindled, they betook themselves to their heels, and fled faster and farther than true chivalry, perhaps, would justify. They remained at a distance until the evening of the next day, when they ventured cautiously to return to camp. The fire was still burning, although faintly; and, after carefully reconnoitering the adjacent ground, they ventured at length to approach the spot, and there beheld the skull and bones of their unfortunate friend!

He had evidently been roasted to death by a party of Indians, and must have been alive at the time when Kenton and his companions approached on the preceding day. It was a subject of deep regret to the party that they had not reconnoitered the spot more closely, as it was probable that their friend might have been rescued. The number of Indians might have been small, and a brisk and unexpected attack might have dispersed them. Regret, however, was now unavailing; and they sadly retraced their steps to their camp at Washington, pondering upon the uncertainty of their own condition and upon the danger to which they were hourly exposed from the numerous bands of hostile Indians who were prowling around them in every direction.

They remained at Washington, entirely undisturbed, until the month of September; when, again visiting the Lick, they saw a white man, who informed them that the interior of the country was already occupied by the whites, and that there was a thriving settlement at Boonesborough. Highly gratified at this intelligence, and anxious once more to enjoy the society of men, they broke up their encampment at Washington and visited the different stations which had been formed in the country. Kenton sustained two sieges in Boonesborough, and served as a spy, with equal diligence and success, until the summer of 1778, when Boone, returning from captivity, as has already been mentioned, concerted an expedition against the small Indian town on Paint Creek.

Kenton acted as a spy on this expedition; and, after

crossing the Ohio, being some distance in advance of the rest, he was suddenly startled by hearing a loud laugh from an adjoining thicket, which he was just about to enter. Instantly halting, he took his station behind a tree, and waited anxiously for a repetition of the noise. In a few minutes, two Indians approached the spot where he lay, both mounted upon a small pony, and chatting and laughing in high good humor. Having permitted them to approach within good rifle distance, he raised his gun, and, aiming at the breast of the foremost, pulled the trigger. Both Indians fell— one shot dead, the other severely wounded.

Their frightened pony galloped back into the cane, giving the alarm to the rest of the party, who were some distance in the rear. Kenton instantly ran up to scalp the dead man and to tomahawk his wounded companion, according to the usual rule of western warfare; but, when about to put an end to the struggles of the wounded Indian, who did not seem disposed to submit very quietly to the operation, his attention was attracted by a rustling of the cane on his right, and, turning rapidly in that direction, he beheld two Indians within twenty steps of him, very deliberately taking aim at his person. A quick spring to one side, on his part, was instantly followed by the flash and report of their rifles; the balls whistled close to his ears, causing him involuntarily to duck his head, but doing him no injury.

Not liking so hot a neighborhood, and being ignorant of the number which might yet be behind, he lost no time in regaining the shelter of the wood, leaving the dead Indian unscalped and the wounded man to the care of his friends. Scarcely had he treed, when a dozen Indians appeared on the edge of the canebrake, and seemed disposed to press upon him with more vigor than was consistent with the safety of his present position. His fears, however, were instantly relieved by the appearance of Boone and his party, who came running up as rapidly as a due regard to the shelter of their persons would permit, and, opening a brisk fire upon the Indians, quickly compelled them to regain the shelter of the canebrake, with the loss of several wounded, who, as usual, were carried off. The dead Indian, in the hurry of the retreat, was abandoned, and Kenton at last had the gratification of taking his scalp.

Boone, as has already been mentioned, instantly retraced his steps to Boonesborough; but Kenton and his friend Montgomery determined to proceed alone to the Indian town, and at least obtain some recompense for the trouble of their journey. Approaching the village with the cautious and stealthy pace of the cat or panther, they took their stations upon the edge of the cornfield, supposing that the Indians would enter it as usual to gather roasting-ears. They remained here patiently all day; but did not see a single Indian, and heard only the voices of some children, who were playing near them. Being disappointed in the hope of getting a shot, they entered the Indian town in the night, and, stealing four good horses, made a rapid night's march for the Ohio, which they crossed in safety, and, on the second day afterward, reached Logan's Fort with their booty.

Scarcely had he returned, when Colonel Bowman ordered him to take his friend Montgomery, and another young man named Clark, and go on a secret expedition to an Indian town on the Little Miami, against which the colonel meditated an expedition, and of the exact condition of which he wished to have certain information. They instantly set out, in obedience to their orders, and reached the neighborhood of the town without being discovered. They examined it attentively, and walked around the houses during the night with perfect impunity. Thus far all had gone well; and had they been contented to return after the due execution of their orders, they would have avoided the heavy calamity which awaited them.

But, unfortunately, during their nightly promenade, they stumbled upon a pound in which were a number of Indian horses. The temptation was not to be resisted. They each mounted a horse; but, not satisfied with that, they could not find it in their hearts to leave a single animal behind them, and, as some of the horses seemed indisposed to change masters, the affair was attended with so much fracas that at last they were discovered. The cry ran through the village at once that the Long Knives were stealing their horses right before the doors of their wigwams; and old and young, squaws, boys, and warriors, all sallied out with loud screams to save their property from these greedy spoilers. Kenton and his friends quickly discovered that they had overshot the mark, and that they must ride for their lives; but, even in this extremity, they could not bring themselves to give up a single horse which they had haltered, and while two of them rode in front and led, I know not how many horses, the other brought up the rear, and, plying his whip from right to left, did not permit a single animal to lag behind.

In this manner they dashed through the woods at a furious rate, with the hue and cry after them, until their course was suddenly stopped by an impenetrable swamp. Here, from necessity, they paused for a few moments and listened attentively. Hearing no sounds of pursuit, they resumed their course; and, skirting the swamp for some distance in the vain hope of crossing it, they bent their course in a straight direction toward the Ohio. They rode during the whole night without resting a moment; and, halting for a few minutes at daylight, they continued their journey throughout the day, and the whole of the following night, and by this uncommon expedition, on the morning of the second day, they reached the northern bank of the Ohio River.

Crossing the river would now insure their safety; but this was likely to prove a difficult undertaking, and the close pursuit which they had reason to expect rendered it necessary to lose as little time as possible. The wind was high and the river rough and boisterous. It was determined that Kenton should cross with the horses, while Clark and Montgomery should construct a raft in order to transport their guns, baggage, and ammunition to the opposite shore. The necessary preparations were soon made, and Kenton, after forcing his horses into the river, plunged in himself and swam by their side. In a very few minutes the high waves completely overwhelmed him and forced him considerably below the horses, that stemmed the current much more vigorously than himself.

The horses, being thus left to themselves, turned about and swam again to the Ohio shore, where Kenton was compelled to follow them. Again he forced them into the water; and again they returned to the same spot—until Kenton became so exhausted by repeated efforts as to be unable to swim. A council was then held and the question proposed, "What was to be done?" That the Indians would pursue them, was certain; that the horses would not, and could not be made to cross the river in its present state, was equally certain. Should they abandon their horses and cross on the raft, or remain with their horses and take such fortune as heaven should send them? The latter alternative was unanimously adopted. Death or captivity might be tolerated, but the loss of so beautiful a lot of horses, after having worked so hard for them, was not to be thought of for a moment.

As soon as it was determined that themselves and horses were to share the same fate, it again became necessary to fix upon some probable plan of saving them. Should they move up or down the river, or remain where they were? The latter course was adopted. It was supposed that the wind would fall at sunset, and the river become sufficiently calm to admit of their passage; and, as it was supposed probable that the Indians might be upon them before night, it was determined to conceal the horses in a neighboring ravine, while they should take their stations in the adjoining wood. A more miserable plan could not have been adopted. If they could not consent to sacrifice their horses in order to save their own lives, they should have moved either up or down the river, and thus have preserved the distance from the Indians which their rapidity of movement had gained.

The Indians would have followed their trail, and being twenty-four hours' march behind them, could never have overtaken them. But neglecting this obvious consideration, they stupidly sat down until sunset, expecting that the river would become more calm. The day passed away in tranquillity, but at night the wind blew harder than ever, and the water became so rough, that even their raft would have been scarcely able to cross. Not an instant more should have been lost, in moving from so dangerous a post; but as if totally infatuated, they remained where they were until morning; thus wasting twenty-four hours of most precious time in total idleness. In the morning, the wind abated and the river became calm—but it was now too late. Their horses, recollecting the difficulty of the passage on the preceding day, had become as obstinate and heedless as their masters, and positively and repeatedly refused to take the water.

Finding every effort to compel them entirely unavailing, their masters at length determined to do what ought to have been done at first. Each resolved to mount a horse, and make the best of his way down the river to Louisville. Had even this resolution, however tardily adopted, been executed with decision, the party would probably have been saved, but after they were mounted, instead of leaving the ground instantly, they went back upon their own trail, in the vain effort to regain possession of the rest of their horses, which had broken from them in the last effort to drive them into the water. They wearied out their good genius, and literally fell victims to their love for horse-flesh.

They had scarcely ridden one hundred yards (Kenton in the center, the others upon the flanks, with an interval of two hundred yards between them), when Kenton heard a loud halloo, apparently coming from the spot which they had just left. Instead of getting out of the way as fast as possible, and trusting to the speed of his horse, and the thickness of the wood for safety, he put the last capping-stone to his imprudence, and dismounting, walked leisurely back to meet his pursuers, and thus give them as little trouble as possible. He quickly beheld three Indians, and one white man, all well mounted. Wishing to give the alarm to his companions, he raised his rifle to his shoulder, took a steady aim at the breast of the foremost Indian, and drew the trigger. His gun had become wet on the raft, and flashed.

The enemy were instantly alarmed, and dashed at him. Now, at last, when flight could be of no service, Kenton betook himself to his heels, and was pursued by four horsemen at full speed. He instantly directed his steps to the thickest part of the wood, where there was much fallen timber and a rank growth of underwood, and had succeeded, as he thought, in baffling his pursuers, when, just as he was leaving the fallen timber and entering the open wood, an Indian on horseback galloped round the corner of the wood, and approached him so rapidly as to render flight useless. The horseman rode up, holding out his hand and calling out, "Brother! brother!" in a tone of great affection. Kenton observes that if his gun would have made fire, he would have "brothered" him to his heart's content, but being totally unarmed, he called out that he would surrender if they would give him quarter and good treatment.

Promises were cheap with the Indian, and he showered them out by the dozen, continuing all the while to advance with extended hands and a writhing grin upon his countenance, which was intended for a smile of courtesy. Seizing Kenton's hand, he grasped it with violence. Kenton, not liking the manner of his captor, raised his gun to knock him down, when an Indian who had followed him closely through the brushwood, instantly sprung upon his back, and pinioned his arms to his side. The one who had just approached him, then seized him by the hair and shook him until his teeth rattled, while the rest of the party coming up, they all fell upon Kenton with their tongues and ramrods, until he thought they would scold or beat him to death. They were the owners of the horses which he had carried off, and now took ample revenge for the loss of their property. At every stroke of their ramrods over his head (and they were neither few nor far between), they would repeat, in a tone of strong indignation, "Steal Indian hoss! hey!"

Their attention, however, was soon directed to Montgomery, who, having heard the noise attending Kenton's capture, very gallantly hastened up to his assistance; while Clark very prudently consulted his own safety in betaking himself to his heels, leaving his unfortunate companions to shift for themselves. Montgomery halted within gunshot, and appeared busy with the pan of his gun, as if preparing to fire. Two Indians instantly sprung off in pursuit of him, while the rest attended to Kenton. In a few minutes Kenton heard the crack of two rifles in quick succession, followed by a halloo, which announced the fate of his friend. The Indians quickly returned, waving the bloody scalp of Montgomery, and with countenances and gestures which menaced him with a similar fate.

They then proceeded to secure their prisoner. They first compelled him to lie upon his back, and stretched out his arms to their full length. They then passed a stout stick at right angles across his breast, to each extremity of which his wrists were fastened by thongs made of Buffalo's hide. Stakes were then driven into the earth near his feet, to which they were fastened in a similar manner. A halter was then tied around his neck and fastened to a sapling which grew near; and, finally, a strong rope was passed under his belly, lashed strongly to the pole which lay transversely upon his breast, and finally wrapped around his arms at the elbows in such a manner as to pinion them to the pole with a painful violence, and render him literally incapable of moving hand, foot, or head in the slightest manner.

During the whole of this severe operation, neither their tongues nor hands were by any means idle. They cuffed him from time to time with great heartiness, until his ears rang again; and abused him for a "tief! a hoss steal! a rascal!" and finally, for a "d——d white man!" I may here observe that all the western Indians had picked up a good many English words, particularly our oaths, which, from the frequency with which they were used by our hunters and traders, they probably looked upon as the very root and foundation of the English language. Kenton remained in this painful attitude throughout the night, looking forward to certain death, and most probably torture, as soon as he should reach their towns. Their rage against him seemed to increase, rather than abate from indulgence, and in the morning it displayed itself in a form at once ludicrous and cruel.

Among the horses which Kenton had taken, and which their original owners had now recovered, was a fine but wild young colt, totally unbroken, and with all his honors of mane and tail undocked. Upon him Kenton was mounted, without saddle or bridle, with his hands tied behind him and his feet fastened under the horse's belly. The country was rough and bushy, and Kenton had no means of protecting his face from the brambles through which it was expected that the colt would dash. As soon as the rider was firmly fastened to his back, the colt was turned loose, with a sudden lash; but, after executing a few curvets and caprioles, to the great distress of his rider, but to the infinite amusement of the Indians, he appeared to take compassion on his rider, and, falling into a line with the other horses, avoided the brambles entirely, and went on very well. In this manner he rode through the day. At night he was taken from the horse and confined as before.

On the third day they came within a few miles of Chillicothe. Here the party halted and dispatched a messenger to inform the village of their arrival, in order, I suppose, to give them time to prepare for his reception. In a short time, Blackfish, one of their chiefs, arrived, and, regarding Kenton with a stern countenance, thundered out, in very good English, "You have been stealing horses?" "Yes, sir." "Did Captain Boone tell you to steal our horses?" "No, sir; I did it of my own accord." This frank confession was too irritating to be borne. Blackfish made no reply; but, brandishing a hickory switch which he held in his hand, he applied it so briskly to Kenton's naked back and shoulders as to bring the blood freely and occasion acute pain.

Thus, alternately beaten and scolded, he marched on to the village. At the distance of a mile from Chillicothe, he saw every inhabitant of the town, men, women, and children, running out to feast their eyes with a view of the prisoner. Every individual, down to the smallest child, appeared in a paroxysm of rage. They whooped, they yelled, they hooted, they clapped their hands, and poured upon him a flood of abuse to which all that he had yet received was gentleness and civility. With loud cries they demanded that their prisoner should be tied to the stake. The hint was instantly complied with.

A stake was quickly fastened into the ground. The remnant of Kenton's shirt and breeches were torn from his person (the squaws officiating with great dexterity in both operations); and his hands, being tied together and raised above his head, were fastened to the top of the stake. The whole party then danced around him until midnight, yelling and screaming in their usual frantic manner, striking him with switches, and slapping him with the palms of their hands. He expected every moment to undergo the torture of fire; but *that* was reserved for another time. They wished to prolong the pleasure of tormenting him as much as possible, and, after having caused him to anticipate the bitterness of death until a late hour of the night, they released him from the stake and conveyed him to the village.

Early in the morning he beheld the scalp of Montgomery, stretched upon a hoop and drying in the air, before the door of one of their principal houses. He was quickly led out and ordered to run the gauntlet. A row of boys, women, and men extended to the distance of a quarter of a mile. At the starting-place stood two grim-looking warriors, with butcher-knives in their hands; at the extremity of the line was an Indian, beating a drum; and a few paces beyond the drum was the door of the council-house. Clubs, switches, hoe-handles, and tomahawks were brandished along the whole line, causing the sweat involuntarily to stream from his pores at the idea of the discipline which his naked skin was to receive during the race.

The moment for starting arrived; the great drum at

the door of the council-house was struck, and Kenton sprung forward in the race. A scene, precisely resembling a splendid picture in the "Last of the Mohicans," now took place. Kenton avoided the row of his enemies, and, turning to the east, drew the whole party in pursuit of him. He doubled several times with great activity, and at length, observing an opening, he darted through it, and pressed forward to the council-house with a rapidity which left his pursuers far behind. One or two of the Indians succeeded in throwing themselves between him and the goal, and from these alone he received a few blows, but was much less injured than he could at first have supposed possible.

As soon as the race was over, a council was held, in order to determine whether he should be burnt to death on the spot or carried round to the other villages and exhibited to every tribe. The arbiters of his fate sat in a circle on the floor of the council-house, while the unhappy prisoner, naked and bound, was committed to the care of a guard in the open air. The deliberation commenced. Each warrior sat in silence, while a large war-club was passed round the circle. Those who were opposed to burning the prisoner on the spot were to pass the club in silence to the next warrior; those in favor of burning were to strike the earth violently with the club before passing it.

A teller was appointed to count the votes. This dignitary quickly reported that the opposition had prevailed; that his execution was suspended for the present, and that it was determined to take him to an Indian town on Mad River, called Waughcotomoco. His fate was quickly announced to him by a renegade white man, who acted as interpreter. Kenton felt rejoiced at the issue; but naturally became anxious to know what was in reserve for him at Waughcotomoco. He accordingly asked the white man, "What the Indians intended to do with him upon reaching the appointed place?" "Burn you, G——d d——n you!" was the ferocious reply. He asked no further question, and the scowling interpreter walked away.

Instantly preparations were made for his departure,

and, to his great joy as well as astonishment, his clothes were restored to him and he was permitted to remain unbound. Thanks to the ferocious intimation of the interpreter, he was aware of the fate in reserve for him, and secretly determined that he would never reach Waughcotomoco alive if it was possible to avoid it. Their route lay through an unpruned forest, abounding in thickets and undergrowth. Unbound as he was, it would not be impossible to escape from the hands of his conductors; and if he could once enter the thickets, he thought that he might be enabled to baffle his pursuers. At the worst, he could only be retaken; and the fire would burn no hotter after an attempt to escape than before. During the whole of their march he remained abstracted and silent, often meditating an effort for liberty and as often shrinking from the peril of the attempt.

At length he was aroused from his reverie by the Indians firing off their guns, and raising the shrill scalp halloo. The signal was soon answered, and the deep roll of a drum was heard far in front, announcing to the unhappy prisoner that they were approaching an Indian town, where the gauntlet certainly, and perhaps the stake, awaited him. The idea of a repetition of the dreadful scenes which he had already encountered, completely banished the indecision which had hitherto withheld him, and, with a sudden and startling cry, he sprung into the bushes, and fled with the speed of a wild deer. The pursuit was instant and keen; some on foot, some on horseback. But he was flying for his life; the stake and the hot iron, and the burning splinters were before his eyes, and he soon distanced the swiftest hunter that pursued him.

But fate was against him at every turn. Thinking only of the enemy behind, he forgot that there might also be enemies before; and, before he was aware of what he had done, he found that he had plunged into the center of a fresh party of horsemen, who had sallied from the town at the firing of the guns, and happened, unfortunately, to stumble upon the poor prisoner, now making a last effort for freedom. His heart sunk at once from the ardor of hope to the very pit of despair, and he was again haltered and driven before them to town like an ox to the slaughter-house.

Upon reaching the village (Pickaway), he was fastened to a stake, near the door of the council-house, and the warriors again assembled in debate. In a short time they issued from the council-house, and, surrounding him, they danced, yelled, etc., for several hours, giving him once more a foretaste of the bitterness of death. On the following morning their journey was continued, but the Indians had now become watchful, and gave him no opportunity of even attempting an escape. On the second day he arrived at Waughcotomoco. Here he was again compelled to run the gauntlet, in which he was severely hurt; and, immediately after this ceremony, he was taken to the council-house, and all the warriors once more assembled to determine his fate.

He sat silent and dejected upon the floor of the cabin, awaiting the moment which was to deliver him to the stake, when the door of the council-house opened, and Simon Girty, James Girty, John Ward, and an Indian came in with a woman (Mrs. Mary Kennedy) as a prisoner, together with seven children and seven scalps. Kenton was instantly removed from the council-house, and the deliberations of the assembly were protracted to a very late hour, in consequence of the arrival of the last-named party with a fresh drove of prisoners.

At length he was again summoned to attend the council-house, being informed that his fate was decided. Regarding the mandate as a mere prelude to the stake and fire, which he knew was intended for him, he obeyed it with the calm despair which had now succeeded the burning anxiety of the last few days. Upon entering the council-house, he was greeted with a savage scowl, which, if he had still cherished a spark of hope, would have completely extinguished it. Simon Girty threw a blanket upon the floor, and harshly ordered him to take a seat upon it. The order was not immediately complied with, and Girty, impatiently seizing his arm, jerked him roughly upon the blanket, and pulled him down upon it.

In the same rough and menacing tone, Girty then interrogated him as to the condition of Kentucky. "How many men are there in Kentucky?" "It is impossible for me to answer that question," replied Kenton, "but I can tell you the number of officers, and their respective ranks; you can then judge for yourself." "Do you know William Stewart?" "Perfectly well; he is an old and intimate acquaintance." "What is your own name?" "Simon Butler!" replied Kenton. Never did the annunciation of a name produce a more powerful effect. Girty and Kenton (then bearing the name of Butler) had served as spies, together, in Dunmore's expedition. The former had not then abandoned the society of the whites for that of the savages, and had become warmly attached to Kenton during the short period of their services together. As soon as he heard the name, he became strongly agitated; and, springing from his seat, he threw his arms around Kenton's neck, and embraced him with much emotion.

Then turning to the assembled warriors, who remained astonished spectators of this extraordinary scene, he addressed them in a short speech, which the deep earnestness of his tone, and the energy of his gesture, rendered eloquent. He informed them that the prisoner, whom they had just condemned to the stake, was his ancient comrade and bosom friend: that they had traveled the same war-path, slept upon the same blanket, and dwelt in the same wigwam. He entreated them to have compassion upon his feelings; to spare him the agony of witnessing the torture of an old friend by the hands of his adopted brothers; and not to refuse so trifling a favor, as the life of a white man, to the earnest intercession of one who had proved, by three years' faithful service, that he was sincerely and zealously devoted to the cause of the Indians.

The speech was listened to in unbroken silence. As soon as he had finished, several chiefs expressed their approbation by a deep guttural interjection, while others were equally as forward in making known their objections to the proposal. They urged that his fate had already been determined in a large and solemn council, and that they would be acting like squaws to change their mind every hour. They insisted upon the flagrant misdemeanors of Kenton; that he had not only stolen their horses, but had flashed his gun at one of their young men; that it was in vain to suppose that so bad a man could ever become an Indian at heart, like their brother Girty; that the Kentuckians were all alike, very bad people, and ought to be killed as fast as they were taken; and finally, they observed, that many of their people had come from a distance solely to assist at the torture of the prisoner, and pathetically painted the disappointment and chagrin with which they would hear that all their trouble had been for nothing.

Girty listened, with obvious impatience, to the young warriors who had so ably argued against a reprieve, and starting to his feet as soon as the others had concluded, he urged his former request with great earnestness. He briefly but strongly recapitulated his own services, and the many and weighty instances of attachment which he had given. He asked if *he* could be suspected of partiality to the whites? When had he ever before interceded for any of that hated race? Had he not brought seven scalps home with him from the last expedition? And had he not submitted seven white prisoners that very evening to their discretion? Had he expressed a wish that a single one of the captives should be saved? *This* was his first and should be his last request: for if they refused to *him* what was never refused to the intercession of one of their natural chiefs, he would look upon himself as disgraced in their eyes, and considered as unworthy of confidence. Which of their own natural warriors had been more zealous than himself? From what expedition had he ever shrunk? What white man had ever seen his back? Whose tomahawk had been bloodier than his? He would say no more. He asked it as a first and last favor—as an evidence that they approved of his zeal and fidelity—that the life of his bosom friend might be spared. Fresh speakers arose upon each side, and the debate was carried on, for an hour and a half, with great heat and energy.

During the whole of this time, Kenton's feelings may readily be imagined. He could not understand a syllable of what was said. He saw that Girty spoke with deep earnestness, and that the eyes of the assembly were often turned upon himself, with various expressions. He felt satisfied that his friend was pleading for his life, and that he was violently opposed by a large part of the council. At length the war-club was produced, and the final vote taken. Kenton watched its progress with thrilling emotion, which yielded to the most rapturous delight as he perceived that those who struck the floor of the council-house were decidedly inferior in number to those who passed it in silence. Having thus succeeded in his benevolent purpose, Girty lost no time in attending to the comfort of his friend. He led him into his own wigwam, and from his own store gave him a pair of moccasins and leggins, a breech-cloth, a hat, a coat, a handkerchief for his neck, and another for his head.

The whole of this remarkable scene is in the highest degree honorable to Girty, and is in striking contrast to most of his conduct after his union with the Indians. No man can be completely hardened, and no character is at all times the same. Girty had been deeply offended with the whites; and knowing that his desertion to the Indians had been universally and severely reprobated, and that he himself was regarded with detestation by his former countrymen, he seems to have raged against them, from these causes, with a fury which resembled rather the paroxysm of a maniac than the deliberate cruelty of a naturally ferocious temper. Fierce censure never reclaims, but rather drives to still greater extremities; and this is the reason that renegadoes are so much fiercer than natural foes—and when females fall, they fall irretrievably.

For the space of three weeks, Kenton lived in perfect tranquillity. Girty's kindness was uniform and indefatigable. He introduced Kenton to his own family, and accompanied him to the wigwams of the principal chiefs, who seemed all at once to have turned from the extremity of rage to the utmost kindness and cordiality. Fortune, however, seemed to have selected him for her football, and to have snatched him from the frying-pan only to throw him into the fire. About twenty days after his most providential deliverance from the stake, he was walking in company with Girty and an Indian named Redpole, when another Indian came from the village toward them, uttering repeatedly a whoop of peculiar intonation. Girty instantly told Kenton that it was the distress halloo, and that they must all go instantly to the council-house. Kenton's heart involuntarily fluttered at the intelligence, for he dreaded all whoops, and hated all council-houses, firmly believing that neither boded him any good. Nothing, however, could be done to avoid whatever fate awaited him, and he sadly accompanied Girty and Redpole back to the village.

Upon approaching the Indian who had hallooed, Girty and Redpole shook hands with him. Kenton likewise offered his hand, but the Indian refused to take it, at the same time scowling upon him ominously. This took place within a few paces of the door of the council-house. Upon entering, they saw that the house was unusually full. Many chiefs and warriors from the distant towns were present; and their countenances were grave, severe, and forbidding. Girty, Redpole, and Kenton, walked around, offering their hands successively to each warrior. The hands of the two first were cordially received; but when poor Kenton anxiously offered *his* hand to the first warrior, it was rejected with the same scowling eye as before. He passed on to the second, but was still rejected; he persevered, however, until his hand had been refused by the first six; when, sinking into despondence, he turned off and stood apart from the rest.

The debate quickly commenced. Kenton looked eagerly toward Girty, as his last and only hope. His friend looked anxious and distressed. The chiefs from a distance arose one after another, and spoke in a firm and indignant tone, often looking at Kenton with an eye of death. Girty did not desert him, but his eloquence appeared wasted upon the distant chiefs. After a warm debate, he turned to Kenton and said, "Well, my friend, *you must die!*" One of the stranger chiefs instantly seized him by the collar, and the others surrounding him, he was strongly pinioned, committed to a guard, and instantly marched off.

His guard were on horseback, while the prisoner was driven before them on foot, with a long rope round his neck, the other end of which was held by one of the guard. In this manner they had marched about two and a half miles, when Girty passed them on horseback, informing Kenton that he had friends at the next village, with whose aid he hoped to be able to do something for him. Girty passed on to the town, but finding that nothing could be done, he would not see his friend again, but returned to Waughcotomoco by a different route.

They passed through the village without halting, and, at the distance of two and a half miles beyond it, Kenton had again an opportunity of witnessing the fierce hate with which these children of nature regard an enemy. At the distance of a few paces from the road a squaw was busily engaged in chopping wood, while her lord and master was sitting on a log, smoking his pipe and directing her labors with the indolent indifference common to the natives when not under the influence of some exciting passion. The sight of Kenton, however, roused him to fury. He hastily sprang up, with a sudden yell, snatched the ax from the squaw, and, rushing upon the prisoner so rapidly as to give him no opportunity of escape, dealt him a blow with the ax which cut through his shoulder, breaking the bone and almost severing the arm from his body. He would instantly have repeated the blow, had not Kenton's conductors interfered and protected him, severely reprimanding the Indian for attempting to rob them of the amusement of torturing the prisoner at ———.

They soon reached a large village upon the head-waters of Scioto, where Kenton, for the first time, beheld the celebrated Mingo chief, Logan, so honorably mentioned in Mr. Jefferson's "Notes on Virginia." Logan walked gravely up to the place where Kenton stood, and the following short conversation ensued: "Well, young man, these young men seem very mad at you!" "Yes, sir, they certainly are." "Well, do n't be disheartened, I am a great chief. You are to go to Sandusky; they speak of burning you there, but I will send two runners to-morrow to speak good for you." Logan's form was striking and manly, his countenance calm and noble, and he spoke the English language with fluency and correctness. Kenton's spirits instantly rose at the address of the benevolent chief, and he once more looked upon himself as providentially rescued from the stake.

On the following morning two runners were despatched to Sandusky, as the chief had promised, and until their return Kenton was kindly treated, being permitted to spend much of his time with Logan, who conversed with him freely and in the most friendly manner. In the evening the two runners returned, and were closeted with Logan. Kenton felt the most burning anxiety to know what was the result of their mission, but Logan did not visit him again until the next morning. He then walked up to him, accompanied by Kenton's guards, and, giving him a piece of bread, told him that he was instantly to be carried to Sandusky; and, without uttering another word, turned upon his heel and left him.

Again Kenton's spirits sank. From Logan's manner he supposed that his intercession had been unavailing, and that Sandusky was destined to be the scene of his final suffering. This appears to have been the truth. But fortune, who, to use Lord Lovat's expression, had been playing at cat and mouse with him for the last month, had selected Sandusky for the display of her strange and capricious power. He was driven into the town as usual, and was to have been burnt on the following morning, when an Indian agent, named Drewyer, interposed, and once more rescued him from the stake. He was anxious to obtain intelligence for the British commandant at Detroit, and so earnestly insisted upon

Kenton's being delivered up to him, that the Indians at length consented, upon the express condition that, after the required information had been obtained, he should again be placed at their discretion. To this Drewyer consented, and without further difficulty Kenton was transferred to his hands. Drewyer lost no time in removing him to Detroit.

On the road he informed Kenton of the condition upon which he had obtained possession of his person, assuring him, however, that no consideration should induce him to abandon a prisoner to the mercy of such wretches. Having dwelt at some length upon the generosity of his own disposition, and having sufficiently magnified the service which he had just rendered him, he began, at length, to cross-question Kenton as to the force and condition of Kentucky, and particularly as to the number of men at Fort McIntosh. Kenton very candidly declared his inability to answer either question, observing that he was merely a private, and by no means acquainted with matters of an enlarged and general import; that his great business had heretofore been to endeavor to take care of himself, which he had found a work of no small difficulty. Drewyer replied that he believed him, and from that time Kenton was troubled with no more questions.

His condition at Detroit was not unpleasant. He was compelled to report himself every morning to an English officer, and was restricted to certain boundaries through the day, but in other respects he scarcely felt that he was a prisoner. His battered body and broken arm were quickly repaired, and his emaciated limbs were again clothed with a proper proportion of flesh. He remained in this state of easy restraint from October, 1777, until June, 1778, when he meditated an escape. There was no difficulty in leaving Detroit, but he would be compelled to traverse a wilderness of more than two hundred miles, abounding with hostile Indians, and affording no means of subsistence beyond the wild game, which could not be killed without a gun. In addition to this, he would certainly be pursued, and, if retaken by the Indians, he might expect a repetition of all that he had undergone before, without the prospect of a second interposition on the part of the English.

These considerations deterred him for some time from the attempt, but at length his impatience became uncontrollable, and he determined to escape, or perish in the attempt. He took his measures with equal secrecy and foresight. He cautiously sounded two young Kentuckians then at Detroit, who had been taken with Boone at the Blue Licks, and had been purchased by the British. He found them as impatient as himself of captivity, and resolute to accompany him. Charging them not to breathe a syllable of their design to any other prisoners, he busied himself for several days in making the necessary preparations. It was absolutely necessary that they should be provided with arms, both for the sake of repelling attack and procuring the means of subsistence; and, at the same time, it was very difficult to obtain them without the knowledge of the British commandant.

By patiently waiting their opportunity, however, all these preliminary difficulties were overcome. Kenton formed a close friendship with two Indian hunters, deluged them with rum, and bought their guns for a mere trifle. After carefully hiding them in the woods, he returned to Detroit, and managed to procure another rifle, together with powder and balls, from a Mr. and Mrs. Edgar, citizens of the town. They then appointed a night for the attempt, and agreed upon a place of rendezvous. All things turned out prosperously. They met at the time and place appointed without discovery, and, taking a circuitous route, avoided pursuit; and, traveling only during the night, they at length arrived safely at Louisville, after a march of thirty days.

Thus terminated one of the most remarkable adventures in the whole range of Western history. A fatalist would recognize the hand of destiny in every stage of its progress. In the infatuation with which Kenton refused to adopt proper measures for his safety while such were practicable; in the persevering obstinacy with which he remained upon the Ohio shore until flight became useless; and afterward, in that remarkable succession of accidents by which, without the least exertion on his part, he was alternately tantalized with a prospect of safety, and then plunged again into the deepest despair. He was eight times exposed to the gauntlet, three times tied to the stake, and as often thought himself upon the eve of a terrible death.

All the sentences passed upon him, whether of mercy or condemnation, seemed to have been only pronounced in one council in order to be reversed in another. Every friend that Providence raised up in his favor was immediately followed by some enemy, who unexpectedly interposed, and turned his short glimpse of sunshine into deeper darkness than ever. For three weeks he was seesawing between life and death, and during the whole time he was perfectly passive. No wisdom, or foresight, or exertion, could have saved him. Fortune fought his battle from first to last, and seemed determined to permit nothing else to interfere. Scarcely had he reached Kentucky, when he embarked in a new enterprise.

Colonel George Rogers Clark had projected an expedition against the hostile posts of Vincennes and Kaskaskia, and invited all Kentuckians, who had leisure and inclination, to join him. Kenton instantly repaired to his standard, and shared in the hardship and glory of one of the boldest, most arduous, and successful expeditions which have ever graced the American arms. The results of the campaign are well known. Secrecy and celerity were eminently combined in it, and Clark shared with the common soldier in encountering every fatigue and braving every danger. Kenton, as usual, acted as a spy, and was eminently serviceable; but no incident occurred of sufficient importance to obtain a place in these sketches.

From that time until the close of the Indian war in the West, Kenton was actively employed, generally in a frontier station, and occasionally in serious expeditions. He accompanied Edwards in his abortive expedition against the Indian towns in 1785, and shared in Wayne's decisive campaign of 1794.

McDonald, in his extended sketch of Kenton, informs us that he settled, about the year 1802, in Urbana, Champaign County, Ohio, remaining there for some years; was elected a brigadier-general of the militia, and in 1810 became a member of the Methodist Church. In 1813, when Governor Shelby reached that place, at the head of the Kentucky troops, Kenton joined the army as a private (but a privileged member of the governor's military family), and was present at the glorious battle of the Moravian Town, where ended his military career. About 1820, he moved to the head of Mad River, in Logan County, Ohio, near to the site of Old Wapatomika (now Zanesville), where he died, in April, 1836, being nearly eighty-one years old.

"General Kenton was of fair complexion, six feet one inch in height. He stood and walked very erect; and, in the prime of life, weighed about one hundred and ninety. He was never inclined to be corpulent, although of sufficient size to form a graceful person. He had a soft, tremulous voice, very pleasing to the hearer, and laughing, gray eyes, which appeared to fascinate the beholder. He was a pleasant, good-humored, and obliging companion. When excited or provoked to anger (which was seldom the case) the fiery glance of his eye would almost curdle the blood of those with whom he came in contact. In his dealings, he was perfectly honest; his confidence in man, and his credulity were such, that the same man might cheat him twenty times, and, if he professed friendship, he might cheat him still."

Such was Simon Kenton, to whose memory be it said, that, "if a long life of hardy adventures—with a courage that never quailed at danger, and patriotism that never ceased its exertion in his country's cause—deserves the title of illustrious, then stands the name of General Kenton in the first rank of worthies."

CHAPTER IV.

AMONG the earliest and most respectable of the emigrants to Kentucky, was General BENJAMIN LOGAN. His father was an Irishman, who had left his own country early in the eighteenth century, and settled in Pennsylvania, from which he subsequently removed to Augusta County, Virginia. Here he shortly afterward died. Young Logan, as the eldest son, was entitled, by the laws of Virginia, to the whole of the landed property, (his father having died intestate). He refused, however, to avail himself of this circumstance, and, as the farm upon which the family resided was too small to admit of a division, he caused it to be sold, and the money to be distributed among his brothers and sisters, reserving a portion for his mother. At the age of twenty-one, he removed from Augusta County to the banks of the Holston, where, shortly afterward, he purchased a farm and married.

In 1774 he accompanied Dunmore in his expedition, probably as a private. In 1775, he removed to Kentucky, and soon became particularly distinguished. His person was striking and manly, his hair and complexion very dark, his eye keen and penetrating, his countenance grave, thoughtful, and expressive of a firmness, probity, and intelligence, which were eminently displayed throughout his life. His education was very imperfect, and confined, we believe, simply, to the arts of reading and writing. Having remained in Kentucky, in a very exposed situation, until the spring of 1776, he returned for his family, and brought them out to a small settlement, called Logan's Fort, not far from Harrodsburgh. The Indians during this summer were so numerous and daring in their excursions, that

Logan was compelled to remove his wife and family for safety to Harrodsburgh, while he himself remained at his cabins and cultivated a crop of corn.

In the spring of 1777, his wife returned to Logan's Fort; and several settlers having joined him, he determined to maintain himself there at all risk. His courage was soon put to the test. On the morning of the twentieth of May, a few days after his wife had rejoined him, the women were milking the cows at the gate of the little fort, and some of the garrison attending them, when a party of Indians appeared and fired upon them. One man was shot dead, and two more wounded, one of them mortally. The whole party, including one of the wounded men, instantly ran into the fort and closed the gate. The enemy quickly showed themselves upon the edge of a canebrake, within close rifle-shot of the gate, and seemed numerous and determined. Having a moment's leisure to look around, they beheld a spectacle which awakened the most lively interest and compassion.

A man named Harrison had been severely wounded, and still lay near the spot where he had fallen, within full view both of the garrison and the enemy. The poor fellow was, at intervals, endeavoring to crawl in the direction of the fort, and had succeeded in reaching a cluster of bushes, which, however, were too thin to shelter his person from the enemy. His wife and family were in the fort, and in deep distress at his situation. The enemy undoubtedly forebore to fire upon him, from the supposition that some of the garrison would attempt to save him, in which case they held themselves in readiness to fire upon them from the canebrake. The case was a very trying one. It seemed impossible to save him without sacrificing the lives of several of the garrison, and their numbers already were far too few for an effectual defense, having originally amounted only to fifteen men, three of whom had already been put *hors de combat.*

Yet the spectacle was so moving, and the lamentation of his family so distressing, that it seemed equally impossible not to make an effort to relieve him.

Logan endeavored to persuade some of his men to accompany him in a sally, but so evident and appalling was the danger, that all at first refused; one Herculean fellow observing that he was a "weakly man," and another declaring that he was sorry for Harrison, " but that the skin was closer than the shirt." At length John Martin collected his courage, and declared his willingness to accompany Logan, saying, that "he could only die once, and that he was as ready now as he ever would be." The two men opened the gate and started upon their forlorn expedition, Logan leading the way.

They had not advanced five steps, when Harrison, perceiving them, made a vigorous effort to rise, upon which Martin, supposing him able to help himself, immediately sprung back within the gate. Harrison's strength almost instantly failed, and he fell at full length upon the grass. Logan paused a moment after the desertion of Martin, then suddenly sprung forward to the spot where Harrison lay, rushing through a tremendous shower of rifle-balls which was poured upon him from every spot around the fort capable of covering an Indian. Seizing the wounded man in his arms, he ran with him to the fort, through the same heavy fire, and entered it unhurt, although the gate and picketing near him were riddled with balls, and his hat and clothes pierced in several places.

The fort was now vigorously assailed in the Indian manner, and as vigorously defended by the garrison. The women were all employed in molding bullets, while the men were constantly at their posts. The weakness of the garrison was not their only grievance. A distressing scarcity of ammunition prevailed, and no supply could be procured nearer than Holston. But how was it to be obtained? The fort was closely blockaded, the Indians were swarming in the woods, and chances were sadly against the probability of the safe passage of any courier through so many dangers! Under these circumstances, Logan determined to take the dangerous office upon himself. After encouraging the men as well as he could, with the prospect of a safe and speedy return, he took advantage of a dark night, and crawled through the Indian encampment without discovery.

Shunning the ordinary route through Cumberland Gap, he arrived at Holston by by-paths which no white man had yet trodden; through canebrakes and thickets; over tremendous cliffs and precipices, where the deer could scarcely obtain footing, and where no vestige of any of the human family could be seen. Having obtained a supply of powder and lead, he returned through the same almost inaccessible paths to the fort, which he found still besieged, and now reduced to extremity. The safe return of their leader inspired them with fresh courage, and in a few days the appearance of Colonel Bowman's party compelled the Indians to retire.

During the whole of this and the next year, the Indians were exceedingly troublesome. The Shawnees particularly distinguished themselves by the frequency and inveterate nature of their incursions; and as their capital, Chillicothe, was within striking distance, an expedition was set on foot against it in 1779, in which Logan served as second in command. Captain James Harrod and John Bulger accompanied the expedition; the former of whom, shortly afterward, perished in a lonely ramble; and the latter was killed at the Blue Licks. Colonel Bowman commanded in chief. The detachment amounted to one hundred and sixty men; consisted entirely of volunteers, accustomed to Indian warfare, and was well officered, but not so fortunate in its commander.

They left Harrodsburg in July, and took their preliminary measures so well, that they arrived within a mile of Chillicothe, without giving the slightest alarm to the enemy. Here the detachment halted at an early hour in the night, and, as usual, sent out spies to examine the condition of the village. Before midnight they returned, and reported that the enemy remained unapprised of their being in the neighborhood, and were in the most unmilitary security. The army was instantly put in motion. It was determined that Logan, with one-half of the men, should turn to the left and march half way around the town, while Bowman, at the head of the remainder, should make a corresponding march to the right; that both parties should proceed in silence, until they had met at the opposite extremity of the village, when, having thus completely encircled it, the attack was to commence.

Logan, who was bravery himself, performed his part of the combined operation, with perfect order, and in profound silence; and having reached the designated spot, awaited with impatience the arrival of his commander. Hour after hour stole away, but Bowman did not appear. At length daylight appeared. Logan, still expecting the arrival of his colonel, ordered the men to conceal themselves in the high grass, and await the expected signal to attack. No orders, however, arrived. In the meantime, the men, in shifting about through the grass, alarmed an Indian dog, the only sentinel on duty. He instantly began to bay loudly, and advanced in the direction of the man who had attracted his attention. Presently a solitary Indian left his cabin, and walked cautiously toward the party, halting frequently, rising upon tiptoes, and gazing around him.

Logan's party lay close, with the hope of taking him without giving the alarm; but at that instant a gun was fired in an opposite quarter of the town, as was afterward ascertained, by one of Bowman's party, and the Indian, giving one shrill whoop, ran swiftly back to the council-house. Concealment was now impossible. Logan's party instantly sprung up from the grass, and rushed upon the village, not doubting for a moment that they would be gallantly supported. As they advanced, they perceived Indians of all ages and of both sexes, running to the great cabin, near the center of the town, where they collected in full force and appeared determined upon an obstinate defense. Logan instantly took possession of the houses which had been deserted, and rapidly advancing from cabin to cabin, at length established his detachment within close rifle shot of the Indian redoubt.

He now listened impatiently for the firing which should have been heard from the opposite extremity of the town, where he supposed Bowman's party to be, but to his astonishment, every thing remained quiet in that quarter. In the meantime his own position had become critical. The Indians had recovered from their panic, and kept up a close and heavy fire upon the cabins which covered his men. He had pushed his detachment so close to the redoubt, that they could neither advance nor retreat without great exposure. The enemy outnumbered him, and gave indications of a disposition to turn both flanks of his position and thus endanger his retreat.

Under these circumstances, ignorant of the condition of his commander, and cut off from communication with him, he formed the bold and judicious resolution, to make a movable breastwork of the planks which formed the floor of the cabins, and under cover of it, to rush upon the stronghold of the enemy and carry it by main force. Had this gallant determination been carried into effect, and had the movement been promptly seconded, as it ought to have been by Bowman, the conflict would have been bloody, and the victory decisive. Most probably not an Indian would have escaped, and the consternation which such signal vengeance would have spread throughout the Indian tribes, might have repressed their incursions for a considerable time. But before the necessary steps could be taken, a messenger arrived from Bowman, with orders "to retreat!"

Astonished at such an order, at a time when honor and safety required an offensive movement on their part, Logan hastily asked if Bowman had been overpowered by the enemy? No! Had he ever beheld an enemy? No! What, then, was the cause of this extraordinary abandonment of a design so prosperously begun? He did not know: the colonel had ordered a retreat! Logan, however reluctantly, was compelled to obey. A retreat is always a dispiriting movement, and, with militia, is almost certain to terminate in a complete rout. As soon as the men were informed of the order, a most irregular and tumultuous scene commenced. Not being buoyed up by the mutual confidence which is the offspring of discipline, and which sustains regular soldiers under all circumstances, they no longer acted in concert.

Each man selected the time, manner, and route of his retreat for himself. Here a solitary Kentuckian would start up from behind a stump, and scud away through the grass, dodging and turning to avoid the balls which whistled around him. There a dozen men would run from a cabin, and scatter in every direction, each anxious to save himself, and none having leisure to attend to their neighbors. The Indians, astonished at seeing men rout themselves in this manner, sallied out of their redoubts and pursued the stragglers, as sportsmen would cut up a scattered flock of wild geese. They soon united themselves to Bowman's party, who from some unaccountable panic of their commander, or fault in themselves, had stood stock still near the spot where Logan had left them the night before.

All was confusion. Some cursed their colonel; some reproached other officers; one shouted one thing, one bellowed another; but all seemed to agree that they ought to make the best of their way home, without the loss of a moment's time. By great exertions on the part of Logan, well seconded by Harrod, Bulger, and the late Maj. G. M. Bedinger, of the Blue Licks, some degree of order was restored, and a tolerably respectable retreat commenced. The Indians, however, soon surrounded them on all sides, and kept up a hot fire, which began to grow fatal. Colonel Bowman appeared quite bewildered, and sat upon his horse like a pillar of stone, neither giving an order, nor taking any measures to repel the enemy. The sound of the rifle-shots had, however, completely restored the men to their senses, and they readily formed in a large hollow square, took trees, and returned the fire with equal vivacity. The enemy was quickly repelled, and the troops recommenced their march.

But scarcely had they advanced half a mile, when the Indians re-appeared, and again opened a fire upon the front, rear, and both flanks. Again a square was formed, and the enemy repelled; but scarcely had the harassed troops recommenced their march, when the same galling fire was opened upon them from every tree, bush, and stone capable of concealing an Indian. Matters now began to look serious. The enemy were evidently endeavoring to detain them, until fresh Indians could come up in sufficient force to compel them to lay down their arms. The men began to be unsteady, and the panic was rapidly spreading from the colonel to the privates. At this crisis, Logan, Harrod, Bedinger, etc., selected the boldest and best-mounted men, and dashing into the bushes on horseback, scoured the woods in every direction, forcing the Indians from their coverts, and cutting down as many as they could overtake.

This decisive step completely dispersed the enemy, and the weary and dispirited troops continued their retreat unmolested. They lost nine killed and a few others wounded. But the loss of reputation on the part of the colonel was incalculable, for, as usual, *he* was the scapegoat upon whose head the disgrace of the miscarriage was laid. No good reason has ever been assigned for the extraordinary failure of his own detachment; and the subsequent panic which he displayed when harassed in the wood, affords room for suspicion that either the darkness of the night, or the cry of an owl (for he did not see the face of an enemy), had robbed the colonel of his usual presence of mind.

It may be here remarked, that the propriety of combined operations with irregular troops, is at least doubtful. Different corps, moving by different routes upon the same point, are liable to miscarriage from so many causes, that the measure is scarcely ever attended with success, unless when the troops are good, the officers intelligent and unanimous, and the ground perfectly understood. The intervention of a creek, the ignorance of a guide, or the panic of an officer, as in the case of Bowman, may destroy the *unity* of the operation, and expose the detachment which has reached its station in proper time to be cut off.

The signal failure of Washington at Germantown, may, in a great measure, be attributed to the complicated plan of attack, as the several divisions arrived at different times, attacked without concert, and were beaten in detail. I can scarcely recollect a single instance, save the affair of Trenton, in which raw troops have succeeded by combined operations, and many miscarriages in our own annals may be attributed to that circumstance. Logan returned to Kentucky with a reputation increased, rather than diminished, by the failure of the expedition. His conduct was placed in glaring contrast to that of his unfortunate commander, and the praise of the one was in exact correspondence to the censure of the other.

No other affair of consequence occurred until the rash and disastrous battle of the Blue Licks, in which, as we have seen, Logan was unable to share. He seems to have remained quietly engaged in agricultural pursuits until the summer of 1788, when he conducted an expedition against the north-western tribes, which, as usual, terminated in burning their villages, and cutting up their corn-fields; serving to irritate, but not to subdue the enemy. A single incident attending this expedition, deserves to be commemorated. Upon approaching a large village of the Shawnees, from which, as usual, most of the inhabitants had fled, an old chief, named Moluntha, came out to meet them, fantastically dressed in an old cocked hat, set jauntily upon one side of his head, and a fine shawl thrown over his shoulders. He carried an enormous pipe in one hand, and a tobacco pouch in the other, and strutted out with the air of an old French beau to smoke the pipe of peace with his enemies, whom he found himself unable to meet in the field.

Nothing could be more striking than the fearless confidence with which he walked through the foremost ranks of the Kentuckians, evidently highly pleased with his own appearance, and enjoying the admiration which he doubted not that his cocked hat and splendid shawl inspired. Many of the Kentuckians were highly amused at the mixture of dandyism and gallantry which the poor old man exhibited, and shook hands with him very cordially. Unfortunately, however, he at length approached Major McGary, whose temper, never particularly sweet, was as much inflamed by the sight of an Indian, as that of a wild bull by the waving of a red flag. It happened, unfortunately, too, that Moluntha had been one of the chiefs who commanded at the Blue Licks, a disaster which McGary had not yet forgotten.

Instead of giving his hand as the others had done, McGary scowled upon the old man, and asked him if "he recollected the Blue Licks?" Moluntha smiled, and merely repeated the word "Blue Licks!" when McGary instantly drew his tomahawk, and cleft him to the brain. The old man received the blow without flinching for a second, and fell dead at the feet of his destroyer. Great excitement instantly prevailed in the army. Some called it a ruthless murder; and others swore that he had done right; that an Indian was not to be regarded as a human being, but ought to be shot down as a wolf whenever and wherever he appeared. McGary himself raved like a madman at the reproach of his countrymen, and declared, with many bitter oaths, that he would not only kill every Indian whom he met, whether in peace or war, at church or market, but that he would equally as readily tomahawk the man who blamed him for the act.

Nothing else, worthy of being mentioned, occurred during the expedition, and Logan, upon his return, devoted himself exclusively to the civil affairs of the country, which about his time began to assume an important aspect.

The reader who is desirous of understanding the gradations by which, from a simple society of woodsmen, Kentucky became transformed into a boiling vortex of political fury, intrigue, and dissension, will do well to consult Mr. Marshall's history, which, although possessing some peculiarities of opinion, and occasional eccentricities of style, will be found to contain a strong, clear, and sagacious view of the political events which succeeded the peace of 1783.

CHAPTER V.

DURING the whole of the Revolutionary war, the Indians had been extremely troublesome to the back counties of Pennsylvania and Virginia, particularly to those of Washington, Youghiogheny, and Westmoreland. In the early part of the year 1782, however, these irregular excursions became so galling that an expedition was concerted against the Wyandott village, lying upon the waters of the Sandusky. Great exertions were made to procure volunteers. Every man who should equip himself with a horse and rifle, was to be exempted from two tours of militia duty; and any loss, either of arms or horses, was to be repaired out of the plunder of the Indian towns. The volunteers were to rendezvous on the twentieth of May, at an old Mingo village, on the western shore of the Ohio, about forty miles above Fort Pitt, and the unfortunate Colonel WILLIAM CRAWFORD was unanimously selected as the leader of the expedition.

On the appointed day, four hundred and fifty mounted volunteers assembled at the Mingo village, and impatiently awaited the arrival of their colonel. Crawford instantly accepted the appointment, which had been so unanimously pressed upon him, and a few days before the day of rendezvous, passed through Pittsburgh, on his way to the appointed place. He there prevailed upon Dr. Knight to accompany the detachment as surgeon, and having provided such medical stores as were likely to be useful on the expedition, he lost no time in putting himself at the head of the troops.

On Saturday, the twenty-fifth of May, the little army commenced its march, striking at once into a pathless wilderness, and directing their course due west. On the fourth day, they halted at the ruins of the old Moravian town, about sixty miles from the Ohio, where a few of the volunteers gave a sample of the discipline which was to be expected from the party, by abandoning the detachment and returning home. The main body, however, still seemed eager to prosecute the expedition, and the march was continued with unabated spirit. On the morning of the thirtieth, Major Brunton and Captain Bean, being a few hundred yards in advance of the troops, observed two Indians skulking through the woods, apparently observing the motions of the detachment. They instantly fired upon them, but without success. Secrecy now being out of the question, it only remained to press forward with all practicable dispatch, and afford the enemy as little time for preparation as possible. As the wilderness began to deepen around them, and the critical moment approached in which their courage would be tried, it became evident that the ardor of the men was considerably cooled.

On the eleventh day of their march, they reached the spot where the town of Sandusky had formerly stood, but from which the Indians had lately removed to a spot about eighteen miles below. Here the detachment halted, and here the insubordinate spirit of the army first displayed itself. They insisted upon returning home, alleging the tired condition of their horses, and the fact, that their provisions were likely soon to be exhausted. The officers, yielding to the wishes of their *constituents* (for the troops had elected their own officers), determined, in council, that they would continue their march for one day longer, and, if no Indians appeared, they would then return home! What other results than these which we are now about to record could have been anticipated from such officers and such men?

Just as the council broke up, a single light-horseman belonging to the advanced guard rode in at a gallop, announcing that a large body of Indians were formed in an open wood, a few miles in advance, and seemed determined to arrest the farther progress of the invaders. Instant preparations were made for battle. The troops, notwithstanding their previous murmurs, advanced with alacrity, and soon came up with the lighthorsemen, who were slowly retiring within view of the enemy. The country was generally open, and well adapted to the operations of cavalry. Here and there a thin copse of woodland appeared, generally free from undergrowth, and giving to each party a full view of their enemy's movements. The Indians had partially obtained possession of one of these copses, although their full force had not yet come up.

The importance of seizing the wood was instantly seen, and Crawford hastily ordered his men to dismount, tie their horses, and force the enemy from their position before their reinforcements could arrive. This judicious order was promptly and effectually obeyed. Both flanks of the Indian position were immediately turned, and a rapid and threatening movement upon their front quickly compelled them to give way. Crawford now took possession of the wood, but scarcely had he done so, when the main body of the enemy hurried up to the assistance of their van, and outflanking Crawford in turn, opened a heavy and galling fire upon his men, from which they found it very difficult to obtain proper shelter.

The action now became sharp and serious; Crawford maintaining his ground, and the enemy (who were hourly increasing in number) making the most strenuous efforts to regain the wood. From four in the evening until dusk, the firing was very heavy, and the loss considerable. During the whole of this time, scarcely an Indian was visible, unless for a moment, when shifting his position. Their number could only be ascertained from the many wreaths of smoke, which arose from every bush, tree, or tuft of grass within view. At night the enemy drew off, and Crawford's party slept upon their arms on the field of battle.

On the next day the attack was renewed, but at a more respectful distance. The Indians had apparently sustained some loss on the close firing of the preceding evening, and seemed now determined to await the arrival of additional reinforcements. Occasional shots were fired through the day on both sides, but without much injury to either. As soon as it was dark, the field officers assembled in council; and, as the numbers of the enemy were evidently increasing every moment, it was unanimously determined to retreat by night, as rapidly as was consistent with order, and the preservation of the wounded. The resolution was quickly announced to the troops, and the necessary dispositions made for carrying it into effect. The outposts were silently withdrawn from the vicinity of the enemy, and as fast as they came in, the troops were formed in three parallel lines, with the wounded borne upon biers, in the center. By nine o'clock at night, all necessary arrangements had been made, and the retreat began in good order.

Unfortunately, they had scarcely moved a hundred paces, when the report of several rifles were heard in the rear, in the direction of the Indian encampment. The troops soon became very unsteady At length, a solitary voice, in the front rank, called out that their design was discovered, and that the Indians would soon be upon them. Nothing more was necessary. The cavalry were instantly broken; and, as usual, each man endeavored to save himself as he best could. A prodigious uproar ensued, which quickly communicated to the enemy, that the white men had routed themselves, and that they had nothing to do but pick up stragglers. The miserable wounded, notwithstanding the piercing cries with which they supplicated to be taken with them, were abandoned to the mercy of the enemy, and soon put out of pain.

Dr. Knight, the surgeon of the detachment, was in the rear when the flight commenced, but seeing the necessity of dispatch, he put spurs to his horse and galloped through the wood as fast as the darkness of the night would permit. He had not advanced more than three hundred yards, when he heard the voice of Colonel Crawford, a short distance in front, calling aloud for his son John Crawford, his son-in-law

Major Harrison, and his two nephews, Major Rose and William Crawford. Dr. Knight replied, in the same loud tone, that he believed the young men were in front. "Is that you, doctor?" asked Crawford, eagerly; for no features could be recognized in the darkness. "Yes, colonel! I am the hindmost man, I believe!" "No, no!" replied Crawford, ' anxiously, "my son is in the rear yet: I have not been able to hear of him in front! Do not leave me, doctor, my horse has almost given out; I can not keep up with the troops, and wish a few of my best friends to stay with me."

Knight assured him that he might rely upon his support in any extremity, and drew up his horse by his side. Colonel Crawford still remained upon the same spot, calling loudly for his son, until the last straggler had passed. He then, in strong language, reprobated the conduct of the militia in breaking their ranks and abandoning the wounded, but quickly returned to the subject of his son, and appeared deeply agitated at the uncertainty of his fate. Perceiving, however, that further delay must terminate in death or captivity, the party set spurs to their horses and followed the route of the troops. Presently an old man and a lad joined them. Crawford eagerly asked if they had seen his son or nephews? They assured him that they had not, upon which he sighed deeply, but made no reply.

At this instant a heavy fire was heard at the distance of a mile in front, accompanied by yells, screams, and all the usual attendants of battle. Not a doubt was entertained that the Indians had intercepted the retreat of the main body, and were now engaged with them. Having lost all confidence in his men, Crawford did not choose to unite his fortune to theirs, and changed his course to the northward, in such a manner as to leave the combatants upon the right. He continued in this direction for nearly an hour, until he supposed himself out of the immediate line of the enemy's operations, when he again changed his course to the eastward, moving as rapidly as possible, with an interval of twenty paces between them, and steadily regulating their route by the north star. The boy who accompanied them was brisk and active; but the old man constantly lagged behind, and as constantly shouted aloud for them to wait for him. They often remonstrated with him on the impropriety of making so much noise at a time when all their lives depended upon secrecy and celerity, and he repeatedly promised to do so no more.

At length, upon crossing Sandusky Creek, the old man found himself once more considerably in the rear, and once more shouted aloud for them to wait until he could come up. Before they could reply, a halloo was heard in the rear of their left, and apparently not more than one hundred paces from the spot where the old man stood. Supposing it to be the cry of an Indian, they remained still and silent for several minutes, looking keenly around them in the expectation of beholding an enemy. Every thing, however, continued silent. The old man was heard no more; and whether he escaped, or was killed, could never be ascertained. The party continued their flight until daybreak, when Colonel Crawford's horse, and that of the boy, sunk under their riders and were abandoned.

Continuing their journey on foot, they quickly fell in with Captain Biggs, an expert woodsman and gallant officer, who, in the universal scattering, had generously brought off a wounded officer—Lieutenant Ashley—upon his own horse, and was now composedly walking by his side, with a rifle in his hand and a knapsack upon his shoulders. This casual meeting was gratifying to both parties, and they continued their journey with renewed spirits. At three o'clock in the afternoon a heavy rain fell, and compelled them to encamp. A temporary shelter was quickly formed by barking several trees, after the manner of the Indians, and spreading the bark over poles, so as to form a roof. A fire was then kindled, and the rain continued to pour down in torrents. They remained here through the night without any accident.

Continuing their route on the following morning, at the distance of three miles from the camp, they found a deer which had recently been killed and skinned. The meat was neatly sliced and bundled up in the skin—and a tomahawk lay near—giving room for suspicion that Indians were in the neighborhood. As the whole party had fasted for thirty-six hours, this was a very acceptable treat; and, lifting the skin, with the meat inclosed, from the ground, they carried it with them until they had leisure to cook it. Having advanced a mile further, they observed a smoke in the woods before them. The party instantly halted, while Colonel Crawford and Dr. Knight advanced to reconnoiter.

Cautiously approaching the fire, they found it burning brightly, but abandoned, from which they inferred that a party had encamped there the preceding night, and had retired a few minutes before their approach. Having carefully examined the bushes around, and discovered no Indian sign, they directed their friends in the rear to come up, and quickly set about preparing breakfast. In a few minutes they observed a white man skulking in the rear, examining the trail, and apparently very shy of approaching them. Calling out to him in a friendly tone, they invited him to approach without fear, assuring him that they were countrymen and friends. The man instantly complied, and informed them that he had killed the deer which they were cooking, but hearing them approach, he had taken them for enemies, and had fled into the bushes for concealment.

Highly pleased at this further accession to their strength, the party breakfasted heartily upon the deer, and continued their march. By noon, they had reached the path by which the army had marched a few days before in their advance upon the Indian towns, and some discussion took place as to the propriety of taking that road homeward. Biggs and the doctor strenuously insisted upon continuing their course through the woods, and avoiding all paths; but Crawford overruled them, assuring them that the Indians would not urge the pursuit beyond the plains, which were already far behind. Unfortunately, the colonel prevailed; and, abandoning their due eastern course, the party pursued the beaten path. Crawford and Knight moved one hundred and fifty yards in front, Biggs and his wounded friend Ashley were in the center, both on horseback, the doctor having lent Biggs his horse, and the two men on foot brought up the rear.

They soon had reason to repent their temerity. Scarcely had they advanced a mile when several Indians sprung up within twenty yards of Knight and Crawford, presented their guns, and in good English ordered them to stop. Knight instantly sprung behind a large black-oak, cocked his gun, and began to take aim at the foremost. Crawford, however, did not attempt to conceal himself; but, calling hastily to Knight, ordered him twice not to fire. Instantly, the Indian at whom Knight had taken aim, ran up to the colonel with every demonstration of friendship, shook his hand cordially, and asked how he did. Knight still maintaining a hostile attitude behind the tree, Crawford called to him again, and ordered him to put down his gun, which the doctor very reluctantly obeyed.

Biggs and Ashley, seeing the condition of their friends, halted; while the two men in the rear very prudently took to their heels and escaped. One of the Indians then told Crawford to order Biggs to come up and surrender or they would kill him. The colonel complied; but Biggs, feeling no inclination to obey his commander in the present instance, very coolly cocked his rifle, took deliberate aim at one of the Indians, and fired, although without effect. He and Ashley then put spurs to their horses and for the time escaped. The two prisoners were then taken to the Indian camp, which stood within a few miles of the place where they were taken; and, on the next evening, five Delawares came in with the scalps and horses of Biggs and Ashley, who it appeared had returned to the road, and were intercepted a few miles further on.

On the following morning, the tenth of June, Crawford and Knight, together with nine more prisoners, were conducted by their captors, seventeen in number, to the old town of Sandusky, about thirty-three miles distant. The main body halted at night within eight miles of the village; but as Colonel Crawford expressed great anxiety to speak with Simon Girty, who was then at Sandusky, he was permitted to go on that evening, under the care of two Indians. On Tuesday morning, the eleventh of June, Colonel Crawford was brought back from Sandusky, on purpose to march into town with the other prisoners. Knight eagerly accosted him and asked if he had seen Girty.

The colonel replied in the affirmative; and added that Girty had promised to use his utmost influence for his (the colonel's) safety, but was fearful of the consequences, as the Indians generally, and particularly Captain Pipe, one of the Delaware chiefs, were much incensed against the prisoners, and were endeavoring to have them all burned. The colonel added that he had heard of his son-in-law, Colonel Harrison, and his nephew, William Crawford, both of whom had been taken by the Shawnees and admitted to mercy. Shortly after this communication, their capital enemy, Captain Pipe, appeared. His appearance was by no means unprepossessing, and he exhibited none of the ferocity which Knight, from Girty's account, had been led to expect.

On the contrary, his manners were bland and his language flattering. But one ominous circumstance attended his visit: with his own hand, he *painted every prisoner black!* While in the act of painting the doctor, he was as polite as a French valet, assuring him that he should soon go to the Shawnoe town and see his friends; and while painting the colonel, he told him that his head should be shaved, *i. e.*, he should be adopted, as soon as he arrived at the Wyandott town. As soon as the prisoners were painted, they were conducted toward the town, Captain Pipe walking by the side of Crawford, and treating him with the utmost kindness; while the other prisoners, with the exception of Dr. Knight, were pushed on ahead of him.

As they advanced, they were shocked at observing the bodies of four of their friends, who had just left them, lying near the path, tomahawked and scalped, with an interval of nearly a mile between each. They had evidently perished in running the gauntlet. This spectacle was regarded as a sad presage of their own fate. In a short time they overtook the five prisoners who remained alive. They were seated on the ground, and appeared much dejected. Nearly seventy squaws and Indian boys surrounded them, menacing them with knives and tomahawks, and exhausting upon them every abusive epithet which their language afforded. Crawford and Knight were compelled to sit down apart from the rest; and immediately afterward, the doctor was given to a Shawnee warrior, to be conducted to their town, while the colonel remained stationary.

The boys and squaws then fell upon the other prisoners and tomahawked them in a moment. Among them was Captain McKinley, who had served with reputation throughout the Revolutionary war until the capture of Cornwallis. An old withered hag approached him, brandishing a long knife, and, seizing him by the hair, instantly cut off his head and kicked it near the spot where Crawford sat in momentary expectation of a similar fate. Another destiny, however, was reserved for him. After having sufficiently exhausted their rage upon the lifeless bodies of the five prisoners, the whole party started up, and, driving Crawford before them, marched toward the village.

Presently, Girty appeared on horseback, coming from Sandusky. He stopped for a few moments and spoke to Crawford, then passing to the rear of the party, addressed Knight. "Is this the doctor?" inquired he, with an insulting smile. "Yes! Mr. Girty, I am glad to see you!" replied poor Knight, advancing toward him and anxiously extending his hand. But Girty cursed him in a savage tone, ordered him to be gone, and not to suppose that he would give his hand to such a —— rascal. Upon this, the Shawnee warrior who had him in custody, dragged him along by a rope. Girty followed on horseback, and informed him that he was to go to Chillicothe. Presently they came to a spot where there was a large fire, around which about thirty warriors, and more than double that number of boys and squaws, were collected.

As soon as the colonel arrived, they surrounded him,

stripped him naked, and compelled him to sit on the ground near the fire. They then fell upon him and beat him severely with sticks and their fists. In a few minutes a large stake was fixed in the ground, and piles of hickory poles, rather thicker than a man's thumb, and about twelve feet in length, were spread around it. Colonel Crawford's hands were then tied behind his back; a strong rope was produced, one end of which was fastened to the ligature between his wrists and the other tied to the bottom of the stake. The rope was long enough to permit him to walk around the stake several times and then return. Fire was then applied to the hickory poles, which lay in piles at the distance of six or seven yards from the stake.

The colonel, observing these terrible preparations, called to Girty, who sat on horseback, at the distance of a few yards from the fire, and asked if the Indians were going to burn him. Girty very coolly replied in the affirmative. The colonel heard the intelligence with firmness, merely observing that he would bear it with fortitude. When the hickory poles had been burnt asunder in the middle, Captain Pipe arose and addressed the crowd, in a tone of great energy, and with animated gestures, pointing frequently to the colonel, who regarded him with an appearance of unruffled composure. As soon as he had ended, a loud whoop burst from the assembled throng, and they all rushed at once upon the unfortunate Crawford. For several seconds the crowd was so great around him, that Knight could not see what they were doing; but in a short time they had dispersed sufficiently to give him a view of the colonel.

His ears had been cut off, and the blood was streaming down each side of his face. A terrible scene of torture now commenced. The warriors shot charges of powder into his naked body, commencing with the calves of his legs and continuing to his neck. The boys snatched the burning hickory poles and applied them to his flesh. As fast as he ran around the stake to avoid one party of tormentors, he was promptly met at every turn by others, with burning poles, red-hot irons, and rifles loaded with powder only; so that in a few minutes nearly one hundred charges of powder had been shot into his body, which had become black and blistered in a dreadful manner. The squaws would take up a quantity of coals and hot ashes, and throw them upon his body, so that in a few minutes he had nothing but fire to walk upon.

In the extremity of his agony, the unhappy colonel called aloud upon Girty, in tones which rang through Knight's brain with maddening effect: "Girty! Girty! shoot me through the heart! Quick! quick! Do not refuse me!" "Don't you see I have no gun, colonel?" replied the monster, bursting into a loud laugh, and then, turning to an Indian beside him, he uttered some brutal jests upon the naked and miserable appearance of the prisoner. While this awful scene was being enacted, Girty rode up to the spot where Dr. Knight stood, and told him that he now had a foretaste of what was in reserve for him at the Shawnee towns. He swore that he need not expect to escape death, but should suffer it in all the extremity of torture!

Knight, whose mind was deeply agitated at the sight of the fearful scene before him, took no notice of Girty, but preserved an impenetrable silence. Girty, after coldly contemplating the colonel's sufferings for a few moments, turned again to Knight, and indulged in a bitter invective against a certain Colonel Gibson, from whom, he said, he had received deep injury, and dwelt upon the delight with which he would see him undergo such tortures as those which Crawford was then suffering. He observed, in a taunting tone, that most of the prisoners had said that the white people would not injure him, if the chance of war was to throw him into their power; but that, for his own part, he should be loath to try the experiment. "I think," added he, with a laugh, "that they would roast me alive with more pleasure than those red fellows are now broiling the colonel! What is your opinion, doctor? Do you think they would be glad to see me?" Still Knight made no answer, and in a few minutes Girty rejoined the Indians.

The terrible scene had now lasted more than two hours, and Crawford had become much exhausted. He walked slowly around the stake, spoke in a low tone, and earnestly besought God to look with compassion upon him, and pardon his sins. His nerves had lost much of their sensibility, and he no longer shrank from the firebrands with which they incessantly touched him. At length he sank in a fainting fit upon his face, and lay motionless. Instantly an Indian sprang upon his back, knelt lightly upon one knee, made a circular incision with his knife upon the crown of his head, and, clapping the knife between his teeth, tore the scalp off with both hands. Scarcely had this been done, when a withered hag approached with a board full of burning embers, and poured them upon the crown of his head, now laid bare to the bone. The colonel groaned deeply, arose, and again walked slowly around the stake. But why continue a description so horrible? Nature at length could endure no more, and at a late hour in the night he was released by death from the hands of his tormentors.

At sunset Dr. Knight was removed from the ground, and taken to the house of Captain Pipe, where, after having been securely bound, he was permitted to sleep unmolested. On the next morning, the Indian fellow to whose care he had been committed unbound him, again painted him black, and told him he must instantly march off for the Shawnee village. The doctor was a small, weak man, and had sunk much under the hardship to which he had been exposed; and this, probably, was the cause of his having been committed, unbound, to the guardianship of a single Indian. They quickly left Sandusky, and in a few minutes passed by the spot where Crawford had been tortured. His flesh had been entirely consumed, and his bones, half burnt and blackened by the fire, lay scattered around the stake. The Indian fellow who guarded him uttered the scalp halloo as he passed the spot, and insultingly told Knight that "these were the bones of his Big Captain!" Knight was on foot, the Indian mounted on a pony and well armed; yet the doctor determined to effect his escape, or compel his enemy to shoot him dead upon the spot.

The awful torture which Crawford had undergone had

left a deep impression upon his mind. The savage intimation of Girty was not forgotten, and he regarded death by shooting as a luxury compared with the protracted agony of the stake. Anxious, however, to lull the suspicious temper of the Indian, who appeared to be extremely vigilant, he spoke to him in a cheerful, confident tone, and pretended to be entirely ignorant of the fate which awaited him at the Shawnee town. He found the fellow very sociable, and apparently as simple as he could wish. Upon his asking if they were not to live together in the same cabin like brothers, as soon as they arrived at the end of their journey, the Indian seemed pleased, and replied, "Yes." He then asked the doctor if he could make a wigwam. The doctor boldly asserted that he was a capital workman in wood, and could build a wigwam to which their most spacious council-houses were mere hovels. This assertion evidently elevated him in the Indian's esteem, and they continued to chat in a very friendly manner, each probably thinking that he had made a dupe of the other.

After traveling about twenty-five miles they encamped for the night, when Knight permitted himself to be bound. The Indian then informed him that they would reach the Shawnee village about the middle of the next day, and seemed to compose himself to rest. Knight frequently attempted to untie himself, but was as often frustrated by the incessant vigilance of the Indian, whose dark eyes were rolling around him throughout the whole night. At daylight the Indian arose and unbound his prisoner, who instantly determined to attempt an escape without further delay. His conductor did not immediately leave the spot, but began to rekindle their fire, which had burned low, and employed himself diligently in giving battle to the myriads of gnats that swarmed around him and fastened upon his naked body with high relish. Knight, seeing him rub his back with great energy, muttering petulantly in the Indian tongue, asked if he should make a smoke behind him, in order to drive the gnats away.

The Indian told him to do so, and Knight, arising from his seat, took the end of a dogwood fork, about eighteen inches in length, and, putting a coal of fire between it and another stick, went behind the Indian as if to kindle a fire. Gently laying down the coal, he paused a moment to collect his strength, and then struck the Indian a furious blow upon the back of the head with the dogwood stick. The fellow stumbled forward, and fell with his hands in the fire; but, instantly rising again, ran off with great rapidity, howling most dismally. Knight instantly seized the rifle which his enemy had abandoned, and pursued him, intending to shoot him dead on the spot, and thus prevent pursuit; but, in drawing back the cock of the gun too violently, he injured it so much that it would not go off, and the Indian, frightened out of his wits, and leaping and dodging with the activity of a wild cat, at length effected his escape.

On the same day, about noon, as Knight afterward learned from a prisoner who effected his escape, the Indian arrived at the Shawnee village, with his head dreadfully cut, and his legs torn by the briers. He proved to be a happy mixture of the braggadocio and coward, and treated his fellows with a magnificent description of his contest with Knight, whom he represented as a giant in stature (five feet seven inches!), and a buffalo in strength and fierceness. He said that Knight prevailed upon him to untie him, and that while they were conversing like brothers, and while he himself was suspecting no harm, his prisoner suddenly seized a dogwood sapling, and belabored him, now on this side of his head, now on the other (here his gestures were very lively), until he was scarcely able to stand. That, nevertheless, he made a manful resistance, and stabbed his gigantic antagonist twice, once in the back, and once in the belly; but, seeing that his knife made no impression upon the strength of the prisoner, he was at length compelled to leave him, satisfied that the wounds which he had inflicted must at length prove mortal. The Indians were much diverted at his account of the affair, and laughed loud and long, evidently not believing a syllable of the tale, at least so far as his own prowess was concerned.

In the meantime, Knight, finding it useless to pursue the Indian, to whom terror had lent wings, hastily returned to the fire, and taking the Indian's blanket, moccasins, bullet bag, and powder horn, lost no time in moving off, directing his course toward the north-east. About half an hour by sun, he came to the plains already mentioned, which were about sixteen miles wide. Not choosing to cross them by daylight, he lay down in the high grass until dark; then, guided by the north star, he crossed them rapidly, and before daylight had reached the woods on the other side. Without halting for a moment, he continued his march until late in the afternoon, crossing nearly at right angles the path by which the troops had advanced, and moving steadily to the northward, with the hope of avoiding the enemy, who might still be lingering upon the rear of the troops.

In the evening he felt very faint and hungry, having tasted nothing for three days, and very little since his captivity. Wild gooseberries grew very abundantly in the woods, but, being still green, they required mastication, which he was unable to perform, his jaws having been much injured by a blow from the back of a tomahawk. There was a weed, however, which grew in the woods, the juice of which was grateful to the palate and nourishing to the body. Of this he sucked plentifully, and finding himself much refreshed, was enabled to continue his journey Supposing that he had now advanced sufficiently to the northward to baffle his pursuers, he changed his course and steered due east.

Wishing, if possible, to procure some animal food, he often attempted to rectify the lock of his gun, supposing that it was only wood-bound; but, having no knife, he was unable to unscrew it, and was at length reluctantly compelled to throw it away as a useless burden. His jaw rapidly recovered, and he was enabled to chew green gooseberries, upon which, together with two young unfledged blackbirds, and one land terrapin (both devoured raw), he managed to subsist for twenty-one days. He swam the Muskingum a few miles below Fort Lawrence, and, crossing all paths, directed his steps to the Ohio River. He struck it at a few miles below Fort

McIntosh on the evening of the twenty-first day, and on the morning of the twenty-second reached the fort in safety.

Such was the lamentable expedition of Colonel Crawford, rashly undertaken, injudiciously prosecuted, and terminating with almost unprecedented calamity. The insubordinate spirit of the men, together with the inadequacy of the force, were the great causes of the failure. The first was incident to the nature of the force, but the second might have been remedied by a little consideration. Repeated disasters, however, were necessary to convince the Americans of the necessity of employing a sufficient force, and it was not until they had suffered by the experience of ten more years that this was at length done. The defeat of Braddock had been bloody, but not disgraceful. Officers and soldiers died in battle, and with arms in their hands. Not a man offered to leave the ground until a retreat was ordered. Crawford, on the contrary, perished miserably at the stake, as did most of his men. They were taken in detail, skulking through the woods to avoid an enemy whom they might have vanquished by union, steadiness, and courage. It stands upon record as one of the most calamitous and disgraceful expeditions which has ever stained the American arms.

CHAPTER VI.

DURING the old French war, JOHN SLOVER, a native of Virginia, was taken by a party of Miami Indians, on the banks of White River, and immediately conducted to the Indian town of Sandusky. Here he resided from his eighth to his twentieth year. At the treaty of Pittsburgh, in the fall of 1773, he came in with the Shawnee nation, and accidentally meeting with some of his relations, he was recognized and earnestly exhorted to relinquish his connection with the Indians, and return to his friends. He yielded with some reluctance, having become strongly attached to a savage life; and having probably but little relish for labor on a farm, after the easy life which he had led in Ohio, he enlisted in the continental army, and served two campaigns with credit, as a sharp-shooter. Having been properly discharged, he settled in Westmoreland County, and when the unfortunate expedition of Crawford was set on foot, was strongly urged to attend in the capacity of a guide.

Conquering the distaste which he naturally felt at the idea of conducting a hostile army against his former friends, he yielded to the persuasion of his neighbors, and shared in all the dangers of the army. At the moment when the rout took place, Slover was in the immediate neighborhood of the enemy, attending to a number of horses that were grazing on the plain. But the uproar in front, occasioned by the tumultuous flight of more than four hundred men, soon warned him of his danger. He hastily mounted the best horse within reach, and put him to his utmost speed. He soon overtook the main body, and was among the foremost when the Indians attempted to intercept them. A deep bog crossed the line of retreat, and occasioned immense confusion.

Those who first reached it, plunged in without hesitation, but after struggling for a few minutes, their horses stuck fast, and were necessarily abandoned. The darkness of the night, and the hurry of the retreat, prevented the rear from profiting by the misfortune of the van. Horseman after horseman plunged madly into the swamp, and in a few minutes a scene which baffles all attempt at description took place. Not one-tenth part of the horses were able to struggle through. Their riders dismounted and endeavored, on foot, to reach the opposite side. The Indians pressed upon them, pouring an incessant fire upon the mass of fugitives, some of whom were completely mired, and sunk gradually to the chin, in which condition they remained until the following morning; others, with great difficulty, effected a passage, and continued their flight on foot.

Slover, having struggled for several minutes to disengage his horse, was at length compelled to abandon him, and wade through the morass as he best could, on foot. After incredible fatigue and danger, he at length reached the firm ground, covered with mud, and frightened not a little at hearing the yells of the enemy immediately behind him and upon each flank, many of them having crossed a few hundred yards above, where the mud was not so deep. In a few minutes he overtook a party of six men on foot, having been compelled like himself to abandon their horses, and two of them having even lost their guns. Finding themselves hard pressed by the enemy, who urged the pursuit with great keenness, they changed their course from an eastern to a western direction, almost turning upon their own trail, and bending their steps toward Detroit. In a short time they struck the same swamp, although considerably higher up, and were compelled to wait until daylight in order to find their way across. Having succeeded at length in reaching the opposite side, they traveled, throughout the day, directly toward the Shawnee towns. This, as the event proved, was finessing rather too much. They would certainly avoid

John Slover hiding, in the grass, from Indians. [See page 147.]

their pursuers, but they were plunging into the midst of the Indian settlements, and must expect to meet with roving bands of Indians in every direction.

At ten o'clock they halted for breakfast, having eaten nothing for two days. While busily engaged with their ration of cold pork and corn bread, they were alarmed by hearing a halloo immediately behind them, which was instantly answered by two others upon each flank. Hastily dropping their wallets, they fled into the grass, and falling upon their faces, awaited with beating hearts the approach of the enemy. Presently, seven or eight Indians appeared, talking and laughing in high spirits, evidently ignorant of the presence of the fugitives. In a few minutes they had passed, and the party cautiously returned to their wallets. The fright, however, had completely spoiled their appetites, and hastily gathering up the remnant of their provisions, they continued their journey, changing their course a little to the north, in order to avoid the party who had just passed.

By twelve o'clock they reached a large prairie, which it was necessary for them to cross, or return upon their own footsteps. In the prairie they would be much exposed, as an enemy could see them at a vast distance, but to return to the spot from which they had started was so melancholy an alternative that, after a short and anxious consultation, it was determined at all risks to proceed. They accordingly entered the vast plain, which stretched for many miles before them, affording no means of concealment but the grass, and advanced rapidly but cautiously, until about one o'clock, when the man in front called their attention to a number of moving objects ahead, which seemed to approach them. The grass was high, and the objects indistinct.

They might be Indians, or elk, or buffalo; but whoever or whatever they were, it would be as well perhaps not to await their coming. They accordingly crawled aside, and again lay down in the grass, occasionally lifting their heads in order to reconnoiter the strangers. As they drew near, they perceived them to be a party of Indians, but from the loose and straggling manner in which they walked, and the loudness of their voices, they were satisfied that they had not been detected. The Indians quickly passed them and disappeared in the grass. The party then arose and continued their journey, looking keenly around them, in hourly expectation of another party of the enemy.

In the evening a heavy rain fell, the coldest that they had ever felt, and from which it was impossible to find a shelter. Drenched to the skin and shivering with cold, they waded on through the grass until near sunset, when to their great joy they saw a deep forest immediately in front, where they could obtain shelter as well from the storm as the enemy. The rain, however, which had poured in torrents while they were exposed to it, ceased at once as soon as they had reached a shelter. Considering this a good omen, they encamped for the night, and on the following morning, recommenced their journey with renewed spirits. They were much delayed, however, by the infirmity of two of their men, one of whom had burnt his foot severely, and the other's knees were swollen with the rheumatism.

The rheumatic traveler, at length, fell considerably behind. The party halted, hallooed for him, and whistled loudly upon their chargers, but in vain. They saw him no more on their march, although he afterward reached Wheeling in safety, while his stronger companions, as we shall quickly see, were not so fortunate. They had now again shifted their course, and were marching in a straight direction toward Pittsburgh. They had passed over the most dangerous part of the road, and had, thus far, got the first view of every enemy who appeared.

On the morning of the third day, however, a party of Indians, who had secretly dogged them from the prairie (through which their trail had been broad and obvious), had now outstripped them, and lay in ambush on their road. The first intimation which Slover had of their existence, was a close discharge of rifles, which killed two of their party. The four survivers instantly ran to the trees, but two of their guns had been left in the swamp, so that two only remained fit for service. Slover, whose gun was in good order, took aim at the foremost Indian, who, raising his hand warningly, told him not to fire and he should be treated kindly. Slover and his two unarmed companions instantly surrendered, but John Paul, a youth, refused to be included in the capitulation, and being equally bold and active, completely baffled his pursuers and came safely into Wheeling.

One of the Indians instantly recognized Slover, having been present at his capture many years before, and having afterward lived with him at Sandusky. He called him by his Indian name (Mannuchcothe), and reproached him indignantly for bearing arms against his brothers. Slover was somewhat confused at the charge, fearing that his recognition would be fatal to him when he should reach the Indian towns. They were taken back to the prairie, where the Indians had left their horses, and each mounting a horse, they moved rapidly toward the nearest town, which proved to be Waughcotomoco, the theater of Kenton's adventure, four years before. Upon approaching the town, the Indians, who had heretofore been very kind to them, suddenly began to look sour, and put themselves into a passion by dwelling upon their injuries. Presently, as usual, the squaws, boys, etc., came out, and the usual scene commenced. They soon became tired of abusing and switching them, and, having selected the oldest of the three, they blacked his face with coal and water. The poor fellow was much agitated, and cried bitterly, frequently asking Slover if they were not going to burn him. The Indians, in their own language, hastily forbid Slover to answer him, and coming up to their intended victim, patted him upon the back, and with many honeyed epithets assured him that they would not hurt him. They then marched on to the large town, about two miles beyond the small one (both bearing the same name), having, as usual, sent a runner in advance to inform the inhabitants of their approach.

The whole village presently flocked out, and a row was formed for the gauntlet. The man who had been blacked attracted so much attention, that Slover and his companion scarcely received a blow. The former preceded them by twenty yards, and was furiously attacked by every individual. Loads of powder were shot into his body, deep wounds were inflicted with knives and tomahawks, and sand was thrown into his eyes, and he was several times knocked down by cudgels. Having heard that he would be safe on reaching the council-house, he forced his way with gigantic strength through all opposition, and grasped the post with both hands, his body burnt with powder and covered with blood.

He was furiously torn from his place of refuge, however, and thrust back among his enemies. When finding that they would give him no quarter, he returned their blows with a fury equal to their own, crying piteously the whole time, and frequently endeavoring to wrest a tomahawk from his enemies. This singular scene continued for nearly half an hour, when the prisoner was at length beaten to death. Slover and his companion reached the post in safety, and were silent spectators of the fate of their friend. As soon as he was dead, the Indians cut up his body, and stuck the head and quarters upon poles in the center of the town.

On the same evening he beheld the dead bodies of young Crawford and Colonel Harrison, and a third, whom he supposed to be Colonel McClelland, the second in command. Their bodies were black and mangled, like that of their unfortunate companion, having been beaten to death a few hours before their arrival. As he passed by the bodies, the Indians smiled maliciously, and asked if he knew them. He mentioned their names, upon which they nodded with much satisfaction. In the evening, all the dead bodies were dragged beyond the limits of the town, and abandoned to the dogs and wolves. In twenty four hours, their bones only were to be seen.

On the following morning, Slover's only surviving companion was marched off to a neighboring town, and never heard of afterward. Slover, himself, was summoned in the evening to attend at the council-house, and give an account of his conduct. Heretofore he had generally been treated with kindness, and on the first day of the council he saw no symptoms of a disposition to put him to death. But on the second day James Girty arrived, from Crawford's execution, and instantly threw the whole weight of his influence into the scale against the prisoner. He dwelt, with much emphasis, upon the ingratitude of Slover in serving as a spy against those who had formerly treated him with such distinguished kindness, and scrupled not to affirm that in a confidential conversation, which he had had with the prisoner on that morning, he had asked him "how he would like to live again with his old friends?"— upon which Slover had laughed and replied, that "he would stay until he had an opportunity of taking a scalp, and would then steal a horse and return to the whites."

Slover knew many of his judges by name, spoke their language fluently, and made a vigorous defense. He said that, during the whole twelve years of his former captivity among them, he had given ample proofs of his fidelity to the Indians. That, although he had a thousand opportunities, he had never once attempted an escape; and there were several now present who could testify that at the treaty of Fort Pitt he had left them with reluctance, in compliance with the earnest solicitations of his family. That he had then taken leave of them publicly, in broad daylight, in time of profound peace, and with their full approbation. That he then had no idea of the existence of a future war; but when war came, it was his duty to accompany his countrymen to the field against the Indians, precisely as he would have accompanied the Indians formerly against the whites. That it was the undoubted duty of every warrior to serve his country, without regard to his own private feelings of attachment; that he had done so; and if the Indians thought it worthy of death, they could inflict the penalty upon him!—he was alone, and in their power. That Mr. Girty's assertion was positively false: he had not exchanged a syllable with him, beyond a brief and cold salutation, when they had met in the morning, not to mention the absurdity of supposing that, if he had really entertained such an idea, he would have communicated it to Girty!—the sworn enemy of the whites, and, as he believed, his own personal enemy.

This vigorous and natural defense seemed to make some impression upon his enemies. Girty's assertion was so strikingly improbable that very few gave it credit, and some of Slover's old friends exerted themselves actively in his behalf. The council suspended their decision for several days, and, in the meantime, endeavored to gain information from him as to the present condition of Virginia. Slover informed them that Cornwallis had been captured, together with his whole army, which astonished them much, and compelled them to utter some deep guttural interjections. But Girty and McKey became very angry, swore that it was a lie, and renewed their exertions, with increased ardor, to have him brought to the stake. While his trial was pending, he was unbound and unguarded, was invited to all their dances, and suffered to reside, as an inmate, in the cabin of an old squaw, who treated him with great affection.

Girty was blustering, ferocious, and vulgar in his manners; but McKey was silent, grave and stern, never addressing Slover, and seldom speaking in council. He lived apart from the rest in a handsome house, built of white-oak logs, elegantly hewed, and neatly covered with shingles. His hatred to the whites was deep and inveterate, and his influence was constantly exerted against every prisoner who came before him. They spared no pains in endeavoring to entrap Slover into some unguarded words, which might injure him with the Indians. A white man one morning asked Slover to walk out with him, as he had something of importance to communicate.

As soon as they had gained the fields, the fellow halted, and, in a confidential tone, informed Slover that he had two brothers living upon the banks of the Potomac, whom he was desirous of seeing again; that the Indians had given him his life for the present, but they were such capricious devils that there was no confidence to be placed in them, and he felt disposed to escape while it was in his power, if Slover would accompany him. Slover heard him coldly, and, with an appearance of great surprise, blamed him for entertaining so rash a project, and assured him that *he* was determined to encounter no such risk. The emissary of Girty and McKey returned instantly to the council, and reported that Slover had eagerly entered into the project, and was desirous of escaping that evening.

Two days afterward, a very large council was held, being composed of warriors from the Shawnee, Delaware, Wyandott, Chippewa, and Mingo tribes. Two Indians came to the wigwam, in order to conduct Slover once more before his judges, but the old squaw concealed him beneath a large bear-skin, and fell upon the two messengers so fiercely with her tongue that they were compelled to retreat with some precipitation. This zeal in his service, on the part of the old squaw, was rather alarming than gratifying to Slover, for he rightly conjectured that something evil was brewing, which he knew that she would be unable to avert. He was not long in suspense. Within two hours, Girty came into the hut, followed by more than forty warriors, and seizing Slover, stripped him naked, bound his hands behind him, painted his body black, and bore him off with great violence. Girty exulted greatly in the success of his efforts, and loaded him with curses and reproaches, assuring him that he would now get what he had long deserved.

The prisoner was borne off to a town at the distance of five miles from Waughcotomoco, where he was met, as usual, by all the inhabitants, and beaten, in the ordinary manner, for one hour. They then carried him to another little village, about two miles distant, where a stake and hickory poles had been prepared, in order to burn him that evening. The scene of his intended execution was the council-house, a part of which was covered with shingles, and the remainder entirely open at the top, and very slightly boarded at the sides. In the open space, a pole had been sunk in the ground, and the faggots collected. Slover was dragged to the stake, his hands bound behind him, and then fastened to the pole, as in Crawford's case.

Fire was quickly applied to the faggots, which began to blaze briskly. An orator then, as usual, addressed the assembly, in order to inflame their passions to the proper height. Slover, seeing his fate inevitable, rallied his courage, and prepared to endure it with firmness. For the last half hour the wind had been high, but the clouds were light, and appeared drifting rapidly away. While the orator was speaking, however, the wind suddenly lulled, and a heavy shower of rain fell, which instantly extinguished the fire, and drenched the prisoner and his enemies to the skin. Poor Slover, who had been making preparations to battle with fire, was astonished at finding himself deluged, all at once, with so different an element, and the enemy seemed no less so. They instantly ran under the covered part of the house, and left the prisoner to take the rain freely, assuring him, from time to time, that he should be burned on the following morning.

As soon as the rain ceased, they again surrounded him, dancing around the stake, kicking him severely, and striking him with sticks, until eleven o'clock at night. A tall young chief, named "Half Moon," then stooped down and asked the prisoner if "he was not sleepy?" Slover, somewhat astonished at such a question, and at such a time, replied in the affirmative. Half Moon then untied him, conducted him into a strong block-house, pinioned his arms until the buffalo tug was buried in the flesh, and then, passing another thong around his neck, and tying the other end to one of the beams of the house, left him under a strong guard, exhorting him to sleep soundly, for that he must "eat fire in the morning."

The prisoner, on the contrary, never closed his eyes, awaiting anxiously until his guard should fall asleep. They showed, however, no inclination to indulge him. Two of them lay down a little after midnight, but the third sat up talking and smoking until nearly daylight. He endeavored to entertain Slover, by speculations upon his (Slover's) ability to bear pain, handling the painful subject with the zest of an amateur, and recounting to the prisoner the particulars of many ex-

hibitions of the same kind which he had witnessed.
He dwelt upon the entertainment which he had no
doubt Slover would afford, exhorting him to bear it
like a man, and not forget that he had once been an
Indian himself. Upon this torturing subject he
talked, and smoked, and talked again, until the prisoner's nerves tingled, as if the hot irons were actually
hissing against his flesh.

At length the tedious old man's head sunk gradually
upon his breast, and Slover heard him snoring loudly.
He paused a few moments, listening intently. His
heart beat so strongly, that he was fearful lest the
Indians should hear it, and arrest him in his last
effort to escape. They did not stir, however, and with
trembling hands he endeavored to slip the cords from
his arms over his wrists. In this he succeeded without
much difficulty, but the thong around his neck was
more obstinate. He attempted to gnaw it in two, but
it was as thick as his thumb, and as hard as iron,
being made of a seasoned buffalo's hide. Daylight
was faintly breaking in the east, and he expected every
moment that his tormentors would summon him to the
stake. In the agony and earnestness of his feelings,
the sweat rolled in big drops down his forehead, and
the quickness of his breathing awakened the old man.

Slover lay still, fearful of being detected, and kept
his arms under his back. The old Indian yawned,
stretched himself, stirred the fire, and then lay down
again, and began to snore as loudly as ever. Now
was the time or never! He seized the rope with both
hands, and giving it several quick jerks, could scarcely
believe his senses when he saw the knot come untied,
and felt himself at liberty. He arose lightly, stepped
silently over the bodies of the sleeping Indians, and
in a moment stood in the open air. Day was just
breaking, and the inhabitants of the village had not
yet arisen. He looked around for a moment to see
whether he was observed, and then ran hastily into a
cornfield in order to conceal himself. On the road he
had nearly stumbled upon a squaw and several children, who were asleep under a tree.

Hastily avoiding them, he ran through the cornfield, and observing a number of horses on the other side, he paused a moment, untied the cord which still confined his right arm, and hastily fitting it into a halter, approached a fine strong colt, about four years old, that fortunately proved as gentle as he could wish. Fancying that he heard a door open behind him, he sprung upon his back as lightly as a squirrel, although every limb was bruised and swollen by the severe beating of the preceding night, and as the woods were open and the ground level, he put his horse to his utmost speed, and was soon out of sight. Confident that pursuit would not be delayed more than fifteen minutes, he never slackened his speed until about ten o'clock in the day, when he reached the Scioto, at a point fully fifty miles distant from the village which he had left at daylight.

He here paused a moment, and allowed the noble animal, who had borne him so gallantly, to breathe for a few minutes. Fearing, however, that the enemy had pursued him with the same mad violence, he quickly mounted his horse again, and plunged into the Scioto, which was now swollen by the recent rains. His horse stemmed the current handsomely, but began to fail in ascending the opposite bank. He still, however, urged him to full speed, and by three o'clock had left the Scioto more than twenty miles behind, when his horse sunk under him, having galloped upwards of seventy miles. Slover instantly sprang from his back, and ran on foot until sunset. Halting for a moment, he heard a halloo far behind him, and seeing the keenness of the pursuit, he continued to run until ten o'clock at night, when he sunk upon the ground, and vomited violently. In two hours the moon arose, which he knew would enable the enemy to follow his trail through the night; and again starting up, he ran forward until day.

During the night, he had followed a path; but in the morning, he abandoned it, and, changing his course, followed a high ridge, covered with rank grass and weeds, which he carefully put back with a stick as he passed through it, in order to leave as indistinct a trail as possible. On that evening he reached some of the tributaries of the Muskingum, where his naked and blistered skin attracted millions of mosquitoes, that followed him day and night, effectually prevented his sleeping, and carefully removed such particles of skin as the nettles had left, so that, if his own account is to be credited, upon reaching the Muskingum, which he did on the third day, he had been completely peeled from head to foot. Here he found a few wild raspberries, which was the first food he had tasted for four days. He had never felt hunger, but suffered much from faintness and exhaustion. He swam the Muskingum at Old Comer's town, and, looking back, thought that he put a great deal of ground between himself and the stake at which he had been bound near Waughcotomoco; and that it would be very strange if, having been brought thus far, he should again fall into the power of the enemy.

On the next day, he reached Stillwater, where he caught two crawfish, and devoured them raw. Two days afterward, he struck the Ohio River immediately opposite Wheeling, and perceiving a man standing upon the island, he called to him, told him his name, and asked him to bring over a canoe for him. The fellow at first was very shy; but Slover having told the names of many officers and privates, who had accompanied the expedition, he was at length persuaded to venture across, and the fugitive was safely transported to the Virginia shore, after an escape which has few parallels in real life, and which seems even to exceed the bounds of probable fiction.

CHAPTER VII.

IN the present chapter, we shall notice several circumstances in the order in which they occurred, none of which, singly, are of sufficient importance to occupy a chapter to themselves. In the autumn of 1779, a number of keel-boats were ascending the Ohio under the command of Major Rodgers, and had advanced as far as the mouth of Licking without accident. Here, however, they observed a few Indians, standing upon the southern extremity of a sand bar, while a canoe, rowed by three others, was in the act of putting off from the Kentucky shore, as if for the purpose of taking them aboard. Rodgers instantly ordered the boats to be made fast on the Kentucky shore, while the crew, to the number of seventy men, well armed, cautiously advanced in such a manner as to encircle the spot where the enemy had been seen to land. Only five or six Indians had been seen, and no one dreamed of encountering more than fifteen or twenty enemies.

When Rodgers, however, had, as he supposed, completely surrounded the enemy, and was preparing to rush upon them from several quarters at once, he was thunderstruck at beholding several hundred savages suddenly spring up in front, rear, and upon both flanks! They instantly poured in a close discharge of rifles, and then, throwing down their guns, fell upon the survivors with the tomahawk. The panic was complete and the slaughter prodigious. Major Rodgers, together with forty-five of his men, were almost instantly destroyed. The survivors made an effort to regain their boats, but the five men who had been left in charge of them had immediately put off from shore in the hindmost boat, and the enemy had already gained possession of the others. Disappointed in the attempt, they turned furiously upon the enemy, and, aided by the approach of darkness, forced their way through their lines, and with the loss of several severely wounded, at length effected their escape to Harrodsburg.

Among the wounded was Captain ROBERT BENHAM. Shortly after breaking through the enemy's line, he was shot through both hips, and, the bones being shattered, he instantly fell to the ground. Fortunately, a large tree had lately fallen near the spot where he lay, and with great pain, he dragged himself into the top, and lay concealed among the branches. The Indians, eager in pursuit of the others, passed him without notice, and by midnight all was quiet. On the following day, the Indians returned to the battle-ground, in order to strip the dead and take care of the boats. Benham, although in danger of famishing, permitted them to pass without making known his condition, very correctly supposing that his crippled legs would only induce them to tomahawk him upon the spot, in order to avoid the trouble of carrying him to their town.

He lay close, therefore, until the evening of the second day, when, perceiving a raccoon descending a tree near him, he shot it, hoping to devise some means of reaching it, when he could kindle a fire and make a meal. Scarcely had his gun cracked, however, when he heard a human cry, apparently not more than fifty yards off. Supposing it to be an Indian, he hastily reloaded his gun, and remained silent, expecting the approach of an enemy. Presently the same voice was heard again, but much nearer. Still Benham made no reply, but cocked his gun, and sat ready to fire as soon as an object appeared. A third halloo was quickly heard, followed by an exclamation of impatience and distress, which convinced Benham that the unknown must be a Kentuckian. As soon, therefore, as he heard the expression, "Whoever you are, for God's sake, answer me!" he replied with readiness, and the parties were soon together.

Benham, as we have already observed, was shot through both legs. The man who now appeared had escaped from the same battle, *with both arms broken!* Thus each was enabled to supply what the other wanted. Benham, having the perfect use of his arms, could load his gun and kill game with great readiness, while his friend, having the use of his legs, could kick the game to the spot where Benham sat, who was thus enabled to cook it. When no wood was near them, his companion would rake up brush with his feet, and gradually roll it within reach of Benham's hands, who constantly fed his companion, and dressed *his* wounds as well as his own—tearing up both of their shirts for that purpose. They found some difficulty in procuring water at first; but Benham, at length, took his own hat, and placing the rim between the teeth of his companion, directed him to wade into the Licking up to his neck, and dip the hat into the water by sinking his own head. The man who could walk was thus enabled to bring water, by means of his teeth, which Benham could afterward dispose of as was necessary.

In a few days, they had killed all the squirrels and birds within reach, and the man with the broken arms was sent out to drive game within gunshot of the spot to which Benham was confined. Fortunately, wild turkeys were abundant in those woods, and his companion would walk around and drive them toward Benham, who seldom failed to kill two or three of each flock. In this manner they supported themselves for several weeks, until their wounds had healed so as to enable them to travel. They then shifted their quarters, and put up a small shed at the mouth of the Licking, where they encamped until late in November, anxiously expecting the arrival of some boat which should convey them to the Falls of Ohio.

On the twenty-seventh of November, they observed a flat-boat moving leisurely down the river. Benham instantly hoisted his hat upon a stick and hallooed loudly for help. The crew, however, supposing them to be Indians—at least suspecting them of an attempt to decoy them ashore—paid no attention to their signals of distress, but instantly put over to the opposite side of the river, and, manning every oar, endeavored to pass them as rapidly as possible. Benham beheld them pass him with a sensation bordering on despair; for the place was much frequented by Indians, and the approach of winter threatened them with destruction unless speedily relieved. At length, after the boat had passed him nearly half a mile, he saw a canoe put off from its stern, and cautiously approach the Kentucky shore, evidently reconnoitering them with great suspicion.

He called loudly upon them for assistance, mentioned his name, and made known his condition. After a long parley, and many evidences of reluctance on the part of the crew, the canoe at length touched the shore, and Benham and his friend were taken on board. Their appearance excited much suspicion. They were almost entirely naked, and their faces were garnished with six weeks' growth of beard. The one was barely able to hobble upon crutches, and the other could manage to feed himself with one of his hands. They were instantly taken to Louisville, where their clothes (which had been carried off in the boat which deserted them) were restored to them, and after a few weeks confinement, both were perfectly restored.

Benham afterward served in the North-west throughout the whole of the Indian war, accompanied the expeditions of Harmer and Wilkinson, shared in the disaster of St. Clair, and afterward in the triumph of Wayne. Upon the return of peace, he bought the land upon which Rodgers had been defeated, and ended his days in tranquillity, amid the scenes which had witnessed his sufferings.

Early in the spring of 1780, Mr. ALEXANDER MCCONNEL, of Lexington, Ky., went into the woods on foot, to hunt deer. He soon killed a large buck, and returned home for a horse, in order to bring it in. During his absence, a party of five Indians, on one of their usual skulking expeditions, accidentally stumbled on the body of the deer, and perceiving that it had been recently killed, they naturally supposed that the hunter would speedily return to secure the flesh.

Three of them, therefore, took their stations within close rifle shot of the deer, while the other two followed the trail of the hunter, and waylaid the path by which he was expected to return. McConnel, expecting no danger, rode carelessly along the path which the two scouts were watching, until he had come within view of the deer, when he was fired upon by the whole party, and his horse killed. While laboring to extricate himself from the dying animal, he was seized by his enemies, instantly overpowered, and borne off as a prisoner.

His captors, however, seemed to be a merry, good-natured set of fellows, and permitted him to accompany them unbound; and, what was rather extraordinary, allowed him to retain his gun and hunting accouterments. He accompanied them with great apparant cheerfulness through the day, and displayed his dexterity in shooting deer for the use of the company, until they began to regard him with great partiality. Having traveled with them in this manner for several days, they at length reached the banks of the Ohio River. Heretofore, the Indians had taken the precaution to bind him at night, although not very securely; but on that evening, he remonstrated with them on the subject, and complained so strongly of the pain which the cords gave him, that they merely wrapped the buffalo tug loosely around his wrists, and having tied it in an easy knot, and attached the extremities of the rope to their own bodies, in order to prevent his moving without awakening them, they very composedly went to sleep, leaving the prisoner to follow their example or not, as he pleased.

McConnel determined to effect his escape that night, if possible, as on the following night they would cross the river, which would render it much more difficult. He, therefore, lay quietly until near midnight, anxiously ruminating upon the best means of effecting his object. Accidentally casting his eyes in the direction of his feet, they fell upon the glittering blade of a knife, which had escaped its sheath, and was now lying near the feet of one of the Indians. To reach it with his hands, without disturbing the two Indians, to whom he was fastened, was impossible, and it was very hazardous to attempt to draw it up with his feet. This, however, he attempted. With much difficulty he grasped the blade between his toes, and after repeated and long-continued efforts, succeeded at length in bringing it within reach of his hands.

To cut his cords, was then but the work of a moment, and gradually and silently extricating his person from the arms of the Indians, he walked to the fire and sat down. He saw that his work was but half done; that if he should attempt to return home, without destroying his enemies, he would assuredly be pursued and probably overtaken, when his fate would be certain. On the other hand, it seemed almost impossible for a single man to succeed in a conflict with five Indians, even although unarmed and asleep. He could not hope to deal a blow with his knife so silently and fatally, as to destroy each one of his enemies in turn, without awakening the rest. Their slumbers were proverbially light and restless; and if he failed with a single one, he must instantly be overpowered by the survivors. The knife, therefore, was out of the question.

After anxious reflection for a few minutes, he formed his plan. The guns of the Indians were stacked near the fire; their knives and tomahawks were in sheaths by their sides. The latter he dared not touch for fear of awakening their owners; but the former he carefully removed, with the exception of two, and hid them in the woods, where he knew the Indians would not readily find them. He then returned to the spot where the Indians were still sleeping, perfectly ignorant of the fate preparing for them, and taking a gun in each hand, he rested the muzzles upon a log within six feet of his victims, and having taken deliberate aim at the head of one and the heart of another, he pulled both triggers at the same moment.

Both shots were fatal. At the report of their guns the others sprung to their feet, and stared wildly around them. McConnel, who had run instantly to the spot where the other rifles were hid, hastily seized one of them and fired at two of his enemies, who happened to stand in a line with each other. The nearest fell dead, being shot through the center of the body; the second fell also, bellowing loudly, but quickly recovering, limped off into the woods as fast as possible. The fifth, and only one who remained unhurt, darted off like a deer, with a yell which announced equal terror and astonishment. McConnel, not wishing to fight any more such battles, selected his own rifle from the stack, and made the best of his way to Lexington, where he arrived safely within two days.

Shortly afterward, Mrs. Dunlap, of Fayette, who had been several months a prisoner amongst the Indians on Mad River, made her escape, and returned to Lexington. She reported that the survivor returned to his tribe with a lamentable tale. He related that they had taken a fine young hunter near Lexington, and had brought him safely as far as the Ohio; that while encamped upon the bank of the river, a large party of white men had fallen upon them in the night, and killed all his companions, together with the poor, defenseless prisoner, who lay bound hand and foot, unable either to escape or resist!

Early in May, 1781, McAfee's Station, in the neighborhood of Harrodsburgh, was alarmed. On the morning of the ninth, SAMUEL MCAFEE, accompanied by another man, left the fort in order to visit a small plantation in the neighborhood, and at the distance of three hundred yards from the gate, they were fired upon by a party of Indians in ambush. The man who accompanied him instantly fell, and McAfee attempted to regain the fort. While running rapidly for that purpose, he found himself suddenly intercepted by an Indian, who, springing out of the canebrake, planted himself directly in his path. There was no time for compliments. Each glared upon the other for an instant in silence, and both raising their guns at the same moment, pulled the triggers together. The Indian's rifle snapped, while McAfee's ball passed directly through his brain. Having no time to reload his gun, he sprang over the body of his antagonist, and continued his flight to the fort.

When within one hundred yards of the gate, he was met by his two brothers, ROBERT and JAMES, who, at the report of the guns, had hurried out to the assistance of their brother. Samuel hastily informed them of their danger, and exhorted them instantly to return. James readily complied, but Robert, deaf to all remonstrances, declared that he must have a view of the dead Indian. He ran on, for that purpose, and having regaled himself with that spectacle, was hastily returning by the same path, when he saw five or six Indians between him and the fort, evidently bent upon taking him alive. All his activity and presence of mind was now put in requisition. He ran rapidly from tree to tree, endeavoring to turn their flank, and reach one of the gates, and after a variety of turns and doublings in the thick wood, he found himself pressed by only one Indian. McAfee, hastily throwing himself behind a fence, turned upon his pursuer, and compelled him to take shelter behind a tree.

Both stood still for a moment, McAfee having his gun cocked, and the sight fixed upon the tree, at the spot where he supposed the Indian would thrust out his head in order to have a view of his antagonist. After waiting a few seconds he was gratified. The Indian slowly and cautiously exposed a part of his head, and began to elevate his rifle. As soon as a sufficient mark presented itself McAfee fired, and the Indian fell. While turning, in order to continue his flight, he was fired on by a party of six, which compelled him again to tree. But scarcely had he done so, when, from the opposite quarter he received the fire of three more enemies, which made the bark fly around him, and knocked up the dust about his feet. Thinking his post rather too hot for safety, he neglected all shelter, and ran directly for the fort, which, in defiance of all opposition, he reached in safety, to the inexpressible joy of his brothers, who had despaired of his return.

The Indians now opened a heavy fire upon the fort, in their usual manner; but finding every effort useless, they hastily decamped, without any loss beyond the two who had fallen by the hands of the brothers, and without having inflicted any upon the garrison. Within half an hour, Major McGary brought up a party from Harrodsburg at full gallop, and uniting with the garrison, pursued the enemy with all possible activity. They soon overtook them, and a sharp action ensued. The Indians were routed in a few minutes, with the loss of six warriors left dead upon the ground, and many others wounded, who, as usual, were borne off. The pursuit was continued for several miles, but from the thickness of the woods, and the extreme activity and address of the enemy, was not very effectual. McGary lost one man dead upon the spot, and another mortally wounded.

About the same time, Bryant's Station was much harassed by small parties of the enemy. This, as we have already remarked, was a frontier post, and generally received the brunt of Indian hostility. It had been settled in 1779 by four brothers from North Carolina, one of whom, William, had married a sister of Colonel Daniel Boone. The Indians were constantly lurking in the neighborhood, waylaying the paths, stealing their horses, and butchering their cattle. It at length became necessary to hunt in parties of twenty or thirty men, so as to be able to meet and repel those attacks, which were every day becoming more bold and frequent.

One afternoon, about the twentieth of May, WILLIAM BRYANT, accompanied by twenty men, left the fort on a hunting expedition down the Elkhorn Creek. They moved with caution, until they had passed all the points where ambuscades had generally been formed, when, seeing no enemy, they became more bold, and determined, in order to sweep a large extent of country, to divide their company into two parties. One of them, conducted by Bryant in person, was to descend the Elkhorn on its southern bank, flanking out largely, and occupy as much ground as possible. The other, under the orders of JAMES HOGAN, a young farmer in good circumstances, was to move down in a parallel line upon the north bank. The two parties were to meet at night, and encamp together at the mouth of Cane Run.

Each punctually performed the first part of their plans. Hogan, however, had traveled but a few hundred yards, when he heard a loud voice behind him exclaim, in very good English, "Stop, boys!" Hastily looking back, they saw several Indians, on foot, pursuing them as rapidly as possible. Without halting to count numbers, the party put spurs to their horses, and dashed through the woods at full speed, the Indians keeping close behind them, and at times gaining upon them. There was a led horse in company, which had been brought with them for the purpose of packing game. This was instantly abandoned, and fell into the hands of the Indians. Several of them lost their hats in the eagerness of flight; but quickly getting into the open woods, they left their pursuers so far behind, that they had leisure to breathe, and inquire of each other whether it was worth while to kill their horses before they had ascertained the number of the enemy.

They quickly determined to cross the creek, and await the approach of the Indians. If they found them superior to their own and Bryant's party united, they would immediately return to the fort; as, by continuing their march to the mouth of Cane Run, they would bring a superior enemy upon their friends, and endanger the lives of the whole party. They accordingly crossed the creek, dismounted, and awaited the approach of the enemy. By this time it had become dark. The Indians were distinctly heard approaching the creek upon the opposite side, and, after a short halt, a solitary warrior descended the bank, and began to wade through the stream.

Hogan waited until he had emerged from the gloom

of the trees which grew upon the bank, and as soon as he had reached the middle of the stream, where the light was more distinct, he took deliberate aim and fired. A great splashing in the water was heard, but presently all became quiet. The pursuit was discontinued, and the party, remounting their horses, returned home. Anxious, however, to apprise Bryant's party of their danger, they left the fort before daylight on the ensuing morning, and rode rapidly down the creek, in the direction of the mouth of Cane. When within a few hundred yards of the spot where they supposed the encampment to be, they heard the report of many guns in quick succession, Supposing that Bryant had fallen in with a herd of buffalo, they quickened their march, in order to take part in the sport.

The morning was foggy, and the smoke of the guns lay so heavily upon the ground that they could see nothing until they had approached within twenty yards of the creek, when they suddenly found themselves within pistol-shot of a party of Indians, very composedly seated upon their packs, and preparing their pipes. Both parties were much startled, but quickly recovering, they sheltered themselves as usual, and the action opened with great vivacity. The Indians maintained their ground for half an hour with some firmness, but being hard pressed in front, and turned in flank, they at length gave way, and being closely pursued, were ultimately routed, with considerable loss, which, however, could not be distinctly ascertained. Of Hogan's party, one man was killed on the spot, and three others wounded, none mortally.

. It happened that Bryant's company had encamped at the mouth of Cane, as had been agreed upon, and were unable to account for Hogan's absence. That, about daylight, they had heard a bell at a distance, which they immediately recognized as the one belonging to the led horse which had accompanied Hogan's party, and which, as we have seen, had been abandoned to the enemy the evening before. Supposing their friends to be bewildered in the fog, and unable to find their camp, Bryant, accompanied by Grant, one of his men, mounted a horse, and rode to the spot where the bell was still ringing. They quickly fell into an ambuscade, and were fired upon. Bryant was mortally, and Grant severely wounded, the first being shot through the hip and both knees, the latter through the back.

Being both able to keep the saddle, however, they set spurs to their horses, and arrived 'at the station shortly after breakfast. The Indians, in the meantime, had fallen upon the encampment, and instantly dispersed it; and, while preparing to regale themselves after their victory, were suddenly attacked, as we have seen, by Hogan. The timidity of Hogan's party, at the first appearance of the Indians, was the cause of the death of Bryant. The same men who fled so hastily in the evening, were able the next morning, by a little firmness, to vanquish the same party of Indians. Had they stood at first, an equal success would probably have attended them, and the life of their leader would have been preserved.

We have now to notice an adventure of a different kind, and which, from its singularity, is entitled to a place in our pages. In 1783, Lexington was only a cluster of cabins, one of which, near the spot where the court-house now stands, was used as a school-house. One morning in May, McKINNEY, the teacher, was sitting alone at his desk, busily engaged in writing, when, hearing a slight noise at the door, he turned his head and beheld—what do you suppose, reader? A tall Indian in his war paint, brandishing his tomahawk or handling his knife? No! an enormous cat, with her forefeet upon the step of the door, her tail curled over her back, her bristles erect, and her eyes glancing rapidly through the room, as if in search of a mouse.

McKinney's position at first completely concealed him, but a slight and involuntary motion of his chair, at sight of this shaggy inhabitant of the forest, attracted puss's attention, and their eyes met. McKinney having heard much of the power of "the human face divine," in quelling the audacity of wild animals, attempted to disconcert the intruder by a frown. But puss was not to be bullied. Her eyes flashed fire, her tail waved angrily, and she began to gnash her teeth, evidently bent upon serious hostility. Seeing his danger, McKinney hastily arose and attempted to snatch a cylindrical rule from a table which stood within reach, but the cat was too quick for him.

Darting upon him with the proverbial activity of her tribe, she fastened upon his side with her teeth, and began to rend and tear with her claws like a fury. McKinney's clothes were, in an instant, torn from his side, and his flesh dreadfully mangled by the enraged animal, whose strength and ferocity filled him with astonishment. He in vain attempted to disengage her from his side. Her long sharp teeth were fastened between his ribs, and his efforts served but to enrage her the more Seeing his blood flow very copiously from the numerous wounds in his side, he became seriously alarmed, and not knowing what else to do, he threw himself upon the edge of the table, and pressed her against the sharp corner with the whole weight of his body.

The cat now began to utter the most wild and discordant cries, and McKinney at the same time lifting up his voice in concert, the two together sent forth notes so doleful as to alarm the whole town. Women, who are always the first in hearing or spreading news, were now the first to come to McKinney's assistance. But so strange and unearthly was the harmony within the school-house, that they hesitated long before they ventured to enter. At length the boldest of them rushed in, and seeing McKinney bending over the corner of the table, and writhing his body as if in great pain, she at first supposed that he was laboring under a severe fit of the colic; but quickly perceiving the cat, which was now in the agonies of death, she screamed out, "Why, good heaven! Mr. McKinney, what is the matter?"

"I have caught a cat, madam!" replied he, gravely turning around, while the sweat streamed from his face, under the mingled operation of fright, and fatigue, and agony. Most of the neighbors had now arrived, and attempted to disengage the dead cat from her antagonist; but so firmly were her tusks locked between his ribs, that this was a work of no small difficulty. Scarcely had it been effected, when McKinney became very sick, and was compelled to go to bed. In a few days, however, he had totally recovered, and so late as 1820 was alive, and a resident of Bourbon County, Ky., where he was often heard to affirm, that he, at any time, had rather fight two Indians than one wild cat.

About the same time, a conflict more unequal, and equally remarkable, took place in another part of the country. DAVID MORGAN, a relation of the celebrated General Daniel Morgan, had settled upon the Monongahela during the earlier period of the Revolutionary war, and at this time had ventured to occupy a cabin at the distance of several miles from any settlement. One morning, having sent his younger children out to a field, at a considerable distance from the house, he became uneasy about them, and repaired to the spot where they were working, armed, as usual, with a good rifle. While sitting upon the fence, and giving some directions as to their work, he observed two Indians upon the other side of the field, gazing earnestly upon the party. He instantly called to the children to make their escape, while he should attempt to cover their retreat.

The odds were greatly against him, as, in addition to other circumstances, he was nearly seventy years of age, and, of course, unable to contend with his enemies in running. The house was more than a mile distant, but the children, having two hundred yards the start, and being effectually covered by their father, were soon so far in front that the Indians turned their attention entirely to the old man. He ran, for several hundred yards, with an activity which astonished himself, but perceiving that he would be overtaken long before he could reach his home, he fairly turned at bay, and prepared for a strenuous resistance. The woods, through which they were running, were very thin, and consisted almost entirely of small trees, behind which it was difficult to obtain proper shelter.

When Morgan adopted the above-mentioned resolution, he had just passed a large walnut, which stood like a patriarch among the saplings which surrounded it, and it became necessary to run back about ten steps in order to regain it. The Indians became startled at the sudden advance of the fugitive, and were compelled to halt among a cluster of saplings, where they anxiously strove to shelter themselves. This, however, was impossible; and Morgan, who was an excellent marksman, saw enough of the person of one of them to justify him in risking a shot. His enemy instantly fell, mortally wounded. The other Indian, taking advantage of Morgan's empty gun, sprung from his shelter and advanced rapidly upon him. The old man, having no time to reload his gun, was compelled to fly a second time. The Indian gained rapidly upon him, and when within twenty steps, fired, but with so unsteady an aim that Morgan was totally unhurt, the ball having passed over his shoulder.

He now again stood at bay, clubbing his rifle for a blow; while the Indian, dropping his empty gun, brandished his tomahawk and prepared to throw it at his enemy. Morgan struck with the butt of his gun and the Indian whirled his tomahawk at one and the same moment. Both blows took effect, and both were at once wounded and disarmed. The breech of the rifle was broken against the Indian's skull, and the edge of the tomahawk was shattered against the barrel of the rifle, having first cut off two of the fingers of Morgan's left hand. The Indian then attempting to draw his knife, Morgan grappled him and bore him to the ground. A furious struggle ensued, in which the old man's strength failed, and the Indian succeeded in turning him.

Planting his knee in the breast of his enemy, and yelling loudly, as is usual with them upon any turn of fortune, he again felt for his knife, in order to terminate the struggle at once; but having lately stolen a woman's apron, and tied it around his waist, his knife was so much confined that he had great difficulty in finding the handle. Morgan, in the meantime, being a regular pugilist, according to the custom of Virginia, and perfectly at home in a ground struggle, took advantage of the awkwardness of the Indian, and got one of the fingers of his right hand between his teeth. The Indian tugged and roared in vain, struggling to extricate it. Morgan held him fast, and began to assist him in hunting for the knife. Each seized it at the same moment, the Indian by the blade and Morgan by the handle, but with a very slight hold.

The Indian, having the firmest hold, began to draw the knife further out of its sheath, when Morgan, suddenly giving his finger a furious bite, twitched the knife dexterously through his hand, cutting it severely. Both now sprang to their feet, Morgan brandishing his adversary's knife, and still holding his finger between his teeth. In vain the poor Indian struggled to get away, rearing, plunging, and bolting, like an unbroken colt. The teeth of the white man were like a vise, and he at length succeeded in giving him a stab in the side. The Indian received it without falling, the knife having struck his ribs; but a second blow, aimed at the stomach, proved more effectual, and the savage fell. Morgan thrust the knife, handle and all, into the cavity of the body, directed it upward, and starting to his feet, made the best of his way home.

The neighborhood was quickly alarmed; and, hurrying to the spot where the struggle had taken place, they found the first Indian lying where he had fallen, but the second had disappeared. A broad trail of blood, however, conducted to a fallen tree-top, within one hundred yards of the spot, into which the poor fellow had dragged himself, and where he now lay bleeding, but still alive. He had plucked the knife from his wound, and was endeavoring to dress it with the stolen apron—which had cost him his life—when his enemies approached. The love of life appeared still strong within him, however. He greeted them with what was intended for an insinuating smile, held out his hand and exclaimed, in broken English, "How de do, broder?

how de do? Glad to see you!" But, poor fellow! the love was all on his side. Their brotherhood extended only to tomahawking, scalping, and skinning him, all of which operations were performed within a few minutes after the meeting. To such an extent had mutual injury inflamed both parties.

About the middle of July, 1782, seven Wyandotts crossed the Ohio a few miles above Wheeling, and committed great depredations upon the southern shore, killing an old man whom they found alone in his cabin, and spreading terror throughout the neighborhood. Within a few hours after their retreat, eight men assembled from different parts of the small settlement, and pursued the enemy with great expedition. Among the most active and efficient of the party were two brothers, ANDREW and ADAM POE. Andrew was particularly popular. In strength, action, and hardihood, he had no equal, being finely formed, and inured to all the perils of the woods. They had not followed the trail far before they became satisfied that the depredators were conducted by Big Foot, a renowned chief of the Wyandott tribe, who derived his name from the immense size of his feet.

His height considerably exceeded six feet, and his strength was represented as Herculean. He had also five brothers, but little inferior to himself in size and courage, and as they generally went in company, they were the terror of the whole country. Andrew Poe was overjoyed at the idea of measuring his strength with that of so celebrated a chief, and urged the pursuit with a keenness which quickly brought him into the vicinity of the enemy. For the last few miles, the trail had led them up the southern bank of the Ohio, where the foot-prints in the sand were deep and obvious; but when within a few hundred yards of the point at which the whites as well as the Indians were in the habit of crossing, it suddenly diverged from the stream and stretched along a rocky ridge, forming an obtuse angle with its former direction.

Here Andrew halted for a moment and directed his

brother and the other young men to follow the trail with proper caution, while he himself still adhered to the river path, which led through clusters of willows directly to the point where he supposed the enemy to lie. Having examined the priming of his gun, he crept cautiously through the bushes, until he had a view of the point of embarkation. Here lay two canoes, empty and apparently deserted. Being satisfied, however, that the Indians were close at hand, he relaxed nothing of his vigilance, and quickly gained a jutting cliff, which hung immediately over the canoes. Hearing a low murmur below, he peered cautiously over, and beheld the object of his search. The gigantic Big Foot lay below him, in the shade of a willow, and was talking in a low, deep tone to another warrior, who seemed a mere pigmy by his side.

Andrew cautiously drew back and cocked his gun. The mark was fair, the distance did not exceed twenty feet, and his aim was unerring. Raising his rifle slowly and cautiously, he took a steady aim at Big Foot's breast and drew the trigger. His gun flashed. Both Indians sprang to their feet with a deep interjection of surprise, and for a single second, all three stared upon each other. This inactivity, however, was soon over. Andrew was too much hampered by the bushes to retreat, and, setting his life upon a cast of the die, he sprung over the bush which had sheltered him, and, summoning all his powers, leaped boldly down the precipice and alighted upon the breast of Big Foot with a shock that bore him to the earth.

At the moment of contact, Andrew had also thrown his right arm around the neck of the smaller Indian, so that all three came to the earth together. At that moment a sharp firing was heard among the bushes above, announcing that the other parties were engaged; but the trio below were too busy to attend to any thing but themselves. Big Foot was for an instant stunned by the violence of the shock, and Andrew was enabled to keep them both down. But the exertion necessary for that purpose was so great that he had no leisure to use his knife. Big Foot quickly recovered, and, without attempting to rise, wrapped his long arms around Andrew's body, and pressed him to his breast with the crushing force of a boa-constrictor. Andrew, as we have already remarked, was a powerful man, and had seldom encountered his equal; but never had he yet felt an embrace like that of Big Foot.

He instantly relaxed his hold of the small Indian, who sprang to his feet. Big Foot then ordered him to run for his tomahawk, which lay within ten steps, and kill the white man, while he held him in his arms. Andrew, seeing his danger, struggled manfully to extricate himself from the folds of the giant, but in vain. The lesser Indian approached with his uplifted tomahawk, but Andrew watched him closely, and as he was about to strike, gave him a kick so sudden and violent as to knock the tomahawk from his hand, and send him staggering back into the water. Big Foot uttered an exclamation in a tone of deep contempt at the failure of his companion, and raising his voice to its highest pitch, thundered out several words in the Indian tongue, which Andrew could not understand, but supposed to be a direction for a second attack.

The lesser Indian now again approached, carefully shunning Andrew's heels, and making many motions with his tomahawk, in order to deceive him as to the point where the blow would fall. This lasted for several seconds, until a thundering exclamation from Big Foot compelled his companion to strike. Such was Andrew's dexterity and vigilance, however, that he managed to received the tomahawk in a glancing direction upon his left wrist, wounding him deeply, but not disabling him. He now made a sudden and desperate effort to free himself from the arms of the giant, and succeeded. Instantly snatching up a rifle (for the Indian could not venture to shoot for fear of hurting his companion), he shot the lesser Indian through the body.

But scarcely had he done so, when Big Foot arose, and placing one hand upon his collar and the other upon his hip, pitched him ten feet into the air, as he himself would have pitched a child. Andrew fell upon his back at the edge of the water, but before his antagonist could spring upon him, he was again upon his feet; and stung with rage at the idea of being handled so easily, he attacked his gigantic antagonist with a fury which for a time compensated for inferiority of strength. It was now a fair fist fight between them, for in the hurry of the struggle neither had leisure to draw their knives. Andrew's superior activity and experience as a pugilist, gave him great advantage. The Indian struck awkwardly, and finding himself rapidly dropping to leeward, he closed with his antagonist, and again hurled him to the ground.

They quickly rolled into the river, and the struggle continued with unabated fury, each attempting to drown the other. The Indian being unused to such violent exertion, and having been much injured by the first shock in his stomach, was unable to exert the same powers which had given him such a decided superiority at first; and, Andrew seizing him by the scalp-lock, put his head under water, and held it there, until the faint struggles of the Indian induced him to believe that he was drowned, when he relaxed his hold and attempted to draw his knife. The Indian, however, to use Andrew's own expression, "had only been POSSUMING!"

He instantly regained his feet, and in his turn put his adversary under. In the struggle both were carried out into the current, beyond their depth, and each was compelled to relax his hold and swim for his life. There was still one loaded rifle upon the shore, and each swam hard in order to reach it, but the Indian proved the most expert swimmer, and Andrew seeing that he should be too late, turned and swam out into the stream, intending to dive and thus frustrate his enemy's intention. At this instant, Adam, having heard that his brother was alone in a struggle with two Indians, and in great danger, ran up hastily to the edge of the bank above, in order to assist him. Another white man followed him closely, and seeing Andrew in the river, covered with blood, and swimming rapidly from shore, mistook him for an Indian and fired upon him, wounding him dangerously in the shoulder.

Andrew turned, and seeing his brother, called loudly upon him to "shoot the big Indian upon the shore." Adam's gun, however, was empty, having just been discharged. Fortunately, Big Foot had also seized the gun with which Andrew had shot the lesser Indian, so that both were upon an equality. The contest now was who should load first. Big Foot poured in his powder first, and drawing his ramrod out of its sheath in too great a hurry, threw it into the river, and while he ran to recover it, Adam gained an advantage. Still, the Indian was but a second too late, for his gun was at his shoulder, when Adam's ball entered his breast. The gun dropped from his hands, and he fell forward upon his face upon the very margin of the river.

Adam, now alarmed for his brother, who was scarcely able to swim, threw down his gun and rushed into the river in order to bring him ashore; but Andrew, more intent upon securing the scalp of Big Foot as a trophy, than upon his own safety, called loudly upon his brother to leave him alone and scalp the big Indian, who was now endeavoring to roll himself into the water, from a romantic desire, peculiar to the Indian warrior, of securing his scalp from the enemy. Adam, however, refused to obey, and insisted upon saving the living, before attending to the dead. Big Foot, in the meantime, had succeeded in reaching the deep water before he expired, and his body was borne off by the waves, without being stripped of the ornament and pride of an Indian warrior.

Not a man of the Indians had escaped. Five of Big Foot's brothers, the flower of the Wyandott nation, had accompanied him in the expedition, and all perished. It is said that the news of this calamity threw the whole tribe into mourning. Their remarkable size, their courage, and their superior intelligence, gave them immense influence, which, greatly to their credit, was generally exerted on the side of humanity. Their powerful interposition had saved many prisoners from the stake, and had given a milder character to the warfare of the Indians in that part of the country. A chief of the same name was alive in that part of the country so late as 1792, but whether a brother or son of Big Foot, is not known. Andrew Poe recovered of his wounds, and lived many years after his memorable conflict; but never forgot the tremendous "hug" which he sustained in the arms of Big Foot.

CHAPTER VIII.

THE present, like the preceding chapter, will be devoted to miscellaneous items of intelligence, arranged in chronological order. About the middle of the summer of 1792, a gentleman named Woods, imprudently removed from the neighborhood of a station, and for the benefit of his stock, settled on a lonely heath, near Beargrass. One morning he left his family, consisting of a wife, a daughter not yet grown, and a lame negro man, and rode off to the nearest station, not expecting to return until night. Mrs. Woods, while engaged in her dairy, was alarmed at seeing several Indians rapidly approaching the house. She instantly screamed loudly in order to give the alarm, and ran with her utmost speed, in order to reach the house before them. In this she succeeded, but had not time to close the door until the foremost Indian had forced his way into the house. As soon as he entered, the lame negro grappled him and attempted to throw him upon the floor, but was himself hurled to the ground with violence, the Indian falling upon him.

Mrs. Woods was too busily engaged in keeping the door closed against the party without, to attend to the combatants, but the lame negro, holding the Indian in his arms, called to the young girl to cut his head off with a very sharp ax which lay under the bed. She attempted to obey, but struck with so trembling a hand that the blow was ineffectual. Repeating her efforts under the direction of the negro, however, she at length wounded the Indian so badly, that the negro was enabled to arise and complete the execution. Elated with success, he then called to his mistress and told her to suffer another Indian to enter and they would kill them all one by one. While deliberating upon this proposal, however, a sharp firing was heard without, and the Indians quickly disappeared. A party of white men had seen them at a distance, and having followed them cautiously, had now interposed, at a very critical moment, and rescued a helpless family from almost certain destruction.

In the spring of 1784, three young Kentuckians, DAVIS, CAFFREE, and McCLURE, pursued a party of southern Indians, who had stolen horses from Lincoln County, and finding it impossible to overtake them, they determined to go on to the nearest Indian settlement, and make reprisals, horse stealing being at that time a very fashionable amusement, and much practiced on both sides. After traveling several days, they came within a few miles of an Indian town near the Tennessee River, called Chicacaugo. Here they fell in with three Indians. Finding themselves equal in point of numbers, the two parties made signs of peace, shook hands, and agreed to travel together. Each, however, was evidently suspicious of the other. The Indians walked upon one side of the road and the whites upon the other, watching each other attentively.

At length the Indians spoke together in tones so low and earnest, that the whites became satisfied of their treacherous intentions, and determined to anticipate them. Caffree being a very powerful man, proposed that he himself should seize one Indian, while Davis and McClure should shoot the other two. The plan was a bad one, but was unfortunately adopted. Caffree sprung boldly upon the nearest Indian, grasped his throat firmly, hurled him to the ground, and drawing a cord from his pocket attempted to tie him. At the same instant Davis and McClure attempted to perform their respective parts. McClure killed his man, but Davis's gun missed fire. All three, *i. e.*, the two white men and the Indian at whom Davis had flashed, immediately took trees, and prepared for a skirmish, while

Caffree remained upon the ground with the captured Indian, both exposed to the fire of the others. In a few seconds, the savage at whom Davis had flashed, shot Caffree as he lay upon the ground and gave him a mortal wound, and was instantly shot in turn by McClure, who had reloaded his gun. Caffree becoming very weak, called upon Davis to come and assist him in tying the Indian, and instantly afterward expired. As Davis was running up to the assistance of his friend, the Indian, now released by the death of his captor, sprung to his feet, and seizing Caffree's rifle, presented it menacingly at Davis, whose gun was not in order for service, and who ran off into the forest, closely pursued by the Indian. McClure hastily reloaded his gun, and taking up the rifle which Davis had dropped, followed them for some distance into the forest, making all those signals which had been concerted between them in case of separation. All, however, was vain ; he saw nothing more of Davis, nor could he ever afterward learn his fate. As he never returned to Kentucky, however, he probably perished.

McClure, finding himself alone in the enemy's country, and surrounded by dead bodies, thought it prudent to abandon the object of the expedition and return to Kentucky. He accordingly retraced his steps, still bearing Davis's rifle in addition to his own. He had scarcely marched a mile, before he saw advancing from the opposite direction an Indian warrior, riding a horse with a bell around its neck, and accompanied by a boy on foot. Dropping one of the rifles, which might have created suspicion, McClure advanced with an air of confidence, extending his hand and making other signs of peace. The opposite party appeared frankly to receive his overtures, and, dismounting, seated himself upon a log, and drawing out his pipe, gave a few puffs himself, and then handed it to McClure.

In a few minutes another bell was heard, at the distance of half a mile, and a second party of Indians appeared upon horseback. The Indian with McClure now coolly informed him by signs that when the horsemen arrived, he (McClure) was to be bound and carried off as a prisoner with his feet tied under the horse's belly. In order to explain it more fully, the Indian got astride of the log, and locked his legs together underneath it. McClure, internally thanking the fellow for his excess of candor, determined to disappoint him, and while his enemy was busily engaged in riding the log, and mimicking the actions of a prisoner, he very quietly blew his brains out, and ran off into the woods. The Indian boy instantly mounted the belled horse, and rode off in an opposite direction.

McClure was fiercely pursued by several small Indian dogs, that frequently ran between his legs and threw him down. After falling five or six times, his eyes became full of dust, and he was totally blind. Despairing of escape, he doggedly lay upon his face, expecting every instant to feel the edge of the tomahawk. To his astonishment, however, no enemy appeared, and even the Indian dogs, after tugging at him for a few minutes, and completely stripping him of his breeches, left him to continue his journey unmolested. Finding every thing quiet, in a few moments he arose, and taking up his gun, continued his march to Kentucky. He reached home in safety, and in 1820 was still alive. This communication is from his own lips, and may be relied upon as correct.

In the course of the next year, many families came down the Ohio in boats, landed at Maysville, and continued their route by land, in such parts of the country as pleased them. Out of a number of incidents which attended the passage of boats down the river, I shall select two, as worthy of being mentioned. Colonel THOMAS MARSHALL, formerly commander of the Third Virginia Regiment on continental establishment, and subsequently holding the same rank in the Virginia artillery, embarked with a numerous family on board of a flat-bottomed boat, and descended the Ohio without any incident worthy of notice, until he had passed the mouth of Kenawha. Here, about ten o'clock at night, he was hailed from the northern shore by a man who spoke good English, and quickly announced himself as James Girty, the brother of Simon, both of whom have already been repeatedly mentioned. The boat dropped slowly down within one hundred and fifty yards of the shore, and Girty making a corresponding movement on the beach, the conference was kept up for several minutes. He began by mentioning his name, and inquiring that of the master of the boat.

Having been satisfied upon this head, he assured him that he knew him well, respected him highly, etc., and concluded with some rather extraordinary remarks. "He had been posted there," he said, "by the order of his brother Simon, to warn all boats of the danger of permitting themselves to be decoyed ashore. The Indians had become jealous of him, and he had lost that influence which he formerly held among them. He deeply regretted the injury which he had inflicted upon his countrymen, and wished to be restored to their society. In order to convince them of the sincerity of his regard, he had directed him to warn all boats of the snares spread for them. Every effort would be made to draw passengers ashore. White men would appear on the bank, and children would be heard to supplicate for mercy. But," continued he, "do you keep the middle of the river, and steel your heart against every mournful application which you may receive." The colonel thanked him for his intelligence, and continued his course.

From this it would appear, that Girty's situation was by no means enviable. The superior intelligence which had first given him influence, gradually attracted envy. Combinations were probably formed against him, as they are in civilized life, against every man who is guilty of the unpardonable offense of mounting rapidly above his fellows. Ambition, jealousy, intrigue, combinations for particular objects, prevail as strongly among savages as among civilized beings, and spring in each from the same source—a tender, passionate, inordinate love of self—a passion the most universal, deeply rooted, and infinitely diversified in its operations, of any in existence—a passion as strong and easily offended in the degraded Hottentot, as in the Emperor Napoleon, in the superannuated old woman as in the blooming belle—the only human passion which age can not tame, or misery extinguish, or experience cure, or philosophy expel; which flutters as strongly in the jaws of death as in the vigor of life, and is as buoyant and ridiculous in the breast of the philosopher, as in that of a village beauty. Nothing more was ever heard of Girty's wish to be restored to his station in society; but his warning, by whatever motive dictated, was of service to many families.

About the same time, Captain JAMES WARD, at present a highly respectable citizen of Mason County, Ky., (1832), was descending the Ohio, under circumstances which rendered a rencounter with the Indians peculiarly to be dreaded. He, together with half a dozen others, one of them his nephew, embarked in a crazy boat, about forty-five feet long and eight feet wide, with no other bulwark than a single pine plank above each gunwale. The boat was much encumbered with baggage, and seven horses were on board. Having seen no enemy for several days, they had become secure and careless, and permitted the boat to drift within fifty yards of the Ohio shore. Suddenly several hundred Indians showed themselves on the bank, and running down boldly to the water's edge, opened a heavy fire upon the boat. The astonishment of the crew may be conceived.

Captain Ward and his nephew were at the oars when the enemy appeared, and the captain, knowing that their safety depended upon their ability to regain the middle of the river, kept his seat firmly, and exerted his utmost powers at the oar; but his nephew started up at sight of the enemy, seized his rifle, and was in the act of leveling it, when he received a ball in the breast and fell dead in the bottom of the boat. Unfortunately, his oar fell into the river, and the captain, having no one to pull against him, rather urged the boat nearer to the hostile shore than otherwise. He quickly seized a plank, however, and giving his own oar to another of the crew, he took the station which his nephew had held, and, unhurt by the shower of bullets which flew around him, continued to exert himself until the boat had reached a more respectable distance. He then for the first time looked around him, in order to observe the condition of the crew.

His nephew lay in his blood, perfectly lifeless; the horses had been all killed or mortally wounded. Some had fallen overboard, others were struggling violently, and causing their frail bark to dip water so abundantly as to excite the most serious apprehensions. But the crew presented the most singular spectacle. A captain, who had served with reputation in the continental army, seemed now totally bereft of his faculties. He lay upon his back in the bottom of the boat with hands uplifted, and a countenance in which terror was personified, exclaiming, in a tone of despair, "Oh, Lord! Oh, Lord!" A Dutchman, whose weight might amount to about three hundred pounds, was anxiously engaged in endeavoring to find shelter for his bulky person, which, from the lowness of the gunwales, was a very difficult undertaking. In spite of his utmost efforts, a portion of his posterial luxuriance appeared above the gunwale, and afforded a mark to the enemy, which brought a constant shower of balls around it.

In vain he shifted his position. The hump still appeared, and the balls still flew around it, until the Dutchman, losing all patience, raised his head above the gunwale, and, in a tone of querulous remonstrance, called out, "Oh, now! quit tat tamned nonsense tere, will you?" Not a shot was fired from the boat. At one time, after they had partly regained the current, Captain Ward attempted to bring his rifle to bear upon them, but so violent was the agitation of the boat from the furious struggles of the horses, that he could not steady his piece within twenty yards of the enemy, and, quickly laying it aside, returned to the oar. The Indians followed them down the river for more than an hour, but, having no canoes, they did not attempt to board; and as the boat was at length transferred to the opposite side of the river, they at length abandoned the pursuit and disappeared. None of the crew, save the young man already mentioned, were hurt, although the Dutchman's seat of honor served as a target for the space of an hour, and the continental captain was deeply mortified at the sudden and, as he said, "unaccountable" panic which had seized him. Captain Ward himself was protected by a post, which had been fastened to the gunwale, and behind which he sat while rowing.

In the month of August, 1786, Mr. FRANCIS DOWNING, then a mere lad, was living in a fort, where subsequently some iron works were erected by Mr. Jacob Myers, now (in 1832) known by the name of "Slate Creek Works," and are the property of Colonel Thomas Dye Owings. About the sixteenth, a young man belonging to the fort called upon Downing, and requested his assistance in hunting for a horse which had strayed away on the preceding evening. Downing readily complied, and the two friends traversed the woods in every direction, until at length, toward evening, they found themselves in a wild valley, at the distance of six or seven miles from the fort. Here Downing became alarmed, and repeatedly assured his elder companion, whose name was Yates, that he heard sticks cracking behind them, and was confident that Indians were dogging them. Yates, being an experienced hunter, and from habit grown indifferent to the dangers of the woods, diverted himself freely at the expense of his young companion, often inquiring at what price he rated his scalp, and offering to insure it for sixpence.

Downing, however, was not so easily satisfied. He observed that in whatever direction they turned the same ominous sounds continued to haunt them, and as Yates still treated his fears with the most perfect indifference, he determined to take his measures upon his own responsibility. Gradually slackening his pace, he permitted Yates to advance twenty or thirty steps in front of him, and immediately after descending a gentle hill, he suddenly sprang aside and hid himself in a thick cluster of whortleberry bushes. Yates, who at that time was performing some woodland ditty to the full extent of his lungs, was too much pleased with his own voice to attend either to Downing or the Indians, and was quickly out of sight. Scarcely had he disappeared, when Downing, to his unspeakable terror, beheld two savages put aside the stalks of a canebrake and look out cautiously in the direction which Yates had taken.

Fearful that they had seen him step aside, he determined to fire upon them and trust to his heels for safety; but so unsteady was his hand, that, in raising his gun to his shoulder, it went off before he had taken aim. He lost no time in following its example, and after having run fifty yards he met Yates, who, alarmed at the report, was hastily retracing his steps. It was not necessary to inquire what was the matter. The enemy were in full view, pressing forward with great rapidity, and "devil take the hindmost" was the order of the day. Yates would not outstrip Downing, but ran by his side, although in so doing he risked both of their lives. The Indians were well acquainted with the country, and soon took a path that diverged from the one which the whites followed at one point and rejoined it at another, bearing the same relation to it that the string does to the bow.

The two paths were at no point distant from each other more than one hundred yards, so that Yates and Downing could easily see the enemy gaining rapidly upon them. They reached the point of reunion first, however, and quickly came to a deep gully, which it was necessary to cross or retrace their steps. Yates cleared it without difficulty, but Downing, being much exhausted, fell short, and falling with his breast against the opposite brink, rebounded with violence and fell at full length on the bottom. The Indians crossed the ditch a few yards below him, and, eager for the capture of Yates, continued the pursuit, without appearing to notice Downing. The latter, who at first had given himself up for lost, quickly recovered his strength, and began to walk slowly along the ditch, fearing to leave it, lest the enemy should see him. As he advanced,

A Bear assists Downing to escape from an Indian. [See page 189.]

however, the ditch became more shallow, until at length it ceased to protect him at all.

Looking around cautiously, he saw one of the Indians returning, apparently in quest of him. Unfortunately, he had neglected to reload his gun while in the ditch, and as the Indian instantly advanced upon him, he had no resource but flight. Throwing away his gun, which was now useless, he plied his legs manfully in ascending a long ridge which stretched before him, but the Indian gained upon him so rapidly that he lost all hope of escape. Coming at length to a large poplar which had been blown up by the roots, he ran along the body of the tree upon one side, while the Indian followed it upon the other, doubtless expecting to intercept him at the root. But here the supreme dominion of fortune was manifested.

It happened that a large she-bear was suckling her cubs in a bed which she had made at the root of the tree, and as the Indian reached that point first, she instantly sprang upon him, and a prodigious uproar took place. The Indian yelled, and stabbed with his knife; the bear growled, and saluted him with one of her most endearing "hugs," while Downing, fervently wishing her success, ran off through the woods, without waiting to see the event of the struggle. Downing reached the fort in safety, and found Yates reposing after a hot chase, having eluded his pursuers, and gained the fort two hours before him. On the next morning they collected a party and returned to the poplar tree, but no traces, either of the Indian or bear, were to be found. They both probably escaped with their lives, although not without injury.

On the night of the eleventh of April, 1787, the house of a widow, in Bourbon County, became the scene of an adventure which, we think, deserves to be related. She occupied what is generally called a double cabin in a lonely part of the county, one room of which was tenanted by the old lady herself, together with two grown sons and a widowed daughter (at that time suckling an infant), while the other was occupied by two unmarried daughters, from sixteen to twenty years of age, together with a little girl not more than half-grown. The hour was eleven o'clock at night. One of the unmarried daughters was still busily engaged at the loom, but the other members of the family, with the exception of one of the sons, had retired to rest. Some symptoms of an alarming nature had engaged the attention of the young man for an hour before any thing of a decided character took place.

The cries of owls were heard in the adjoining wood, answering each other in rather an unusual manner. The horses, which were inclosed as usual in a pound near the house, were more than commonly excited, and by repeated snorting and galloping announced the presence of some object of terror. The young man was often upon the point of awakening his brother, but was as often restrained by the fear of incurring ridicule and the reproach of timidity, at that time an unpardonable blemish in the character of a Kentuckian. At length hasty steps were heard in the yard, and, quickly afterward, several loud knocks at the door, accompanied by the usual exclamation, "Who keeps house?" in very good English. The young man, supposing from the language that some benighted settlers were at the door, hastily arose, and was advancing to withdraw the bar which secured it, when his mother, who had long lived upon the frontiers, and had probably detected the Indian tone in the demand for admission, instantly sprang out of bed and ordered her son not to admit them, declaring that they were Indians.

She instantly awakened her other son, and the two young men, seizing their guns, which were always charged, prepared to repel the enemy. The Indians, finding it impossible to enter under their assumed characters, began to thunder at the door with great violence, but a single shot from a loop-hole compelled them to shift the attack to some less exposed point, and, unfortunately, they discovered the door of the other cabin, which contained the three daughters. The rifles of the brothers could not be brought to bear upon this point, and, by means of several rails taken from the yard fence, the door was forced from its hinges, and the three girls were at the mercy of the savages. One was instantly secured, but the eldest defended herself desperately with a knife which she had been using at the loom, and stabbed one of the Indians to the heart before she was tomahawked.

In the meantime, the little girl, who had been overlooked by the enemy in their eagerness to secure the others, ran out into the yard, and might have effected her escape had she taken advantage of the darkness and fled; but, instead of that, the terrified little creature ran around the house, wringing her hands, and crying out that her sisters were killed. The brothers, unable to hear her cries without risking every thing for her rescue, rushed to the door, and were preparing to sally out to her assistance, when their mother threw herself before them, and calmly declared that the child must be abandoned to its fate; that the sally would sacrifice the lives of all the rest without the slightest benefit to the little girl. Just then the child uttered a loud scream, followed by a few faint moans, and all was again silent. Presently the crackling of flames was heard, accompanied by a triumphant yell from the Indians, announcing that they had set fire to that division of the house which had been occupied by the daughters, and of which they held undisputed possession.

The fire was quickly communicated to the rest of the building, and it became necessary to abandon it or perish in the flames. In the one case there was a possibility that some might escape; in the other, their fate would be equally certain and terrible. The rapid approach of the flames cut short their momentary suspense. The door was thrown open, and the old lady, supported by her eldest son, attempted to cross the fence at one point, while her daughter, carrying her child in her arms, and attended by the younger of the brothers, ran in a different direction. The blazing roof shed a light over the yard but little inferior to that of day, and the savages were distinctly seen awaiting the approach of their victims. The old lady was permitted to reach the stile unmolested, but in the act of crossing, received several balls in her breast and fell dead. Her son, providentially, remained unhurt, and by extraordinary agility effected his escape.

The other party succeeded also in reaching the fence unhurt, but, in the act of crossing, were vigorously assailed by several Indians, who, throwing down their guns, rushed upon them with their tomahawks. The young man defended his sister gallantly, firing upon the enemy as they approached, and then wielding the butt of his rifle with a fury that drew their whole attention upon himself, and gave his sister an opportunity of effecting her escape. He quickly fell, however, under the tomahawks of his enemies, and was found, at daylight, scalped and mangled in a shocking manner. Of the whole family, consisting of eight persons when the attack commenced, only three escaped. Four were killed upon the spot, and one (the second daughter) carried off as a prisoner.

The neighborhood was quickly alarmed, and by daylight about thirty men were assembled under the command of Colonel Edwards. A light snow had fallen during the latter part of the night, and the Indian trail could be pursued at a gallop. It led directly into the mountainous country bordering upon Licking, and afforded evidences of great hurry and precipitation on the part of the fugitives. Unfortunately, a hound had been permitted to accompany the whites, and as the trail became fresh and the scent warm, she followed it with eagerness, baying loudly and giving the alarm to the Indians. The consequences of this imprudence were soon displayed. The enemy, finding the pursuit keen, and perceiving that the strength of the prisoner began to fail, instantly sunk their tomahawks in her head, and left her, still warm and bleeding, upon the snow.

As the whites came up, she retained strength enough to wave her hand in token of recognition, and appeared desirous of giving them some information with regard to the enemy, but her strength was too far gone. Her brother sprang from his horse and knelt by her side, endeavoring to stop the effusion of blood, but in vain. She gave him her hand, muttered some inarticulate words, and expired within two minutes after the arrival of the party. The pursuit was renewed with additional ardor, and in twenty minutes the enemy was within view. They had taken possession of a steep narrow ridge, and seemed desirous of magnifying their numbers in the eyes of the whites, as they ran rapidly from tree to tree, and maintained a steady yell in their most appalling tones. The pursuers, however, were too experienced to be deceived by so common an artifice, and being satisfied that the number of the enemy must be inferior to their own, they dismounted, tied their horses, and flanking out in such a manner as to inclose the enemy, ascended the ridge as rapidly as was consistent with a due regard to the shelter of their persons.

The firing quickly commenced, and now, for the first time, they discovered that only two Indians were opposed to them. They had voluntarily sacrificed themselves for the safety of the main body, and had succeeded in delaying pursuit until their friends could reach the mountains. One of them was instantly shot dead, and the other was badly wounded, as was evident from the blood upon his blanket, as well as that which filled his tracks in the snow for a considerable distance. The pursuit was re-commenced, and urged keenly until night, when the trail entered a running stream and was lost. On the following morning the snow had melted, and every trace of the enemy was obliterated. This affair must be regarded as highly honorable to the skill, address, and activity of the Indians, and the self-devotion of the rear guard is a lively instance of that magnanimity of which they are at times capable, and which is more remarkable in them, from the extreme caution, and tender regard for their own lives, which usually distinguishes their warriors.

A few weeks after this melancholy affair, a very remarkable incident occurred in the same neighborhood. One morning about sunrise, a young man of wild and savage appearance suddenly arose from a cluster of bushes in front of a cabin, and hailed the house in a barbarous dialect, which seemed neither exactly Indian nor English, but a collection of shreds and patches from which the graces of both were carefully excluded. His skin had evidently once been white, although now grievously tanned by constant exposure to the weather. His dress in every respect was that of an Indian, as were his gestures, tones, and equipments, and his age could not be supposed to exceed twenty years. He talked volubly but uncouthly, placed his hand upon his breast, gestured vehemently, and seemed very earnestly bent upon communicating something. He was invited into the cabin, and the neighbors quickly collected around him.

He appeared involuntarily to shrink from contact with them; his eyes rolled rapidly around with a distrustful expression from one to the other, and his whole manner was that of a wild animal, just caught, and shrinking from the touch of its captors. As several present understood the Indian tongue, they at length gathered the following circumstances, as accurately as they could be translated out of a language which seemed to be an *omnium gatherum* of all that was mongrel, uncouth, and barbarous. He said that he had been taken by the Indians when a child, but could neither recollect his name nor the country of his birth; that he had been adopted by an Indian warrior, who brought him up with his other sons, without making the slightest difference between them, and that under his father's roof he had lived happily until within the last month.

A few weeks before that time, his father, accompanied by himself and a younger brother, had hunted for some time upon the waters of the Miami, about forty miles from the spot where Cincinnati now stands, and after all their meat, skins, etc., had been properly secured, the old man determined to gratify his children by taking them upon a war expedition to Kentucky. They accordingly built a bark canoe, in which they crossed the Ohio near the mouth of Licking, and having buried it, so as to secure it from the action of the sun, they advanced into the country and encamped at the distance of fifteen miles from the river. Here their father was alarmed by hearing an owl cry in a peculiar tone, which he declared boded death or captivity to themselves if they continued their expedition, and announced his intention of returning without delay to the river.

Both of his sons vehemently opposed this resolution, and at length prevailed upon the old man to disregard the owl's warning, and conduct them, as he had promised, against the frontiers of Kentucky. The party then composed themselves to sleep, but were quickly awakened by their father, who had again been warned, in a dream, that death awaited them in Kentucky, and again besought his children to release him from his promise, and lose no time in returning home. Again they prevailed upon him to disregard the warning and persevere in the march. He consented to gratify them, but declared he would not remain a moment longer in the camp which they now occupied; and, accordingly, they left it immediately, and marched on through the night, directing their course toward Bourbon County.

In the evening they approached a house—that which he had hailed and in which he was now speaking. Suddenly the desire of rejoining his people occupied his mind so strongly as to exclude every other idea; and, seizing the first favorable opportunity, he had concealed himself in the bushes, and neglected to reply to all the signals which had been concerted for the purpose of collecting their party when scattered. This account appeared so extraordinary, and the young man's appearance was so wild and suspicious, that many of the neighbors suspected him of treachery, and thought that he should be arrested as a spy. Others opposed this resolution, and gave full credit to his narrative. In order to satisfy themselves, however, they insisted upon his instantly conducting them to the spot where the canoe had been buried. To this the young man objected most vehemently, declaring that although he had deserted his father and brother, yet he would not betray them.

These feelings were too delicate to meet with much

sympathy from the rude borderers who surrounded him, and he was given to understand that nothing short of conducting them to the point of embarkation would be accepted as an evidence of his sincerity. With obvious reluctance he at length complied. From twenty to thirty men were quickly assembled, mounted upon good horses, and under the guidance of the deserter, they moved rapidly toward the mouth of Licking. On the road, the young man informed them that he would first conduct them to the spot where they had encamped when the scream of the owl alarmed his father, and where an iron kettle had been left, concealed in a hollow tree. He was probably induced to do this from the hope of delaying the pursuit so long as to afford his friends an opportunity of crossing the river in safety.

But if such was his intention, no measure could have been more unfortunate. The whites approached the encampment in deep silence, and quickly perceived two Indians—an old man and a boy—seated by the fire, and busily employed in cooking some venison. The deserter became much agitated at the sight of them, and so earnestly implored his countrymen not to kill them, that it was agreed to surround the encampment and endeavor to secure them as prisoners. This was accordingly attempted; but so desperate was the resistance of the Indians, and so determined were their efforts to escape, that the whites were compelled to fire upon them, and the old man fell mortally wounded, while the boy, by an incredible display of address and activity, was enabled to escape. The deserter beheld his father fall, and throwing himself from his horse, he ran up to the spot where the old man lay, bleeding but still sensible, and falling upon his body, besought his forgiveness for being the unwilling cause of his death, and wept bitterly.

His father evidently recognized him, and gave him his hand, but almost instantly afterward expired. The white men now called upon him to conduct them at a gallop to the spot where the canoe was buried, expecting to reach it before the Indian boy and intercept him. The deserter in vain implored them to compassionate

Mrs. Merril's Defense against a Midnight Attack. [See page 197.]

his feelings. He urged that he had already sufficiently demonstrated the truth of his former assertions, at the expense of his father's life, and earnestly entreated them to permit his younger brother to escape. His companions, however, were inexorable. Nothing but the blood of the young Indian would satisfy them, and the deserter was again compelled to act as a guide. Within two hours they reached the designated spot. The canoe was still there, and no track could be seen upon the sand, so that it was evident that their victim had not yet arrived.

Hastily dismounting, they tied their horses and concealed themselves within close rifle-shot of the canoe. Within ten minutes after their arrival, the Indian appeared in sight, walking swiftly toward them. He went straight to the spot where the canoe had been buried, and was in the act of digging it up when he received a dozen balls through his body, and leaping high into the air, fell dead upon the sand. He was instantly scalped and buried where he fell, without having seen his brother, and, probably, without having known the treachery by which he and his father had lost their lives. The deserter remained but a short time in Bourbon, and never regained his tranquillity of mind. He shortly afterward disappeared, but whether to seek his relations in Virginia or Pennsylvania, or whether, disgusted by the ferocity of the whites, he returned to the Indians, has never yet been known. He was never heard of afterward.

During the summer, the house of Mr. JOHN MERRIL, of Nelson County, Ky., was attacked by the Indians, and defended with singular address and good fortune. Merril was alarmed by the barking of a dog about midnight, and, upon opening the door in order to ascertain the cause of the disturbance, he received the fire of six or seven Indians, by which his arm and thigh were both broken. He instantly sunk upon the floor and called upon his wife to close the door. This had scarcely been done, when it was violently assailed by the tomahawks of the enemy, and a large breach soon effected. Mrs. Merril, however, being a perfect Amazon, both in strength and courage, guarded it with an ax, and successively killed or badly wounded four of the enemy as they attempted to force their way into the cabin.

The Indians then ascended the roof, and attempted to enter by way of the chimney; but here again they were met by the same determined enemy. Mrs. Merril seized the only feather bed which the cabin afforded, and, hastily ripping it open, poured its contents upon the fire. A furious blaze and stifling smoke instantly ascended the chimney, and brought down two of the enemy, who lay for a few moments at the mercy of the lady. Seizing the ax, she quickly dispatched them, and was instantly afterward summoned to the door, where the only remaining savage now appeared, endeavoring to effect an entrance while Mrs. Merril was engaged at the chimney. He soon received a gash in the cheek, which compelled him, with a loud yell, to relinquish his purpose, and return hastily to Chillicothe, where, from the report of a prisoner, he gave an exaggerated account of the fierceness, strength, and courage of the "long-knife squaw."

CHAPTER IX.

IN the month of April, 1792, a number of horses, belonging to Captain LUTHER CALVIN, of Mason County, were stolen by the Indians; and, as usual, a strong party volunteered to go in pursuit of the enemy, and recover the property. The party consisted of thirty-seven men, commanded by Captains CALVIN and KENTON, and was composed chiefly of young farmers, most of whom had never yet met an enemy. The present Captain CHARLES WARD, deputy sheriff of Mason, in 1832, was one of the volunteers, and was at that time a mere lad, totally unacquainted with Indian warfare. They rendezvoused upon the Kentucky shore, immediately opposite Ripley, and crossing the river, in a small ferry-boat, pursued the trail for five or six miles with great energy. Here, however, a specimen of the usual caprice and uncertainty attending the motions of militia was given.

One of the party, whose voice had been loud and resolute while on the Kentucky shore, all at once managed to discover that the enterprise was rash, ill-advised, and, if prosecuted, would certainly prove disastrous. A keen debate ensued, in which young Spencer Calvin, then a lad of eighteen, openly accused the gentleman alluded to of cowardice, and even threatened to take the measure of his shoulders with a ramrod, on the spot. By the prompt interference of Kenton and the elder Calvin, the young man's wrath was appeased for the time, and all those who preferred safety to honor were invited instantly to return. The permission was promptly accepted, and no less than fifteen men, headed by the recreant already mentioned, turned their horses heads and recrossed the river. The remainder, consisting chiefly of experienced warriors, continued the pursuit.

The trail led them down on the Miami, and, about noon on the second day, they heard a bell in front, apparently from a horse grazing. Cautiously approaching it, they quickly beheld a solitary Indian, mounted on horseback, and leisurly advancing toward them. A few of their best marksm n fired upon him, and brought him to the ground. After a short consultati n, it was then determined to follow his back tiail, and ascertain whether there were more in the neighborhood. A small, active, resolute woodsman, named McIntyre, accompanied by three others, was pushed on in advance, in order to give them early notice of the enemy's appearance, while the main body followed at a more leisurely pace. Within an hour, McIntyre returned, and reported that they were then within a short distance of a large party of Indians, supposed to be greatly superior to their own; that they were encamped in a bottom, upon the borders of a creek, and were amusing themselves, apparently awaiting the arrival of the Indian whom they had just killed, as they would occasionally halloo loudly, and then laugh immoderately, supposing, probably, that their comrade had lost his way.

This intelligence fell like a shower-bath upon the spirits of the party, who, thinking it more prudent to put a greater interval between themselves and the enemy, set spurs to their horses, and galloped back in the direction from which they had come. Such was the panic, that one of the footmen, a huge, hulking fellow, six feet high, in his zeal for his own safety, sprang up behind Captain Calvin (who was then mounted on Captain Ward's horse, the captain having dismounted in order to accommodate him), and nothing, short of a threat to blow his brains out, could induce him to dismount. In this orderly manner they scampered through the woods for several miles, when, in obedience to the orders of Kenton and Calvin, they halted and prepared for re istance, in case (as was probable) the enemy had discovered them, and were engaged in the pursuit. Kenton and Calvin were engaged apart in earnest consultation. It was proposed, that a number of saplings should be cut down, and a temporary breastwork erected; and, while the propriety of these measures was under discussion, the men were left to themselves.

Captain Ward, as we have already observed, was, then, very young, and perfectly raw. He had been in the habit of looking up to one man as a perfect Hector, having always heard him represented, in his own neighborhood, as a man of redoubted courage, and a perfect Anthropophagus among the Indians. When they halted, therefore, he naturally looked around for his friend, hoping to read safety, courage, and assurance of success in that countenance, usually so ruddy and confident. But, alas! the gallant warrior was wofully chop-fallen. There had, generally, been a ruddy tinge upon the tip of his nose, which some ascribed to the effervescence of a fiery valor, while others, more maliciously inclined, attributed it to the fumes of brandy. Even this burning beacon had been quenched, and had assumed a livid ashy hue, still deeper, if possible, than that of his lips. Captain Ward, thinking that the danger must be appalling which could damp the ardor of a man like him, instantly became grievously frightened himself, and the contagion seemed spreading rapidly, when Kenton and Calvin rejoined them, and speaking in a cheerful, confident tone, completely re-animated their spirits.

Finding themselves not pursued by the enemy, as they had expected, it was determined that they should remain in their present position until night, when a rapid attack was to be made, in two divisions, upon the Indian camp, under the impression that the darkness of the night, and the surprise of the enemy, might give them an advantage which they could scarcely hope for in daylight. Accordingly, every thing remaining quiet, at dusk they again mounted, and advanced rapidly, but in profound silence, upon the Indian camp. It was ascertained that the horses which the enemy had stolen, were grazing in a rich bottom, below their camp. As they were advancing to the attack, therefore, Calvin detached his son, with several halters, which he had borrowed from the men, to regain their own horses, and be prepared to carry them off in case the enemy should overpower them. The attack was then made in two divisions.

Calvin conducted the upper, and Kenton the lower party. The wood was thick, but the moon shone out clearly, and enabled them to distinguish objects with sufficient precision. Calvin's party came first in contact with the enemy. They had advanced within thirty yards of a large fire, in front of a number of tents, without having seen a single Indian, when a dog, which had been watching them for several minutes, sprang forward to meet them, baying loudly. Presently an Indian appeared, approaching cautiously toward them, and occasionally speaking to the dog in the Indian tongue. This sight was too tempting to be borne, and Calvin heard the tick of a dozen rifles, in rapid succession, as his party cocked them in order to fire. The Indian was too close to permit him to speak, but, turning to his men, he earnestly waved his hand, as a warning to be quiet. Then, cautiously raising his own rifle, he fired with a steady aim, just as the Indian had reached the fire, and stood fairly exposed to its light.

The report of the rifle instantly broke the stillness of the night, and their ears were soon deafened by the yells of the enemy. The Indian at whom Calvin had fired, fell forward into the burning pile of faggots, and by his struggling to extricate himself, scattered the brands so much as almost to extinguish the light. Several dusky forms glanced rapidly before them for a moment, which drew a volley from his men, but with what effect could not be ascertained. Calvin, having discharged his piece, turned so rapidly as to strike the end of his ramrod against a tree behind him, and drive it into its sheath with such violence, that he was unable to extricate it for several minutes, and finally fractured two of his teeth in the effort.

A heavy fire now commenced from the Indian camp, which was returned with equal spirit by the whites, but without much effect on either side. Trees were barked very plentifully, dogs bayed, the Indians yelled, the whites shouted, the squaws screamed, and a prodigious uproar was maintained for about fifteen minutes, when it was reported to Calvin that Kenton's party had been overpowered and was in full retreat. It was not necessary to give orders for a similar movement. No sooner had the intelligence been received, than the Kentuckians of the upper division broke their ranks, and every man attempted to save himself as he best could. They soon overtook the lower division, and a hot scramble took place for horses. One called upon another to wait for him until he could catch his horse, which had broken his bridle, but no attention was paid to the request. Some fled upon their own horses, others mounted those of their friends. "First come, first served," seemed to be the order of the night, and a sad confusion of property took place, in consequence of which, to their great terror, a few were compelled to return on foot. The flight was originally caused by the panic of an individual. As the lower division moved up to the attack, most of the men appeared to advance with alacrity.

Captain Ward, however, happened to be stationed next to McIntyre, whom we have already had occasion to mention as a practiced woodsman and peculiarly expert marksman. Heretofore, he had always been foremost in every danger, and had become celebrated for the address, activity, and boldness with which he had acquitted himself. As they were ascending the gentle acclivity upon which the Indian camp stood, however, he appeared much dejected, and spoke despondingly of their enterprise. He declared that it had been revealed to him in a dream, on the preceding night, that their efforts would be vain, and that he himself was destined to perish; that he was determined to fight, as long as any man of the party stood his ground, but if the whites were wise, they would instantly abandon the attempt upon the enemy, and recross the Ohio as rapidly as possible.

These observations made but little impression upon Ward, but seemed to take deep root in the mind of the gentleman whose pale face had alarmed the company at the breastwork. The action quickly commenced, and at the first fire from the Indians, Barre, a young Kentuckian, was shot by ——'s side. This circumstance completed the overthrow of his courage, which had declined visibly since the first encounter in the morning, and elevating his voice to its shrillest notes, he shouted aloud, "Boys! it won't do for us to be here; Barre is killed, and the Indians are crossing the creek!" Bonaparte has said, that there is a critical period in every battle, when the bravest men will eagerly seize an excuse to run away. The remark is doubly true with regard to militia.

No sooner had this speech been uttered by one who had never yet been charged with cowardice, than the rout instantly took place, and all order was disregarded. Fortunately, the enemy were equally frightened, and probably would have fled themselves had the whites given them time. No pursuit took place for several hours, nor did they then pursue the trail of the main body of fugitives. But it unfortunately happened that McIntyre, instead of accompanying the rest, turned off from the main route, and returned to the breastwork, where some flour and venison had been left. The Indians quickly became aware of the circumstance, and following with rapidity, overtook, tomahawked, and scalped him, while engaged in preparing breakfast on the following morning. Thus was his dream verified. The prediction in this case, as in many others, probably produced its own accomplishment by confounding his mind, and depriving him of his ordinary alertness and intelligence. He certainly provoked his fate, by his own extraordinary rashness.

It is somewhat remarkable that a brother of Captain Ward was in the Indian camp at the moment when it was attacked. He had been taken by the Indians in 1758, being at that time only three years old, had been adopted as a member of the Shawnee tribe, and had married an Indian woman by whom he had several children, all of whom, together with their mother, were then in camp. Captain Ward has informed the writer of this narrative that, a few seconds before the firing began, while he stood within rifle-shot of the encampment, an Indian girl, apparently fifteen years of age, attracted his attention. She stood for an instant in an attitude of alarm in front of one of the tents, and gazed intently upon the spot where he then stood. Not immediately perceiving that it was a female, he raised his gun, and was upon the point of firing, when her open bosom announced her sex, and her peculiarly light complexion caused him to doubt for a moment whether she could be an Indian by birth. He afterward ascertained that she was his brother's child.

It appears still more remarkable that, exactly one year afterward, John Ward, the adopted Indian, should have been opposed to another one of his brothers, Captain JAMES WARD, of Mason, in a night skirmish somewhat resembling that which we have just detailed. Captain James Ward, together with Kenton, Baker, and about thirty others, while engaged in pursuit of some stolen horses, fell upon a fresh trail of Indians, that crossed the road which they were then pursuing. Instantly abandoning their former object, they followed the fresh trail with great eagerness, and a short time after dark arrived at an encampment. Having carefully reconnoitered it, they determined to remain quiet until daylight, and then fall upon the enemy as before, in two divisions, one to be commanded by Kenton and the other by Baker. Every thing remained quiet until four o'clock in the morning, when Baker moved at the head of his party, in order to take the appointed position (which was very advantageous, and, in conjunction with Kenton's, completely surrounded the enemy), while Kenton remained stationary, awaiting the signal of attack.

By some mistake, Baker moved in a false direction, and to the surprise of both parties, instead of inclosing the Indian camp, he fell directly upon it. A heavy firing, and the usual yelling, quickly announced the fact to Kenton, who moved hastily up to the assistance of his friends. It was still perfectly dark, and the firing was of course at random. Baker, in whose fiery character courage predominated over every thing else, lost all patience at the restraint under which they lay, and urged strenuously that they should rush upon the enemy, and decide the affair at once with the tomahawk; but Kenton, whom repeated misfortunes had rendered extremely cautious, opposed it so vehemently that it was not done.

One of their men had fallen, and they could hear one of the enemy, apparently not more than thirty yards from them, groan deeply, and occasionally converse with his companions in the Indian tongue. The wounded man was the unfortunate John Ward, whose hard fate it was to fight against the whites in a battle in which his own father was killed, to encounter two of his brothers in the field, and finally to fall mortally wounded in a night skirmish when his brother was opposed to him, and was within hearing of his groans. His father perished in the long battle at the "Point," as it was called, near the mouth of the Kenawha. The whole force of the Shawnees was assembled at that point, and John Ward was then nineteen years of age, so that there can be but little doubt of his having been present.

CHAPTER X.

MR. JOHN MAY, a gentleman of Virginia, had, at an early period, been appointed surveyor of the Kentucky lands, and had become so extensively involved in business as to require the aid of a clerk. In 1789 he employed Mr. CHARLES JOHNSTON, a young man scarcely twenty years of age, in that capacity. Johnston accompanied his employer to Kentucky in the summer of 1789, and returned to Virginia in the autumn of the same year, without any adventure worthy of notice; and in the month of February, 1790, it became necessary for them to return to Kentucky, in order to complete the business which had been left unfinished on the former trip. Heretofore they had traveled by land, but on the present occasion May determined to descend the Great Kenawha and Ohio by water. They accordingly traveled by the usual route to Green Briar Courthouse, where the town of Lewisburgh has since been built, and from thence crossed the wilderness which lay between that point and the Great Kenawha.

After suffering much from the weather, which was intensely cold, they at length reached Kelly's Station upon the Kenawha, from which point May proposed to embark. Having purchased a boat—such as was then used for the navigation of the Western waters—they embarked, in company with Mr. JACOB SKYLES, a gentleman of Virginia, who had at that time a stock of dry goods intended for Lexington, and, without any accident, in the course of a few days they arrived at Point Pleasant. Here there was an accession to their number of three persons; a man named FLINN and two sisters of the name of Fleming. Flinn was a hardy borderer, accustomed from his youth to all the dangers of the frontiers, and the two Miss Flemings were women of low station and doubtful character. They were all natives of Pittsburgh, and were on their way to Kentucky.

During their short stay at Point Pleasant, they learned that roving bands of Indians were constantly hovering upon either bank of the Ohio, and were in the habit of decoying boats ashore under various pretenses, and murdering or taking captive all who were on board; so that, upon leaving Point Pleasant, they determined that no consideration should induce them to approach either shore, but, steeling their hearts against every entreaty, that they would resolutely keep the middle of the current, and leave distressed individuals to shift for themselves. How firmly this resolution was maintained the sequel will show. The spring freshet was in its height at the time of their embarkation, and their boat was wafted rapidly down the stream. There was no occasion to use the side oars, and it was only necessary for one individual at a time to watch throughout the night, at the steering oar, in order to keep the boat in the current. So long as this could be done, they entertained no dread of any number of Indians on either shore, as boarding had hitherto formed no part of their plans, and was supposed to be impracticable so long as arms were on board of the boat.

On the morning of the twentieth of March, when near the junction of the Scioto, they were awakened at daylight by Flinn, whose turn it was to watch, and informed that danger was at hand. All instantly sprang to their feet, and hastened upon deck without removing their nightcaps or completing their dress. The cause of Flinn's alarm was quickly evident. Far down the river a smoke was seen, ascending in thick wreaths above the trees, and floating in thinner masses over the bed of the river. All instantly perceived that it could only proceed from a large fire; and who was there to kindle a fire in the wilderness which surrounded them? No one doubted that Indians were in front, and the only question to be decided was upon which shore they lay, for the winding of the river, and their distance from the smoke, rendered it impossible at first to ascertain this point. As the boat drifted on, however, it became evident that the fire was upon the Ohio shore, and it was instantly determined to put over to the opposite side of the river. Before this cou'd be done, however, two white men ran down upon the beach, and, clasping their hands in the most earnest manner, implored the crew to take them on board.

They declared that they had been taken by a party of Indians in Kennedy's Bottom a few days before; had been conducted across the Ohio, and had just effected their escape. They added that the enemy was in close pursuit of them, and that their death was certain unless admitted on board. Resolute in their purpose on no account to leave the middle of the stream, and strongly suspecting the suppliants of treachery, the party paid no attention to their entreaties, but steadily pursued their course down the river, and were soon considerably ahead of them. The two white men ran down the bank in a line parallel with the course of the boat, and their entreaties were changed into the most piercing cries and lamentations upon perceiving the obstinacy with which their request was disregarded.

Instantly the obduracy of the crew began to relax. Flinn and the two females, accustomed from their youth to undervalue danger from the Indians, earnestly insisted upon going ashore and relieving the white men, and even the incredulity of May began to yield to the persevering importunity of the suppliants. A parley took place. May called to them from the deck of the boat, where he stood in his nightcap and drawers, and demanded the cause of the large fire the smoke of which had caused so much alarm. The white men positively denied that there was any fire near them. This falsehood was so palpable that May's former suspicions returned with additional force, and he positively insisted upon continuing their course without paying the slightest attention to the request of the men. This resolution was firmly seconded by Johnston and Skyles, and as vehemently opposed by Flinn and the Miss Flemings, for, contrary to all established rules of policy, the females were allowed an equal vote with the males on board of the boat.

Flinn urged that the men gave every evidence of real distress which could be required, and recounted too many particular circumstances attending their capture and escape, to give color to the suspicion that their story was invented for the occasion, and added that it would be a burning shame to them and theirs forever, if they should permit two countrymen to fall a sacrifice to the savages when so slight a risk on their part would suffice to relieve them. He acknowledged that they had lied in relation to the fire, but declared himself satisfied that it was only because they were fearful of acknowledging the truth, lest the crew should suspect that Indians were concealed in the vicinity. The controversy became warm, and during its progress the boat drifted so far below the men, that they appeared to relinquish their pursuit in despair.

At this time Flinn made a second proposal, which, according to his method of reasoning, could be carried into effect without the slightest risk to any one but himself. They were now more than a mile below the pursuers. He proposed that May should only touch the hostile shore long enough to permit him to jump out; that it was impossible for Indians, even admitting that they were at hand, to arrive in time to arrest the boat, and, even should any appear, they could immediately put off from shore and abandon him to his fate; that he was confident of being able to outrun the red devils if they saw him first, and was equally confident of being able to see them as soon as they could see him. May remonstrated upon so unnecessary an exposure, but Flinn was inflexible, and in an evil hour the boat was directed to the shore.

They quickly discovered, what ought to have been known before, that they could not float as swiftly after leaving the current as while borne along by it, and they were nearly double the time in making the shore that they had calculated upon. When within reach Flinn leaped fearlessly upon the hostile bank, and the boat grated upon the sand. At that moment five or six savages ran up out of breath, from the adjoining wood, and instantly seizing Flinn, began to fire upon the boat's crew. Johnston and Skyles sprang to their arms, in order to return the fire, while May, seizing an oar, attempted to regain the current. Fresh Indians arrived, however, in such rapid succession that the beach was quickly crowded with them, and May called out to his companions to cease firing and come to the oars. This was instantly done, but it was too late.

The river, as we have already observed, was very high, and their clumsy and unwieldy boat had become entangled in the boughs of the trees which hung over the water, so that, after the most desperate efforts to get her off, they were compelled to relinquish the attempt in despair. During the whole of this time the Indians were pouring a heavy fire into the boat, at a distance not exceeding ten paces. Their horses, of which they had a great number on board, had broken their halters, and, mad with terror, were plunging so furiously as to expose them to a danger scarcely less dreadful than that which menaced them from shore. In addition to this, none of them had ever beheld a hostile Indian before, with the exception of May, and the furious gestures and appalling yells of the enemy, struck a terror to their hearts which had almost deprived them of their faculties.

Seeing it impossible to extricate themselves, they all lay down upon their faces in such parts of the boat as would best protect them from the horses, and awaited in passive helplessness the approach of the conquerors. The enemy, however, still declined boarding, and contented themselves with pouring in an incessant fire, by which all the horses were killed, and which at length began to grow fatal to the crew. One of the females received a ball in her mouth which had passed immediately over Johnston's head, and almost instantly expired. Skyles, immediately afterward, was severely wounded in both shoulders, the ball striking the right shoulder blade and ranging transversely along his back. The fire seemed to grow hotter every moment, when at length May arose and waved his nightcap above his head as a signal of surrender. He instantly received a ball in the middle of the forehead, and fell perfectly dead by the side of Johnston, covering him with his blood.

Now—at last—the enemy ventured to board. Throwing themselves into the water, with their tomahawks in their hands, a dozen or twenty swam to the boat, and began to climb the sides. Johnston stood ready to do the honors of the boat, and, presenting his hand to each Indian in succession, he helped them over the side to the number of twenty. Nothing could *appear* more cordial than the meeting. Each Indian shook him by the hand, with the usual salutation of "How de do?" in passable English, while Johnston encountered every visitor with an affectionate squeeze, and a forced smile, in which terror struggled with civility. The Indians then passed on to Skyles and the surviving Miss Fleming, where the demonstrations of mutual joy were not quite so lively. Skyles was writhing under a painful wound, and the girl was sitting by the dead body of her sister.

Having shaken hands with all of their captives, the Indians proceeded to scalp the dead, which was done with great coolness, and the reeking scalps were stretched and prepared upon hoops, for the usual process of drying, immediately before the eyes of the survivors. The boat was then drawn ashore, and its contents examined with great greediness. Poor Skyles, in addition to the pain of his wounds, was compelled to witness the total destruction of his property by the hands of these greedy spoilers, who tossed his silks, cambric, and broadcloth into the dirt with the most reckless indifference. At length they stumbled upon a keg of whisky. The prize was eagerly seized, and every thing else abandoned. The Indian who had found it instantly carried it ashore, and was followed by the rest with tumultuous delight. A large fire, nearly fifty feet long, was quickly kindled, and victors and vanquished indiscriminately huddled around it.

As yet no attempt had been made to strip the prisoners, but, unfortunately, Johnston was handsomely dressed in a broadcloth surtout, red vest, fine ruffled shirt, and a pair of new boots. The Indians began to eye him attentively, and at length one of them, whose name he afterward learned was Chickatommo, a Shawnee chief, came up to him and gave the skirt of his coat two or three hard pulls, accompanied by several gestures which were not to be mistaken. Johnston instantly stripped off his coat and very politely handed it to him. His red waistcoat was now exposed to full view, and attracted great attention. Chickatommo instantly exclaimed, "Hugh! you big cappatain!" Johnston hastily assured him that he was mistaken; that he was no officer, nor had any connection with military affairs whatever. The Indian then drew himself up, pointed with his finger to his breast, and exclaimed, "Me cappatain! all dese"—pointing to his men—"my sogers!" The red waistcoat accompanied the surtout, and Johnston quickly stood shivering in his shirt and pantaloons.

An old Indian then came up to him, and placing one hand upon his own shirt (a greasy, filthy garment, which had not, probably, been washed for six months), and the other upon Johnston's ruffles, cried out in English, "Swap! swap!" at the same time giving the ruffles a gentle pull with his dirty fingers. Johnston, conquering his disgust at the proposal, was about to comply, and had drawn his shirt over his head, when it was violently pulled back by another Indian, whose name he afterward learned was Tom Lewis. His new ally then reproached the other Indian severely for wishing to take the shirt from a prisoner's back in such cold weather, and instantly afterward threw his own blanket over Johnston's shoulders. The action was accompanied by a look so full of compassion and kindness, that Johnston, who had expected far different treatment, was perfectly astonished. He now saw that native kindness of heart, and generosity of feeling, was by no means rare, even among savages.

The two white men who had decoyed them ashore, and whose names were Divine and Thomas, now appeared, and took their seats by the side of the captives. Sensible of the reproach to which they had exposed themselves, they hastened to offer an excuse for their conduct. They declared that they really *had* been taken in Kennedy's Bottom a few days before, and that the Indians had compelled them, by threats of instant death in case of refusal, to act as they had done. They concluded by some common-place expressions of regret for the calamity which they had occasioned, and declared that their own misery was aggravated at beholding that of their countrymen! In short, words were cheap with them, and they showered them out in profusion. But Johnston's and Skyles' sufferings had been, and still were, too severe to permit their resentment to be appeased by such light atonement.

Their suspicions of the existence of willful and malignant treachery on the part of the white men (at least one of them), were confirmed by the report of a negro, who quickly made his appearance, and who, as it appeared, had been taken in Kentucky a few days before. He declared that Thomas had been extremely averse to having any share in the treachery, but had been overruled by Divine, who alone had planned, and was most active in the execution of the project, having received a promise from the Indians that, in case of success, his own liberty should be restored to him. This report has been amply confirmed by subsequent testimony. Mr. Thomas is now living near Maysville, and has always sustained an excellent reputation. [This was written in 1832.]

In a few minutes, six squaws, most of them very old, together with two white children, a girl and a boy, came down to the fire and seated themselves. The children had lately been taken from Kentucky. Skyles' wound now became excessively painful, and Flinn, who, in the course of his adventurous life, had picked up some knowledge of surgery, was permitted to examine it. He soon found it necessary to make an incision, which was done very neatly with a razor. An old squaw then washed the wound, and having caught the bloody water in a tin cup, presented it to Skyles, and requested him to drink it, assuring him that it would greatly accelerate the cure. He thought it most prudent to comply.

During the whole of this time, the Indians remained

silently smoking or lounging around the fire. No sentinels were posted in order to prevent a surprise, but each man's gun stood immediately behind him, with the breech resting upon the ground, and the barrel supported against a small pole, placed horizontally upon two forks. Upon the slighest alarm, every man could have laid his hand upon his own gun. Their captors were composed of small detachments from several tribes. Much the greater portion belonged to the Shawnees, but there were several Delawares, Wyandotts, and a few wandering Cherokees. After smoking, they proceeded to the division of their prisoners. Flinn was given to a Shawnee warrior; Skyles to an old, crabbed, ferocious Indian of the same tribe, whose temper was sufficiently expressed in his countenance; while Johnston was assigned to a young Shawnee chief, whom he represents as possessed of a disposition which would have done him honor in any age or in any nation; his name was Messhawa, and he had just reached the age of manhood. His person was tall, and expressive rather of action than strength; his air was noble, and his countenance mild, open, and peculiarly prepossessing. He evidently possessed great influence among those of his own tribe, which, as the sequel will show, he exerted with great activity on the side of humanity. The surviving Miss Fleming was given to the Cherokees, while the Wyandotts and the Delawares were allowed no share in the distribution. No dissatisfaction, however, was expressed. The division had been proclaimed by an old chief in a loud voice, and a brief guttural monosyllable announced their concurrence. After the distribution of their captives, Flinn, Divine, and Thomas, were ordered to prepare four additional oars, for the boat which they had taken, as they had determined to man it, and assail such other boats as should be encountered during their stay on the Ohio. These and several other preparations occupied the rest of the day.

On the next morning, the Indians arose early, and prepared for an encounter, expecting, as usual, that boats would be passing. They dressed their scalp-tufts, and painted their faces in the most approved manner, before a pocket-glass which each carried with him, grimacing and frowning in order to drill their features to the expression of the most terrific passions. About ten o'clock, a canoe containing six men was seen, slowly and laboriously ascending the river on the Kentucky shore. All the prisoners were instantly ordered to descend the bank to the water's edge, and decoy the canoe within reach of the Indian guns. Johnston, with whatever reluctance, was compelled to accompany the rest. Divine, on this, as on the former occasion, was peculiarly active and ingenious in stratagems. He invented a lamentable story of their canoe having been overset, and of their starving condition, destitute as they were of either guns or axes.

It was with agony that Johnston beheld the canoe put off from the Kentucky shore, and move rapidly toward them, struggling with the powerful current, which bore them so far below them that they could not distinguish the repeated signs which Johnston made, warning them to keep off. The Indians, perceiving how far the canoe was driven below them, ran rapidly down the river, under cover of the woods, and concealed themselves among the willows which grew in thick clusters upon the bank. The unsuspecting canoe-men soon drew near, and when within sixty yards, received a heavy fire, which killed every man on board. Some fell into the river, and overset the canoe, which drifted rapidly down the current, as did the bodies of the slain. The Indians sprang into the water, and dragging them ashore, tomahawked two of them who gave some signs of life, and scalped the whole.

Scarcely had this been done, when a more splendid booty appeared in view. It happened that Captain Thomas Marshall, of the Virginia Artillery, in company with several other gentlemen, was descending the Ohio, having embarked only one day later than May. They had three boats, weakly manned, but heavily laden with horses and dry goods, intended for Lexington. About twelve o'clock on the second day of

Johnston's captivity, the little flotilla appeared about a mile above the point where the Indians stood. Instantly all was bustle and activity. The additional oars were fixed to the boat, the savages instantly sprang on board, and the prisoners were compelled to station themselves at the oars, and were threatened with instant death unless they used their utmost exertions to bring them along-side of the enemy. The three boats came down very rapidly, and were soon immediately opposite their enemy's. The Indians opened a heavy fire upon them, and stimulated their rowers to their utmost efforts.

The boats became quickly aware of their danger, and a warm contest of skill and strength took place. There was an interval of one hundred yards between each of the three boats in view. The hindmost was for a time in great danger. Having but one pair of oars, and being weakly manned, she was unable to compete with the Indian boat, which greatly outnumbered her, both in oars and men. The Indians quickly came within rifle-shot, and swept the deck with an incessant fire, which rendered it extremely dangerous for any of the crew to show themselves. Captain Marshall was on board of the hindmost boat, and maintained his position at the steering-oar in defiance of the shower of balls which flew around him. He stood in his shirt sleeves, with a red silk handkerchief bound around his head, which afforded a fair mark to the enemy, and steered the boat with equal steadiness and skill, while the crew below relieved each other at the oars.

The enemy lost ground from two circumstances. In their eagerness to overtake the whites, they left the current, and attempted to cut across the river from point to point, in order to shorten the distance. In doing so, however, they lost the force of the current, and quickly found themselves dropping astern. In addition to this, the whites conducted themselves with equal coolness and dexterity. The second boat waited for the hindmost, and received their crew on board, abandoning the goods and horses, without scruple, to the enemy. Being now more strongly manned, she shot rapidly ahead, and quickly overtook the foremost boat, which, in like manner, received her crew on board, abandoning the cargo as before; and having six pair of oars, and being powerfully manned, she was soon beyond the reach of the enemy's shot. The chase lasted more than an hour. For the first half hour, the fate of the foremost boat hung in mournful suspense, and Johnston, with agony, looked forward to the probability of its capture. The prisoners were compelled to labor hard at the oars, but they took care never to pull together, and by every means in their power, endeavored to favor the escape of their friends.

At length, the Indians abandoned the pursuit, and turned their whole attention to the boats which had been deserted. The booty surpassed their most sanguine expectations. Several fine horses were on board, and flour, sugar, and chocolate in profusion. Another keg of whisky was found, and excited the same immoderate joy as at first. It was unanimously determined to regale themselves in a regular feast, and instant preparations were made to carry their resolution into effect. A large kettle of chocolate and sugar, of which the sugar formed the greater part, was set upon the fire, which an old squaw stirred with a dirty stick. Johnston was promoted on the spot to the rank of cook, and received orders to bake a number of flour cakes in the fire. A deer-skin, which had served for a saddle blanket, and was most disgustingly stained by having been applied to a horse's sore back, was given him as a tray, and being repeatedly ordered to "make haste," he entered upon his new office with great zeal.

By mixing a large portion of sugar with some dumplings, which he had boiled in chocolate, he so delighted the palates of the Indians, that they were enthusiastic in their praises, and announced their intention of keeping him in his present capacity as long as he remained with them. The two kegs, which had been carefully guarded, were now produced, and the mirth began to border on the "fast and furious." A select band, as usual, remained sober, to maintain order and guard against surprise, but the prisoners were invited to get drunk with their red brothers. Johnston and Skyles declined the invitation, but Flinn, without waiting to be asked twice, instantly joined the revelers, and quickly became as drunk as any of them. In this situation he entered into a hot dispute with an Indian, which, after much abuse on both sides, terminated in blows, and his antagonist received a sad battering. Several of his tribe drew their knives, and rushed upon Flinn with fury, but were restrained amid peals of laughter by the others, who declared that Flinn had proved himself a man, and should have fair play.

In the meantime, Johnston and Skyles had been bound and removed to a convenient distance from the drinking party, with the double design of saving their lives, and guarding against escape. While lying in this manner, and totally unable to help themselves, they beheld, with terror, one of the revelers staggering toward them, with a drawn knife in his hand, and muttering a profusion of drunken curses. He stopped within a few paces of them, and harangued them with great vehemence, for nearly a minute, until he had worked himself up to a state of insane fury, when, suddenly uttering a startling yell, he sprung upon the prostrate body of Skyles, and seizing him by the hair endeavored to scalp him. Fortunately he was too much intoxicated to exert his usual dexterity, and before he had succeeded in his design, the guard ran up at full speed, and seizing him by the shoulders, hurled him violently backwards to the distance of several yards. The drunken beast rolled upon the ground, and with difficulty recovering his feet, staggered off, muttering curses against the white man, the guard himself, and the whole world. Skyles had only felt the point of the knife, but had given up his scalp for lost, and rubbed the crown of his head several times with feverish apprehensions, before he could be satisfied that his scalp was still safe.

No other incident occurred during the night, and on the following morning the Indians separated. Those to whom Flinn belonged, remained at the river in expectation of intercepting other boats, while Johnston's party struck through the wilderness, in a steady direction for their towns. During their first day's march, he afforded much amusement to his captors. In the boat abandoned by Captain Marshall, they had found a milk cow, haltered in the usual manner. Upon leaving the river, they committed her to the care of Johnston, requiring him to lead her by the halter. Being totally unaccustomed to this method of traveling, she proved very refractory, and perplexed him exceedingly. When he took one side of a tree, she regularly chose the other. Whenever he attempted to lead her, she planted her feet firmly before her, and refused to move a step. When he strove to drive her, she ran off into the bushes, dragging him after her, to the no small injury of his person and dress.

The Indians were in a roar of laughter throughout the whole day, and appeared highly to enjoy his perplexity. At night they arrived at a small encampment, where they had left their women and children. Here, to his great joy, Johnston was relieved of his charge, and saw her slaughtered with the utmost gratification. At night, he suffered severely by the absence of the benevolent Messhawa, to whose charge, as we have already said, he had been committed. The Indians were apprehensive of pursuit, and directed Messhawa, at the head of several warriors, to bring up the rear, and give them seasonable warning of any attempt on the part of the whites to regain their prisoners. In his absence, he had been committed to an Indian of very different character.

While his new master was engaged in tying his hands, as usual, for the night, he ventured to complain that the cord was drawn too tight, and gave him unnecessary pain. The Indian flew into a passion, exclaiming, "D——n you soul!" and drew the cord with all the violence of which he was capable, until it was completely buried in the flesh. Johnston, in consequence, did not sleep for a moment, but passed the whole night in exquisite torture. In the morning,

Messhawa came up, and finding his prisoner in a high fever, and his hands excessively swollen, instantly cut the cords, and exchanged some high words with the other Indian upon the subject.

The march was recommenced, and Johnston could not avoid congratulating himself every moment upon his good fortune in having Messhawa for his guide. Skyles' master seemed to take pleasure in tormenting him. In addition to an enormous quantity of baggage, he compelled him to carry his rifle, by which his raw wound was perpetually irritated, and prevented from healing. Messhawa permitted Johnston to share his own mess upon all occasions; while the savage to whom Skyles belonged, would scarcely permit him to eat a dozen mouthfuls a day, and never without imbittering his meat with curses and blows. In a few days they arrived at the Scioto River, which, from the recent rains, was too high to admit of being forded. The Indians were instantly employed in constructing a raft, and it was necessary to carry one very large log several hundred yards.

Two Indians with a handspike supported the lighter end, while the butt was very charitably bestowed upon Johnston alone. Not daring to murmur, he exerted his utmost strength, and, aided by several Indians, with some difficulty succeeded in placing the enormous burden upon his shoulder. He quickly found, however, that the weight was beyond his strength, and, wishing to give his two companions in front warning of his inability to support it, he called to them in English to "take care!" They did not understand him, however, and continued to support it, when, finding himself in danger of being crushed to death, he dropped the log so suddenly that both the Indians were knocked down, and lay for a time without sense or motion. They soon sprang up, however, and, drawing their tomahawks, would instantly have relieved Johnston of all his troubles had not the other Indians, amid peals of laughter, restrained them and compelled them to vent their spleen in curses, which were showered upon "Ketepels," as he was called, for the space of an hour, with great fury.

After crossing the Scioto, the Indians displayed a disposition to loiter and throw away time, but little in unison with Johnston's feelings, who was anxious to reach their towns as speedily as possible, flattering himself with the hope that some benevolent trader would purchase him of the Indians and restore him to liberty. They amused themselves at a game called "Nosey," with a pack of cards which had been found in one of the abandoned boats. The pack is equally divided between two of them, and by some process which Johnston did not understand, each endeavored to get all the cards into his own possession. The winner had a right to ten fillips at his adversary's nose, which the latter was required to sustain with inflexible gravity, as the winner was entitled to ten additional fillips for every smile which he succeeded in forcing from him. At this game they would be engaged for a whole day, with the keenest interest, the bystanders looking on with a delight scarcely inferior to that of the gamblers themselves, and laughing immoderately when the penalty was exacted.

When gaming, they were unusually kind to their prisoners; but this ray of sunshine was frequently very suddenly overcast. Johnston ventured to ask an old Shawnee chief how far they would be forced to travel before reaching his village. The old man very good-naturedly assured him, by drawing a diagram upon the sand with a stick, pointing out the situation of the Ohio River, of the Scioto, and of the various Indian villages, and pointing to the sun, he waved his hand once for every day which they would employ in the journey. Johnston then ventured to ask "how many inhabitants his village contained." The old man replied that the Shawnees had once been a great nation; but (and here his eyes flashed fire, and he worked himself into a furious passion) the long-knives had killed nearly the whole of his nation. "However," continued he, "so long as there is a Shawnee alive, we will *fight! fight! fight!* When no Shawnee, then no fight."

The prisoners were also in great danger whenever the Indians passed through a forest which had been surveyed, and where the marks of the ax upon the trees were evident. They would halt upon coming to such a tree, and after a few minutes' silence, would utter the most terrible yells, striking the trees with their hatchets, and cursing the prisoners with a fierceness which caused them often to abandon all hopes of life. On one occasion, they passed suddenly from the most ferocious state of excitement to the opposite extreme of merriment, at a slight disaster which befell Johnston. They were often compelled to ford creeks; but upon one occasion, they attempted to pass upon a log. The morning was bitterly cold and frosty, and the log having been barked, was consequently very slippery.

In passing upon this bridge, Johnston's foot slipped and he fell into the cold water with an outcry so sudden and shrill that the whole party, which the instant before had been inflamed with rage, burst at once into loud laughter, which, at intervals, was maintained for several miles. Sometimes they amused themselves by compelling their prisoners to dance, causing them to pronounce, in a tone bordering on music, the words, "Komne-kah! He-kah-kah! Was-sat-oo—Hos-ses-kah!" and this monotonous and fatiguing exercise was occasionally relieved by the more exciting one of springing over a large fire when the blaze was at its highest, in which they could only escape injury by great activity.

Their painful journey had now lasted nearly a month, and the Indian towns were yet at a great distance. Hitherto, Skyles and Johnston had remained together; but by the whimsical fancy of their captors, they were now separated. Skyles was borne off to the Miami towns, while Johnston was destined for Sandusky. A few days after this separation, Johnston's party fell in with a Wyandott, and a negro man who, having run away from Kentucky, had been taken up by the Wyandott and retained as an assistant in a very lucrative trade which he was at that time carrying on with the Indians of the interior. He was in the habit of purchasing whisky, powder, blankets, etc., at Detroit, generally upon credit, packing them upon horses into the interior, and exchanging them, at a profit of nearly one thousand per cent., for furs and hides. This casual rencounter in the wilderness was followed by great demonstrations of joy on both sides. The trader produced his rum, the Shawnees their merchandise, and a very brisk exchange ensued.

Johnston's boots, for which he had paid eight dollars in Virginia, were gladly given for a pint of rum; and other articles were sold at a proportionate price. Johnston, as before, was removed from the immediate neighborhood of the revelers, and committed to the care of two sober Indians, with strict injunctions to prevent his escape. They accordingly bound him securely, and, passing the ends of the cord under their own bodies, lay down to sleep—one upon each side of their prisoner. At midnight, Johnston was awakened by a heavy rain, although his guards slept on with most enviable composure. Unable to extricate himself, and fearful of awakening them, he was endeavoring to submit with patience, when the negro appeared, and very courteously invited him to take shelter in his tent, which stood within fifty yards of the spot where he lay.

Johnston was beginning to explain to his black friend the impossibility of moving without the consent of his guards, when they suddenly sprang to their feet, and, seizing the negro by the throat, and at the same time grasping Johnston's collar, they uttered the alarm-hailoo in the most piercing tones. The whole band of drunken Indians instantly repeated the cry, and ran up, tomahawk in hand, and with the most ferocious gestures. Johnston gave himself up for lost, and the negro looked white with terror; but their enemies conducted themselves with more discretion than, from their drunken condition, could have been anticipated. They seized Johnston, bore him off a few paces into the woods, and questioned him closely as to the conference between himself and the negro. He replied by simply and clearly stating the truth. They then grappled the negro, and, menacing him with their knives, threatened to take his scalp on the spot if he did not tell the truth. His story agreed exactly with Johnston's, and the Indians became satisfied that no plot had been concerted.

The incident, however, had completely sobered them, and for several hours the rum-cask gave way to the dancing-ring, which was formed in front of the negro's tent, where Johnston had been permitted, after the alarm subsided, to take shelter from the rain. He quickly fell asleep, but was grievously tormented by the nightmare. He dreamed that he was drowning in the middle of the creek which he had crossed on that morning; and his respiration became so laborious and painful that he at length awoke. The song and the dance were still going on around him, and the cause of his unpleasant dream was made manifest. A huge Indian had very composedly seated himself upon his breast, and was smoking a long pipe and contemplating the dancers, apparently very well satisfied with his seat. Johnston turned himself upon his side and threw the Indian off. He did not appear to relish the change of place much, but soon settled himself and continued to smoke with uninterrupted gravity.

At daylight, a new scene presented itself. The warriors painted themselves in the most frightful colors, and performed a war-dance with the usual accompaniments. A stake, painted in alternate stripes of black and vermilion, was fixed in the ground, and the dancers moved in rapid but measured evolutions around it. They recounted, with great energy, the wrongs which they had received from the whites: Their lands had been taken from them, their corn cut up, their villages burnt, their friends slaughtered; every injury which they had received was dwelt upon, until their passions had become inflamed beyond all control. Suddenly, Chickatommo darted from the circle of dancers, and, with eyes flashing fire, ran up to the spot where Johnston was sitting calmly contemplating the spectacle before him. When within reach, he struck him a furious blow with his fist, and was preparing to repeat it, when Johnston seized him by the arms and hastily demanded the cause of such unprovoked violence.

Chickatommo, grinding his teeth with rage, shouted, "Sit down! sit down!" Johnston obeyed, and the Indian, perceiving the two white children within ten steps

(the Mingo) should either procure her another husband or lay down his own life as a penalty for the slain Wyandott.

He added that he was too poor to procure her another husband, unless he should take that honorable office upon himself—for which he had but small inclination, the squaw in question being well stricken in years, tolerably crooked, and withal a most terrible scold—and that he must submit to the other alternative and lay down his life, unless the Shawnees would have compassion upon him, and give him Johnston, who (he said) being young and handsome, would doubtless be acceptable to the squaw aforesaid, and console her faithful heart for the loss of her former husband. He urged his suit with so much earnestness that the Shawnees relented and assured him that Johnston should instantly be delivered into his hands. This was accordingly done, without the slightest regard to the prisoner's inclination; and within an hour the whole party took leave of him, shaking him heartily by the hand and congratulating him upon his approaching happiness, telling him that there was a fine squaw waiting for him in the Wyandott town.

Johnston would have liked the adoption better without the appendage of the bride, but thinking that, if she were one of the furies, her society would be preferable to the stake and hot irons, he determined to make the best of his condition, and wear his shackles as easily as possible, until an opportunity offered of effecting his escape. His new master, after lingering around the late encampment, until late in the day, at length shouldered his wallet, and moved off by the same route which the Shawnees had taken. By noon, on the following day, they came up with them, when a curious scene ensued. As soon as the Shawnees had become sober, they repented their late liberality, and determined to reclaim their prisoner; the Mingo stoutly demurred, and a long argument took place, accompanied by animated gestures, and not a few oaths, on both sides. At length Messhawa put an end to the wrangling by seizing a horse by the halter and ordering Johnston instantly to mount. He then sprang upon another, and, applying the lash smartly to both horses, he quickly bore the prisoner beyond the sound of the Mingo's voice.

An hour's ride brought them to Upper Sandusky, where Messhawa dismounted, and awaited the arrival of Chickatommo. He soon appeared, accompanied by his party, and followed by the discontented Mingo. This man regarded Johnston, from time to time, with so earnest a countenance, and appeared so desirous of approaching him, that the later became alarmed, lest, in the rage of disappointment, he should inflict upon the prisoner the vengeance which he dared not indulge against the Shawnees. But his fears were quickly relieved. The Mingo dogged him so faithfully, that he at length came upon him while alone, and, approaching him with a good-natured smile, presented a small pamphlet, which Johnston had dropped on the preceding day. Having done this, he shook him by the hand, and immediately left the village.

At Sandusky, Johnston became acquainted with Mr. Duchouquet, a French trader, who had, for several years, resided among the Indians, and was extensively engaged in the fur trade. To him he recounted his adventures, and earnestly solicited his good offices in delivering him from the Indians. Duchouquet promptly assured him that every exertion should be used for that purpose, and lost no time in redeeming his pledge. That evening he spoke to Chickatommo, and offered a liberal ransom for the prisoner, but his efforts were fruitless. The Shawnee chief did not object to the price, but declared that no sum should induce them to give him up until they had first taken him to their towns. This answer was quickly reported to Johnston, and filled him with despair. But, as the Shawnee party were engaged in another drinking-bout, he entreated Duchouquet to seize the favorable moment, when their hearts were mellowed by rum, and repeat his offer. The Frenchman complied, and was again peremptorily refused. Johnston now desired him to inquire, of Chickatommo, the name of the town to which he was to be taken, and the fate which was in reserve for him, upon his arrival there.

To the first question, Chickatommo promptly replied that the prisoner was to be carried to the Miami villages; but to the second, he gave no satisfactory answer, being probably ignorant himself upon the subject. The mention of the Miami villages completely extinguished every spark of hope which still existed in Johnston's breast, as those towns had, heretofore, been the grave of every white prisoner who had visited them. He had also heard that the Indians carefully concealed from their victims the fate which awaited them, either from some instinctive feelings of compassion, or, more probably, from policy, in order to prevent the desperate efforts to escape, which were usual with prisoners who were informed of their destiny. Under these circumstances, he gloomily abandoned himself to despair, and lay down in helpless expectation of his fate. But no sooner had he abandoned the case, than fortune, as usual, put in her oar, and displayed that capricious but omnipotent power for which she has so long and so deservedly been celebrated. The same Wyandott trader, who had encountered them in the wilderness, now again appeared at Sandusky, with several horses laden with kegs of rum, and, in the course of two days, completely stripped them of every skin, blanket, and article of merchandise which had escaped his rapacity before.

On the morning of the third day, Chickatommo and his party awoke, as from a dream, and found themselves poor, destitute, ragged, and hungry, without the means of supplying any of their wants. Ashamed to return to their village in this condition, after having sent before them so magnificent a description of their wealth, they determined to return to the Ohio, in hopes of again replenishing their purses, at the expense of emigrants. They accordingly appeared, of their own accord, before Duchouquet, and declared that, as the scalp of their prisoner would be transported more easily than his person, they had determined to burn him on that evening; but, if he still wished to purchase him, they would forego the expected entertainment for his sake, and let him have the prisoner upon good terms. Duchouquet eagerly accepted the offer, and instantly counted down six hundred silver brooches, the ordinary price of a prisoner. The Indians lost no time in delivering him into the trader's hands, and, having taken an affectionate leave of him, they instantly set out for the Ohio.

Johnston's gratification may easily be conceived, but on the following day his apprehensions returned with renewed vigor. To his great surprise, Chickatommo and his party again made their appearance at Sandusky, having abandoned their contemplated trip to the Ohio, and loitered about the village for several days, without any visible cause for such capricious conduct. Johnston, recollecting their former whimsical bargain with the Mingo, was apprehensive that the same scene was to be repeated, and, resolving not to be taken alive, he armed himself, and awaited, calmly, their determination. His suspicions, however, were entirely groundless. They passed him several times without the slightest notice, and at length set off, in earnest, for Detroit, leaving him at full liberty with his friend Duchouquet.

On the evening of their departure, a Delaware arrived from the Miami villages, with the heart-rending intelligence, that his unfortunate companion, Flinn, had been burned at the stake a few days before. The savage declared that he himself had been present at the spectacle, had assisted in torturing him, and had afterward eaten a portion of his flesh, which, he declared, "was sweeter than bear's meat." The intelligence was fully confirmed on the following day, by a Canadian trader, who had just left the Miami towns. He stated that Flinn had been taken to their villages, and, at first, had entertained strong hopes of being adopted, as his bold, frank, and fearless character had made considerable impression upon his enemies. But the arrival of some wild chiefs, from the extreme northern tribes, most of whom were cannibals, had completely changed his prospects. A wild council was held, in which the most terrible sentiments, with regard

to the whites, were uttered. The custom of adopting prisoners was indignantly reprobated as frivolous and absurd, and the resolution proclaimed, that henceforth no quarter should be given, to any age, sex or condition.
Flinn was accordingly seized and fastened to the stake. The trader was one of the spectators. Flinn quickly observed him, and asked if he was not ashamed to witness the distress of a fellow-creature, in that manner, without making some effort to relieve him; upon which he instantly ran to the village and brought out several kegs of rum, which he offered, as a ransom, for the prisoner. The Indians, who, by this time, were in a terrible rage, rejected the offer with fierceness, and split the heads of the kegs with their tomahawks, suffering the liquor to flow unheeded upon the ground. The disappointed trader again returned to the village, and brought out six hundred silver brooches. They, in turn, were rejected with additional fury, and not without a threat of treating him in the same manner if he again interfered. The trader, finding every effort vain, communicated his ill success to Flinn, who heard him with composure, and barely replied, "Then all I have to say is, *God have mercy upon my soul!*"

The scene of torture then commenced, amid whoops and yells, which struck terror to the heart of the trader, but which the prisoner bore with the most heroic fortitude. Not a groan escaped him. He walked calmly around the stake for several hours, until his flesh was roasted, and the fire had burned down. An old squaw then approached, in order to rekindle it, but Flinn, watching his opportunity, gave her so furious a kick in the breast that she fell back totally insensible, and for several minutes she was unable to take any further share in the ceremony. The warriors then bored his ankles, and passing thongs through the sinews, confined them closely to the stake, so that he was unable afterward to offer the same resistance. His sufferings continued for many hours, until they were at length terminated by the tomahawk.

Within a few days he also heard of Skyles. After leaving Johnston, this gentleman had been conducted to one of the towns on the Miami of the lake, near the scene of Flinn's execution, where, as usual, he was compelled to run the gauntlet. The Indian boys were his chief tormentors. One of the little urchins displayed particular address and dexterity in his infernal art. He provided himself with a stout switch taken from a thorn-tree, upon which one of the largest thorns had been permitted to remain. As Skyles passed him, he drove the keen instrument up to the head in his naked back. The switch was rested from his grasp, and was borne by Skyles, sticking in his back, to the end of his painful career. He continued in the hands of the same crabbed master who had taken such pleasure in tormenting him upon the march through the wilderness; but had found means to make himself so acceptable to his squaw, that his time was rendered more agreeable than he could have anticipated.

He carried water for her, gathered her wood, and soothed her sullen temper by a thousand artifices, so that her husband, who stood in some awe of his helpmate, was compelled to abate somewhat of his churlishness. He at length reaped the fruit of his civility. The squaw returned one evening alone to the wigwam, and informed Skyles, in confidence, that his death had been determined on in council, and that the following day had been appointed for his execution. He at first doubted the truth of this startling intelligence, and retiring to rest as usual, feigned to be asleep, but listened attentively to the conversation of the old squaw with her daughter, a young girl of fifteen. His doubts were quickly dispelled. His approaching execution was the subject of conversation between them, and their language soon became warm. The old lady insisted upon it that he was a good man, and ought to be saved; while the girl exulted at the idea of witnessing his agonies, declaring repeatedly that the "white people were all devils," and ought to be put to death.

At length they ceased wrangling, and composed themselves to rest. Skyles then arose, took down his master's rifle, shot bag, and corn pouch, and, stepping lightly over the bodies of the family, quickly gained the wood, and bent his steps to the bank of the Miami River. Without an instant's delay, he plunged into the stream and swam to the opposite side. In doing so, however, he completely ruined his rifle, and was compelled to throw it away. Retaining the wallet of parched corn, he directed his steps to the southward, intending, if possible, to strike the settlements in Kentucky, but so poor a woodsman was he that, after a hard march of six hours, he again stumbled upon the Miami, within one hundred yards of the spot where he had crossed it before. While anxiously meditating upon the best means of avoiding the dangers which surrounded him, he heard the tinkle of a bell, within a few hundred yards of the spot where he stood, and directing his steps toward it, he saw a horse grazing quietly upon the rank grass of the bottom.

Instantly mounting him, he again attempted to move in a southern direction, but was compelled by the thickness of the wood, and the quantity of fallen timber, to change his course so frequently that he again became bewildered, and, abandoning his horse, determined to prosecute his journey on foot. Daylight found him in a deep forest, without a path to direct him, without the means of procuring food, and without the slightest knowledge of any of those signs by which an experienced woodsman is enabled to direct his course through a trackless wilderness with such unerring certainty. Fearful of stumbling unawares upon some Indian town, he lay concealed all day, and at night recommenced his journey. But fresh perplexities awaited him at every step. He was constantly encountering either a small village or a solitary wigwam, from which he was frequently chased by the Indian dogs with such loud and furious barking that he more than once considered detection inevitable.

In this manner he wandered through the woods for several days, until, faint with hunger, he determined at all risks to enter an Indian village, and either procure food or perish in the attempt. Having adopted this resolution, he no longer loitered on the way, but throwing himself boldly upon the first path which presented itself, he followed it at a brisk and steady pace, careless of where it might lead. About four o'clock in the afternoon, he came so suddenly upon a village that it was impossible to retreat without exposing himself to detection, and, as he considered it madness to enter it in daylight, he concealed himself among some old logs until nightfall, when he sallied out like an owl or a wolf in search of something to allay the piercing pangs of hunger. Nothing could be picked up upon the skirts of the village, as neither roasting-ears nor garden fruit were in season, and it became necessary to enter the town or perish of hunger.

Fortunately, the embers of a decayed fire lay near him, in which he found a sufficient quantity of coal with which to black his face and hands; and, having completely disguised himself in this manner, he boldly marched into the hostile town to take such fate as it should please heaven to send. He luckily had with him the remnant of a blanket, which he disposed about his person in the usual Indian manner, and imitating at the same time their straggling gait, he kept the middle of the street and passed unquestioned by squaw or warrior. Fortunately for him, the streets were almost entirely deserted, and, as he afterward learned, most of the warriors were absent. Security, however, was not his present object so much as food, which, indeed, had now become indispensable. Yet how was he to obtain it? He would not have hesitated to steal, had he known where to look for the larders; nor to beg, had he not known that he would have been greeted with the tomahawk.

While slowly marching through the village, and ruminating upon some feasible plan of satisfying his wants, he saw light in a wigwam at some distance, which gave it the appearance of a trader's booth. Cautiously approaching, he satisfied himself of the truth of his conjecture. A white man was behind a counter dealing out various articles to several squaws who stood around him. After some hesitation, Skyles entered the shop, and in bad English asked for rum. The trader regarded him carelessly, and without appearing surprised at either his dress or manner, replied that he had no rum in the house, but would go and bring him some, if he could wait a few moments. So saying, he leaped carelessly over the counter and left the shop. Skyles instantly followed him, and stopping him in the street, briefly recounted his story, and throwing himself upon his mercy, earnestly implored his assistance.

The trader appeared much astonished, and visibly hesitated. Quickly recovering himself, however, he assured Skyles that he would use every effort to save him, although in doing so he himself would incur great risk. He then informed him that a band of Shawnees had appeared at the village on that very morning in keen pursuit of a prisoner, who (they said) had escaped a few days before, and whom they supposed to be still in the neighborhood, from the zigzag manner in which he had traveled. Many of the warriors of the town were at that moment assisting the Shawnees in hunting for him. He added that they might be expected to return in the morning, in which case, if discovered, his death would be certain. Skyles listened in great alarm to his account of the danger which surrounded him. If he left the village, he could scarcely expect to escape the numerous bands who were ranging the forest in search of him. If he remained where he was, the danger was still more imminent.

Under these circumstances, he earnestly requested the advice of the trader as to the best means of avoiding his enemies. The man replied that he must instantly leave the village, as keen eyes would be upon him in the morning, and his design would be penetrated; that he must conceal himself in a hazel thicket, which he pointed out to him, where in a short time he would join him with food, and where they could arrange some feasible plan of escape. They then separated, the trader returning to his shop, and Skyles repairing to the friendly thicket. Here within a few minutes he was joined by his friend, who informed him that he saw but one possible mode of escape; that it would be impossible for him either to remain where he was, or to attempt to reach the white settlements through the woods; but he declared that if he was diligent and active, he might overtake a boat which had left them that morning for Lake Erie, and offered him his own skiff for that purpose.

He added that the boat was laden with furs, and was commanded by an English captain, who would gladly receive him on board. Skyles eagerly embraced the offer, and they proceeded without a moment's delay to the river shore, where a handsome skiff with two oars lay in readiness for the water. Having taken an affectionate leave of the trader, Skyles put off from shore, and quickly gaining the current, rowed until daylight with the zeal of a man who knew the value of life and liberty. His greatest apprehension was that his flight would be discovered in time to prevent his reaching the boat; and at every rustling of the bushes on the bank of the river, or at every cry of the owl wh'ch arose from the deep forest around him, the blood would rush back to his heart, and he would fancy that his enemies were upon him. At length, between dawn and sunrise, he beheld the boat, which he had pursued so eagerly, only a few hundred yards in front, drifting slowly and calmly down the stream.

He redoubled his exertions, and in half an hour was within hailing distance. He called aloud for them to halt, but no answer was returned. Upon coming alongside he was unable to see a single man on board. Supposing her crew asleep, he mounted the side of the vessel, and saw the man at the helm enjoying a very comfortable nap with the most enviable disregard to the dangers which might await him in the waters of Lake Erie, which were then in sight. The helmsman started up, rubbed his eyes, looked around him, and after saluting his visitor, observed that "he had almost fallen asleep." Skyles agreed with him, and anxiously inquired for the captain. The latter soon made his appearance in a woolen nightcap, and the negotiation commenced. The captain asked who he was, and what was the cause of so early a visit? Skyles was fearful of committing himself by a premature disclosure of his real character, and replied, that he was an adventurer who had been looking for land upon the Auglaize; but that he had been driven from the country by the apprehension of outrage from the Indians, who had lately become unusually incensed against the whites.

The captain coolly replied that he had heard of one white man having been burned a few days before at one of the Miami villages, and had understood that another had avoided the same fate only by running away into the woods, where, unless retaken, it was supposed he would perish, as he had shown himself a miserable woodsman, and as numerous parties were in search of him. After a moment's hesitation, Skyles frankly acknowledged himself to be that miserable fugitive, and threw himself at once upon their mercy. The English captain heard him apparently without surprise, and granted his request without hesitation. All was done with the utmost *sang froid*. In a short time they arrived at Detroit, where, to his no small astonishment, he beheld Chickatommo, Messhawa, and their party, who had just arrived from Sandusky, after the sale of Johnston. Carefully avoiding them, he lay close in the house of a trader until the following day, when another large party arrived in pursuit of him (having traced him down the river to Lake Erie), and paraded the streets for several days, uttering loud complaints against those who had robbed them of their prisoner. Poor Skyles entertained the most painful apprehensions for several days, but was at length relieved by their departure. As soon as possible, he obtained a passage to Montreal, and returned in safety to the United States.

In noticing the fate of the companions of Johnston's captivity, we are naturally led to say something of the only female of the party. The reader can not have forgotten that one of the Miss Flemings was killed upon the Ohio, and that the other became a prisoner and was assigned to the Cherokees. Johnston had been much surprised at the levity of her conduct, when first taken. Instead of appearing dejected at the dreadful death of her sister, and the still more terrible fate of her friends, she never appeared more lively or better reconciled to her fate than while her captors lingered upon the banks of the Ohio. Upon the breaking up of the party, the Cherokees conducted their prisoner toward the Miami villages, and Johnston saw nothing more of her until after his own liberation. While he remained at the house of Mr. Duchouquet, the small party of Cherokees to whom she belonged, suddenly made their appearance in the village, in a condition so tattered and dilapidated as to satisfy every one that all their booty had been wasted with their usual improvidence.

Miss Fleming's appearance, particularly, had been entirely changed. All the levity which had astonished Johnston so much on the banks of the Ohio, was completely gone. Her dress was tattered, her cheeks sunken, her eyes discolored by weeping, and her whole manner expressive of the most heartfelt wretchedness. Johnston addressed her with kindness, and inquired the cause of so great a change, but she only replied by wringing her hands, and bursting into tears. Her master quickly summoned her away, and on the morning after her arrival, she was compelled to leave the village, and accompany them to Lower Sandusky. Within a few days, Johnston, in company with his friend Duchouquet, followed them to that place, partly upon business, partly with the hope of procuring her liberation. He found the town thronged with Indians of various tribes, and there, for the first time, he learned that his friend Skyles had effected his escape. Upon inquiring for the Cherokees, he learned that they were encamped with their prisoner within a quarter of a mile of the town, holding themselves aloof from the rest, and evincing the most jealous watchfulness over their prisoner.

Johnston instantly applied to the traders of Sandusky for their good offices, and, as usual, the request was promptly complied with. They went out in a body to the Cherokee camp, accompanied by a white man named Whittaker, who had been taken from Virginia when a child, and had become completely naturalized among the Indians. This Whittaker was personally known to Miss Fleming, having often visited Pittsburgh, where her father kept a small tavern, much frequented by Indians and traders. As soon as she beheld him, therefore, she ran up to the spot where he stood, and bursting into tears, implored him to save her from the cruel fate which she had no doubt awaited her. He engaged very zealously in her service, and finding that all the offers of the traders were rejected with determined obstinacy, he returned to Detroit, and solicited the intercession of an old chief known among the whites by the name of "Old King Crane," assuring him (a lie which we can scarcely blame) that the woman was his sister.

King Crane listened with gravity to the appeal of Whittaker, acknowledged the propriety of interfering in the case of so near a relative, and very calmly walked out to the Cherokee camp, in order to try the efficacy of his own eloquence in behalf of the white squaw. He found her master, however, perfectly inexorable. The argument gradually waxed warm, until at length the Cherokees became enraged, and told the old man that it was a disgrace to a chief like him to put himself upon a level with "white people," and that they looked upon him as no better than "dirt." At this insupportable insult, King Crane became exasperated in turn, and a very edifying scene ensued, in which each bespattered the other with a profusion of abuse for several minutes, until the Old King recollected himself sufficiently to draw off for the present, and concert measures for obtaining redress. He returned to the village in a towering passion, and announced his determination to collect his young men and rescue the white squaw by force; and if the Cherokees dared to resist, he swore that he would take their scalps upon the spot.

Whittaker applauded this doughty resolution, but warned him of the necessity of dispatch, as the Cherokees, alarmed at the idea of losing their prisoner, might be tempted to put her to death without further delay. This advice was acknowledged to be of weight, and before daylight on the following morning, King Crane assembled his young men and advanced cautiously upon the Cherokee encampment. He found all but the miserable prisoner buried in sleep. *She* had been stripped naked, her body painted black, and in this condition had been bound to a stake, around which hickory poles had already been collected, and every other disposition made for burning her alive at daylight. She was moaning in a low tone as her deliverers approached, and was so much exhausted as not to be aware of their approach until King Crane had actually cut the cords which bound her, with his knife. He then ordered his young men to assist her in putting on her clothes, which they obeyed with the most stoical indifference.

As soon as her toilet had been completed, the King awakened her masters, and informed them that the squaw was *his!* that if they submitted quietly, it was well—if not, his young men and himself were ready for them. The Cherokees, as may readily be imagined, protested loudly against such unrighteous proceedings, but what could words avail against drawn tomahawks and superior numbers? They finally expressed their willingness to resign the squaw, but hoped that King Crane would not be such a "beast" as to refuse them the ransom which he had offered them on the preceding day. The king replied coolly, that he had the squaw now in his own hands, and would serve them only right if he refused to pay a single brooch; but that he disdained to receive any thing at their hands without paying an equivalent, and would give them six hundred silver brooches. He then returned to Lower Sandusky, accompanied by the liberated prisoner. She was instantly painted as a squaw by Whittaker, and sent off under care of two trusty Indians to Pittsburgh, where she arrived in safety in the course of the following week.

The Cherokees, in the evening, paraded the streets of Sandusky, armed and painted, as if upon a war party, and loudly complained of the violence which had been offered to them. They declared that they would not leave town until they had shed the blood of a white man, in revenge for the loss of their prisoner. Johnston and Duchouquet were compelled to remain closely at home for several days, until, to their great joy, the Cherokees finally left the village and were seen no more.

The remainder of Johnston's narrative is easily dispatched. He soon after left Lower Sandusky, and embarked in a boat laden with fur for Detroit. After remaining here a few days he took passage to Montreal, and for the first and last time had an opportunity of beholding the tremendous Falls of Niagara.* Having arrived at Montreal in safety, he remained a few days in order to arrange his affairs, and as soon as possible continued his journey by way of Fort Stanwix to New York. There he had an interview with President Washington, who, having been informed of his escape, sent for him, in order to make a number of inquiries as to the strength of the tribes through which he had passed, the force and condition of the British garrisons, and the degree of countenance which they had afforded to the hostile Indians. Having given all the information of which he was possessed, he was dismissed with great kindness, and in the course of the following week he found himself once more in the bosom of his family.

As the reader may probably take some interest in the fate of the Indians whom we have mentioned, we are enabled to add something upon that subject. Chickatommo was killed at the decisive battle of the "Fallen Timber," where the united force of the North-western tribes was defeated by General Wayne. Messhawa fought at the same place, but escaped, and afterward became a devoted follower of the celebrated Tecumseh. He fought at Tippecanoe, Raisin, and finally at the River Thames, where it is supposed he was killed. King Crane lived to a great age, was present at St. Clair's defeat, and at the "Fallen Timber," but finally became reconciled to the Americans, and fought under Harrison at Thames. Whittaker, the white man, was in St. Clair's defeat, and afterward with the Indians against Wayne. He has been dead many years. Tom Lewis fought against the Americans in all the north-western battles, until the final peace in 1796, and

---

* This was an Iroquois word, and in their language signifies "The Thunder of the Waters." It is pronounced O-ni-aa-gaa-ra.

then was one of the deputation who came on to Washington City, where Johnston saw him in 1797. He afterward rose to the rank of chief among the Shawnees, but having an incurable propensity to rum and thieving, he was degraded from his rank, and removed, with a band of his countrymen, to the country west of the Mississippi.

CHAPTER XI.

IN the year 1791, while the Indians were yet troublesome, especially on the banks of the Ohio, Captain WILLIAM HUBBELL, who had previously emigrated to Kentucky from the State of Vermont, and who, after having fixed his family in the neighborhood of Frankfort, then a frontier settlement, had been compelled to go to the eastward on business, was a second time on his way to this country. On one of the tributary streams of the river Monongahela, he procured a flat-bottomed boat, and embarked, in company with Mr. Daniel Light and Mr. William Plascut and his family, consisting of a wife and eight children, destined for Limestone, Kentucky. On their progress down the river Ohio, and soon after passing Pittsburgh, they saw evident traces of Indians along the banks, and there is every reason to believe that a boat which they overtook, and which through carelessness was suffered to run aground on an island, became a prey to these merciless savages.

Though Captain Hubbell and his party stopped some time for it in a lower part of the river, it did not arrive, and it has never, to their knowledge, been heard of since. Before they reached the mouth of the Great Kenawha, they had, by several successive additions, increased their number to twenty, consisting of nine men, three women, and eight children. The men, besides those mentioned above, were one John Stoner, an Irishman and a Dutchman whose names are not recollected, Messrs. Ray and Tucker, and a Mr. Kilpatrick, whose two daughters also were of the party. Information received at Gallipolis confirmed the expectation which appearances previously raised, of a serious conflict with a large body of Indians, and, as Captain Hubbell had been regularly appointed commander of the boat, every possible preparation was made for a formidable and successful resistance of the anticipated attack.

The nine men were divided into three watches for the night, which were alternately to continue awake and be on the lookout for two hours at a time. The arms on board, which consisted principally of old muskets much out of order, were collected, loaded, and put in the best possible condition for service. At about sunset on that day (the twenty-third day of March, 1791), our party overtook a fleet of six boats descending the river in company, and intended to have continued with them; but, as their passengers seemed to be more disposed to dancing than fighting, and as, soon after dark, notwithstanding the remonstrances of Captain Hubbell, they commenced fiddling and dancing instead of preparing their arms and taking the necessary rest preparatory to battle, it was wisely considered more hazardous to be in such company than to be alone.

It was therefore determined to proceed rapidly forward by aid of the oars, and to leave those thoughtless fellow-travelers behind. One of the boats, however, belonging to the fleet, commanded by a Captain Greathouse, adopted the same plan, and for awhile kept up with Captain Hubbell; but, all its crew at length falling asleep, that boat also ceased to be propelled by the oars, and Captain Hubbell and his party proceeded steadily forward *alone*. Early in the night a canoe was dimly seen floating down the river, in which were probably Indians reconnoitering, and other evident indications were observed of the neighborhood and hostile intentions of a formidable party of savages.

It was now agreed that should the attack, as was probable, be deferred till morning, every man should be up before the dawn, in order to make as great a show as possible of numbers and of strength; and that, whenever the action should take place, the women and children should lie down on the cabin floor, and be protected as well as they could by the trunks and other baggage which might be placed around them. In this perilous situation they continued during the night, and the captain, who had not slept more than one hour since he left Pittsburgh, was too deeply impressed with the imminent danger which surrounded him to obtain any rest at that time.

Just as daylight began to appear in the east, and before the men were up and at their posts agreeably to arrangement, a voice at some distance below them in a plaintive tone repeatedly solicited them to come on shore, as there were some white persons who wished to obtain a passage in their boat. This the captain very naturally and correctly concluded to be an Indian artifice, and its only effect was to rouse the men and place every one on his guard. The voice of entreaty was soon changed into the language of indignation and insult, and the sound of distant paddles announced the approach of the savage foe. At length three Indian canoes were seen through the mist of the morning rapidly advancing. With the utmost coolness the captain and his companions prepared to receive them. The chairs, tables, and other incumbrances were thrown into the river, in order to clear the deck for action.

Every man took his position, and was ordered not to fire till the savages had approached so near that (to use the words of Captain Hubbell) "the flash from the guns might singe their eyebrows," and a special caution was given that the men should fire successively, so that there might be no interval. On the arrival of the canoes, they were found to contain about twenty-five or thirty Indians each. As soon as they had approached within the reach of musket-shot, a general fire was given from one of them, which wounded Mr. Tucker through the hip so severely that his leg hung only by the flesh, and shot Mr. Light just below the ribs. The three canoes placed themselves at the bow, stern, and on the right side of the boat, so that they had an opportunity of raking in every direction. The fire now commenced from the boat, and had a powerful effect in checking the confidence and fury of the Indians.

The captain, after firing his own gun, took up that of one of the wounded men, raised it to his shoulder, and was about to discharge it, when a ball came and took away the lock. He coolly turned round, seized a brand of fire from the kettle which served for a caboose, and, applying it to the pan, discharged the piece with effect. A very regular and constant fire was now kept up on both sides. The captain was just in the act of raising his gun a third time, when a ball passed through his right arm, and for a moment disabled him. Scarcely had he recovered from the shock and re-acquired the use of his hand, which had been suddenly *drawn up* by the wound, when he observed the Indians in one of the canoes just about to board the boat in its bow, where the horses were placed belonging to the party. So near had they approached, that some of them had actually seized with their hands the side of the boat.

Severely wounded as he was, he caught up a pair of horsemen's pistols, and rushed forward to repel the attempt at boarding. On his approach the Indians fell back, and he discharged a pistol with effect at the foremost man. After firing the second pistol he found himself without arms, and was compelled to retreat; but, stepping back upon a pile of small wood which had been prepared for burning in the kettle, the thought struck him that it might be made use of in repelling the foe, and he continued for some time to strike them with it so forcibly and actively, that they were unable to enter the boat; and at length he wounded one of them so severely, that with a yell they suddenly gave way. All the canoes instantly discontinued the contest, and directed their course to Captain Greathouse's boat, which was then in sight. Here a striking contrast was exhibited to the firmness and intrepidity which had been displayed.

Instead of resisting the attack, the people on board of this boat retired to the cabin in dismay. The Indians entered it without opposition and rowed it to the shore, where they instantly killed the captain and a lad of about fourteen years of age. The women they placed in the center of their canoes, and, manning them with fresh hands, again pursued Captain Hubbell and party. A melancholy alternative now presented itself to these brave but almost desponding men—either to fall a prey to the savages themselves, or to run the risk of shooting the women, who had been placed in the canoes in the hope of deriving protection from their presence. But "self-preservation is the first law of nature," and the captain very justly remarked there would not be much humanity in preserving their lives at such a sacrifice, merely that they might become victims of savage cruelty at some subsequent period.

There were now but four men left on board of Captain Hubbell's boat capable of defending it, and the captain himself was severely wounded in two places. The second attack, however, was resisted with almost incredible firmness and vigor. Whenever the Indians would rise to fire, their opponents would commonly give them the first shot, which in almost every instance would prove fatal. Notwithstanding the disparity of numbers, and the exhausted condition of the defenders of the boat, the Indians at length appeared to despair of success, and the canoes successively retired to the shore. Just as the last one was departing, Captain Hubbell called to the Indian who was standing in the stern, and, on his turning round, discharged his piece at him. When the smoke, which for a moment obstructed the vision, was dissipated, he was seen lying on his back, and appeared to be severely, perhaps mortally, wounded.

Unfortunately, the boat now drifted near to the shore where the Indians were collected, and a large concourse, probably between four and five hundred, were seen rushing down on the bank. Ray and Plascut, the only men remaining unhurt, were placed at the oars, and, as the boat was not more than twenty yards from shore, it was deemed prudent for all to lie down in as safe a position as possible, and attempt to push forward with the utmost practicable rapidity. While they continued in this situation, nine balls were shot into one oar, and ten into the other, without wounding the rowers, who were hidden from view and protected by the side of the boat and the blankets in its stern. During this dreadful exposure to the fire of the savages, which continued about twenty minutes, Mr. Kilpatrick observed a particular Indian, whom he thought a favorable mark for his rifle, and, notwithstanding the solemn warning of Captain Hubbell, rose to shoot him. He immediately received a ball in his mouth, which passed out at the back part of his head, and was almost at the same moment shot through the heart. He fell among the horses that about the same time were killed, and presented to his afflicted daughters and fellow-travelers, who were witnesses of the awful occurrence, a spectacle of horror which we need not further attempt to describe.

The boat was now providentially and suddenly carried out into the middle of the stream, and taken by the current beyond the reach of the enemy's balls. Our little band, reduced as they were in numbers, wounded, afflicted, and almost exhausted by fatigue, were still unsubdued in spirit, and being assembled in all their strength—men, women, and children—with an appearance of triumph gave three hearty cheers, calling to the Indians to come on again if they were fond of the sport.

Thus ended this awful conflict, in which, out of nine men, two only escaped unhurt. Tucker and Kilpatrick were killed on the spot, Stoner was mortally wounded and died on his arrival at Limestone, and all the rest, excepting Ray and Plascut, were severely wounded. The women and children were all uninjured, excepting a little son of Mr. Plascut, who, after the battle was over, came to the captain and with great coolness requested him to take a ball out of his head. On examination, it appeared that a bullet which had passed through the side of the boat, had penetrated the forehead of this little hero, and remained under the skin. The captain took it out, and the youth, observing, "*That is not all,*" raised his arm, and exhibited a piece of bone at the point of his elbow, which had been shot off and hung only by the skin. His mother exclaimed, "Why did you not tell me of this?" "Because," he coolly replied, "the captain directed us to be silent during the action, and I thought you would be likely to make a noise if I told you."

The boat made the best of its way down the river, and the object was to reach Limestone that night. The captain's arm had bled profusely, and he was compelled to close the sleeve of his coat in order to retain the blood and stop its effusion. In this situation, tormented by excruciating pain and faint through loss of blood, he was under the necessity of steering the boat with his left arm, till about ten o'clock that night, when he was relieved by Mr. William Brooks, who resided on the bank of the river, and who was induced by the calls of the suffering party to come out to their assistance. By his aid and that of some other persons who were in the same manner brought to their relief, they were enabled to reach Limestone about twelve o'clock that night.

Immediately on the arrival of Mr. Brooks, Captain Hubbell, relieved from labor and responsibility, sunk under the weight of pain and fatigue, and became for a while totally insensible. When the boat reached Limestone, he found himself unable to walk, and was obliged to be carried up to the tavern. Here he had his wound dressed and continued several days, until he acquired sufficient strength to proceed homeward.

On the arrival of our party at Limestone, they found a considerable force of armed men, about to march against the same Indians from whose attacks they had so severely suffered. They now learned that, the Sunday preceding, the same party of savages had cut off a detachment of men ascending the Ohio from Fort Washington, at the mouth of Licking River, and had killed with their tomahawks, without firing a gun, twenty-one out of twenty-two men, of which the detachment consisted.

Crowds of people, as might be expected, came to witness the boat which had been the scene of so much heroism, and such horrid carnage, and to visit the resolute little band by whom it had been so gallantly and perseveringly defended. On examination, it was found that the sides of the boat were literally filled with bullets and with bullet holes. There was scarcely a space of two feet square in the part above water, which had not either a ball remaining in it or a hole through which a ball had passed. Some persons, who had the curiosity to count the number of holes in the blankets which were hung up as curtains in the stern of the boat, affirmed that in the space of five feet square there were one hundred and twenty-two. Four horses out of five were killed, and the escape of the fifth amidst such a shower of balls appears almost miraculous.

The day after the arrival of Captain Hubbell and his companions, the five remaining boats, which they had passed on the night preceding the battle, reached Limestone. Those on board remarked, that during the action they distinctly saw the flashes, but could not hear the reports of the guns. The Indians, it appears, had met with too formidable a resistance from a single boat to attack a fleet, and suffered them to pass unmolested; and since that time, it is believed that no boat has been assailed by Indians on the Ohio.

The force which marched out to disperse this formidable body of savages, discovered several Indians dead on the shore near the scene of action. They also found the bodies of Captain Greathouse and several others, men, women, and children, who had been on board of his boat. Most of them appeared to have been *whipped to death*, as they were found stripped, tied to trees, and marked with the appearance of lashes, and large rods which seemed to have been worn with use were observed lying near them.

CHAPTER XII.

HERETOFORE our narrative has chiefly been confined to the adventures of individuals, or, at most, to the irregular *forays* of independent volunteers. We come now, however, to events upon a large scale, and to a detail of national, not individual efforts. Before entering, however, upon such a brief notice as our limits will permit, of the events of the North-western campaign, it will be necessary to premise a few observations upon the causes of the long-continued warfare to which the Western States were exposed, while those upon the borders of the Atlantic enjoyed all the blessings of peace.

At the general pacification of 1783, there were several stipulations upon both sides, which were not complied with. Great Britain had agreed, as speedily as possible, to evacuate all the North-western posts which lay within the boundaries of the United States; while, on the other hand, Congress had stipulated that no *legal* impediments should be thrown in the way, in order to prevent the collection of debts due to British merchants before the declaration of war. Large importations had been made by American merchants, upon *credit*, in 1773 and 1774; and as all civil intercourse between the two countries had ceased until the return of peace, the British creditors were unable to collect their debts. Upon the final ratification of the treaty, they naturally became desirous of recovering their property, while their debtors as naturally were desirous of avoiding payment.

Congress had stipulated that no legal barrier should be thrown in the way; but, as is well known, Congress, under the old confederation, was much more prolific in

"Resolutions," or rather "Recommendations," than acts. The States might or might not comply with them, as suited their convenience. Accordingly, when Congress recommended the payment of all debts to the State Legislatures, the Legislatures determined that it was inexpedient to comply. The British creditor complained to his Government; the Government remonstrated with Congress upon so flagrant a breach of one of the articles of pacification; Congress appealed to the Legislatures; the Legislatures were deaf and obstinate, and there the matter rested. When the question was agitated as to the evacuation of the posts, the British, in turn, became refractory, and determined to hold them until the acts of the State Legislatures, preventing the legal collection of debts, were repealed. Many remonstrances were exchanged, but all to no purpose.

In the meantime, the Indians were supplied, as usual, by the British agents, and if not openly encouraged, were undoubtedly secretly countenanced, in their repeated depredations upon the frontier inhabitants. These, at length, became so serious, as to demand the notice of Government. Accordingly, in the autumn of 1790, General Harmer was detached at the head of three hundred regular troops, and more than one thousand militia, with orders to march upon their towns bordering upon the lakes, and inflict upon them such signal chastisement as should deter them from future depredations. On the twentieth of September, the various troops designed for the expedition rendezvoused at Fort Washington, now Cincinnati, and on the following day commenced their march to the Miami villages. The country was rough, swampy, and in many places almost impassable, so that seventeen days were consumed before the main body could come within striking distance of the enemy. In the meantime, the great scarcity of provisions rendered it necessary for the general to sweep the forest with numerous small detachments, and as the woods swarmed with roving bands of Indians, most of these parties were cut off.

At length, the main body, considerably reduced by this petty warfare, came within a few miles of their towns. Here the general ordered Captain Armstrong, at the head of thirty regulars, and Colonel Hardin, of Kentucky, with one hundred and fifty militia, to advance and reconnoiter. In the execution of this order they suddenly found themselves in the presence of a superior number of Indians, who suddenly arose from the bushes and opened a heavy fire upon them. The militia instantly gave way; while the regulars, accustomed to more orderly movements, attempted a regular retreat. The enemy rushed upon them, tomahawk in hand, and completely surrounded them. The regulars attempted to open a passage with the bayonet, but in vain. They were all destroyed, with the exception of their captain and one lieutenant.

Captain Armstrong was remarkably stout and active, and succeeded in breaking through the enemy's line, although not without receiving several severe wounds. Finding himself hard pressed, he plunged into a deep and miry swamp, where he lay concealed during the whole night, within two hundred yards of the Indian camp, and witnessed the dances and joyous festivity with which they celebrated their victory. The lieutenant (Hartshorn) escaped by accidentally stumbling over a log and falling into a pit, where he lay concealed by the rank grass which grew around him. The loss of the militia was very trifling. Notwithstanding this severe check, Harmer advanced with the main body upon their villages, which he found deserted and in flames, the Indians having fired them with their own hands. Here he found several hundred acres of corn, which was completely destroyed. He then advanced upon the adjoining villages, which he found deserted and burned as the first had been. Having destroyed all the corn which he found, the army commenced its retreat from the Indian country, supposing the enemy sufficiently intimidated.

After marching about ten miles on the homeward route, General Harmer received information which induced him to suppose that a body of Indians had returned and taken possession of the village which he had just left. He detached, therefore, eighty regular troops under the orders of Major Wyllys, and nearly the whole of his militia, under Colonel Hardin, with orders to return to the village and destroy such of the enemy as presented themselves. The detachment accordingly countermarched and proceeded, with all possible dispatch, to the appointed spot, fearful only that the enemy might hear of their movement and escape before they could come up. The militia, in loose order, took the advance; the regulars, moving in a hollow square, brought up the rear. Upon the plain in front of the town, a number of Indians were seen, between whom and the militia a sharp action commenced. After a few rounds, with considerable effect upon both sides, the savages fled in disorder, and were eagerly and impetuously pursued by the militia, who, in the ardor of the chase, were drawn into the woods to a considerable distance from the regulars.

Suddenly, from the opposite quarter several hundred Indians appeared, rushing with loud yells upon the unsupported regulars. Major Wyllys, who was a brave and experienced officer, formed his men in a square, and endeavored to gain a more favorable spot of ground, but was prevented by the desperate impetuosity with which the enemy assailed him. Unchecked by the murderous fire which was poured upon them from the diff·rent sides of the square, they rushed in masses up to the points of the bayonets, hurled their tomahawks with fatal accuracy, and putting aside the bayonets with their hands, or clogging them with their bodies, they were quickly mingled with the troops, and handled their long knives with destructive effect. In two minutes the bloody struggle was over. Major Wyllys fell, together with seventy-three privates and one lieutenant. One captain, one ensign, and seven privates—three of whom were wounded—were the sole survivors of this short but desperate encounter.

The Indian loss was nearly equal, as they sustained several heavy fires which the closeness of their masses rendered very destructive, and as they rushed upon the bayonets of the troops with the most astonishing disregard to their own safety. Their object was to overwhelm the regulars before the militia could return to their support, and it was as boldly executed as it had been finely conceived. In a short time the militia returned from the pursuit of the flying party, which had decoyed them to a distance; but it was now too late to retrieve the fortune of the day. After some sharp skirmishing, they effected their retreat to the main body, with the loss of one hundred and eight killed and twenty-eight wounded. This dreadful slaughter so reduced the strength and spirits of Harmer's army that he was happy in being permitted to retreat unmolested, having totally failed in accomplishing the objects of the expedition, and by obstinately persevering in the ruinous plan of acting in detachments, having thrown away the lives of more than half of his regular force. This abortive expedition served only to encourage the enemy and to give additional rancor to their incursions.

Before detailing the important events which followed, however, we shall pause for a few moments to dwell upon the singular adventure of an individual who attended Harmer in his expedition. JACKSON JOHONNET was born in Connecticut in May, 1774. His father was a farmer, and managed, upon a very small and by no means fertile farm, to bring up a large family with credit and decency. Jackson, the eldest son, at the age of sixteen, became desirous of engaging in some business upon his own account; and, as his father could well spare his labor upon the farm, he took leave of his family in the spring of 1790, and embarked on board of a coasting schooner for Boston. Having arrived in this large city, and for the first time in his life finding himself without friends, money, or employment of any kind, he began to entertain some uncomfortable apprehensions of want. After wandering through the streets for several days with a very disconsolate air, he was at length accosted by a dexterous recruiting officer, who, seeing him to be a perfect greenhorn, determined to enlist him if he could.

Accosting him with great frankness, he soon became acquainted with his real condition, and after some preliminary observations upon the gayety, recklessness, and happiness of a soldier's life, he proposed that he should enlist in his company and march out to the West, assuring him that if he was active and diligent he would make an immense fortune in one year. Jackson at first shrunk from the idea of "enlisting;" but his imagination became gradually heated at the glowing description of the fertility of the Western country, and the facility with which land could be acquired to any extent by a successful soldier. He finally promised him a sergeant's commission on the spot, and held out to him the prospect of a lieutenancy in case of good behavior. Jackson at length yielded to the eloquence of this modern Kite, and in a few days found himself on the road to Pittsburgh, and highly charmed with his martial appearance when arrayed in the uniform of his corps.

Embarking on board of a flat-boat at Pittsburgh, he descended the Ohio as far as Fort Washington (Cincinnati), where he found his regiment preparing to accompany Harmer. A few days after his arrival, the march commenced. Here he, for the first time, awoke from the pleasant dream in which he had indulged. He had thought that war was a succession of battles and triumphs, leading naturally to wealth and glory. Splendid uniforms, gay music, waving plumes, and showy parades had floated in splendid confusion before his fancy, until the march commenced. He now found that war was made up of dreadful fatigue, constant exposure to all weather, hard words and harder blows from his superiors, and the whole crowned by the constant gnawings of hunger without the means of satisfying it.

On the tenth day of their march (having been promoted to the rank of sergeant), he was detached upon an exploring expedition, at the head of ten regular soldiers. Being all equally ignorant of Indian warfare, they were quickly decoyed into an ambuscade and made prisoners by a party of Kickapoo Indians. Having been bound and secured in the usual manner, they were driven before their captors like a herd of bullocks, and, with scarcely a morsel of food, were forced to make the most exhaustive marches in the direction of the Kickapoo village. On the second day, George Aikins, one of his companions, a native of Ireland, was unable to endure his sufferings any longer, and sunk under his pack in the middle of the path. They instantly scalped him as he lay, and, stripping him naked, pricked him with their knives in the most sensitive parts of the body until they had aroused him to a consciousness of his situation, when they tortured him to death in the usual manner.

The march then recommenced, and the wretched prisoners, faint and famished as they were, were so shocked at the fate of their companion, that they bore up for eight days under all their sufferings. On the ninth, however, they reached a small village, where crowds of both sexes came out to meet them, with shrieks and yells which filled them with terror. Here they were compelled, as usual, to run the gauntlet, and as they were much worn down by hunger and fatigue, four of the party, viz: Durgee, Forsythe, Deloy, and Benton, all of New England, were unable to reach the council-house, but fainted in the midst of the course. The boys and squaws instantly fell upon them, and put them to death by torture.

Here they remained in close confinement, and upon very scanty diet, for several days, in the course of which the news of Harmer's defeat arrived. Piles of scalps, together with canteens, sashes, military hats, etc., were brought into the village, and several white women and children were taken through the town on their way to the villages farther west. At the same time, four more of his companions were led off to the western villages, and never heard of afterward. Himself and a corporal, named Sackville, were now the only survivors. They remained in close confinement two weeks longer. Their rations were barely sufficient to sustain life, and upon the receipt of any unpleasant intelligence, they were taken out, whipped severely, and compelled to run the gauntlet.

At length, on the fourteenth night of their confinement, they determined to make an effort to escape. Sackville had concealed a sharp penknife in a secret pocket, which the Indians had been unable to discover. They were guarded by four warriors and one old hag of seventy, whose temper was as crooked as her person. The prisoners having been securely bound, the warriors lay down about midnight to sleep, ordering the old squaw to sit up during the rest of the night. Their guns stood in the corner of the hut, and their tomahawks, as usual, were attached to their sides. Their hopes of escape were founded upon the probability of eluding the vigilance of the hag, cutting their cords, and either avoiding or destroying their guard. The snoring of the warriors quickly announced them asleep, and the old squaw hung in a drowsy attitude over the fire. Sackville cautiously cut his own cords, and after a few minutes delay, succeeded in performing the same office for Jackson.

But their work was scarcely begun yet. It was absolutely necessary that the old squaw should fall asleep, or be *silenced in some other way*, before they could either leave the hut, or attack the sleeping warriors. They waited impatiently for half an hour, but perceiving that, although occasionally dozing, she would rouse herself at short intervals, and regard them suspiciously, they exchanged looks of intelligence (being afraid even to whisper), and prepared for the decisive effort. Jackson suddenly sprang up as silently as possible, and grasping the old woman by the throat, drew her head back with violence, when Sackville, who had watched his movements attentively, instantly cut her throat from ear to ear. A short gurgling moan was the only sound which escaped her, as the violence with which Jackson grasped her throat effectually prevented her speaking.

The sleepers were not awakened, although they appeared somewhat disturbed at the noise; and the two adventurers, seizing each a rifle, struck at the same moment with such fury as to disable two of their enemies. The other two instantly sprang to their feet, but before they could draw their tomahawks, or give the alarm, they were prostrated by the blows of the white men, who attacked them at the moment that they had gained their feet. Their enemies, although stunned, were not yet dead. They drew their tomahawks from their sides, therefore, and striking each Indian repeatedly upon the head, completed the work by piercing the heart of each with his own scalping knife. Selecting two rifles from the corner, together with their usual appendages, and taking such provisions as the hut afforded, they left the village as rapidly as possible, and fervently invoking the protection of heaven, committed themselves to the wilderness.

Neither of them were good woodsmen, nor were either of them expert hunters. They attempted a south-eastern course, however, as nearly as they could ascertain it, but were much embarassed by the frequent recurrence of impassable bogs, which compelled them to change their course, and greatly retarded their progress. Knowing that the pursuit would be keen and persevering, they resorted to every method of baffling their enemies. They waded down many streams, and occasionally surmounted rocky precipices, which, under other circumstances, nothing could have induced them to attempt. Their sufferings from hunger were excessive, as they were so indifferently skilled in hunting as to be unable to kill a sufficient quantity of game, although the woods abounded with deer, beaver, and buffalo.

On the fourth day, about ten o'clock, A. M., they came to a fine spring, where they halted and determined to prepare their breakfast. Before kindling a fire, however, Sackville, either upon some vague suspicion of the proximity of an enemy, or from some other cause, thought proper to ascend an adjoining hillock and reconnoiter the ground around the spring. No measure was ever more providential. Jackson presently beheld him returning cautiously and silently to the spring, and being satisfied from his manner that danger was at hand, he held his rifle in readiness for action at a moment's warning. Sackville presently rejoined him with a countenance in which anxiety and resolution were strikingly blended. Jackson eagerly inquired the cause of his alarm. His companion, in a low voice, replied that they were within one hundred yards of four Indian warriors, who were reposing upon the bank of the little rivulet on the other side of the hillock; that they were about kindling a fire in order to prepare their breakfast, and that two white men lay bound hand and foot within twenty feet of them.

He added that they were evidently prisoners, exposed to the same dreadful fate which *they* had just escaped; and concluded by declaring that, if Jackson would stand by him faithfully, he was determined to rescue them or perish in the attempt. Jackson gave him his hand and expressed his readiness to accompany him. Sackville then looked carefully to the priming of his gun, loosened his knife in the sheath, and desired Jackson to follow him, without making the slightest noise.

They, accordingly, moved in a stooping posture up a small and bushy ravine, which conducted them to the top of the gentle hill. When near the summit, they threw themselves flat upon the ground, and crawled into a thick cluster of whortleberry bushes, from which they had a fair view of the enemy. The Indians had not changed their position, but one of the white men was sitting up, and displayed the countenance of a young man, apparently about twenty-five, pale, haggard, and exhausted. Two Indians, with uplifted tomahawks, sat within three feet of him. One lay at full length upon the ground, while the remaining one was in the act of lighting a fire.

Sackville cocked his gun, and in a low voice directed Jackson to fire at one of the guards, who, from the quantity of beads and silver about his head, appeared to be a chief, while he selected the other guard for a mark. Each presented at the same moment, took a steady aim, and fired. Both Indians fell—the chief shot dead, the other mortally wounded. The other two Indians squatted in the grass like terrified partridges when the hawk hovers over them, and lay still and motionless. Sackville and Jackson reloaded their guns as rapidly as possible, and shifted their position a few paces in order to obtain a better view of the enemy. In the meantime, the two Indians cautiously elevated their heads above the grass, and glanced rapidly around in order to observe from what quarter the fatal shots were discharged. The thin wreaths of smoke which curled above the bushes where our adventurers lay, betrayed their hiding-place to the enemy. Before they could take advantage of it, however, they were ready to fire again, and this second volley proved fatal to one of their enemies, who lay without motion, but the other was only slightly wounded, and endeavored to reach the bushes upon the opposite side of the brook.

Sackville and Jackson now sprang to their feet, and rushed upon him, but the desperate savage shot Sackville through the heart, as he advanced, and flourished his tomahawk so menacingly at Jackson, that he was compelled to pause and reload his gun. The savage seized this opportunity to grasp the two rifles belonging to the Indians who had been first killed, and Jackson, in consequence, was compelled to retreat to the friendly shelter of the bushes, which he had too hastily abandoned. At this instant, the two prisoners, having burst the cords which confined them, sprang to their feet and ran toward the bushes for protection. Before they could reach them, however, the Indian shot one dead, and fired his last gun at the other, but without effect. Jackson having loaded again, fired upon their desperate enemy and wounded him in the neck, from which he could see the blood spouting in a stream. Nothing daunted, the Indian rapidly reloaded his gun and again fired without effect.

The prisoner who had escaped now seized Sackville's gun, and he and Johonnet, having reloaded, once more left the bushes and advanced upon their wounded enemy. The savage, although much exhausted from loss of blood, sat up at their approach, and, flourishing a tomahawk in each hand, seemed at least determined to die game. Johonnet was anxious to take him alive, but was prevented by his companion, who, leveling his gun as he advanced, shot his adversary through the head, and thus put an end to the conflict. It was a melancholy victory to the survivors. Johonnet had lost his gallant comrade, and the rescued white man had to lament the death of his fellow captive. The last Indian had certainly inflicted a heavy penalty upon his enemies, and died amply revenged. The rescued prisoner proved to be George Sexton, of Newport, Rhode Island, a private in Harmer's army.

Fortunately for Johonnet, his new comrade was an excellent woodsman, and very readily informed his deliverer of their present situation, and of the proper course to steer. He said, that in company with three others, he had been taken by a party of Wabash Indians, in the neighborhood of Fort Jefferson; that two of his comrades, having sunk under their sufferings, had been tomahawked and scalped upon the spot; that himself and his dead companion had been in hourly expectation of a similar fate; and concluded with the warmest expressions of gratitude for the gallantry with which he had been rescued, So lively, indeed, was his sense of obligation, that he would not permit Jackson to carry his own baggage, nor would he suffer him to watch more than three hours in the twenty-four. On the following day they fortunately fell in with a small detachment from Fort Jefferson, by which they were safely conducted to the fort, Here Jackson remained until summoned to attend St. Clair in his disastrous expedition against the same Miami villages, where he had lately suffered so much.

CHAPTER XIII.

WE now come to one of the heaviest disasters which occurs in the annals of Indian warfare. The failure of Harmer made a deep impression upon the American nation, and was followed by a loud demand for a greater force, under the command of a more experienced general. General ARTHUR ST. CLAIR was, at that time, Governor of the North-western Territory, and had a claim to the command of such forces as should be employed within his own limits. This gentleman had uniformly ranked high as an officer of courage and patriotism, but had been more uniformly unfortunate than any other officer in the American service. He had commanded at Ticonderoga, in the spring of 1777, and had conducted one of the most disastrous retreats which occurred during the Revolutionary War. Notwithstanding his repeated misfortunes, he still commanded the respect of his brother officers, and the undiminished confidence of Washington. He was now selected as the person most capable of restoring the American affairs in the North-west, and was placed at the head of a regular force, amounting to near fifteen hundred men, well furnished with artillery, and was empowered to call out such reinforcements of militia as might be necessary. Cincinnati, as usual, was the place of rendezvous.

In October, 1791, an army was assembled at that place, greatly superior, in numbers, officers, and equipments, to any which had yet appeared in the west. The regular force was composed of three complete regiments of infantry, two companies of artillery, and one of cavalry. The militia, who joined him at Fort Washington, amounted to upwards of six hundred men, most of whom had long been accustomed to Indian warfare. The general commenced his march, from Cincinnati, on the —— of October, and, following the route of Harmer, arrived at Fort Jefferson without material loss, although not without having sustained much inconvenience from scarcity of provisions. The Kentucky Rangers, amounting to upwards of two hundred men, had encountered several small parties of Indians, but no serious affair had as yet taken place. Shortly after leaving Fort Jefferson, one of the militia regiments, with their usual disregard to discipline, determined that it was inexpedient to proceed farther, and, detaching themselves from the main body, returned rapidly to the fort, on their way home. This ill-timed mutiny not only discouraged the remainder, but compelled the general to detach the first regiment in pursuit of them, if not to bring them back, at least to prevent them from injuring the stores collected at the fort for the use of the army. With the remainder of the troops, amounting in all to about twelve hundred men, he continued his march to the great Miami villages.

On the evening of the third of November he encamped upon a very commanding piece of ground, upon the bank of one of the tributaries of the Wabash, where he determined to throw up some slight works, for the purpose of protecting their knapsacks and baggage, having to move upon the Miami villages, supposed to be within twelve miles, as soon as the first regiment should rejoin them. The remainder of the evening was employed in concerting the plan of the proposed work with Major Ferguson of the engineers; and when the sentries were posted at night, every thing was as quiet as could have been desired. The troops were encamped in two lines, with an interval of seventy yards between them, which was all that the nature of the ground would permit. The battalions of Majors Butler, Clarke, and Patterson composed the front line, the whole under the orders of Major-General Butler, an officer of high and merited reputation. The front of the line was covered by a creek, its right flank by the river, and its left by a strong corps of infantry.

The second line was composed of the battalions of Majors Gaither and Bedinger, and the second regiment under the command of Lieutenant-Colonel Darke. This line, like the other, was secured upon one flank by the river, and upon the other by the cavalry and pickets.* The night passed away without alarm. The sentinels were vigilant,† and the officers upon the alert.

A few hours before day, St. Clair caused the reveille to be beaten, and the troops to be paraded under arms, under the expectation that an attack would probably be made. In this situation they continued until daylight, when they were dismissed to their tents. Some were endeavoring to snatch a few minutes' sleep, others were preparing for the expected march, when suddenly the report of a rifle was heard from the militia, a few hundred yards in front, which was quickly followed by a sharp, irregular volley in the same direction. The drums instantly beat to arms, the officers flew in every direction, and in two minutes the troops were formed in order of battle. Presently the militia rushed into camp, in the utmost disorder, closely pursued by swarms of Indians, who, in many places, were mingled with them, and were cutting them down with their tomahawks.

Major Butler's battalion received the first shock, and was thrown into disorder by the tumultuous flight of the militia, who in their eagerness to escape, bore down every thing before them. Here Major-General Butler had stationed himself, and here St. Clair directed his attention in order to remedy the confusion which began to spread rapidly through the whole line. The Indians pressed forward with great audacity, and many of them

---

*The militia, amounting to about two hundred and fifty men, were thrown across the creek, about three hundred yards in front of the first line, and a small detachment of regulars, under the orders of Captain Slough, were pushed still farther in advance, in order to prevent the possibility of surprise.

†Captain Slough was alarmed, in the course of the night, by the appearance of an unusual number of the enemy in his front and upon both flanks. A short time before day, they had collected in such numbers as seriously to alarm him, and induced him to fall back upon the militia. He instantly informed General Butler of the circumstance, but that officer, unfortunately, slighted the intelligence, and did not deem it of sufficient importance to inform the commander-in-chief.

were mingled with the troops before their progress could be checked. Major-General Butler was wounded at the first fire, and before his wound could be dressed, an Indian, who had penetrated the ranks of the regiment, ran up to the spot where he lay and tomahawked him before his attendants could interpose. The desperate savage was instantly killed. By great exertions, Butler's battalion was restored to order, and the heavy and sustained fire of the first line compelled the enemy to pause and shelter themselves.

This interval, however, endured but for a moment. An invisible but tremendous fire quickly opened upon the whole front of the encampment, which rapidly extended to the rear, and encompassed the troops on both sides. St. Clair, who at that time was worn down by a fever, and unable to mount his horse, nevertheless, as is universally admitted, exerted himself with a courage and presence of mind worthy of a better fate. He instantly directed his litter to the right of the rear line, where the great weight of fire fell, and where the slaughter, particularly of the officers, was terrible. Here Darke commanded, an officer who had been trained to hard service during the Revolutionary War, and who was now gallantly exerting himself to check the consternation which was evidently beginning to prevail. St. Clair ordered him to make a rapid charge with the bayonet, and rouse the enemy from their covert.

The order was instantly obeyed, and, at first, apparently with great effect. Swarms of dusky bodies arose from the high grass and fled before the regiment, with every mark of consternation; but as the troops were unable to overtake them, they quickly recovered their courage, and kept up so fatal a retreating fire that the exhausted regulars were compelled in their turn to give way. This charge, however, relieved that particular point for some time; but the weight of the fire was transferred to the center of the first line, where it threatened to annihilate every thing within its range. There, in turn, the unfortunate general was borne by his attendants, and ordered a second appeal to the bayonet. This second charge was made with the same impetuosity as at first, and with the same momentary success. But the attack was instantly shifted to another point, where the same charge was made and the same result followed. The Indians would retire before them, still keeping up a most fatal fire, and the continentals were uniformly compelled to retire in turn. St. Clair brought up the artillery, in order to sweep the bushes with grape; but the horses and artillerymen were destroyed by the terrible fire of the enemy before any effect could be produced. They were instantly manned afresh from the infantry, and again swept of defenders.

The slaughter had now become prodigious. Four-fifths of the officers and one-half of the men were either killed or wounded. The ground was covered with bodies, and the little ravine which led to the river was running with blood. The fire of the enemy had not in the least slackened, and the troops were falling in heaps before it in every part of the camp. To have attempted to have maintained his position longer could only have led to the total destruction of his force, without the possibility of annoying the enemy, who never showed themselves unless when charged, and whose numbers (to judge from the weight and extent of the fire) must have greatly exceeded his own. The men were evidently much disheartened; but the officers, who were chiefly veterans of the Revolution, still maintained a firm countenance, and exerted themselves with unavailing heroism to the last. Under these circumstances, St. Clair determined to save the lives of the survivors if possible, and for that purpose collected the remnants of several battalions into one corps, at the head of which he ordered Lieutenant-Colonel Darke to make an impetuous charge upon the enemy, in order to open a passage for the remainder of the army. Darke executed his orders with great spirit, and drove the Indians before him to the distance of a quarter of a mile. The remainder of the army instantly rushed through the opening in order to gain the road, Major Clarke, with the remnant of his battalion, bringing up the rear, and endeavoring to keep the Indians in check.

The retreat soon degenerated into a total rout. Officers who strove to arrest the panic only sacrificed themselves. Clarke, the leader of the rear-guard, soon fell in this dangerous service, and his corps were totally disorganized. Officers and soldiers were now mingled without the slightest regard to discipline, and "devil take the hindmost" was the order of the day. The pursuit at first was keen; but the temptation afforded by the plunder of the camp soon brought them back, and the wearied, wounded, and disheartened fugitives were permitted to retire from the field unmolested. The rout continued as far as Fort Jefferson, twenty-nine miles from the scene of action. The action lasted more than three hours, during the whole of which time the fire was heavy and incessant.

The loss, in proportion to the number engaged, was enormous, and is unparalleled, except in the affair of Braddock. Sixty-eight officers were killed upon the spot, and twenty-eight wounded. Out of nine hundred privates who went into the action, five hundred and fifty were left dead upon the field, and many of the survivors were wounded. General St. Clair was untouched, although eight balls passed through his hat and clothes, and several horses were killed under him.*

The Indian loss was reported by themselves at fifty-eight killed and wounded, which was probably not underrated, as they were never visible after the first attack until charged with the bayonet. At Fort Jefferson, the fugitives were joined by the first regiment, who, as noticed above, had been detached in pursuit of the deserters. Here a council of war was called, which terminated in the unanimous opinion that the junction with the first regiment did not justify an attempt upon the enemy in the present condition of affairs, and that the army should return to Fort Washington without delay. This was accordingly done; and thus closed the second campaign against the Indians.

The unfortunate general was, as usual, assailed from

---

* General St. Clair's horses were killed, as well as those of his aids. He was placed by a few friends upon an exhausted pack-horse that could not be pricked out of a walk, and in this condition followed in the rear of the troops.

one end of the country to the other—but particularly in Kentucky—with one loud and merciless outcry of abuse, and even detestation. All the misfortunes of his life (and they were many and bitter) were brought up in array against him. He was reproached with cowardice, treason, imbecility, and a disposition to prolong the war in order to preserve that authority which it gave him. He was charged with sacrificing the lives of his men and the interests of his country to his own private ambition. Men who had never fired a rifle, and never beheld an Indian, criticised severely the plan of his encampment and the order of his battle; and in short all the bitter ingredients which compose the cup of the unsuccessful general were drained to the dregs.

It seems to be a universal, and, probably, a correct rule that, as the general reaps all the glory of success, so, in like manner, he should sustain all the disgrace of defeat. A victorious general, whether by a lucky blunder or otherwise, is distinguished for life, and an unfortunate one is degraded. No charge in the one case, or excuse in the other, is listened to for a moment. Victory hides every blemish, and misfortune obscures every virtue. This is the popular rule for estimating the merits of a leader, which, for a time, might elevate a noisy *Cleon* to the level of an Alexander. But the historian decides otherwise. Let us look at the unfortunate St. Clair's conduct, and see if it deserves the furious and unbounded censure which has been heaped upon it. It is acknowledged that, although attacked suddenly (all Indian attacks are sudden), he was not surprised; his troops were encamped in order of battle, and formed in a moment.

He can not be charged with remissness, for he had arrayed them in order of battle three hours before daylight, and they had just been dismissed when the attack commenced. He can not be charged with incompetency *during the action*, for all his measures, if allowance be made for the circumstances attending it, were bold, judicious, and military.* He did not suffer his

---

* See Appendix.

men to be shot down in their ranks, as in Braddock's case, but made repeated, desperate, and successful charges against the enemy, which nothing but their overwhelming superiority of numbers prevented from being decisive. The troops, in general, behaved with firmness, the officers were the flower of the old Continental army, and not a man deserted his colors until the order was given to retreat.

The charge of cowardice is unworthy of an answer. It could only be brought by a blind and ignorant populace, stung with rage, as they ever are, at defeat, and pouring upon their unhappy victim every reproach which rage, ignorance, and the malice of interested demagogues may suggest. It may be observed, that St. Clair always stood high in the opinion of Washington, notwithstanding his repeated misfortunes, and that in his last battle, although worn down by a cruel disease, he exposed his person in every part of the action, delivered his orders with coolness and judgment, and was one of the last who arrived at Fort Jefferson in the retreat. His whole life, afterward, was one long and wasting struggle with poverty, reproach, and misfortune.

When demanding a compensation to which he considered himself entitled, before the Congress of the United States, a demand to which he had been compelled by the stern pressure of want, old age, and decrepitude, he was stigmatized by a member of that body as a "pauper!" and his claim rejected—rejected on that same floor where a princely present was bestowed on Lafayette, for services of the same kind which were refused to be acknowledged in the case of the unhappy and really indigent St. Clair! In the one case, their generosity would resound through the world, and gratify national pride. In the other, it would only have been an act of obscure justice. The official letter of St. Clair, at once temperate, mournful, and dignified, is subjoined in the appendix.

It remains only to mention such private incidents as we have been enabled to collect. The late WILLIAM

KENNAN, of Fleming County, at that time a young man of eighteen, was attached to the corps of rangers who accompanied the regular force. He had long been remarkable for strength and activity. In the course of the march from Fort Washington, he had repeated opportunities of testing his astonishing powers in that respect, and was universally admitted to be the swiftest runner of the light corps. On the evening preceding the action, his corps had been advanced, as already observed, a few hundred yards in front of the first line of infantry, in order to give seasonable notice of the enemy's approach. Just as day was dawning, he observed about thirty Indians within one hundred yards of the guard fire, advancing cautiously toward the spot where he stood, together with about twenty rangers, the rest being considerably in the rear.

Supposing it to be a mere scouting party, as usual, and not superior in number to the rangers, he sprang forward a few paces in order to shelter himself in a spot of peculiarly rank grass, and firing with a quick aim upon the foremost Indian, he instantly fell flat upon his face, and proceeded with all possible rapidity to reload his gun, not doubting for a moment but that the rangers would maintain their position and support him. The Indians, however, rushed forward in such overwhelming masses, that the rangers were compelled to fly with precipitation, leaving young Kennan in total ignorance of his danger. Fortunately, the captain of his company had observed him when he threw himself in the grass, and suddenly shouted aloud, "Run, Kennan! or you are a dead man!" He instantly sprang to his feet, and beheld Indians within ten feet of him, while his company was already more than one hundred yards in front.

Not a moment was to be lost. He darted off with every muscle strained to its utmost, and was pursued by a dozen of the enemy with loud yells. He at first pressed straight forward to the usual fording place in the creek which ran between the rangers and the main army, but several Indians who had passed him before he arose from the grass, threw themselves in the way, and completely cut him off from the rest. By the most powerful exertions he had thrown the whole body of pursuers behind him, with the exception of one young chief (probably Messhawa), who displayed a swiftness and perseverance equal to his own. In the circuit which Kennan was obliged to take, the race continued for more than four hundred yards. The distance between them was about eighteen feet, which Kennan could not increase nor his adversary diminish. Each, for the time, put his whole soul in the race.

Kennan, as far as he was able, kept his eye upon the motions of his pursuer, lest he should throw the tomahawk, which he held aloft in a menacing attitude, and at length, finding that no other Indian was immediately at hand, he determined to try the mettle of his pursuer in a different manner, and felt for his tomahawk in order to turn at bay. It had escaped from its sheath, however, while he lay in the grass, and his hair had almost lifted the cap from his head, when he saw himself totally disarmed. As he had slackened his pace for a moment, the Indian was almost within reach of him when he recommenced the race, but the idea of being without arms lent wings to his flight, and for the first time he saw himself gaining ground. He had watched the motions of his pursuer too closely, however, to pay proper attention to the nature of the ground before him, and he suddenly found himself in front of a large tree which had been blown down, and upon which brush and other impediments lay to the height of eight or nine feet.

The Indian (who, heretofore, had not uttered the slightest sound) now gave a short quick yell, as if secure of his victim. Kennan had not a moment to deliberate. He must clear the impediment at a leap or perish. Putting his whole soul into the effort, he bounded into the air with a power which astonished himself, and clearing limbs, brush, and every thing else, alighted in perfect safety upon the other side. A loud yell of astonishment burst from the band of pursuers, not one of whom had the hardihood to attempt the same feat. Kennan, as may be readily imagined, had no leisure to enjoy his triumph, but dashing into the bed of the creek (upon the banks of which his feat had been performed) where the high banks would shield him from the fire of the enemy, he ran up the stream until a convenient place offered for crossing, and rejoined the rangers in the rear of the encampment, panting from the fatigue of exertions which have seldom been surpassed. No breathing time was allowed him, however. The attack instantly commenced, and as we have already observed, was maintained for three hours with unabated fury.

When the retreat commenced Kennan was attached to Major Clarke's battalion, and had the dangerous service of protecting the rear. This corps quickly lost its commander, and was completely disorganized. Kennan was among the hindmost when the flight commenced, but exerting those same powers which had saved him in the morning, he quickly gained the front, passing several horsemen in the flight. Here he beheld a private in his own company, an intimate acquaintance, lying upon the ground, with his thigh broken, and in tones of the most piercing distress, implored each horseman who hurried by to take him up behind him. As soon as he beheld Kennan coming up on foot, he stretched out his arms, and called loud upon him to save him. Notwithstanding the imminent peril of the moment, his friend could not reject so passionate an appeal, but seizing him in his arms, he placed him upon his back, and ran in that manner for several hundred yards. Horseman after horseman passed them, all of whom refused to relieve him of his burden.

At length the enemy was gaining upon him so fast that Kennan saw their death certain, unless he relinquished his burden. He accordingly told his friend that he had used every possible exertion to save his life, but in vain; that he must relax his hold around his neck, or they would both perish. The unhappy wretch, heedless of every remonstrance, still clung convulsively to his back, and impeded his exertions until the foremost of the enemy (armed with tomahawks alone) were within twenty yards of them. Kennan then drew his knife from its sheath and cut the fingers of his com·

panion, thus compelling him to relinquish his hold. The unhappy man rolled upon the ground in utter helplessness, and Kennan beheld him tomahawked before he had gone thirty yards. Relieved from his burden he darted forward with an activity which once more brought him to the van. Here again he was compelled to neglect his own safety in order to attend to that of others.

The late Governor Madison, of Kentucky, who afterward commanded the corps which defended themselves so honorably at Raisin, a man who united the most amiable temper to the most unconquerable courage, was at that time a subaltern in St. Clair's army, and being a man of infirm constitution, was totally exhausted by the exertions of the morning, and was now sitting down calmly upon a log, awaiting the approach of his enemies. Kennan hastily accosted him, and inquired the cause of his delay. Madison, pointing to a wound which had bled profusely, replied that he was unable to walk further, and had no horse. Kennan instantly ran back to a spot where he had seen an exhausted horse grazing, caught him without difficulty, and having assisted Madison to mount, walked by his side until they were out of danger. Fortunately, the pursuit soon ceased, as the plunder of the camp presented irresistible attractions to the enemy. The friendship thus.formed between these two young men, endured without interruption through life. Mr. Kennan never entirely recovered from the immense exertions which he was compelled to make during this unfortunate expedition. He settled in Fleming County, and continued for many years a leading member of the Baptist Church. He died in 1827.

A party of Chickasaws were on their march to join St. Clair, but did not arrive in time to share in the action. One warrior of that nation alone was present, and displayed the most admirable address and activity. He positively refused to stand in the ranks with the soldiers, declaring that the "Shawnees would shoot him down like a wild pigeon," but took refuge behind a log a few yards in front of Butler's battalion, and discharged his rifle eleven times at the enemy with unerring accuracy. He could not be persuaded, however, to forego the pleasure of scalping each Indian as he fell, and in performing this agreeable office, he at length was shot down by the enemy, and scalped in turn.

The leader of the Indian army in this bloody engagement, was a chief of the Mississago tribe, known by the name of the " LITTLE TURTLE." Notwithstanding his name, he was at least six feet high, strong, muscular, and remarkably dignified in his appearance. He was forty years of age, had seen much service, and had accompanied Burgoyne in his disastrous invasion. His aspect was harsh, sour, and forbidding, and his person during the action was arrayed in the very extremity of Indian foppery, having at least twenty dollars worth of silver depending from his nose and ears. The plan of attack was conceived by him alone, in opposition to the opinion of almost every other chief. Notwithstanding his ability, however, he was said to have been unpopular among the Indians, probably in consequence of those very abilities.

Many veteran officers of inferior rank, who had served with distinction throughout the Revolutionary War, were destined to perish in this unhappy action. Among them was the gallant and unrewarded Captain KIRKWOOD, of the old Delaware line, so often and so honorably mentioned in Lee's Memoirs. The State of Delaware having had but one regiment on Continental establishment, and that regiment having been reduced to a company at Camden, it was impossible for Kirkwood to be promoted without a violation of the ordinary rules by which commissions were regulated. He, accordingly, had the mortification of beholding junior officers daily mounting above him in the scale of rank, while he himself, however meritorious, was compelled to remain in his present condition, on account of the small force which his native state could bring into the field.

Notwithstanding this constant source of mortification, he fought with distinguished gallantry throughout the war, and was personally engaged in the battles of Camden, Guilford, Hobkirks, Ninety-six, and Eutaw, the hottest and bloodiest which occurred during the Revolution. At the peace of 1783, he returned with a broken fortune, but a high reputation for courage, honor, and probity, and upon the re-appearance of war in the North-west, he hastened once more to the scene of action, and submitted, without reluctance, to the command of officers who had been boys while he was fighting those severe battles in the South. He fell in a brave attempt to repel the enemy with the bayonet, and thus closed a career as honorable as it was unrewarded.

Lieutenant Colonel DARKE'S escape was almost miraculous. Possessed of a tall, striking figure, in full uniform, and superbly mounted, he headed three desperate charges against the enemy, in each of which he was a conspicuous mark. His clothes were cut in many places, but he escaped with only a slight flesh wound. In the last charge, Ensign Wilson, a youth of seventeen, was shot through the heart, and fell a few paces in the rear of the regiment, which was then rather rapidly returning to its original position. An Indian, attracted by his rich uniform, sprang up from the grass, and rushed forward to scalp him. Darke, who was at that time in the rear of his regiment, suddenly faced about, dashed at the Indian on horseback, and cleft his skull with his broad-sword, drawing upon himself by the act a rapid discharge of more than a dozen rifles. He rejoined his regiment, however, in safety, being compelled to leave the body of young Wilson to the enemy. On the evening of the eighth of November, the broken remains of the army arrived at Fort Washington, and were placed in winter-quarters.

CHAPTER XIV.

AMIDST the almost universal clamor which arose upon the defeat of the unfortunate St. Clair, General Washington himself did not entirely escape censure. The appointment of an old, infirm, and above all, an *unlucky* general to a command which, above all other qualities, required activity, promptitude, and the power of sustaining great fatigue, was reprobated in no measured terms. Public opinion imperiously demanded a better selection for the third offensive campaign, and St. Clair was necessarily superseded. The choice of a proper successor became the theme of general discussion, and was a matter of no small difficulty. The command was eagerly sought by many officers of the Revolution, among whom the most prominent were General WAYNE, of Pennsylvania, and the late General Henry Lee, of Virginia, the celebrated commandant of the Partisan Legion during the war of Independence.

The peculiar fitness of Lee for a command of that kind, seems to have impressed itself strongly upon the mind of Washington, and there is a letter extant which shows that nothing but the discontent which the appointment of so young an officer would naturally have excited in the minds of those who had held a rank above him in the former war, could have prevented his being the successor of St. Clair. This objection did not apply to Wayne, and as he had repeatedly proved himself a bold, active, and energetic commander, his appointment was unacceptable to those only whose claims had been rejected—a description of men very difficult to be pleased. Wayne had entered the army as colonel of a regiment in the Pennsylvania line, and first attracted notice in the Canadian expedition. He there displayed so keen a relish for battle upon all occasions, and upon any terms, exposed his own life as well as those of his men with such recklessness, and was in the habit of swearing so hard in the heat of battle, that he soon obtained among the common soldiers the nickname of "Mad Anthony."

He never enjoyed a high reputation as an officer of prudence, science, and combination, and on one occasion particularly was surprised by the celebrated English partisan, Grey, and routed with a slaughter scarcely inferior to that of St. Clair. As an executive officer, however, he was incomparable. He seemed to be of opinion that the whole science of war consisted in giving and taking hard blows; and we have heard, from one who served under him many years, that his favorite word of command was, "Charge the d—d rascals with the bayonet!" Whenever (as at Stony Point) a bold, brisk onset was all that was required, no better general than Wayne could possibly be selected, but on other occasions his keen appetite for action was apt to hurry him into an imprudent exposure of his troops.

In Virginia he once narrowly escaped total destruction by pressing too eagerly upon Lord Cornwallis, who afterward repeatedly affirmed that one-half hour more of daylight would have sufficed for the destruction of his rash but gallant enemy; and afterward, in the Carolinas, his quarters were broken up, and his whole camp thrown into confusion, by a small party of Creek Indians, who fell upon him as unexpectedly as if they had risen from the earth. Several severe losses, however, which he received in the course of his career, had taught him to temper his courage with a moderate degree of caution, and as he was remarkably popular among the common soldiers (who are better judges of the ordinary quality of courage than the higher military talents) he was supposed to be peculiarly qualified for re-animating the cowering spirits of the troops.

There was an interval of more than a year between the defeat of St. Clair and the appointment of his successor. Wayne lost no time in proceeding to the headquarters of the western army, and arrived at Fort Washington in the spring of 1793. Reinforcements of regular troops were constantly arriving, and, in addition to the usual complement of cavalry and artillery, a strong legionary corps was raised upon continental establishment, and placed under his command. In addition to this, he was authorized to call upon the Governor of Kentucky (Shelby) for as many mounted militia as might be necessary. It was so late in the season, however, before all the various forces could be collected, and all the necessary supplies procured, that he judged it prudent to defer any offensive movement until the spring.

The mounted volunteers were accordingly dismissed with some flattering encomiums upon their zeal and readiness, while the regular forces were placed in winter-quarters. The volunteers returned to Kentucky with a high idea of the efficiency of the regular force under Wayne, and sanguine expectations of a favorable result. The rapid succession of disasters which had heretofore attended the operations of regulars in conjunction with militia, had created a strong disgust to that species of force, and it was with difficulty that a sufficient number of mounted men could be procured for co-operation. But, after witnessing the order, diligence, and energy which characterized Wayne's conduct as an officer, and the indefatigable labor with which he drilled his troops into a ready performance of the necessary movements, this disrelish to a co-operation with regulars completely vanished, and on the following spring the volunteers proffered their services with great alacrity.

During the winter Wayne remained at a fort which he had built upon a western fork of the Little Miami, and to which he had given the name of Greenville. By detachments from the regular troops he was enabled to sweep the country lying between him and the Miami villages, and having taken possession of the ground upon which St. Clair was defeated, he erected a small fort upon it, to which he gave the name of Recovery. His orders were positive to endeavor, if possible, to procure peace upon reasonable terms without resorting to force, and he accordingly opened several conferences with the hostile tribes during the winter.

Many of their chiefs visited him in his camp, and examined his troops, artillery, and equipments with great attention, and from time to time made ample professions of a disposition to bury the hatchet; but nothing definite could be drawn from them, and from the known partiality of Wayne to the decision of the sword, could it be supposed that he pressed the overtures with much eagerness? As the spring approached, the visits of the Indians became more rare, and their professions of friendship waxed fainter. In February they threw aside the mask at once, and made a bold effort to carry the distant outpost at Fort Recovery by a coup-de-main. In this, however, they were frustrated by the vigilance and energy of the garrison; and, finding that Wayne was neither to be surprised nor deceived, they employed themselves in collecting their utmost strength, with a determination to abide the brunt of battle.

In the spring the general called upon the Governor of Kentucky for a detachment of mounted men, who repaired with great alacrity to his standard in two brigades, under Todd and Barbee, the whole commanded by Major-General Scott, amounting to more than fifteen hundred men accustomed to Indian warfare. The regular force, including cavalry and artillery, amounted to about two thousand, so that the general found himself at the head of three thousand men, well provided with every thing, in high spirits, and eager for battle. The Indian force did not exceed two thousand, and was known to have assembled in the neighborhood of the British fort at the rapids of the Miami.

It was late in July before Wayne was ready to march from Greenville, and, from the nature of the country as well as the necessity of guarding against surprise, his progress was very leisurely. On the nineteenth of August, when within a day's march of the enemy's position, he determined to send a messenger, charged with the last offer of peace and friendship which he intended to make. For this dangerous and apparently useless office, he selected a private volunteer named Miller, who had formerly been taken by the Indians, and lived for many years upon the banks of the Miami. Miller, however, appeared to value his own neck much more highly than the general did, as he stoutly remonstrated against the duty, declaring that it would be useless to the army as well as destructive to himself.

He declared confidently that the Indians, from many undoubted signs, were resolutely bent upon battle, and would listen to nothing of which he might be the bearer. He added that he knew them of old, and was satisfied that they would roast him alive, without an instant's hesitation, in defiance of his white flag and sacred character of embassador. Wayne, however, was not to be diverted from his purpose. He assured Miller that he would hold eight or ten Indians, then in his camp, as hostages for his safe return, and, if the enemy roasted him, he swore that a noble hecatomb should be offered to his manes, as he would compel all his prisoners to undergo the same fate; but concluded with an assurance that the Indians, when informed of his determination, would dismiss him in perfect safety, for a regard to the lives of their friends.

Reluctantly, and with many dark prophecies of the fate which awaited him, he at length consented to go upon the mission, and, having taken leave of his friends, he set off at a rapid pace for the Indian camp. When within view of it, he hoisted a white flag upon a pole, and marched boldly forward, knowing that in this, as in most other cases, the boldest is the safest course. As soon as they beheld him approaching, they ran out to meet him with loud yells, brandishing their tomahawks, and crying out, in their own language, "Kill the runaway!" Miller, who well understood their language, instantly addressed them with great earnestness, and in a few words made known the cause of his visit, and the guarantee which Wayne held for his safe return. To the first part of the intelligence they listened with supreme contempt. A long conference ensued, in which many chiefs spoke, but nothing could be determined upon.

On the next day Miller was ordered to return to Wayne with some evasive message, intending to amuse him until they could devise some means of recovering their friends. He accordingly left them with great readiness, and was returning with all possible dispatch, when he met the general in full march upon the enemy, having become tired of waiting for the return of his messenger. Wayne's object in sending Miller is difficult to be conjectured. The Indians had constantly refused to come to any terms; they had sent away their women, and given every indication of a disposition to fight, and were in possession of ground which would give them immense advantages against the regulars. He could scarcely suppose that a treaty could be effected, nor, with the prospect of battle before him, which to him presented all the attractions of a ball to a dandy, or a dinner to an epicure, is it to be supposed that he could have been very desirous of such an event. The ground was well known to many individuals in the army, and Miller's report could have added but little to the knowledge already existing, to say nothing of the strong probability that he might never return from a duty so perilous. The truth is, the old general valued the life of a soldier at an exceedingly low rate, and thought that, even if the mission brought no advantage, it was attended with no other danger than the chance of death to a single soldier, which did not deserve a moment's thought.

The general received the report of Miller without delaying his march for a moment, which was continued in order of battle until he arrived within view of the enemy. The regular force formed the center column, one brigade of mounted volunteers moved upon the left under General Barbee, the other brought up the rear under Brigadier Todd. The right flank was covered by the river, and Major Price, with a selected corps of mounted volunteers, was advanced about five miles in front, with orders to feel the enemy's position, and then fall back upon the main body. About noon, the advanced corps received so heavy a fire from a concealed enemy, as to compel it to retire with precipitation. The heads of the columns quickly reached the hostile ground, and had a view of the enemy. The ground for miles was covered with a thick growth of timber, which rendered the operation of cavalry extremely difficult. The Indians occupied a thick wood in front, where an immense number of trees had been blown down by a hurricane, the branches of which were interlocked in such a manner as greatly to impede the exertions of the regulars.

The enemy were formed in three parallel lines, at right angles to the river, and displayed a front of more than two miles. Wayne rode forward to reconnoiter their positions, and perceiving, from the weight and extent of the fire, that they were in full force, he instantly made dispositions for the attack. The whole of the mounted volunteers were ordered to make a circuit, for the purpose of turning the right flank of the Indians; the cavalry were ordered to move up under cover of the river bank, and if possible, turn their left; while the regular infantry were formed in a thick wood in front of the "Fallen timber," with orders, as soon as the signal was given, to rush forward at full speed, without firing a shot, arousing the enemy from their covert at the point of the bayonet, and *then* to deliver a close fire upon their backs, pressing them so closely as not to permit them to reload their guns. All these orders were executed with precision. The mounted volunteers moved off rapidly to occupy the designated ground, while the first line of infantry was formed under the eye of the commander for the perilous charge in front.

As soon as time had been given for the arrival of the several corps upon their respective points, the order was given to advance, and the infantry, rushing through a tremendous fire of rifles, and overleaping every impediment, hastened to close with their concealed enemy and maintain the struggle on equal terms. Although their loss in this desperate charge was by no means inconsiderable, yet the effect was decisive. The enemy rose and fled before them more than two miles, with considerable loss, as, owing to the orders of Wayne, they were nearly as much exposed as the regulars. Such was the rapidity of the advance, and the precipitation of the retreat, that only a small part of the volunteers could get up in time to share in the action, although there can be no question that their presence and threatening movement contributed equally with the impetuous charge of the infantry to the success of the day.

The broken remains of the Indian army were pursued under the guns of the British fort, and so keen was the ardor of Wayne's men, and so strong their resentment against the English, that it was with the utmost difficulty they could be restrained from storming it upon the spot. As it was, many of the Kentucky troops advanced within gunshot, and insulted the garrison with a select volley of oaths and epithets, which must have given the British commandant a high idea of backwoods gentility. He instantly wrote an indignant letter to General Wayne, complaining of the outrage, and demanding by what authority he trespassed upon the sacred precincts of a British garrison? Now, "Mad Anthony" was the last man in the world to be dragooned into politeness, and he replied in terms little short of those employed by the Kentuckians, and satisfactorily informed Captain Campbell, the British commandant, that his only chance of safety was silence and civility. After some sharp messages on both sides, the war of the pen ceased, and the destruction of property began. Houses, stores, cornfields, orchards, were soon wrapped in flames or leveled with the earth. The dwelling house and store of Colonel McKee, the Indian agent, shared the fate of the rest.

All this was performed before the face of Captain Campbell, who was compelled to look on in silence, and without any effort to prevent it. There remains not the least question *now* that the Indians were not only encouraged in their acts of hostility by the English *traders*, but were actually supplied with arms, ammunition, and provisions, by order of the English commandant at Detroit, Colonel England.* There remains a

---

*This gentleman was remarkable for his immense height and enormous quantity of flesh. After his return from America, the waggish Prince of Wales, who was himself no pigmy, became desirous of seeing him. Colonel England was one day pointed out to him by Sheridan, as he was in the act of dismounting from his horse. The Prince regarded him with marked attention for several minutes, and then turning to Sheridan, said with a laugh, "Colonel England, hey! You should have said *Great Britain!* by G—d!"

correspondence between this gentleman and McKee, in which urgent demands are made for fresh supplies of *ammunition*, and the approach of "the enemy" (as they call Wayne) is mentioned with great anxiety. After the battle of the Rapids, he writes that the Indians are much discouraged, and that "*it will require great efforts to induce them to remain in a body.*" Had Wayne been positively informed of this circumstance, he would scarcely have restrained his men from a more energetic expression of indignation.

The Indian force being completely dispersed, their cornfields cut up, and their houses destroyed, Wayne drew off from the neighborhood of the British post, and in order to hold the Indians permanently in check, he erected a fort at the junction of the Auglaize and Miami, in the very heart of the Indian country, to which he gave the appropriate name of Defiance. As this was connected with Fort Washington by various intermediate fortifications, it could not fail completely to overawe the enemy, who, in a very short time, urgently and unanimously demanded peace.

No victory could have been better timed than that of Wayne. The various tribes of Indians throughout the whole of the United States, encouraged by the repeated disasters of our armies in the North-west, had become very unsteady and menacing in their intercourse with the whites. The Creeks and Cherokees, in the South, were already in arms, while the Oneidas, Tuscaroras, etc., in the North, were evidently preparing for hostilities. The shock of the victory at the Rapids, however, was felt in all quarters. The southern Indians instantly demanded peace; the Oneidas, conscious of their evil intentions, and fearful of the consequences, became suddenly affectionate, even to servility; and within a few months after the victory, all the frontiers enjoyed the most profound peace. Wayne reported his loss at thirty-three killed and one hundred wounded. The Indian loss could not be ascertained, but was supposed to exceed that of the Americans. This, however, is very doubtful, as they gave way immediately, and were not so much exposed as the continentals.

One circumstance attending their flight is remarkable and deserves to be inserted. Three Indians, being hard pressed by the cavalry upon one side, and the infantry upon the other, plunged into the river and attempted to swim to the opposite shore. A runaway negro, who had attached himself to the American army, was concealed in the bushes on the opposite bank, and perceiving three Indians approaching nearer than in his opinion was consistent with the security of his hiding-place, he collected courage enough to level his rifle at the foremost, as he was swimming, and shot him through the head. The other two Indians instantly halted in the water, and attempted to drag the body of their dead companion ashore. The negro, in the meantime, reloaded his gun and shot another dead upon the spot. The survivor then seized hold of both bodies, and attempted, with a fidelity which seems astonishing, to bring them both to land. The negro having had leisure to reload a second time, and firing from his covert upon the surviving Indian, wounded him mortally while struggling with the dead bodies. He then ventured to approach them, and from the striking resemblance of their features, as well as their devoted attachment, they were supposed to have been brothers. After scalping them, he permitted their bodies to float down the stream.

We shall conclude our sketches with an anecdote, which, although partaking somewhat of the marvelous, is too well authenticated to be rejected. Early in the spring of 1793, two boys by the name of JOHNSON, the one twelve, the other nine years of age, were playing on the banks of Short Creek, near the mouth of the Muskingum, and occasionally skipping stones in the water. At a distance, they beheld two men, dressed, like ordinary settlers, in hats and coats, who gradually approached them, and from time to time threw stones into the water, in imitation of the children. At length, when within one hundred yards of the boys, they suddenly threw off the mask, and, rushing rapidly upon them, made them prisoners. They proved to be Indians of the Delaware tribe. Taking the children in their arms, they ran hastily into the woods, and after a rapid march of about six miles encamped for the night. Having kindled a fire and laid their rifles and tomahawks against an adjoining tree, they laid down to rest, each with a boy in his arms.

The children, as may readily be supposed, were too much agitated to sleep. The eldest at length began to move his limbs cautiously, and finding that the Indian who held him remained fast asleep, he gradually disengaged himself from his arms, and walking to the fire, which had burned low, remained several minutes in suspense as to what was next to be done. Having stirred the fire, and ascertained by its light the exact position of the enemy's arms, he whispered softly to his brother to imitate his example, and, if possible, extricate himself from his keeper. The little fellow did as his brother directed, and both stood irresolute for several minutes around the fire. At length, the eldest, who was of a very resolute disposition, proposed that they should kill the sleeping Indians and return home. The eldest pointed to one of the guns, and assured his brother that if he would only pull the trigger of that gun after he had placed it in rest, he would answer for the other Indian.

The plan was soon agreed upon. The rifle was leveled, with the muzzle resting upon a log which lay near, and having stationed his brother at the breech, with positive directions not to touch the trigger until he gave the word, he seized a tomahawk and advanced cautiously to the other sleeper. Such was the agitation of the younger, however, that he touched the trigger too soon, and the report of his gun awakened the other Indian before his brother was quite prepared. He struck the blow, however, with firmness, although, in the hurry of the act, it was done with the blunt part of the hatchet, and only stunned his antagonist. Quickly repeating the blow, however, with the edge, he inflicted a deep wound upon the Indian's head, and after repeated strokes, left him lifeless upon the spot. The younger, frightened at the explosion of his own gun, had already betaken himself to his heels, and was with difficulty overtaken by his brother. Having regained the road by which they had advanced, the elder fixed his hat upon a bush, in order to mark the spot, and by daylight they had regained their homes.

They found their mother in an agony of grief for their loss, and ignorant whether they had been drowned or taken by the Indians. Their tale was heard with astonishment, not unmingled with incredulity, and a few of the neighbors insisted upon accompanying them instantly to the spot where so extraordinary a rencounter had occurred. The place was soon found and the truth of the boy's story placed beyond doubt. The tomahawked Indian lay in his blood, where he fell; but the one who had been shot was not to be found. A broad trail of blood, however, enabled them to trace his footsteps, and he was at length overtaken. His appearance was most ghastly. His under jaw had been entirely shot away, and his hands and breast were covered with clotted blood. Although evidently much exhausted, he still kept his pursuers at bay, and faced them from time to time with an air of determined resolution. Either his gory appearance, or the apprehension that more were in the neighborhood, had such an effect upon his pursuers that, notwithstanding their numbers, he was permitted to escape. Whether he survived, or perished in the wilderness, could never be ascertained; but from the severity of the wound, the latter supposition is most probable.

From the peace of 1794 down to the renewal of war in the North-west, under the auspices of Tecumseh and the Prophet, no event occurred of sufficient importance to claim our notice. The war was over, and even private and individual aggression was of rare occurrence. The country which had been the scene of those fierce conflicts which we have endeavored to relate, became settled with a rapidity totally unprecedented in the annals of the world. The forests became rapidly thinned, and the game equally as rapidly disappeared. Numerous villages, as if by enchantment, were daily springing up in those wild scenes where Kenton, Crawford, Slover, and Johnston had endured such sufferings; and the Indians, from fierce and numerous tribes, were gradually melting down to a few squalid wanderers, hovering like restless spirits around the scenes of their former glory, or driven, with insult, from the doors of the settlers, where they were perpetually calling for food and rum. Such wanderers were frequently murdered by lawless white men, who, like the rovers of old, contended that "there was no peace beyond the line," and as such offenses were rarely punished, the Indians at length became satisfied that they must either retire beyond the reach of the whites or make one last effort to retrieve the sinking fortunes of their race. Tecumseh was the great apostle of this reviving spirit, and to do him justice, displayed a genius and perseverance worthy of a better fate. As these events, however, are beyond our limits, we must refer the young reader, who may have accompanied us thus far, to the histories of the day, where his curiosity will be amply gratified.

APPENDIX.

IN the life of KENTON, we had occasion to refer to various names and circumstances, which, in our anxiety to preserve the unity and connection of the narrative, we passed over very slightly at the time, reserving a more full detail for the present place. We allude to the celebrated war upon the Kenawha, generally known by the name of Dunmore's expedition, in which the names of Logan, Lewis, Girty, Cornstalk, etc., figure conspicuously. Many and various reasons have been assigned for this war. Some have attributed it to the murder of Logan's family by Cresap; others, to the equally atrocious murder of "Bald Eagle," a celebrated Delaware chief. Both, probably, contributed to hasten the rupture, which, however, would unquestionably have taken place without either. The cause of this, as of all other Indian wars, is to be found in the jealousy and uneasiness with which the Indians beheld the rapid extension of the white settlements. After the peace of 1763, large tracts of land, in the West, had been assigned as bounties to such officers and soldiers as had fought throughout the war. Accordingly, as soon as peace was restored, crowds of emigrants hastened to the West, attended by the usual swarm of surveyors, speculators, etc. The inhabitants of the frontiers became mingled with the Indians. They visited and received visits from each other, and frequently met in their hunting parties. Peace existed between the nations, but the old, vindictive feelings, occasioned by mutual injuries, still rankled in the breast of individuals. Civilities were quickly followed by murders, which led to retaliation, remonstrances, promises of amendment, and generally closed with fresh murders.

The murder of "Bald Eagle," an aged Delaware sachem, was peculiarly irritating to that warlike nation. He spoke the English language with great fluency, and being remarkably fond of tobacco, sweetmeats, and rum, all of which were generally offered to him in profusion in the settlements, he was a frequent visitor at the fort erected at the mouth of the Kenawha, and familiarly acquainted even with the children. He usually ascended the river alone, in a bark canoe, and, from the frequency and harmlessness of his visits, his appearance never excited the least alarm. A white man, who had suffered much from the Indians, encountered the old chief one evening alone upon the river, returning peaceably from one of his usual visits. A conference ensued, which terminated in a quarrel, and the old man was killed upon the spot. The murderer, having scalped his victim, fixed the dead body in the usual sitting posture in the stern of the boat, replaced the pipe in his mouth, and, launching the canoe again upon the river, permitted it to float down with its burden undisturbed. Many settlers beheld it descending in this manner, but, from the upright posture of the old man, they supposed that he was only returning, as usual, from a visit to the whites. The truth, however, was quickly discovered, and inflamed his tribe with the most ungovernable rage. Vengeance was vowed for the outrage, and amply exacted.

At length hostilities upon this remote frontier became so serious as to demand the attention of government. One of the boldest of these forays was conducted by Logan in person. Supposing that the inhabitants of the interior would consider themselves secure from the Indians, and neglect those precautions which were generally used upon the frontier, he determined, with a small but select band of followers, to penetrate to the thick settlements upon the head-waters of the Monongahela, and wreak his vengeance upon its unsuspecting inhabitants. The march was conducted with the usual secrecy of Indian warriors, and with great effect. Many scalps and several prisoners were taken, with which, by the signal conduct of their chief, they were enabled to elude all pursuit, and return in safety to their towns.

One of the incidents attending this incursion deserves to be mentioned, as illustrating the character of Logan. While hovering, with his followers, around the skirts of a thick settlement, he suddenly came in view of a small field, recently cleared, in which three men were pulling flax. Causing the greater part of his men to remain where they were, Logan, together with two others, crept up within long shot of the white men and fired. One man fell dead; the remaining two attempted to escape. The elder of the fugitives (Hellew) was quickly overtaken and made prisoner by Logan's associates, while Logan himself, having thrown down his rifle, pressed forward alone in pursuit of the younger of the white men, whose name was Robinson. The contest was keen for several hundred yards, but Robinson, unluckily looking around in order to have a view of his pursuer, ran against a tree with such violence as completely to stun him, and render him insensible for several minutes.

Upon recovering, he found himself bound and lying upon his back, while Logan sat by his side, with unmoved gravity, awaiting his recovery. He was then compelled to accompany them in their further attempts upon the settlements, and in the course of a few days was marched off, with great rapidity, for their villages in Ohio. During the march, Logan remained silent and melancholy, probably brooding over the total destruction of his family. The prisoners, however, were treated kindly, until they arrived at an Indian village upon the Muskingum. When within a mile of the town, Logan became more animated, and uttered the "scalp halloo" several times, in the most terrible tones. The never-failing scene of insult and torture then began. Crowds flocked out to meet them, and a line was formed for the gauntlet.

Logan took no share in the cruel game, but did not attempt to repress it. He, however, gave Robinson, whom he regarded as his own prisoner, some directions as to the best means of reaching the council-house in safety, and displayed some anxiety for his safe arrival, while poor Hellew was left in total ignorance, and permitted to struggle forward as he best could. Robinson, under the patronage of Logan, escaped with a few slight bruises; but Hellew, not knowing where to run, was dreadfully mangled, and would probably have been killed upon the spot had not Robinson (not without great risk on his own part) seized him by the hand, and dragged him into the council-house.

On the following morning a council was called, in order to determine their fate, in which Logan held a conspicuous superiority over all who were assembled. Hellew's destiny came first under discussion, and was quickly decided by an almost unanimous vote of adoption. Robinson's was most difficult to determine. A majority of the council (partly influenced by a natural thirst for vengeance upon at least *one* object, partly, perhaps, by a lurking jealousy of the imposing superiority of Logan's character) were obstinately bent upon putting him to death. Logan spoke for nearly an hour upon the question; and, if Robinson is to be believed, with an energy, copiousness, and dignity which would not have disgraced Henry himself. He appeared at no loss for either words or ideas; his tones were deep and musical, and were heard by the assembly with the silence of death. All, however, was vain. Robinson was condemned, and, within an hour afterwards, was fastened to the stake. Logan stood apart from the crowd with his arms folded, and his eyes fixed upon the scene with an air of stern displeasure.

. When the fire was about to be applied, he suddenly strode into the circle, pushing aside those who stood in the way, and, advancing straight up to the stake, cut the cords with his tomahawk, and taking the prisoner by the hand, led him, with a determined air, to his own wigwam. The action was so totally unexpected, and the air of the chief so determined, that he had reached the door of his wigwam before any one ventured to interfere. Much dissatisfaction was then expressed, and threatening symptoms of a tumult appeared; but so deeply rooted was his authority, that in a few hours all was quiet, and Robinson, without opposition, was permitted to enter an Indian family. He remained with Logan until the treaty of Fort Pitt, in the autumn of the ensuing year, when he returned to Virginia. He ever retained the most unbounded admiration for Logan, and repeatedly declared, that his countenance, when speaking, was the most striking, varied, and impressive that he ever beheld. And when it is recollected that he had often heard Lee and Henry, in all their glory, the compliment must be regarded as a very high one.

This, together with various other marauding expeditions, generally carried on by small parties, determined the governor of Virginia (Dunmore) to assemble a large force, and carry the war into their own territories. The plan of the expedition was soon arranged. Three complete regiments were to be raised west of the Blue Ridge, under the command of General Andrew Lewis; while an equal force, from the interior, was commanded by Dunmore in person. The armies were to form a junction at the mouth of the Great Kenawha, and proceed together, under Dunmore, to the Indian towns in Ohio.

On the first of September, 1774, a part of General Lewis's division, consisting of two regiments, under the orders of Colonel Charles Lewis, his brother, and Colonel William Fleming, of Botetourt, rendezvoused at Camp Union (now Lewisburgh, Va.), where they were joined by an independent regiment of backwoods volunteers, under the orders of Colonel John Fields, a very distinguished officer, who, together with most of those now assembled, had served under Braddock. Here they remained, awaiting the arrival of Colonel Christian, who was busily engaged in assembling another regiment. By the junction of Field, Lewis's force amounted to about eleven hundred men, accustomed to danger, and conducted by the flower of the border officers. General Lewis, as well as his brother, had been present at Braddock's defeat, and were subaltern officers in two companies of Virginia riflemen, who formed the advance of the English army.

We shall here relate some circumstances attending that melancholy disaster, which are not to be found in the regular histories of the period. Braddock's battle-ground was a small bottom, containing not more than two acres, bounded on the east by the Monongahela, and upon the west by a high cliff which rises precipitately above the bottom, and which, together with the river, completely inclosed it. Through this cliff, and near its center, runs a deep gorge or ravine, the sides of which are nearly perpendicular, and the summits of which were at that time thickly covered with timber, rank grass, and thickets of underwood. Upon this cliff the Indian army lay in ambush, awaiting the arrival of their foe. The only passage for the English lay through the ravine, immediately in front of the ford. The two companies of rangers crossed the river in advance of the regulars, and suspecting no danger, immediately entered the mouth of the ravine. Braddock followed in close column, and the devoted army soon stood in the bottom already mentioned, the river in the rear, the cliff in front, and the ravine presenting the only practicable passage to the French fort.

Instantly a tremendous fire opened upon them from the cliff above, and as the small bottom was thronged with red coats, immense execution was done. In the meantime, the two devoted companies of rangers were more than one hundred yards in front, and completely buried in the gorge already mentioned. Upon hearing the firing in their rear, they attempted to rejoin the army, but a select corps of Indian warriors rushed down the steep banks of the ravine and blocked up the passage. A furious struggle ensued. The Indians could not possibly give way, as the banks were too steep to admit of retreat in that direction; and if they retired through the mouth of the ravine into the bottom below, they would have found themselves in the midst of the English ranks. On the other hand, the Virginians were desperately bent upon rejoining their friends, which could only be done over the bodies of the Indians. Thus the gorge became the theater of a separate battle, far more desperate than that which raged in the bottom or upon the cliffs.

In these two companies, were to be found many names afterward highly distinguished both in the Indian and British war. Here was General Lewis and his five brothers; Colonel Matthews, afterward so distinguished at Germantown, together with four of his brothers; Colonel John Field, afterward killed at Point Pleasant; Colonel Grant, of Kentucky; John McDowell, and several others, afterward well known in Virginia and Kentucky. The press was too great to admit of the rifle. Knives and tomahawks were their only weapons, and upon both sides (for the numbers engaged) the slaughter was prodigious. One-half the Virginians were left dead in the pass, and most of the survivors were badly wounded. The Indians suffered equally, and at length became so thinned as to afford room for the Virginians to pass them and rejoin their friends below. There all was dismay and death. Braddock, unable from the nature of the ground to charge with effect, and too proud to retreat before an enemy whom he despised, was actively, and as calmly as if upon parade, laboring to form his troops under a fire which threatened to annihilate every thing within its range. The event is well known.

Upon the fall of Braddock, the troops gave way, and, recrossing the river, rejoined the rear guard of the army, after a defeat, which *then* had no parallel in Indian warfare. Colonel Lewis afterward served as major in Washington's regiment, and ranked peculiarly high in the estimation of his illustrious commander. He accompanied Grant in his unfortunate masquerade, and in a brave attempt with the colonial troops to retrieve the fortune of the day, was wounded and made prisoner by the French. While he and Grant were together at Fort du Quesne, upon parole, a quarrel took place between them, much to the amusement of the French. Grant, in his dispatches, had made Lewis the scapegoat, and thrown the whole blame of the defeat upon him; whereas, in truth, the only execution that was done was effected by his Virginia troops. The dispatches fell into the hands of some Indians, who brought them to the French commandant. Captain Lewis happened to be present when they were opened, and was quickly informed of their contents.

Without uttering a word, he went in search of Grant, reproached him with the falsehood, and putting his hand upon his sword, directed his former commander to draw and defend himself upon the spot. Grant contemptuously refused to comply, upon which Lewis lost all temper, cursed him for a liar and a coward, and in the presence of two French officers *spit in his face*. General Lewis's person considerably exceeded six feet in height, and was at once strongly and handsomely formed. His countenance was manly and stern—strongly expressive of that fearlessness and energy of character which distinguished him through life. His manners were plain, cold, and unbending, and his conversation short, pithy, and touching only upon the "needful." At the general treaty with the Indian tribes, in 1763, General Lewis was present, and his fine military appearance attracted great attention, and inspired somewhat of *awe* among the more pacific deputies. The governor of New York declared that he "looked like the genius of the forest; and that the earth seemed to tremble beneath his footsteps."

Such as we have described him, he was now placed at the head of one thousand men, with orders to meet Dunmore at Point Pleasant. Having waited several days at Lewisburgh for Colonel Christian, without hearing from him, he determined no longer to delay his advance. On the eleventh of September, he left Lewisburgh, and without any adventure of importance, arrived at the concerted place of rendezvous. Dunmore had not yet arrived, and Lewis remained several days in anxious expectation of his approach. At length he received dispatches from the governor, informing him that he had changed his plan, and had determined to move directly upon the Scioto villages, at the same time ordering Lewis to cross the Ohio and join him.

Although not much gratified at this sudden change of a plan which had been deliberately formed, Lewis prepared to obey, and had issued directions for the construction of rafts, boats, etc., in which to cross the Ohio; when, on the morning of the tenth of October, two of his hunters came running into camp, with the intelligence that a body of Indians was at hand, which covered "four acres of ground."

Upon this news, the general (having first lit his pipe) directed his brother, Colonel Charles Lewis, to proceed with his own regiment, and that of Colonel Fleming, and reconnoiter the ground where the enemy had been seen, while he held the remainder of the army ready to support him. Colonel Charles Lewis instantly advanced in the execution of his orders, and at the distance of a mile from camp, beheld a large body of the enemy advancing rapidly in hope of surprising the Virginian camp. The sun was just rising as the rencounter took place, and in a few minutes the action became warm and bloody. Colonel Charles Lewis being much exposed, and in full uniform, was mortally wounded early in the action, as was Colonel Fleming, the second in command. The troops, having great confidence in Colonel Lewis, were much discouraged, and being hard pressed by the enemy, at length gave way, and attempted to regain the camp. At this critical moment, General Lewis ordered up Field's regiment, which, coming handsomely into action, restored the fortune of the day. The Indians, in turn, were routed, and compelled to retire to a spot where they had erected a rough breastwork of logs.

The action was fought in the narrow point of land formed by the junction of the Ohio and Kenawha. The Indian breastwork was formed from one river to the other, so as to inclose the Virginians within the point; of course the breastwork formed the base, and the Virginian camp the vertex of the triangle, of which the rivers were sides. Here they rallied in full force, and appeared determined to abide the brunt of the Virginian force. Logan, Cornstalk, Elenipsico, Red Eagle, and many other celebrated chiefs were present, and were often heard loudly encouraging their warriors. Cornstalk, chief sachem of the Shawnees, and leader of the northern confederacy, was particularly conspicuous. As the repeated efforts of the whites to carry the breastwork became more warm and determined, the Indian line began to waver, and several were seen to give way. Cornstalk, in a moment, was upon the spot, and was heard distinctly to shout, "Be strong! Be strong!" in tones which rose above the din of the conflict. He buried his hatchet in the head of one of his warriors, and indignantly shaming the rest, completely restored the battle, which raged until four o'clock in the afternoon, without any decisive result. The Virginians fought with distinguished bravery, and suffered severely in those repeated charges upon the breastwork, but were unable to make any impression. The Indians, toward evening, dispatched a part of their force to cross both rivers, in order to prevent the escape of a man of the Virginians, should victory turn against them.

At length General Lewis, alarmed at the extent of his loss and the obstinacy of the enemy, determined to make an effort to turn their flank with three companies and attack them in rear. By the aid of a small stream, which empties into the Kenawha a short distance above its mouth, and which at that time had high and bushy banks, he was enabled to gain their rear with a small force, commanded by Captain (afterward governor) Isaac Shelby. Cornstalk instantly ordered a retreat, which was performed in a masterly manner, and with a very slight loss, the Indians alternately advancing and retreating in such a manner as to hold the whites in check until dark, when the whole body disappeared. The loss of the Virginians was severe, and amounted, in killed and wounded, to one-fourth of their whole number. The Indian loss was comparatively trifling. The action was shortly followed by a treaty, at which all the chiefs were present except Logan, who refused to be included in it. He wandered among the North-western tribes for several years, like a restless spirit, and finally, in utter recklessness, became strongly addicted to gaming and the use of ardent spirits. He was at length murdered on a solitary journey from Detroit to the north-eastern part of Ohio, as is generally supposed, by his own nephew.

It is not a little singular that the three celebrated Indian chiefs who commanded in the battle at the Point should all have been murdered, and that two of them should have met their fate upon the same spot which had witnessed their brave efforts to repress the extension of the white settlements. Cornstalk and Elenipsico, his son, were killed during a friendly visit to Point Pleasant in the summer of 1775, only a few months after the action. The circumstances attending the affair are thus related by Colonel Stewart:

A Captain Arbuckle commanded the garrison of the fort erected at Point Pleasant after the battle fought by General Lewis with the Indians at that place, in October, 1774. In the succeeding year, when the revolutionary war had commenced, the agents of Great Britain exerted themselves to excite the Indians to hostility against the United States. The mass of the Shawnees entertained a strong animosity against the Americans. But two of their chiefs, Cornstalk and Red Hawk, not participating in that animosity, visited the garrison at the Point, where Arbuckle continued to command. Colonel Stewart was at the post in the character of a volunteer, and was an eye-witness of the facts which he relates. Cornstalk represented his unwillingness to take a part in the war on the British side, but stated that his nation, except himself and his tribe, were determined on war with us, and he supposed that he and his people would be compelled to go with the stream.

On this intimation, Arbuckle resolved to detain the two chiefs and a third Shawnee who came with them to the fort as hostages, under the expectation of preventing thereby any hostile efforts of the nation. On the day before these unfortunate Indians fell victims to the fury of the garrison, Elenipsico, the son of Cornstalk, repaired to Point Pleasant for the purpose of visiting his father, and on the next day two men belonging to the garrison, whose names were Hamilton and Gillmore, crossed the Kenawha, intending to hunt in the woods beyond it. On their return from hunting, some Indians, who had come to view the position at the Point, concealed themselves in the weeds near the mouth of the Kenawha, and killed Gillmore while endeavoring to pass them. Colonel Stewart and Captain Arbuckle were standing on the opposite bank of the river at that time, and were surprised that a gun had been fired so near the fort, in violation of orders which had been issued inhibiting such an act.

Hamilton ran down the bank and cried out that Gillmore was killed. Captain Hall commanded the company to which Gillmore belonged. His men leaped into a canoe, and hastened to the relief of Hamilton. They brought the body of Gillmore, weltering in blood and the head scalped, across the river. The canoe had scarcely reached the shore, when Hall's men cried out, "Let us kill the Indians in the fort!" Captain Hall placed himself in front of his soldiers, and they ascended the river's bank, pale with rage, and carrying their loaded firelocks in their hands. Colonel Stewart and Captain Arbuckle exerted themselves in vain to dissuade these men, exasperated to madness by the spectacle of Gillmore's corpse, from the cruel deed which they contemplated. They cocked their guns, threatening those gentlemen with instant death if they did not desist, and rushed into the fort.

The interpreter's wife, who had been a captive among the Indians and felt an affection for them, ran to their cabin and informed them that Hall's soldiers were advancing with the intention of taking their lives, because they believed that the Indians who killed Gillmore had come with Cornstalk's son on the preceding day. This the young man solemnly denied, and averred that he knew nothing of them. His father, perceiving that Elenipsico was in great agitation, encouraged him, and advised him not to fear. "If the Great Spirit," said he, "has sent you here to be killed, you ought to die like a man!" As the soldiers approached the door, Cornstalk rose to meet them, and received seven or eight balls, which instantly terminated his existence. His son was shot dead in the seat which he occupied. The Red Hawk made an attempt to climb the chimney, but fell by the fire of some of Hall's men. "The other Indian," says Colonel Stewart, "was shamefully mangled, and I grieved to see him so long dying."

ST. CLAIR'S OFFICIAL LETTER.

"FORT WASHINGTON, *November* 9, 1791.

"*Sir:* Yesterday afternoon the remains of the army under my command got back to this place, and I have now the painful task to give an account of a warm and as unfortunate an action as almost any that has been fought, in which every corps was engaged and worsted except the first regiment, that had been detached upon a service that I had the honor to inform you of in my last dispatch, and had not joined me.

"On the third inst. the army had reached a creek about twelve yards wide, running to the southward of west, which I believe to have been the river St. Mary that empties into the Miami of the lake; arrived at the village about four o'clock in the afternoon, having marched near nine miles, and were immediately encamped upon a commanding piece of ground in two lines, having the above-mentioned creek in front. The right wing, composed of Butler's, Clark's, and Patterson's battalions, commanded by Major-General Butler, formed the first line, and the left wing, consisting of Bedinger and Gaither's battalions, and the second regiment, commanded by Colonel Darke, formed the second line, with an interval between them of about seventy yards, which was all the ground would allow.

"The right flank was pretty well secured by the creek, a steep bank, and Faulkner's corps. Some of the cavalry and their pickets covered the left flank. The militia were sent over the creek, and advanced about one-quarter of a mile, and encamped in the same order. There were a few Indians who appeared on the opposite side of the creek, but fled with the utmost precipitation on the advance of the militia. At this place, which I judged to be about fifteen miles from the Miami villages, I had determined to throw up a slight work, the plan of which was concerted that evening with Major Ferguson, wherein to have deposited the men's knapsacks, and every thing else that was not of absolute necessity, and to have moved on to attack the enemy as soon as the first regiment was come up; but they did not permit me to execute either, for on the fourth, about half an hour before sunrise, and when the men had been just dismissed from the parade (for it was a constant practice to have them all under arms a considerable time before daylight), an attack was made upon the militia, who gave way in a very little time and rushed into camp through Major Butler's battalion, which, together with part of Clark's, they threw into considerable disorder, and which, notwithstanding the exertions of both these officers, was never altogether remedied.

"The Indians followed close at their heels; the fire, however, of the front line checked them; but almost instantaneously a very heavy attack began upon that line, and in a few minutes it was extended to the second likewise. The great weight of it was directed against the center of each, where the artillery was placed, and from which the men were repeatedly driven with great slaughter. Finding no great effect from the fire, and confusion beginning to spread from the great number of men who were fallen in all quarters, it became necessary to try what could be done with the bayonet.

"Lieutenant-Colonel Darke was accordingly ordered to make a charge, with a part of the second line, and to turn the left flank of the enemy. This was executed with great spirit, and at first promised much success. The Indians instantly gave way, and were driven back three or four hundred yards; but for want of a sufficient number of riflemen to pursue this advantage, they soon returned, and the troops were obliged to give back in their turn. At this moment they had entered our camp by the left flank, having pursued back the troops that were posted there.

"Another charge was made here by the second regiment, Butler's and Clark's battalions, with equal effect, and it was repeated several times, and always with success; but in all of them many men were lost, and particularly the officers, which, with some raw troops, was a loss altogether irremediable. In that I just spoke of, made by the second regiment, and Butler's battalion, Major Butler was dangerously wounded, and every officer of the second regiment fell, except three, one of which, Captain Greaton, was shot through the body.

"Our artillery being now silenced, and all the officers killed except Captain Ford, who was badly wounded, more than half of the army fallen, being cut off from the road, it became necessary to attempt the regaining it, and to make a retreat if possible. To this purpose the remains of the army was formed as well as circumstances would admit, toward the right of the encampment; from which, by the way of the second line, another charge was made upon the enemy, as if with the design of turning their right flank, but it was in fact to gain the road. This was effected, and as soon as it was open the militia entered it, followed by the troops, Major Clark, with his battalion, covering the rear.

"The retreat in those circumstances was, you may be sure, a precipitate one. It was in fact a flight. The camp and the artillery were abandoned; but that was unavoidable, for not a horse was left alive to have drawn it off had it otherwise been practicable. But the most disgraceful part of the business is, that the greatest part of the men threw away their arms and accouterments, even after the pursuit (which continued about four miles) had ceased.

"I found the road strewed with them for many miles, but was not able to remedy it; for having had all my horses killed, and being mounted upon one that could not be pricked out of a walk, I could not get forward myself, and the orders I sent forward, either to halt the front, or prevent the men from parting with their arms, were unattended to.

"The rout continued quite to Fort Jefferson, twenty-nine miles, which was reached a little after sunset. The action began about half an hour before sunrise, and the retreat was attempted at half past nine o'clock.

"I have not yet been able to get the returns of the killed and wounded; but Major-General Butler, Lieutenant-Colonel Oldham, of the militia, Majors Ferguson, Hart, and Clark, are among the former.

"I have now, sir, finished my melancholy tale; a tale that will be felt, sensibly felt, by every one that has sympathy for private distress, or for public misfortune. I have nothing, sir, to lay to the charge of the troops but their want of discipline, which, from the short time they had been in service, it was impossible they should have acquired, and which rendered it very difficult, when they were thrown into confusion, to reduce them again to order, and is one reason why the loss has fallen so heavily upon the officers, who did every thing in their power to effect it. Neither were my own exertions wanting; but worn down with illness, and suffering under a painful disease, unable either to mount or dismount a horse without assistance, they were not so great as they otherwise would, or perhaps ought to have been.

"We were overpowered by numbers; but it is no more than justice to observe that, though composed of so many different species of troops, the utmost harmony prevailed through the whole army during the campaign.

"At Fort Jefferson I found the first regiment, which had returned from the service they had been sent upon, without either overtaking the deserters, or meeting the convoy of provisions. I am not certain, sir, whether I ought to consider the absence of this regiment from the field of action as fortunate; for I very much doubt whether, had it been in the action, the fortune of the day had been turned; and if it had not, the triumph of the enemy would have been more complete, and the country would have been destitute of means of defense.

"Taking a view of the situation of our broken troops at Fort Jefferson, and that there were no provisions in the fort, I called on the field officers for their advice what would be proper further to be done; and it was their unanimous opinion, that the addition of the first regiment, unbroken as it was, did not put the army on so respectable a footing as it was in the morning, because a great part of it was now unarmed; that it had been found unequal to the enemy, and should they come on, which was probable, would be found so again; that the troops could not be thrown into the fort, because it was too small, and there was no provision in it; that provisions were known to be upon the road at the distance of one, or at most two, marches; that, therefore, it would be proper to move without loss of time to meet the provisions, when the men might have the sooner an opportunity of some refreshment, and that a proper detachment might be sent back with it, to have it safely deposited in the fort.

"This advice was accepted, and the army was put in motion at ten o'clock, and marched all night, and the succeeding day met with a quantity of flour; part of it was distributed immediately, part taken back to supply the army on the march to Fort Hamilton, and the remainder, about fifty horse-loads, sent forward to Fort Jefferson.

"I have said, sir, in the former part of my communication, that we were overpowered by numbers; of that, however, I had no other evidence but the weight of the fire, which was always a most deadly one, and generally delivered from the ground, few of the enemy showing themselves on foot, except when they were charged, and that in a few minutes our whole camp, which extended above three hundred and fifty yards in length, was entirely surrounded and attacked on all quarters.

"The loss, sir, the public has sustained by the fall of so many officers, particularly General Butler and Major Ferguson, can not be too much regretted; but it is a circumstance that will alleviate the misfortune in some measure, that all of them fell most gallantly doing their duty. I have the honor to be, sir, your most obedient servant,

"ARTHUR ST. CLAIR.

"HON. SECRETARY OF WAR."

Upon a review of the chapter containing St. Clair's defeat, the author is aware that he will probably be charged with undue partiality, and perhaps with a misstatement of facts, particularly as it relates to the force

of the Indian army. Mr. Marshall, in his life of
Washington, reduces the Indian force to an equality
with St. Clair, and Mr. Marshall, of Kentucky, appears
to be of the same opinion. That chapter was written
before I had particularly referred to these excellent authorities, and my own statement of the Indian force
was taken from a book entitled "Indian Wars," which
professes to have derived it from the acknowledgment
of the Indians themselves. Upon reflection, I am satisfied that the gentlemen above mentioned are correct,
and only regret that the error, into which I was led by
insufficient authority, can not now be remedied.

In a private letter from Colonel McKee, the Indian
agent, to Colonel England, at Detroit, the Indian force
assembled at the "Fallen Timber," a few days before
the battle, is estimated at "*one thousand men!*" The
letter concludes with an earnest demand for *reinforcements!* Ten days afterward the battle was fought,
within which period it is difficult to believe that large
reinforcements could arrive from the upper lakes, the
only source from which they were expected. It is absolutely certain, that the Indian force opposed to Wayne
did not exceed fifteen hundred men, although their
whole strength was assembled. From this data, it
would seem impossible that the force employed against
St. Clair (more hastily collected and at shorter warning) could have exceeded twelve or fifteen hundred
men. Mr. Marshall, although evidently disposed to do
that unfortunate gentleman every justice, is, nevertheless, tolerably severe in his strictures upon the order of
battle.

He particularly censures him for posting the militia
in front, in order to receive the first shock, and contends that they should have been formed in the center
of the square, in order to reinforce such parts of the
line as gave away. This, as the event turned out, would
probably have been better than the measure actually
adopted, but St. Clair, at the time, only conformed to
the rule then established, and universally practiced.
Militia was *always* advanced in front of regulars, and
never incorporated with them. This was uniformly

done by Washington, by Green (except upon one occasion, when he placed them in the rear as a reserve, and, when they were wanted, found them too much frightened to be of any use), and by every general who employed them. We criticise St. Clair by the light of forty years' additional experience in Indian warfare, which, at the time of his defeat, was not so well understood, at least so far as relates to the employment of regulars, as now.

The close encampment of the troops was certainly highly improper, as battle was expected, and for battle he should have been always prepared. For the rest, we can see no room for blame. That no *general* charge was made, is true, for the simple reason that the troops, being totally *raw*, could not be brought to *unite* in one, although every possible exertion was made by officers as brave and intelligent as any in America. And even if one *could* have been made, there is every reason to believe that the event of the action would have been the same. The Indians would have given way, but their *retreating* fire was as fatal as any other, and, had the regulars followed throughout the day, they could not have overtaken them, and, without a sufficient body of cavalry, could have made no impression upon so lightfooted and irregular an enemy.

That a general charge succeeded under Wayne, is true. But how different were the circumstances! Wayne was the *assailant;* St. Clair was attacked suddenly, and under great disadvantages. Wayne more than doubled his enemy in numbers; St. Clair was, at best, only equal to his. And, what made an incalculable difference, Wayne was in possession of a poweiful body of mounted men, who alone exceeded the whole body of Indians in the field. *Here* advantages gained by the bayonet could be pressed by a numerous cavalry. The Indians were aware of all these circumstances; they beheld the movement of the mounted men, in order to turn their position, and, finding themselves charged in their coverts, instantly fled, but whether from fear of the bayonets of the infantry or the more rapid movements of the horse, is a question which might admit of discussion. Had Wayne encountered them with the bayonet alone, they would (as in St. Clair's case) have fled, but, like the ancient Parthians, their flight would have been as fatal as their advance. I have not the slightest disposition to detract from the well-merited fame of Wayne. His whole movements, during the campaign, displayed a boldness, vigor, and decision which the miserable decrepitude of St. Clair forbade him to exert; but it can not be denied that he fought with means incomparably beyond those of his predecessor.

N. B.—General St. Clair was of the opinion that his defeat occurred upon the St. Mary, and it is so stated in his official dispatch. It is incorrect. The action was fought upon a small tributary-stream of the Wabash.

INDIAN MANNERS.

THE CHASE.

THE following numbers are chiefly collected from Lewis & Clarke and Major Long's Journal:

"When the trading and planting occupations of the people are terminated, and provisions begin to fail them, which occurs generally in June, the chiefs assemble a council for the purpose of deliberating upon farther arrangements necessary to be made. This assembly decrees a feast to be prepared on a certain day, to which all the distinguished men of the nation are to be invited, and one of their number is appointed to have it prepared in his own lodge. On the return of this individual to his dwelling, he petitions his squaws to have pity on him, and proceed to clean and adjust the department; to spread the mats and skins for seats, and to collect wood, and bring water for cooking. He requests them to provide three or four large kettles to prepare the maize, and to kill their fattest dog for a feast. The squaws generally murmur at this last proposition, being reluctant to sacrifice these animals, which are of great service to them in carrying burdens, like the dogs of the erratic Tartars; but when they are informed of the honor that awaits them, of feasting all the distinguished men, they undertake their duties with pride and satisfaction.

"When they have performed their part, the squaws give notice to the husband, who then calls two or three old public criers to his lodge. He invites them to be seated near him, and, after the ceremony of smoking, he addresses them in a low voice, directing them to pass through the village and invite the individuals whom he names to them, to honor him, by their presence, at the feast which is now prepared. 'Speak in a low voice,' says he, 'and tell them to bring their bowls and spoons.' The criers, having thus received their instructions, sally out together, and, in concert, sing aloud, as they pass in various directions through the village. In this song of invitation, the names of all the elect are mentioned. Having performed this duty, they return to the lodge, and are soon followed by the chiefs and warriors. The host seats himself in the back part of the lodge, facing the entrance, where he remains during the ceremony. If the host is invested with the dignity of chief, he directs those who enter where to seat themselves, so that the chiefs may be arranged on one side, and the warriors on the other: if he is a warrior, he seats the principal chiefs of the village by his side, who whisper, in his ear, the situation which those who enter ought to occupy: this intimation is repeated aloud by the host; when the guests are all arranged, the pipe is lighted, and the indispensable ceremony of smoking proceeds.

"The principal chief then rises, and, extending his expanded hand toward each in succession, gives thanks to them individually, by name, for the honor of their company, and requests their patient attention to what he is about to say. He then proceeds somewhat in the following manner:—'Friends and relatives, we are assembled here for the purpose of consulting respecting the proper course to pursue in our next hunting excursion, or whether the quantity of provisions at present on hand will justify a determination to remain here to weed our maize.' If it be decided to depart immediately, the subject to be then taken into view will be the direction, extent, and object of the route.

"Having thus disclosed the business of the council, he is frequently succeeded by an old chief, who thanks him for his attention to their wants, and advises the assembly to pay great attention to what he has said, as he is a man of truth, of knowledge, and bravery. He further assures them, that they have ample cause to return thanks to the Great Wahconda for having sent such a man among them.

"The assembly then take the subject into their consideration, and, after much conversation, determine upon a route, which the principal chief proposes in a speech. This chief, previous to the council, is careful to ascertain the opinions and wishes of his people, and speaks accordingly.

"He sometimes, however, meets with opposition from persons who propose other hunting-grounds; but their discourses are filled with compliments to his superior knowledge and good sense. *The proceedings of the council are uniformly conducted with the most perfect good order and decorum.*

"*Each speaker carefully abstains from militating against the sensibility of any of his hearers: and uncourteous expressions toward each other, on these occasions, are never heard. Generally, at each pause of the speaker, the audience testify their approbation, aloud, by the interjection* HEH! *and as they believe that he has a just right to his own opinions, however absurd they may appear to be, and opposite to their own, the expression of them excites no reprehension; and, if they can not approve, they do not condemn, unless urged by necessity.*

"The day assigned for their departure having arrived, the squaws load their horses and dogs, and place as great a weight upon their own backs as they can conveniently transport; and, after having closed the entrances to their several habitations, by placing a considerable quantity of brushwood before them, the whole nation departs from the village.

"The men scatter about in every direction, to reconnoiter the country for enemies and game; but notwithstanding the constant activity of the hunters, the people often endure severe privation from want of food, previously to their arrival within view of the bisons, an interval of fifteen or twenty days.

"On coming in sight of the herd, the hunters speak kindly to their horses; applying to them the endearing name of father, brother, uncle, etc.; they petition them not to fear the buffaloes, but to run well, and keep close to them, but at the same time to avoid being gored. The party having approached as near to the herd as they suppose the animals will permit, without taking the alarm, they halt, to give the pipe-bearer an opportunity of smoking; which is considered necessary to their success. He lights his pipe, and remains a short time with his head inclined, and the stem of the pipe extended toward the herd. He then smokes, and puffs the smoke toward the buffaloes, toward the heavens and the earth, and finally to the cardinal points successively. These last they distinguish by the terms, sunrise, sunset, cold country, and warm country; or they designate them collectively by the phrase of the four winds.

"The ceremony of smoking being performed, the word for starting is given by the principal chief. They immediately separate into two bands, who pass in full speed to the right and left, and perform a considerable circuit, with the object of inclosing the herd, at a considerable interval between them. They then close in upon the animals, and each man endeavors to kill as many of them as his opportunity permits.

"It is upon this occasion that the Indians display their horsemanship and dexterity in archery. While in full run, they discharge the arrow with an aim of much certainty, so that it penetrates the body of the animal behind the shoulder. If it should not bury itself so deeply as they wish, they are often known to ride up to the enraged animal and withdraw it. They observe the direction and depth to which the arrow enters, in order to ascertain whether or not the wound is mortal, of which they can judge with a considerable degree of exactness; when a death wound is inflicted the hunter raises a shout of exultation, to prevent others from pursuing the individual of which he considers himself certain. He then passes on in pursuit of another, and so on until his quiver is exhausted, or the game has fled beyond his farther pursuit.

"The force of the arrow, when discharged by a dexterous and athletic Indian, is very great; and we were even credibly informed that, under favorable circumstances, it has been known to pass entirely through the body of a buffalo, and actually to fly some distance, or fall to the ground, on the opposite side of the animal.

"Notwithstanding the apparent confusion of this engagement, and that the same animal is sometimes feathered by arrows from different archers before he is dispatched, or considered mortally wounded, yet, as each man knows his own arrows from all others, and can also estimate the nature of the wound, whether it would produce a speedy death to the animal, quarrels respecting the right of property in the prey seldom occur, and it is consigned to the more fortunate individual, whose weapon penetrated the most vital part. The chase having terminated, each Indian can trace back his devious route to the starting place, so as to recover any small article he may have lost.

"A fleet horse, well trained to hunt, runs at the proper distance, with the reins thrown upon his neck, parallel with the buffalo, turns as he turns, and does not cease to exert his speed until the shoulder of the animal is presented, and the fatal arrow is implanted there. He then complies with the motion of his rider, who leans to one side in order to direct his course to another buffalo. Such horses as these are reserved by their owners exclusively for the chase, and are but rarely subjected to the drudgery of carrying burdens.

"When the herd has escaped, and those that are only wounded or disabled are secured, the hunters proceed to flay and cut up the slain. Every eatable part of the animal is carried to the camp and preserved, excepting the feet and the head; but the brains are taken from the skull for the purpose of dressing the skin, or converting it into Indian leather."

In descending the Ontonagon River, which falls into Lake Superior, Mr. Schoolcraft says: "Our Indian guides stopped on the east side of the river to examine a bear-fall that had been previously set, and were overjoyed to find a large bear entrapped. As it was no great distance from the river, we all landed to enjoy the sight. The animal sat up on his fore paws, facing us, the hinder paws being pressed to the ground by a heavy weight of logs, which had been arranged in such a manner as to allow the bear to creep under, and when, by seizing the bait, he had sprung the trap, he could not extricate himself, although with his fore paws he had demolished a part of the works. After viewing him for some time, a ball was fired through his head, but did not kill him. The bear kept his position, and seemed to growl in defiance. A second ball was aimed at the heart, and took effect; but he did not resign the contest immediately, and was at last dispatched with an ax. As soon as the bear fell, one of the Indians walked up, and addressing him by the name of Muckwah, shook him by the paw with a smiling countenance, saying, in the Indian language, he was sorry he had been under the necessity of killing him, and hoped the offense would be forgiven, particularly as Long-knife* had fired one of the balls."†

THEIR DANCES.

All their dances are distinguished by appropriate names, such as the war dance, the scalp dance, the buffalo dance, the beggar's dance, etc. In Major Long's Journal, the beggar's dance is thus described: "About one hundred Ottoes, together with a deputation of the Ioway nation, who had been summoned by Major O'Fallon (Indian agent for the Government of the United States), presented themselves at our camp. The principal chiefs advanced before their people, and, upon invitation, seated themselves. After a short interval of silence, Shonga-Tonga, the Big Horse, a large, portly

---

*An American.   † Schoolcraft's Journal, p. 183.

Indian, of a commanding presence, arose, and said, 'My father, your children have come to dance before your tent, agreeably to our custom of honoring brave or distinguished persons.'

"After a suitable reply from Major O'Fallon, the amusement of dancing was commenced by the striking up of their rude instrumental and vocal music, the former consisting of a gong made of a large keg, over one end of which a skin was stretched, which was struck by a small stick; and another instrument consisting of a stick of firm wood, notched like a saw, over the teeth of which a smaller stick was rubbed forcibly backward and forward. With these, rude as they were, very good time was preserved with the vocal performers, who sat around them; and by all the natives as they sat, in the inflection of their bodies, or the movements of their limbs. After the lapse of a little time, three individuals leaped up, and danced around for a few minutes; then, at a concerted signal from the master of ceremonies, the music ceased and they retired to their seats, uttering a loud noise, which, by patting the mouth rapidly with the hand, was broken into a succession of similar sounds, somewhat like the hurried barking of a dog. Several sets of dancers succeeded, each terminating as the first.

"In the intervals of the dances, a warrior would step forward and strike a flag-staff they had erected with a stick, whip, or other weapon, and recount his martial deeds. This ceremony is called "striking the post,"* and whatever is then said, may be relied on as truth, being delivered in the presence of many a jealous warrior and witness, who could easily detect, and would immediately disgrace the striker, for exaggeration and falsehood. This is called the beggar's dance, during which some presents are always expected by the performers, as tobacco, whisky, or trinkets. But, on this occasion, as none of these articles were immediately offered, the amusement was not, at first, distinguished by much activity. The master of ceremonies continu-

---

* Of this an explanation will hereafter be given.

ally called aloud to them to exert themselves; but still they were somewhat dull and backward. Ietan (the master of ceremonies) now stepped forward and lashed a post with his whip, declaring that he would thus punish those who would not dance.

"This threat, from one whom they had vested with authority for this occasion, had a manifest effect upon his auditors, who were presently highly wrought up by the sight of two or three little mounds of tobacco twists, which were now laid before them, and appeared to infuse new life. After lashing the post, and making his threat, Ietan went on to relate his martial exploits. He had stolen horses, seven or eight times, from the Konzas; he had first struck the bodies of three of that nation slain in battle. He had stolen horses from the Ietan nation, and had struck one of their dead. He had stolen horses from the Pawnees, and struck the body of one Pawnee Loup. He had stolen horses, several times, from the Omawhaws, and once from the Pimcas. He had struck the bodies of two Sioux. On a war party, in company with the Pawnees, he had attacked the Spaniards, and penetrated into one of their camps. The Spaniards, except a man and a boy, fled. He was at a distance before his party, and was shot at and missed by the man, whom he immediately shot down and struck. 'This, my father,' said he, 'is the only martial act of my life that I am ashamed of.'

"After several rounds of dancing, and of striking at the post, the Miaketa, or the Little Soldier, a war-worn veteran, took his turn to strike the post. He leaped actively about, and strained his voice to the utmost pitch, while he portrayed some of the scenes of blood in which he had acted. He had struck dead bodies of all the red nations around, Osages, Konzas, Pawnee Loups, Pawnee Republicans, Grand Pawnees, Puncas, Omawhaws, Sioux, Paducas, La Plais or Baldheads, Ietans, Sacs, Foxes, and Ioways. He had struck eight of one nation, seven of another, etc. He was proceeding with his account, when Ietan ran up to him, put his hand upon his mouth, and respectfully led him to his seat. This act was no trifling compliment paid to the well-known brave. It indicated, that he had still so many glorious acts to speak of that he would occupy so much time as to prevent others from speaking, and put to shame the other warriors by the contrast of his actions with theirs.

"Their physical action is principally confined to leaping a small distance from the ground, with both feet, the body being slightly inclined; and, upon alighting, an additional slight but sudden inclination of the body is made, so as to appear like a succession of jerks; or the feet are raised alternately, the motions of the body being the same. Such are their movements, in which the whole party corresponds; but in the figures, as they are termed in our assembly rooms, each individual performs a separate part, and each part is a significant pantomimic narrative. In all their variety of action they are careful to observe the musical cadences. In this dance, Ietan represents one who was in the act of stealing horses. He carried a whip in his hand, as did a considerable number of the Indians, and around his neck were thrown several leather thongs, for bridles and halters, the ends of which trailed on the ground behind him.

"After many preparatory maneuvers, he stooped down and, with his knife, represented the act of cutting the hopples of horses; he then rode his tomahawk as children ride their broomsticks, making such use of his whip as to indicate the necessity of rapid movement, lest his foes should overtake him. Wa-sa-ba-jing-ga, or Little Black Bear, after a variety of gestures, threw several arrows, in succession, over his head, thereby indicating his familiarity with the flight of such missiles; he, at the same time, covered his eyes with his hand, to indicate that he was blind to danger. Others represented their maneuvers in battle, seeking their enemy, discharging at him their guns and arrows, etc., etc. Most of the dancers were the principal warriors of the nation, men who had not condescended to amuse themselves or others, in this manner, for years before; but they now appeared in honor of the occasion, and to conciliate, in their best manner, the good will of the representative of the government of the Big-Knives.*

"Among these veteran warriors, Ietan, or Shamone-kussee, Hashea, the Broken Arm, commonly called Cut-nose, and Wa-sa-ba-jing-ga, or Little Black Bear, three youthful leaders, in particular attracted our attention. In consequence of having been appointed soldiers, on this occasion, to preserve order, they were painted entirely black. The countenance of the former indicated much wit, and had, in its expression, something of the character of that of Voltaire. He frequently excited the mirth of those about him by his remarks and gestures. Hashea, called Cutnose, in consequence of having lost the tip of his nose, in a quarrel with Ietan, wore a handsome robe of white wolf-skin, with an appendage behind him called a *crow*. This singular decoration is a large cushion, made of the skin of a crow, stuffed with any light material, and variously ornamented. It has two decorated sticks projecting from it upward, and a pendant one beneath. This apparatus is secured, upon the buttocks, by a girdle passing round the body.

"The other actors in the scene were decorated with paints of several colors, fantastically disposed upon their persons. Several were painted with white clay, which had the appearance of being grooved, in many places. This grooved appearance is given by drawing the finger-nails over the part, so as to remove the pigment from thence in parallel lines. These lines are either rectilinear, undulated, or zigzag: sometimes passing over the forehead transversely, or vertically; sometimes in the same directions, or obliquely, over the whole visage, or upon the breast, arms, etc. Many were painted with red clay, in which the same lines appeared. A number of them had the representation of a black hand, with outspread fingers, on different parts of the body, strongly contrasted with the principal color with which the body was overspread. The hand was depicted in

---

* The appellation by which the Indians distinguish the whites of the United States.

different positions upon the face, breast, and back. The faces of others were colored one-half black and the other white, etc.

"Many colored their hair with red clay; but the eyelids and base of the ears were generally tinged with vermilion. At the conclusion of the ceremony, whisky, which they always expect on similar occasions, was produced, and a small portion given to each. The principal chiefs, of the different nations, who had remained passive spectators of the scene, now directed their people to return to their camp. The word of the chiefs was obeyed, except by a few of the Ioways, who appeared to be determined to keep their places, notwithstanding the reiterated command of the chiefs. Ietan now sprang toward them, with an expression of much ferocity in his countenance, and, it is probable, a tragic scene would have been displayed had not the chiefs requested him to use gentle means, and thus he succeeded, after which the chiefs withdrew."*

EMBASSIES.

Charlevoix says, "In their treaties for peace, and generally in all their negotiations, they discover a dexterity and a nobleness of sentiment which would do honor to the most polished nations." † A specimen of the mode of negotiating peace, among the Missouri Indians, which I shall extract from Major Long's Journal, will, in a considerable degree, sustain the foregoing remark of Charlevoix: it will also convey an idea of the formalities observed, on that occasion, with greater accuracy than any general observations.

"During the stay of our detached party at the Konza village, several chief men of the nation requested Mr. Dougherty to lead a deputation, from them, to their enemies, the Ottoes, Missouries, and Ioways, then dwelling in one village on the Platte. Circumstances then prevented the gratification of their wishes, but he gave them to understand, that if the deputation should

---

* Vol. 1, page 153. † Charlevoix, p. 167.

meet our party near Council Bluff, he would probably then be authorized to bear them company: on which they determined to send a party thither. Accordingly, on the day preceding the arrival of our steamboat at the position chosen for our winter cantonment, a deputation from the Konzas arrived for that purpose. It consisted of six men, lead by Herochche, or the Red War Eagle, one of the principal warriors of the Konza nation.

"Mr. Dougherty having made known their pacific mission to Major O'Fallon, the latter expressed to them his cordial approbation of their intentions, and the following day he dispatched Mr. Dougherty with them, to protect them, by his presence, on their approach to the enemy; and to assist them, by his mediation, in their negotiations, should it be found necessary.

"The distance of the Otto village is about twenty-five miles. On the journey over the prairies, they espied an object at a distance, which was mistaken for a man standing upon an eminence. The Indians immediately halted, when Herochche addressed them with the assurance that they must put their trust in the Master of Life, and in their leaders; and observed, that having journeyed thus far on their business, they must not return until their purpose was accomplished; that if it was their lot to die, no event could save them. 'We have set out, my braves,' said he, 'to eat of the Ottoes victuals, and we must do so or die.' The party then proceeded onward. The Indians are always very cautious when approaching an enemy's village, on any occasion, and this party well knew that their enterprise was full of danger.

"In a short time, they were again brought to a halt by the appearance of a considerable number of men and horses, that were advancing toward them. After some consultation and reconnoitering, they sat down upon the ground, and lighting the peace pipe or calumet, Herochche directed the stem of it toward the object of their suspicion, saying: 'Smoke, friend or foe.' He then directed it toward the Otto village, toward the white people, toward heaven, and toward the earth, successively."

The strangers, however, proved to be drovers, with cattle for the troops, on their way to Council Bluff.

"In consequence of being thus detained, it was late in the afternoon when the party arrived at the Platte River, and as they had still eighteen miles to travel, and it was indispensable to their safety that they should reach the village before dark, Mr. Dougherty urged his horse rapidly forward. The Indians, who were all on foot, ran the whole distance, halting but twice, in order to cross the Elkhorn and Platte Rivers, although one of them was upwards of sixty years of age, and three of the others were much advanced in years.

"As they drew near the Otto village, they were discovered by some boys who were collecting their horses together for the night, and who, in a telegraphic manner, communicated intelligence of their approach to the people of the village, by throwing their robes into the air.

"The party was soon surrounded by the inhabitants, who rushed toward them, riding, and running with the greatest impetuosity. The greatest confusion reigned for some time, the Ottoes, shouting, hallooing, and screaming, while their Konza visitors lamented aloud. Shamonekussee soon arrived, and restored a degree of order, when the business of the mission being made known in a few words, the Konzas were taken up, behind some of the horsemen, and conveyed as rapidly as possible to the lodge of Shonga-Tongo, lest personal violence should be offered them on the way. They did not, however, escape the audible maledictions of the squaws, as they passed, but were stigmatized as wrinkled-faced old men with hairy chins, and ugly faces, and flat noses.

"After running this species of gauntlet, they were quietly seated in the lodge, where they were sure of protection. A squaw, however, whose husband had been recently killed by the Konzas, rushed into the lodge, with the intention of seeking vengeance by killing one of the embassadors on the spot. She stood suddenly before Herochche, and seemed a very demon of fury. She caught his eye, and at the instant, with all her strength, she aimed a blow at his breast with a large knife, which was firmly grasped in her right hand, and which she seemed confident of sheathing in his heart. At that truly hopeless moment, the countenance of the warrior remained unchanged, and even exhibited no emotion whatever; and when the knife approached its destination with the swiftness of lightning, his eye stood firm, nor were its lids seen to quiver; so far from recoiling, or raising his arm to avert the blow, that he even rather protruded his breast to meet that death which seemed inevitable, and which was only averted by the sudden interposition of the arm of one of her nation, that received the weapon to the very bone.

"Thus foiled in her attempt, the squaw was gently led out of the lodge, and no one offered her violence, or even harsh reproof. No further notice was taken of this transaction by either party. Food was then, as usual, placed before the strangers, and soon after a warrior entered with a pipe, which he held, while Herochche smoked, saying in a loud voice, 'You tell us you wish for peace; I say I will give you a horse; let us see which of us will be the liar, you or I.' The horse was presented to him.

"The evening, and much of the night, were passed in friendly conversation, respecting the events of the five years' war which they had waged with each other. On the following morning, the Konzas were called to partake of the hospitality of different lodges, while the principal men of the village were assembled in council, to deliberate upon the subject of concluding a peace.

"At noon, the joint and grand council was held in Crenier's lodge. The Ottoes, Missouries, and Ioways took their seats around the apartment, with the Konzas in the center. Herochche, whose business it was first to speak, holding the bowl of the calumet in his hand, remained immovable for the space of three-fourths of an hour, when he arose, pointed the stem of the calumet toward each of the three nations successively, then toward heaven, and the earth, after which he stretched out his arm, with the palm of the hand toward each of the members in succession. He then proceeded to shake each individual by the hand, after which he returned to his place, and renewed the motion of the hand as before.

"Having performed all these introductory formalities, he stood firm and erect, though perfectly easy and unconstrained, and with a bold expression of countenance, loud voice, and emphatic gesticulation, he thus addressed the council:

"'Fathers, brothers, chiefs, warriors, and brave men—You are all great men: I am a poor, obscure individual. It has, however, become my duty to inform you, that the chiefs and warriors of my nation, some time ago, held a council for the purpose of concerting measures to terminate amicably the cruel and unwelcome war that has so long existed between us, and chosen me, all insignificant as I am, to bring you this pipe which I hold in my hand. I have visited your village, that we might all smoke from the same pipe, and eat from the same bowl, with the same spoon, in token of our future union in friendship.

"'On approaching your village, my friends and relatives, I thought I had not long to live. I expected that you would kill me and these poor men who have followed me. But I received encouragement from the reflection, that if it should be my lot to die to-day, I would not have to die to-morrow, and I relied firmly upon the Master of Life.

"'Nor was this anticipation of death unwarranted by precedent; you may recollect that, five winters ago, six warriors of my nation came to you, as I have now done, and that you killed them all but one, who had the good fortune to escape. This circumstance was vivid in my memory when I yesterday viewed your village in the distance; said I, those warriors who preceded me in the attempt to accomplish this desirable object, although they were greater and more brave than I, yet they were killed by those whom they came to conciliate, and why shall I not share their fate? If so, my bones will bleach near theirs. If, on the contrary, I should escape death, I will visit the bones of my friends. The oldest of my followers here, was father-in-law to the chief of those slaughtered messengers; he is poor and infirm, and has followed us with difficulty; his relatives also are poor, and have been long lamenting the loss of the chief you killed. I hope you will have pity on him, and give him moccasins (meaning a horse) to return home with, for he can not walk. Two or three others of my companions are also in want of moccasins for their journey homeward.

"'My friends, we wish for peace, and we are tired of war. There is a large tract of country intervening between us, from which, as it is so constantly traversed by our respective hostile parties, we can not either of us kill the game in security, to furnish our traders with peltries. I wish to see a large level road over that country, connecting our villages together, near which no one can conceal himself in order to kill passengers, and that our squaws may be enabled to visit from village to village in safety, and not be urged, by fear, to cast off their packs, and betake themselves to the thickets, when they see any person on the route. Our nations have made peace frequently, but a peace has not been of long duration. I hope, however, that which we shall now establish, will continue one day, two days, three days, four days, five days. My friends! what I have told you is true; I was not sent here to tell you lies. That is all I have to say.'

"Herochche then lit his pipe, and presented the stem to the brother of the Crenier, Wasacaruja, or, he who eats raw, who had formerly been his intimate friend. The latter held the end of the stem in his hand, while he looked Herochche full in the face for a considerable space of time. At length, he most emphatically asked, 'Is all true that you have spoken?' The other, striking himself repeatedly and forcibly upon the breast, answered with a loud voice, 'Yes, it is all truth that I have spoken.' Wasacaruja, without any further hesitation, accepted the proffered pipe, and smoked, while Herochche courteously held the bowl of it in his hand; the latter warrior then held it in succession to each member of council, who respectively took a whiff or two, after which the pipe itself was presented to Wasacaruja to retain.

"It is impossible to convey an adequate idea of the energy and propriety with which this speech was delivered, or of the dignity and self-possession of the speaker. Before he commenced, he hesitated, and looked around upon his enemies, probably in order to trace in the lineaments of their countenances, the expressions of their feelings toward him. He then began his address, by raising his voice at once to its full intonation, producing a truly powerful effect upon the ear, by a contrast with the deep and long-continued silence which preceded it. He was at no loss for subject or for words, but proceeded right onwards to the close of his speech, like a full-flowing impetuous stream.

"Wasacaruja, in consequence of having first accepted of the calumet, was now regarded as responsible for the sincerity of his friend Herochche, He, therefore arose, and thus addressed the embassador:—'My friend! I am glad to see you on such an occasion as the present, and to hear that your voice is for peace. A few winters ago, when we were in friendship with each other, I visited your village, and you gave me all your people, saying that all the Konzas were mine. But it was not long afterward, as we hunted near your country, that you stole our horses, and killed some of our people, and I can not but believe that the same course will be again pursued. Nevertheless, I shall again repair to the same place of which I have spoken this autumn, for the purpose of hunting, and in the spring I will again visit your town. You observed that you were apprehensive of being killed as you approached our village, and you most probably would have been so, coming as you did, late in the evening, and without the usual formality of sending a messenger to apprize us of your approach, had you not been accompanied by the Big Knife, with whom you are so well acquainted. But we have now smoked together, and I hope that the peace thus established may long continue. You say that you are in want of moccasins; we will endeavor to give you one or two for your journey home. That is all I have to say.'

"Herochche then apologized for his unceremonious entrance into the village, by saying, that he knew it was customary to send forward a runner, on such an occasion, and he should have done so, but his friend, the Big Knife, whom he had previously consulted with that view, told him that he had full confidence in the magnanimity of the Ottoes. Thus the ceremony was concluded, and peace restored between the two nations."*

WAR EXPEDITIONS.

In this number we shall give a few striking instances of the dexterity and address, as well as the devoted courage, which frequently distinguish their conduct in war.

"In the year 1763, Detroit, containing a British garrison of three hundred men, commanded by Major Gladwyn, was besieged by a confederacy of Indian tribes under Pontiac, an Ottoway chief, who displayed such a boldness in his designs, such skill in negotiation, and such personal courage in war, as to justify us in considering him one of the greatest men who have ever appeared among the Indian tribes of North America. He was the decided and constant enemy of the British government, and excelled all his contemporaries in both mental and bodily vigor. His conspiracy for making himself master of the town of Detroit, and destroying the garrison, although frustrated, is a master-piece among Indian stratagems; and his victory over the British troops at the battle of Bloody Bridge, stands unparalleled in the history of Indian wars, for the decision and steady courage by which it was, in an open fight, achieved.

"As, at the time above mentioned, every appearance of war was at an end, and the Indians seemed to be on a friendly footing, Pontiac approached Detroit without exciting any suspicions in the breast of the governor, or the inhabitants. He encamped at a little distance from it, and let the commandant know that he was

---

* Long's Journal, vol. 1, p. 310.

come to trade; and being desirous of brightening the chain of peace between the English and his nation, desired that he and his chiefs might be admitted to hold a council with him. The governor, still unsuspicious, and not in the least doubting the sincerity of the Indian, granted their general's request, and fixed on the next morning for their reception.

"On the evening of that day, an Indian woman who had been appointed by Major Gladwyn to make a pair of Indian shoes, out of a curious elk-skin, brought them home. The major was so pleased with them, that, intending these as a present for a friend, he ordered her to take the remainder back, and make it into others for himself. He then directed his servant to pay her for those she had done, and dismissed her. The woman went to the door that led to the street, but no further; she there loitered about as if she had not finished the business on which she came. A servant at length observed her, and asked her why she staid there. She gave him, however, no answer.

"Some short time after, the governor himself saw her, and inquired of his servant what occasioned her stay. Not being able to get a satisfactory answer, he ordered the woman to be called in. When she came into his presence, he desired to know what was the reason of her loitering about, and not hastening home before the gates were shut, that she might complete in due time the work he had given her to do. She told him, after much hesitation, that as he had always behaved with great goodness toward her, she was unwilling to take away the remainder of the skin, because he put so great a value upon it; and yet had not been able to prevail upon herself to tell him so. He then asked her why she was more reluctant to do so now than she had been when she made the former pair. With increased reluctance she answered, that she should never be able to bring them back.

"His curiosity was now excited, and he insisted on her disclosing the secret that seemed to be struggling in her bosom for utterance. At last, on receiving a promise that the intelligence she was about to give him should

Indian Woman revealing the Conspiracy of Pontiac. [See page 328.]

not turn to her prejudice, and that, if it appeared to be beneficial, she should be rewarded for it, she informed him, that at the council to be held with the Indians the following day, Pontiac and his chiefs intended to murder him ; and, after having massacred the garrison and inhabitants, to plunder the town. That for this purpose, all the chiefs who were to be admitted into the council-room had cut their guns short, so that they could conceal them under their blankets; with which on a signal given by their general, on delivering the belt, they were all to rise up, and instantly to fire on him and his attendants. Having effected this, they were immediately to rush into the town, where they would find themselves supported by a great number of their warriors, that were to come into it during the sitting of the council under the pretense of trading, but privately armed in the same manner. Having gained from the woman every necessary particular relative to the plot, and also the means by which she acquired a knowledge of them, he dismissed her with injunctions of secrecy, and a promise of fulfilling on his part, with punctuality, the engagements he had entered into.

"The intelligence the governor had just received gave him great uneasiness; and he immediately consulted the officer who was next him in command, on the subject. But this gentleman, considering the information as a story invented for some artful purpose, advised him to pay no attention to it. This conclusion, however, had happily no weight with him. He thought it prudent to conclude it to be true, till he was convinced that it was not so ; and therefore, without revealing his suspicions to any other person, he took every needful precaution that the time would admit of. He walked around the fort the whole night, and saw himself, that every sentinel was upon duty, and every weapon of defence in proper order.

"As he traversed the ramparts that lay nearest to the Indian camp, he heard them in high festivity, and little imagining that their plot was discovered, probably pleasing themselves with the anticipation of success. As soon as the morning dawned, he ordered all the garrison under arms, and then, imparting his apprehension to a few of the principal officers, gave them such directions as he thought necessary. At the same time he sent round to all the traders, to inform them, that as it was expected a great number of Indians would enter the town that day, who might be inclined to plunder, he desired they would have their arms ready, and repel any attempt of that kind.

"About ten o'clock, Pontiac and his chiefs arrived, and were conducted to the council chamber, where the governor and his principal officers, each with pistols in his belt, awaited his arrival. As the Indians passed on, they could not help observing that a greater number of troops than usual were drawn up on the parade, or marching about. No sooner were they entered and seated on the skins prepared for them, than Pontiac asked the governor, on what occasion his young men, meaning the soldiers, were thus drawn up and parading the streets. He received for answer, that it was only intended to keep them perfect in their exercise.

"The Indian chief-warrior now began his speech, which contained the strongest professions of friendship and good-will toward the English; and when he came to the delivery of the belt of wampum, the particular mode of which, according to the woman's information, was to be the signal for the chiefs to fire, the governor and all his attendants drew their swords half way out of their scabbards; and the soldiers at the same instant made a clattering with their arms before the doors, which had been purposely left open. Pontiac, though one of the bravest of men, immediately turned pale and trembled; and instead of giving the belt in the manner proposed, delivered it according to the usual way. His chiefs, who had impatiently expected the signal, looked at each other with astonishment, but continued quiet, waiting the result.

"The governor, in his turn, made a speech, but instead of thanking the great warrior for the professions of friendship he had just uttered, he accused him of being a traitor. He told him that the English, who knew every thing, were convinced of his treachery and villainous designs; and as a proof that they were acquainted with his most secret thoughts and intentions, he stepped towards an Indian chief that sat nearest to him, and drawing aside the blanket, discovered the shortened firelock. This entirely disconcerted the Indians, and frustrated their design.

"He then continued to tell them that, as he had given his word, at the time they desired an audience, that their persons should be safe, he would hold his promise inviolable, though they so little deserved it. However, he desired them to make the best of their way out of the fort, lest his young men, on being acquainted with their treacherous purposes, should cut every one of them to pieces.

"Pontiac endeavored to contradict the accusation, and to make excuses for his suspicious conduct; but the governor, satisfied of the falsity of his protestations, would not listen to him. The Indians immediately left the fort; but, instead of being sensible of the governor's generous behavior, they threw off the mask, and the next day made a regular attack upon it."

Major Gladwyn has not escaped censure for this mistaken lenity: for, probably, had he kept a few of the principal chiefs prisoners, while he had them in his power, he might have been able to have brought the whole confederacy to terms, and prevented a war. But he atoned for his oversight by the gallant defense he made for more than a year, amidst a variety of discouragements.

"During that period some very smart skirmishes happened between the besiegers and garrison, of which the following was the principal and most bloody: Captain Delzel, a brave officer, prevailed on the governor to give him the command of about two hundred men, and to permit him to attack the enemy's camp. This being complied with, he sallied from the town before daybreak; but Pontiac, receiving from some of his swift-footed warriors, who were constantly employed in watching the motions of the garrison, timely intelligence of their deisgn, collected the choicest of his troops, and met the detachment at some distance from his camp, near a place since called Bloody Bridge. As the Indians were vastly superior in number to Captain Delzel's party, he was soon overpowered and driven back. Being now nearly surrounded, he made a vigorous effort to regain the bridge he had just crossed, by which alone he could find a retreat; but in doing this, he lost his life, and many of his men fell with him. However, Major Rogers, the second in command, assisted by Lieutenant Graham, found means to draw off the shattered remains of their little army, and conducted them into the fort.

"Then, considerably reduced, it was with difficulty the major could defend the town, notwithstanding which, he held out against the Indians till he was relieved; as after this they made but few attacks upon the place, and only continued to blockade it. The Gladwyn schooner arrived about this time near the town, with a reinforcement, and necessary supplies. But before this vessel could reach the place of its destination, it was most vigorously attacked by a detachment from Pontiac's army. The Indians surrounded it in their canoes, and made great havoc among the crew.

"At length, the captain of the schooner, with a considerable number of his crew, being killed, and the savages beginning to climb up the sides from every quarter, the lieutenant, being determined that the stores should not fall into the enemy's hands, and seeing no alternative, ordered the gunner to set fire to the powder-room and blow the ship up. This order was on the point of being executed, when a chief of the Hurons, who understood the English language, gave out to his friends the intention of the commander. On receiving this intelligence, the Indians hurried down the sides of the ship with the greatest precipitation and got as far from it as possible; while the commander immediately took advantage of their consternation, and arrived without any further obstruction at the town.

"'This seasonable supply gave the garrison fresh spirits; and Pontiac, being now convinced that it would not be in his power to reduce the place, proposed an accommodation. The governor, wishing much to get rid of such troublesome enemies, listened to his proposals, and having procured advantageous terms, agreed to a peace." *

The massacre of the garrison of Michilimackinac, which occurred also in the year 1763, while it exhibits one of the most shocking instances of Indian barbarity, is at the same time a striking proof of the sagacity and dissimulation of the Indian character. It appears from the very interesting account given of this transaction by Henry, who was an eye-witness, "that the Indians were in the habit of playing at a game called Bag-gat-iway, which is played with a ball and a bat on the principles of our foot-ball, and decided by one of the parties heaving the ball beyond the goal of their adversaries. The king's birthday, the fourth of June, having arrived, the Sacs and Chippeways, who were encamped in great numbers around the fort, turned out upon the green, to play at this game for a high wager, and attracted a number of the garrison and traders to witness the sport. The game of bag-gat-iway is necessarily attended with much violence and noise. In the ardor of contest, the ball, if it can not be thrown to the goal desired, is struck or thrown in any direction by which it can be diverted from that designed by the adversary.

"At such a moment, therefore, nothing could be less liable to excite premature alarm, than that the ball should be tossed over the pickets of the fort, nor, having fallen there, that it should be followed on the instant by all engaged in the game, as well the one party as the other, all eager, all struggling, all shouting, in the unrestrained pursuit of a rude athletic exercise. Nothing, therefore, could be more happily devised, under the circumstances, then a stratagem like this; and it was in fact the stratagem which the Indians employed to obtain possession of the fort, and by which they were enabled to slaughter and subdue its garrison, and such of the other inhabitants as they pleased. To be still

---

* I have extracted this narrative of Pontiac's attempt on Detroit, from Mr. Schoolcraft, who takes it from Carver's Travels.

more certain of success, they had prevailed on as many as they could, by a pretext the least liable to suspicion, to come voluntarily without the pickets; and particularly the commandant and garrison themselves. The Indians, after butchering the garrison, burnt down the fort."

ADDITIONAL SKETCHES

OF

WESTERN ADVENTURE.

THE WETZELS.—LEWIS WETZEL.

[The sketch below is believed to be the most full and accurate ever compiled of Lewis Wetzel, the famous Indian hunter. It embraces, and mainly in their language, all the particulars found in the various accounts given of him by the following writers, or narrators of frontier history, viz: John McDonald, Joseph Pritts, Charles Cist, Major Jacob Fowler, Wills DeHass, John Rodefer, sen., and Joseph Doddridge. The name is frequently, but incorrectly, spelled Whetzel, Whetzell, or Whitzell.]

LEWIS WETZEL was regarded by many of the settlers in the neighborhood of Wheeling, Virginia, between the years 1782 and 1795, as the right arm of their defense. His presence was considered as a tower of strength to the infant settlements, and an object of terror to the fierce and restless savages who prowled about and depredated upon our frontier homes. The memory of Wetzel should be embalmed in the hearts of the people of Western Virginia; for his efforts in defense of their forefathers were without a parallel in border warfare. Among the foremost and most devoted, he plunged into the fearful strife which a bloody and relentless foe waged against the feeble colonists. He threw into the common treasury a soul as heroic, as adventurous, as full of energy, and exhaustless of resources, as ever animated the human breast. Bold, wary, and active, he stood without an equal in the pursuit to which he had committed himself, mind and body. No man on the western frontier was more dreaded by the enemy, and none did more to beat him back into the heart of the forest, and reclaim the expanseless domain which we now enjoy. He was never known to inflict unwonted cruelty upon women and children, as has been charged upon him; and he never was found to torture or mutilate his victim, as many of the traditions would indicate. He was revengeful, because he had suffered deep injury at the hands of that race, and woe to the Indian warrior who crossed his path. He was literally a man without fear. He was brave as a lion, cunning as a fox; "daring where daring was the wiser part —prudent when discretion was valor's better self." He seemed to possess, in a remarkable degree, that intuitive knowledge which can alone constitute a good and efficient hunter, added to which, he was sagacious, prompt to act, and always aiming to render his actions efficient. Such was Lewis Wetzel, the celebrated Indian hunter of Western Virginia.

John Wetzel, the father of Lewis, was one of the first settlers on Wheeling Creek. He had five sons and two daughters, whose names were, respectively, Martin, Lewis, Jacob, John, George, Susan, and Christina.

The elder Wetzel spent much of his time in locating lands, hunting, and fishing. His neighbors frequently admonished him against exposing himself thus to the enemy; but, disregarding their advice, and laughing at their fears, he continued to widen the range of his excursions, until finally he fell a victim to the active vigilance of the tawny foe. He was killed near Captina, in 1787, on his return from Middle Island Creek, under the following circumstances: Himself and companion were in a canoe, paddling slowly near the shore, when they were hailed by a party of Indians, and ordered to land. This they of course refused, when immediately they were fired upon, and Wetzel shot through the body. Feeling himself mortally wounded, he directed his companion to lie down in the canoe, while he (Wetzel), so long as strength remained, would paddle the frail vessel beyond reach of the savages. In this way he saved the life of his friend, while his own was ebbing fast. He died soon after reaching the shore, at Baker's Station, and his humble grave can still be seen near the site of that primitive fortress. A rough stone marks the spot, bearing, in rude but perfectly distinct characters, "J. W., 1787."

At the time of his father's death, Lewis was about twenty-three years of age, and, in common with his brothers, or those who were old enough, swore sleepless vengeance against the whole Indian race. Terribly did he and they carry that resolution into effect. From that time forward, they were devoted to the woods; and an Indian, whether in peace or war, at night or by day, was a doomed man in the presence of either. The name of Wetzel sent a thrill of horror through the heart of the stoutest savage, before whom a more terrible image could not be conjured up than one of these relentless "Long-knives."

The first event worthy of record, in the life of our hero, occurred when he was about fourteen years of age. The Indians had not been very troublesome in the immediate vicinity of his father's, and no great apprehensions were felt, as it was during a season of comparative quietude. On the occasion referred to, Lewis had just stepped from his father's door, and was looking at his brother Jacob playing, when suddenly turning toward the corn-crib, he saw a gun pointing around the corner. Quick as thought he jumped back, but not in time to escape the ball; it took effect upon the breast-bone, carrying away a small portion, and cutting a fearful wound athwart the chest. In an instant, two athletic warriors sprang from behind the crib, and quietly making prisoners of the lads, bore them off without being discovered. On the second day they reached the Ohio, and crossing near the mouth of McMahan's Creek, gained the Big Lick, about twenty miles from the river. During the whole of this painful march, Lewis suffered severely from his wound, but bore up with true courage, knowing that if he complained the tomahawk would be his doom. That night, on lying down, the Indians, contrary to their custom, failed to tie their prisoners.

Lewis now resolved to escape; and, in the course of an hour or two, satisfying himself that the Indians were asleep, touched Jacob, and both arose without disturbing their captors. Lewis, leading the way, pushed into the woods. Finding, however, that he could not travel without moccasins, he returned to camp, and soon came back with two pair, which having fitted on, Lewis said, "Now I must go back for father's gun," which the Indians had carried off. Securing this, the two boys started in the direction of home. Finding the path, they traveled on briskly for some time; but hearing a noise, listened, and ascertained the Indians were in pursuit. The lads stepped aside as the pursuers came up, and then again moved on. Soon they heard the Indians return, and by the same plan effectually eluded them. Before daylight they were again followed by two on horseback, but, resorting to a similar expedient, readily escaped detection. On the following day, about eleven o'clock, the boys reached the Ohio, at a point opposite Zane's Island. Lashing together two logs, they crossed over, and were once more with their friends.

Shortly after Crawford's defeat, a man named Thomas Mills, in escaping from that unfortunate expedition, reached the Indian Spring, about nine miles from Wheeling, on the present National Road, where he was compelled to leave his horse, and proceed to Wheeling on foot. Thence he went to Van Metre's Fort, and, after a day or two of rest, induced Lewis Wetzel to go with him to the spring for his horse. Lewis cautioned him against the danger, but Mills was determined, and the two started. Approaching the spring, they discovered the horse tied to a tree, and Wetzel at once comprehended their danger. Mills walked up to unfasten the animal, when instantly a discharge of rifles followed, and the unfortunate man fell, mortally wounded. Wetzel now turned, and, knowing his only escape was in flight, plunged through the enemy, and bounded off at the very extent of his speed. Four fleet Indians followed in rapid pursuit, whooping in proud exultation of soon overhauling their intended victim. After a chase of half a mile, one of the most active savages approached so close that Wetzel was afraid he might throw his tomahawk, and, instantly wheeling, shot the fellow dead in his tracks. In early youth Lewis had acquired the habit of loading his gun while at a full run, and now he felt the great advantage of it. Keeping in advance of his pursuers during another half mile, a second Indian came up, and, turning to fire, the savage caught the end of his gun, and, for a time, the contest was doubtful. At one moment the Indian, by his great strength and dexterity, brought Wetzel to his knee, and had nearly wrenched the rifle from the hands of his antagonist, when Lewis, by a renewed effort, drew the weapon from the grasp of the savage, and, thrusting the muzzle against the side of his neck, pulled the trigger, killing him instantly. The two other Indians, by this time, had nearly overtaken him; but leaping forward, he kept ahead, until his unerring rifle was a third time loaded. Anxious to have done with that kind of sport, he slackened his pace, and even stopped once or twice to give his pursuers an opportunity to face him. Every time, however, he looked round, the Indians treed, unwilling any longer to encounter his destructive weapon. After running a mile or two farther in this manner, he reached an open piece of ground, and wheeling suddenly, the foremost Indian jumped behind a tree, but which not screening his body, Wetzel fired, and dangerously wounded him. The remaining Indian made an immediate retreat, yelling as he went, "*No catch dat man, him gun always loaded.*"

In the summer of 1786, the Indians having become troublesome in the neighborhood of Wheeling, particularly in the Short Creek Settlement, and a party having killed a man near Mingo Bottom, it was determined to send an expedition after the retreating enemy, of sufficient force to chastise them most effectually. A subscription or pony-purse was made up, and one hundred dollars were offered to the man who should bring in the first Indian scalp. Major McMahan, living at Beach Bottom, headed the expedition, and Lewis Wetzel was one of his men. They crossed the river, on the fifth of August, and proceeded, by a rapid march, to the Muskingum. The expedition numbered about twenty men; and an advance of five were detailed to reconnoiter. This party reported to the commander that they had discovered the camp of the enemy, but that it was far too numerous to think of making an attack. A consultation was thereupon held, and an immediate retreat determined on. During the conference our hero sat upon a log, with his gun carelessly resting across his knees. The moment it was resolved to retreat, most of the party started in disordered haste; but the commander, observing Wetzel still sitting on the log, turned to inquire if he was not going along. "No," was his sullen reply; "I came out to hunt Indians, and now that they are found, I am not going home, like a fool, with my fingers in my mouth. I am determined to take an Indian scalp, or lose my own." All arguments were unavailing, and there they were compelled to leave him: a lone man, in a desolate wilderness, surrounded by an enemy—vigilant, cruel, bloodthirsty, and of horrid barbarity—with no friend but his rifle, and no guide but the sure index which an All-wise Providence has deep set in the heavens above. Once by himself, and looking around, to feel satisfied that they were all gone, he gathered his blanket about him, adjusted his tomahawk and scalping-knife, shouldered his rifle, and moved off in an opposite direction, hoping that a small party of Indians might be met with. Keeping away from the larger streams, he strolled on cautiously, peering into every dell and suspicious cover, and keenly sensitive to the least sound of a suspicious character. Nothing, however, crossed his path that day. The night being dark and chilly, it was necessary to have a fire; but to show a light, in the midst of his enemy, would be to invite to certain destruction. To avoid this, he constructed a small coal-pit out of bark, dried leaves, etc., and covering these with loose earth, leaving an occasional air-hole, he seated himself, encircling the pit with his legs, and then completed the whole by covering his head with the blanket. In this manner he would produce a temperature equal, as he expressed it, to that of a "stove-room." This was certainly an original and ingenious mode of getting up a fire, without, at the same time, endangering himself by a light.

During most of the following day he roamed through the forest without noticing any "signs" of Indians. At length smoke was discovered, and going in the direction of it, he found a camp, but tenantless. It contained two blankets and a small kettle, which Wetzel at once knew belonged to two Indians, who were, doubtless, out hunting. Concealing himself in the matted undergrowth, he patiently awaited the return of the occupants. About sunset, one of the Indians came in and made up the fire, and went to cooking his supper. Shortly after, the other came in. They ate their supper, and began to sing, and amuse themselves by telling comic stories, at which they would burst into roars of laughter. Singing, and telling amusing stories, was the common practice of the white and red men, when lying in their hunting camps. About nine or ten o'clock, one of the Indians wrapped his blanket around him, shouldered his rifle, took a chunk of fire in his hand, and left the camp, doubtless with the intention of going to watch a deer-lick. The fire and smoke would serve to keep off the gnats and musquitoes. It is a remarkable fact, that deer are not alarmed at seeing fire, from the circumstance of meeting it so frequently in the fall and winter seasons, when the leaves and grass are dry, and the woods on fire. The absence of the Indian was a cause of vexation and disappointment to our hero, whose trap was so happily set, that he considered his game secure. He still indulged the hope that the Indian would return to camp before day, but in this he was disappointed. There are birds in the woods which commence chirping just before break of day, and, like the cock, give notice to the woodman that light will soon appear. Lewis heard the wooded songsters begin to chatter, and determined to delay no longer the work of death, for the return of the other Indian. He walked to the camp with a noiseless step, and found his victim buried in profound sleep, lying upon one side. He drew his butcher-knife, and with the utmost force, impelled by revenge, sent the blade through his heart. He said the Indian gave a short quiver, a convulsive motion, and then laid still in the sleep of death. Lewis scalped him, and set out for home. He arrived at the Mingo Bottom only one day after his unsuccessful companions. He claimed and received the reward.

A most fatal decoy, on the frontier, was the turkey-call. On several different occasions men, from the fort at Wheeling, had gone across the hill in quest of a turkey, whose plaintive cries had elicited their attention, and, on more than one occasion, the men never returned. Wetzel suspected the cause, and determined to satisfy himself. On the east side of the Creek Hill, and at a point elevated at least sixty feet above the water, there is a capacious cavern, the entrance to which, at that time, was almost obscured by a heavy growth of vines and foliage. Into this the alluring savage would crawl, and could there have an extensive view of the hill-front on the opposite side. From that cavern issued the decoy of death to more than one incautious soldier and settler. Wetzel knew of the existence and exact locality of the cave, and accordingly started out before day, and, by a circuitous route, reached the spot from the rear. Posting himself so as to command a view of the opening, he waited patiently for the expected cry. Directly the twisted tuft of an Indian warrior slowly rose in the mouth of the cave, and, looking cautiously about, sent forth the long, shrill, peculiar, "cry," and immediately sunk back out of view. Lewis screened himself in his position, cocked his gun, and anxiously waited for a re-appearance of the head. In a few minutes up rose the tuft, Lewis drew a fine aim at the polished head, and the next instant the brains of the savage were scattered about the cave. *That* turkey troubled the inhabitants no longer, and tradition does not say whether the place was ever after similarly occupied.

A singular custom with this daring borderer was to take a fall hunt into the Indian country. Equipping himself, he set out and penetrated to the Muskingum, and fell upon a camp of four Indians. Hesitating a moment, whether to attack a party so much his superior in numerical strength, he determined to make the attempt. At the hour of midnight, when naught was heard but the long, dismal howl of the wolf,

> "Cruel as death, and hungry as the grave,
> Burning for blood, bony, gaunt, and grim,"

he moved cautiously from his covert, and, gliding through the darkness, stealthily approached the camp, supporting his rifle in one hand, and a tomahawk in the other. A dim flicker from the camp-fire faintly revealed the forms of the sleepers, wrapped in that profound slumber, which, to part of them, was to know no waking. There they lay, with their dark faces turned up to the night-sky, in the deep solitude of their own wilderness, little dreaming that their most relentless enemy was hovering over them. Quietly resting his gun against a tree, he unsheathed his knife, and, with an intrepidity that could never be surpassed, stepped boldly forward like the minister of death, and, quick as thought, cleft the skull of one of his sleeping victims. In an instant, a second one was similarly served; and, as a third attempted to rise, confused by the horrid yells with which Wetzel accompanied his blows, he too shared the fate of his companions, and sunk dead at the feet of his ruthless slayer. The fourth darted into the darkness of the wood and escaped, although Wetzel pursued him some distance. Returning to camp, he scalped his victims, and then left for home. When asked, on his return, what luck? "Not much," he replied. "I treed four Indians, but one got away." This unexampled achievement stamped him as one of the most daring, and, at the same time, successful hunters of his day. The distance to and from the scene of this adventure could not have been less than one hundred and seventy miles.

During one of his scouts, in the neighborhood of Wheeling, our hero took shelter, on a stormy evening, in a deserted cabin on the bottom, not far from what was the residence (in 1851) of Mr. Hamilton Woods. Gathering a few broken boards, he prepared a place, in the loft, to sleep. Scarcely had he got himself adjusted for a nap, when six Indians entered, and, striking a fire, commenced preparing their homely meal. Wetzel watched their movements closely, with drawn knife, determined, the moment he was discovered, to leap into their midst, and, in the confusion, endeavor to escape. Fortunately they did not see him; and, soon after supper, the whole six fell asleep. Wetzel now crawled noiselessly down, and hid himself behind a log, at a convenient distance from the door of the cabin. At early dawn, a tall savage stepped from the door, and stretching up both hands in a long, hearty yawn, seemed to draw in new life from the pure, invigorating atmosphere. In an instant Wetzel had his finger upon the trigger, and the next moment the Indian fell heavily to the ground, his life's blood gushing upon the young grass, brilliant with the morning dewdrops. The report of his rifle had not ceased echoing through the valley, ere the daring borderer was far away, secure from all pursuit.

Some time after General Harmar had erected a fort at the mouth of the Muskingum River, where Marietta now stands, about 1789, he employed some white men to go, with a flag, among the nearest Indian tribes, to prevail with them to come to the fort, and there to conclude a treaty of peace. A large number of Indians came, on the general invitation, and encamped on the Muskingum River, a few miles above its mouth. General Harmar issued a proclamation, giving notice that a cessation of arms was mutually agreed upon, between the white and red men, till an effort for a treaty of peace should be concluded.

As treaties of peace with Indians had been so frequently violated, but little faith was placed in the stability of such engagements by the frontiersmen; notwithstanding that they were as frequently the aggressors as were the Indians. Half the backwoodsmen of that day had been born in a fort, and grew to manhood, as it were, in a siege. The Indian war had continued so long, and was so bloody, that they believed war with them was to continue as long as both survived to fight. With these impressions, as they considered the Indians faithless, it was difficult to inspire confidence in the stability of treaties. While General Harmar was diligently engaged with the Indians, endeavoring to make peace, Lewis Wetzel concluded to go to Fort Harmar, and, as the Indians would be passing and re-passing between their camp and the fort, he would have a fair opportunity of killing one. He associated with himself, in this enterprise, a man by the name of Veach Dickerson, who was only a small grade below him in restless daring. As soon as the enterprise was resolved on, they were impatient to put it in execution. The more danger, the more excited and impatient they were to execute their plan. They set off without delay, and arrived at the desired point, and sat themselves down in ambush, near the path leading from the fort to the Indian camp. Shortly after they had concealed themselves by the wayside, they saw an Indian approaching on horse-back, running his horse at full speed. They called to him, but, owing to the clatter of the horse's feet, he did not hear or heed their call, but kept on at a sweeping gallop. When the Indian had nearly passed, they concluded to give him a shot as he rode. They fired; but, as the Indian did not fall, they thought they had missed him. As the alarm would soon be spread that an Indian had been shot at, and as large numbers of them were near at hand, they commenced an immediate retreat to their home. As their neighbors knew the object of their expedition, as soon as they returned, they were asked, what luck? Wetzel answered that they had bad luck —they had seen but one Indian, and he on horseback— that they had fired at him as he rode, but he did not fall, but went off scratching his back, as if he had been stung by a yellowjacket. The truth was, they had shot him through the hips and lower part of the belly. He rode to the fort, and that night expired of his wound. It proved to be a large, fine-looking savage, of considerable celebrity, and known by the name of George Washington.

It was soon rumored, to General Harmar, that Lewis Wetzel was the murderer. General Harmar sent a Captain Kingsbury, with a company of men, to the

Mingo Bottom, with orders to take Wetzel, alive or dead—a useless and impotent order. A company of men could as easily have drawn Beelzebub out of the bottomless pit, as take Lewis Wetzel, by force, from the Mingo Bottom settlement. On the day that Captain Kingsbury arrived, there was a shooting-match in the neighborhood, and Lewis was there. As soon as the object of Captain Kingsbury was ascertained, it was resolved to ambush the captain's barge, and kill him and his company. Happily Major McMahan was present to prevent this catastrophe, who prevailed on Wetzel and his friends to suspend the attack, till he would pay Captain Kingsbury a visit; perhaps he would induce him to return without making an attempt to take Wetzel. With a great deal of reluctance, they agreed to suspend the attack till Major McMahan should return. The resentment and fury of Wetzel and his friends, were boiling and blowing like the steam from a scape-pipe of a steamboat. "A pretty affair this," said they, "to hang a man for killing an Indian, when they are killing some of our men almost every day." Major McMahan informed Captain Kingsbury of the force and fury of the people, and assured him that, if he persisted in the attempt to seize Wetzel, he would have all the settlers in the country upon him; that nothing could save him and his company from massacre, but a speedy return. The captain took his advice, and forthwith returned to Fort Harmar. Wetzel considered the affair now as finally adjusted.

As Lewis was never long stationary, but ranged, at will, along the river from Fort Pitt to the falls of the Ohio, and was a welcome guest and perfectly at home wherever he went, shortly after the attempt to seize him by Captain Kingsbury, he got into a canoe, with the intention of proceeding down the Ohio to Kentucky. He had a friend, by the name of Hamilton Carr, who had lately settled on the island near Fort Harmar. Here he stopped, with the view of lodging for the night. By some means, which never were explained, General Harmar was advised of his being on the island. A guard was sent, who crossed to the island, surrounded

Mr. Carr's house, went in, and, as Wetzel lay asleep, he was seized by numbers; his hands and feet securely bound, and he was hurried off into a boat, and from thence placed in a guard-room, where he was loaded with irons.

The ignominy of wearing iron handcuffs and hobbles, and being chained down, to a man of his independent and resolute spirit, was more painful than death. Shortly after he was confined, he sent for General Harmar, and requested a visit. The general went. Wetzel admitted, without hesitation, "that he had shot the Indian." As he did not wish to be hung like a dog, he requested the general to give him up to the Indians, there being a large number of them present. "He might place them all in a circle, with their scalping knives and tomahawks, and give him a tomahawk and place him in the midst of the circle, and then let him and the Indians fight it out the best way they could." The general told him, "that he was an officer appointed by the law, by which he must be governed. As the law did not authorize him to make such a compromise, he could not grant his request." After a few days' longer confinement, he again sent for the general to come and see him; and he did so. Wetzel said "he had never been confined, and could not live much longer if he was not permitted some room to walk about in."

The general ordered the officer on guard to knock off his iron fetters, but to leave on his handcuffs, and permit him to walk about on the point at the mouth of the Muskingum; but to be sure and keep a close watch upon him. As soon as they were outside the fort-gate, Lewis began to caper about like a wild colt broke loose from the stall. He would start and run a few yards, as if he was about making an escape, then turn round and join the guards. The next start he would run farther, and then stop. In this way he amused the guard for some time, at every start running a little farther. At length he called forth all his strength, resolution, and activity, and determined on freedom or an early grave. He gave a sudden spring forward, and bounded off at the top of his speed for the shelter of his beloved woods. His movement was so quick, and so unexpected, that the guards were taken by surprise, and he got nearly a hundred yards before they recovered from their astonishment. They fired, but all missed; they followed in pursuit, but he soon left them out of sight. As he was well acquainted with the country, he made for a dense thicket, about two or three miles from the fort. In the midst of this thicket, he found a tree which had fallen across a log, where the brush was very close. Under this tree he squeezed his body. The brush was so thick that he could not be discovered unless his pursuers examined very closely. As soon as his escape was announced, General Harmar started the soldiers and Indians in pursuit. After he had lain about two hours in his place of concealment, two Indians came into the thicket, and stood on the same log under which he lay concealed; his heart beat so violently he was afraid they would hear it thumping. He could hear them hallooing in every direction as they hunted through the brush. At length, as the evening wore away the day, he found himself alone in the friendly thicket. But what should he do? His hands were fastened with iron cuffs and bolts, and he knew of no friend, on the same side of the Ohio, to whom he could apply for assistance.

He had a friend who had recently put up a cabin on the Virginia side of the Ohio, who, he had no doubt, would lend him every assistance in his power. But to cross the river was the difficulty. He could not make a raft with his hands bound, and though an excellent swimmer, it would be risking too much to trust himself to the stream in that disabled condition. With the most gloomy foreboding of the future, he left the thicket as soon as the shades of night began to gather, and directed his way to the Ohio, by a circuitous route, which brought him to a lonely spot, three or four miles below the fort. He made to this place, as he expected guards would be set at every point where he could find a canoe. On the opposite shore he saw an acquaintance, Isaac Wiseman by name, fishing in a canoe. Not daring to call to him, as he could not know whether his enemies were not within sound of his voice, he waved his hat for some time to attract the notice of his friend, having previously induced him to direct his eye that course by a gentle splashing in the water. This brought Wiseman to his assistance, who readily aided his escape. Once on the Virginia shore, he had nothing to fear, as he had well-wishers all through the country, who would have shed blood, if necessary, for his defense. It was not, however, until years had elapsed, and General Harmar returned to Philadelphia, that it became safe for Wiseman to avow the act, such was the weakness of civil authority and the absolute supremacy of military rule on the frontier. A file and hammer soon released him from the heavy handcuffs. After the night's rest had recruited his energies, he set out for fresh adventures, his friend having supplied him with a rifle, ammunition, and blanket. He took a canoe and went down the river for Kentucky, where he should feel safe from the grasp of Harmar and his myrmidons.

Subsequently to Wetzel's escape, General Harmar removed his head-quarters to Fort Washington, Cincinnati. One of his first official acts there, was to issue a proclamation, offering considerable rewards for the apprehension and delivery of Lewis at the garrison there. No man, however, was found base or daring enough to attempt this service.

On his way down, Wetzel landed at Point Pleasant, and following his usual humor, when he had no work among Indians on the carpet, ranged the town, for a few days, with as much unconcern as if he were on his own farm. Lieutenant Kingsbury, attached to Harmar's own command, happened to be at the mouth of the Kenawha at the time, and scouting about, while ignorant of Wetzel's presence, met him—unexpectedly to both parties. Lewis, being generally on the *qui vive*, saw Kingsbury first, and halted with great firmness in the path, leaving to the lieutenant to decide his own course of procedure, feeling himself prepared and ready, whatever that might be. Kingsbury, a brave man himself, had too much good feeling toward such a gallant spirit as Wetzel to attempt his injury, if it were even safe to do so. He contented himself with saying, "*Get out of my sight, you Indian killer!*" And Lewis, who was implacable to the savage only, retired slowly and watchfully, as a lion draws off, measuring his steps in the presence of the hunters, being as willing to avoid unnecessary danger as to seek it, when duty called him to act.

He regained his canoe and put off for Limestone, at which place, and at Washington, the county town, he established his head-quarters for some time. Here he engaged on hunting parties, or went out with the scouts after Indians. When not actually engaged in such service, he filled up his leisure hours at shooting-matches, foot-racing, or wrestling with other hunters. Major Fowler, of Washington, who knew him well during this period, described him as a general favorite, no less from his personal qualities than for his services.

While engaged in these occupations at Maysville, Lieutenant Lawler, of the regular army, who was going down the Ohio to Fort Washington, in what was called a Kentucky boat, full of soldiers, landed at Maysville, and found Wetzel sitting in one of the taverns. Returning to the boat, he ordered out a file of soldiers, seized Wetzel and dragged him on board the boat, and, without a moment's delay, pushed off, and that same night delivered him to General Harmar, at Cincinnati, by whom the prisoner was again put in irons, preparatory to his trial and consequent condemnation, for what Lewis disdained to deny or conceal, the killing of the Indian at Marietta. But Harmar, like St. Clair, although acquainted with the routine of military service, was destitute of the practical good sense, always indispensable in frontier settlements, in which such severe measures were more likely to rouse the settlers to flame than to intimidate them; and soon found the country around him in arms.

The story of Wetzel's captivity—captured and liable to punishment for shooting an Indian merely—spread through the settlements like wild-fire, kindling the passions of the frontier men to a high pitch of fury.

Petitions for the release of Wetzel came in to General Harmar, from all quarters and all classes of society. To these, at first, he paid little attention. At length the settlements along the Ohio, and some even of the back counties, began to embody in military array to release the prisoner *vi et armis*. Representations were made to Judge Symmes, which induced him to issue a writ of *habeas corpus* in the case. John Clawson, and other hunters of Columbia, who had gone down to attend his trial, went security for Wetzel's good behavior; and, being discharged, he was escorted with great triumph to Columbia, and treated, at that place, to his supper, etc. Judge Foster, who gave these last particulars, described him at this period (August 26th, 1789) as about twenty-six years of age, about five feet nine inches high. He was full-breasted, very broad across the shoulders; his arms were large; skin, darker than the other brother's; his face, heavily pitted with the small-pox; his hair, of which he was very careful, reached, when combed out, to the calves of the legs; his eyes remarkably black, and, when excited, sparkling with such a vindictive glance as to indicate plainly it was hardly safe to provoke him to wrath. He was taciturn in mixed company, although the fiddle of the party among his social friends and acquaintances. His morals and habits, compared with those of his general associates and the tone of society in the West of that day, were quite exemplary.

Shortly after his return from Kentucky, a relative, from Dunkard Creek, invited Lewis home with him. The invitation was accepted, and the two leisurely wended their way along, hunting and sporting as they traveled. On reaching the home of the young man, what should they see but, instead of the hospitable roof, a pile of smoking ruins! Wetzel instantly examined the trail, and found that the marauders were three Indians and one white man, and that they had taken one prisoner. That captive proved to be the betrothed of the young man, whom nothing could restrain from pushing on in immediate pursuit. Placing himself under the direction of Wetzel, the two strode on, hoping to overhaul the enemy before they had crossed the Ohio. It was found, after proceeding a short distance, that the savages had taken great care to obliterate their trail; but the keen discernment of Wetzel once on the track, and there need not be much difficulty. He knew they would make for the river by the most expeditious route, and therefore, disregarding their trail, he pushed on, so as to head them at the crossing-place. After an hour's hard travel, they struck a path which the deer had made, and which their sagacity had taught them to carry over knolls, in order to avoid the great curves of ravines. Wetzel followed the path because he knew it was in almost a direct line to the point at which he was aiming. Night coming on, the tireless and determined hunters partook of a hurried meal, then again pushed forward, guided by the lamps hung in the heavens above them, until, toward midnight, a heavy cloud shut out their light and obscured the path. Early, on the following morning, they resumed the chase, and descending from the elevated ridge, along which they had been passing for an hour or two, found themselves in a deep and quiet valley, which looked as though human steps had never before pressed its virgin soil. Traveling a short distance, they discovered fresh footsteps in the soft sand, and, upon close examination, the eye of Wetzel's companion detected the impress of a small shoe, with nail-heads around the heel, which he at once recognized as belonging to his affianced. Hour after hour the pursuit was kept up: now tracing the trail across the hills, over alluvian, and often detecting it where the wily captors had taken to the beds of streams. Late in the afternoon, they found themselves approaching the Ohio, and, shortly after dark, discovered, as they struck the river, the camp of the enemy on the opposite side, and just below the mouth of Captina. Swimming the river, the two reconnoitered the position of the camp, and discovered the locality of the captive. Wetzel proposed waiting until daylight before making the attack, but the almost frantic lover was for immediate action. Wetzel, however, would listen to no suggestion, and thus they waited the break of day. At early dawn, the savages were up and preparing to leave, when Wetzel directed his companion to take good aim at the white renegade, while he would make sure work of one of the Indians. They fired at the same moment, and with fatal effect. Instantly the young man rushed forward to release the captive; and Wetzel, reloading, pursued the two Indians who had taken to the woods to ascertain the strength of the attacking party. Wetzel pursued a short distance, and then fired his rifle at random, to draw the Indians from their retreat. The trick succeeded, and they made after him with uplifted tomahawks, yelling at the height of their voices. The adroit hunter soon had his rifle loaded, and wheeling suddenly, discharged its contents through the body of his nearest pursuer. The other Indian now rushed impetuously forward, thinking to dispatch his enemy in a moment. Wetzel, however, kept dodging from tree to tree, and, being more fleet than the Indian, managed to keep ahead until his unerring gun was again loaded, when, turning, he fired, and the last of the party lay dead before him.

Soon after this, our hero determined to visit the extreme South, and for that purpose engaged on a flat-boat about leaving for New Orleans. Many months elapsed before his friends heard any thing of his whereabouts, and then it was to learn that he was in close confinement at New Orleans, under some weighty charge. What the exact nature of this charge was, has never been fully ascertained; but it is very certain he was imprisoned and treated like a felon for nearly two years. The charge is supposed to have been of some trivial character, and has been justly regarded as a great outrage. It was alleged, at the time of his arrest, to have been for uttering counterfeit coin; but this being disproved, it was then charged that he had been guilty of illicit connection with the wife of a Spaniard. Of the nature of these charges, however, but little is known. He was finally released by the intervention of our government, and reached home by way of Philadelphia, to which city he had been sent from New Orleans. He remained but two days on Wheeling Creek after his return. From the settlement he went to Wheeling, where he remained a few days, and then left again for the South, vowing vengeance against the person whom he believed to have been accessory to his imprisonment, and in degrading his person with the vile rust of a felon's chain. During his visit to Wheeling, he remained with George Cookis, a relative. Mrs. Cookis plagued him about getting married, and jocularly asked whether he ever intended to take a wife. "No," he replied, "there is no woman in this world for me, but I expect there is one in heaven."

After an absence of many months, he again returned to the neighborhood of Wheeling; but whether he avenged his real or imaginary wrongs, upon the person of the Spaniard alluded to, is not known. His propensity to roam the woods was still as great as ever; and an incident occurred which showed that he had lost none of his cunning while undergoing incarceration at New Orleans. Returning homeward, from a hunt north of the Ohio, somewhat fatigued and a little careless of his movements, he suddenly espied an Indian, in the very act of raising his gun to fire. Both immediately sprang to trees, and there they stood for an hour, each afraid of the other. What was to be done? To remain there during the whole day, for it was then early in the morning, was out of the question. Now it was that the sagacity of Wetzel displayed itself over the child-like simplicity of the savage. Cautiously adjusting his bear-skin cap to the end of his ramrod—with the slightest, most dubious and hesitating motion, as though afraid to venture a glance, the cap protruded. An instant, a crack, and off was torn the fatal cap, by the sure ball of the vigilant savage. Leaping from his retreat, our hero rapidly advanced upon the astonished Indian, and ere the tomahawk could be brought to its work of death, the tawny foe sprang convulsively into the air, and, straightening as he descended, fell upon his face quite dead.

Wetzel was universally regarded as one of the most efficient scouts and most practiced woodsmen of his day. He was frequently engaged by parties who desired to hunt up and locate lands, but were afraid of the Indians. Under the protection of Lewis Wetzel, however, they felt safe, and thus he was often engaged for months at a time. Of those who became largely interested in western lands, was John Madison, brother of James, afterward President Madison. He employed Lewis Wetzel to go with him through the Kenawha region. During their expedition they came upon a deserted hunter's camp, in which were concealed some goods. Each of them helped himself to a blanket, and that day, in crossing Little Kenawha, they were fired upon by a concealed party of Indians, and Madison killed.

General Clark, the companion of Lewis in the celebrated tour across the Rocky Mountains, had heard much of Lewis Wetzel in Kentucky, and determined to secure his services in the perilous enterprise. A messenger was accordingly sent for him, but he was reluctant to go. However, he finally consented, and accompanied the party during the first three months' travel, but then declined going any farther, and returned home. Shortly after this he left again, on a flat-boat, and never returned. He visited a relative named Philip Sikes, living about twenty miles in the interior from Natchez, and there made his home until the summer of 1808, when he died. The late venerable David McIntyre, of Belmont County, Ohio, one of the most reliable and respectable men in the State, said that he met Lewis Wetzel at Natchez, in April, 1808, and remained with him three days. That Lewis told him he would visit his friends during the then approaching summer. But alas, that visit was never made! His journey was to "that undiscovered country, from whose bourne no traveler returns."

JOHN WETZEL.*

IN the year 1791 or '92, the Indians having made frequent incursions into the settlements, along the river Ohio, between Wheeling and the Mingo Bottom—

---
*The three succeeding sketches are from Pritts' Border Life.

sometimes killing and capturing whole families, at other times stealing all the horses belonging to a station or fort—a company, consisting of seven men, rendezvoused at a place called the Beech Bottom, on the Ohio River, a few miles below where Wellsburg has been erected. This company were John Wetzel, William McCullough, John Hough, Thomas Biggs, Joseph Hedges, Kinzie Dickerson, and a Mr. Linn. Their avowed object was, to go to the Indian town to steal horses. This was then considered a legal, honorable business, as we were then at open war with the Indians. It would only be retaliating upon them in their own way. These seven men were all trained to Indian warfare and a life in the woods, from their youth. Perhaps the western frontier at no time could furnish seven men whose souls were better fitted, and whose nerves and sinews were better strung, to perform any enterprise which required resolution and firmness. They crossed the Ohio, and proceeded, with cautious steps and vigilant glances, on their way through the cheerless, dark, and almost impenetrable forest, in the Indian country, till they came to an Indian town, near where the head-waters of the Sandusky and Muskingum rivers interlock. Here they made a fine haul, and set off homeward with about fifteen horses. They traveled rapidly, only making a short halt, to let their horses graze and breathe a short time, to recruit their strength and activity. In the evening of the second day of their rapid retreat, they arrived at Wells Creek, not far from where the town of Cambridge has been since erected. Here Mr. Linn was taken violently sick, and they must stop their march, or leave him alone to perish in the dark and lonely woods. Our frontier men, notwithstanding their rough and unpolished manners, had too much of my Uncle Toby's "sympathy for suffering humanity," to forsake a comrade in distress. They halted and placed sentinels on their back-trail, who remained there till late in the night without seeing any signs of being pursued. The sentinels on the back-trail returned to the camp; Mr. Linn still lying in excruciating pain. All the simple remedies in their power were administered to the sick man, without producing any effect. Being late in the night, they all lay down to rest, except one who was placed as guard. Their camp was on the bank of a small branch. Just before daybreak the guard took a small bucket and dipped some water out of the stream; on carrying it to the fire, he discovered the water to be muddy. The muddy water awaked his suspicion that the enemy might be approaching them, and were walking down in the stream, as their footsteps would be noiseless in the water. He waked his companions, and communicated his suspicion. They arose, examined the branch a little distance, and listened attentively for some time, but neither saw nor heard any thing, and then concluded it must have been raccoons or some other animals puddling in the stream. After this conclusion, the company all lay down to rest, except the sentinel, who was stationed just outside of the light. Happily for them the fire had burned down, and only a few coals afforded a dim light to point out where they lay. The enemy had come silently down the creek, as the sentinel suspected, to within ten or twelve feet of the place where they lay, and fired several guns over the bank. Mr. Linn, the sick man, was lying with his side toward the bank, and received nearly all the balls which were at first fired. The Indians then, with tremendous yells, mounted the bank with loaded rifles, war-clubs, and tomahawks, rushed upon our men, who fled barefooted and without arms. Mr. Linn, Thomas Biggs, and Joseph Hedges were killed in and near the camp. William McCullough had run but a short distance when he was fired at by the enemy. At the instant the firing was given, he jumped into a quagmire and fell; the Indians, supposing that they had killed him, ran past in pursuit of others. He soon extricated himself out of the mire, and so made his escape. He fell in with John Hough, and came into Wheeling. John Wetzel and Kinzie Dickerson met in their retreat, and returned together. Those who made their escape were without arms, without clothing, or provisions. Their sufferings were great; but this they bore with stoical indifference, as it was the fortune of war. Whether the

Indians who defeated our heroes followed in pursuit from their towns, or were a party of warriors who accidentally happened to fall in with them, has never been ascertained. From the place they had stolen the horses, they had traveled two nights and almost two entire days without halting, except, just a few minutes at a time, to let the horses graze. From the circumstance of their rapid retreat with the horses, it was supposed that no pursuit could possibly have overtaken them, but that fate had decreed that this party of Indians should meet and defeat them. As soon as the stragglers arrived at Wheeling, Captain John M'Cullough collected a party of men, and went to Wells Creek, and buried the unfortunate men who fell in and near the camp. The Indians had mangled the dead bodies at a most barbarous rate. Thus was closed the horse-stealing tragedy.

Of the four who survived this tragedy, none are now living to tell the story of their suffering. They continued to hunt and to fight as long as the war lasted. John Wetzel and Dickerson died in the country near Wheeling. John Hough died about 1842, near Columbia, Hamilton County, Ohio. The brave Captain William M'Cullough fell in 1812, in the battle of Brownstown, in the campaign with General Hull.

JOHN WETZEL AND VEACH DICKERSON.

JOHN WETZEL and Veach Dickerson associated to go on an Indian scout. They crossed the Ohio at the Mingo Bottom, three miles below where the town of Steubenville has since been constructed. They set off with the avowed intention of bringing an Indian prisoner. They painted and dressed in complete Indian style, and could talk some in their language. What induced them to undertake this hazardous enterprise, is unknown; perhaps the novelty and danger of the undertaking prompted them. No reward was given for either prisoners or scalps; nor were they employed or paid by the government. Every man fought on his own hook, furnished his own arms and ammunition, and carried his own baggage. This was, to all intents, a democratic war, as every one fought as often and as long as he pleased; either by himself, or with such company as he could confide in. As the white men on the frontier took but few prisoners, Wetzel and Dickerson concluded to change the practice, and bring in an Indian to make a pet. Whatever whim may have induced them, they set off with the avowed intention of bringing in a prisoner, or losing their own scalps in the attempt. They pushed through the Indian country with silent treads, and a keen lookout, till they went near the head of the Sandusky River, where they came near to a small Indian village. They concealed themselves near to a path which appeared to be considerably traveled. In the course of the first day of their ambush, they saw several small companies of Indians pass them. As it was not their wish to raise an alarm among the enemy, they permitted them to pass undisturbed. In the evening of the next day, they saw two Indians coming sauntering along the road, in quite a merry mood. They immediately stepped into the road, and, with a confident air, as if they were meeting friends, went forward until they came within reach of the enemy. Wetzel drew his tomahawk, and, with one sweep, knocked an Indian down; at the same instant, Dickerson grasped the other in his arms, and threw him on the ground. By this time Wetzel had killed the other, and turned his hand to aid in fastening the prisoner. This completed, they scalped the dead Indian, and set off with the prisoner for home. They traveled, all that night, on the warpath leading toward Wheeling. In the morning they struck off from the beaten path, taking diverse courses, and keeping on the hardest ground, where their feet would make the least impression, as this would render their trail more difficult to follow in case they should be pursued. They pushed along till they had crossed the Muskingum some distance, when their prisoner began to show a restive, stubborn disposition; he finally threw himself on the ground and refused to rise. He held down his head, and told them they might tomahawk him as soon as they pleased, for he was determined to go no farther. They used every argument they could think of, to induce him to proceed, but without any effect. He said "he would prefer dying in his native woods, than to preserve his life a little longer, and, at last, be tortured by fire, and his body mangled for sport, when they took him to their towns." They assured him his life would be spared, and that he would be well used, and treated with plenty. But all their efforts would not induce him to rise to his feet. The idea that he would be put to death for sport, or in revenge, in presence of a large number of spectators, who would enjoy, with raptures, the scenes of his torture and death, had taken such a strong hold of his mind, that he determined to disappoint the possibility of their being gratified at his expense. As it was not their wish to kill him, from coaxing, they concluded to try if a hickory, well applied, would not bend his stubborn soul. This, too, failed to have any effect. He appeared to be as callous and indifferent to the lash as if he had been a cooper's horse. What invincible resolution and fortitude was evinced by this son of the forest! Finding all their efforts to urge him forward ineffectual, they determined to put him to death. They then tomahawked and scalped him, and left his body a prey to the wild beasts of the forest, and to the birds of the air. Our heroes then returned home with their two scalps; but vexed and disappointed that they could not bring with them the prisoner.

JACOB WETZEL AND SIMON KENTON.

THE following relation I had from General Kenton: Kenton and Wetzel made arrangements to make a fall hunt together; and for that purpose they went into the hilly country, near the mouth of the Kentucky River. When they arrived in that part of the country in which they intended to make their hunt, they discovered some signs of Indians having pre-occupied the ground. It would have been out of character in a Kenton and a Wetzel to retreat, without first ascertaining the description and number of the enemy. They determined to find the Indian camp, which they believed was at no great distance from them, as they had heard reports of guns late in the evening, and early the next morning, in the same direction. This convinced them that the camp was at no great distance from the firing. Our heroes moved cautiously about, making as little sign as possible, that they might not be discovered by the enemy. Toward evening of the second day after they arrived on the ground, they discovered the Indian camp. They kept themselves concealed, determined, as soon as night approached, to reconnoiter the situation and number of the enemy; and then govern their future operations as prudence might dictate. They found five Indians in the camp. Having confidence in themselves, and in their usual good fortune, they concluded to attack them boldly. Contrary to military rules, they agreed to defer the attack till light. In military affairs it is a general rule to avoid night fights, except where small numbers intend to assault a larger force. The night is then chosen, as the darkness, the numbers of the assailants being uncertain, may produce panics and confusion, which may give the victory to far inferior numbers. Our heroes chose daylight and an open field for the fight. There was a large fallen tree lying near the camp; this would serve as a rampart for defense, and would also serve to conceal them from observation till the battle commenced. They took their station behind the log, and there lay till broad daylight, when they were able to draw a clear bead. Jacob Wetzel had a double-barreled rifle. Their guns were cocked—they took aim, and gave the preconcerted signal—fired, and two Indians fell. As quick as thought, Wetzel fired his second load, and down fell the third Indian. Their number was equal, and they bounded over the log, screaming and yelling at the highest pitch of their voices, to strike terror into their remaining enemies; and were among them before they recovered from the sudden surprise. The two remaining Indians, without arms, took to their heels, and ran in different directions. Kenton pursued one, whom he soon overhauled, tomahawked and scalped, and then returned, with the bloody trophy, to the camp. Shortly after, Wetzel returned with the scalp of the fifth Indian. This was a wholesale slaughter that but few, except such men as a Kenton and a Wetzel, would have attempted.

MAJOR SAMUEL McCOLLOCH.*

FIRST SIEGE OF WHEELING.

AMONG the earliest settlers on Short Creek, not far from Wheeling, Virginia, was the McColloch family, composed of three brothers, Abraham, Samuel, and John, and two sisters — the latter as lovely, devoted, and gentle as the brothers were bold, brave, and generous. No men were more respected by their neighbors, or more dreaded by the Indians. At an early age, Samuel, the second son, distinguished himself as a bold and efficient borderer. As an "Indian hunter," he had few superiors. He seemed to track the wily red man with a sagacity as remarkable as his efforts were successful. He was almost constantly engaged in excursions against the enemy, or "scouting" for the security of the settlements. It was mainly to these energetic operations that the frontier was so often saved from savage depredation; and by cutting off their retreat, attacking their hunting camps, and annoying them in various other ways, he rendered himself so great an object of fear and hatred. For these they marked him, and vowed sleepless vengeance against the name. In consideration of his very many efficient services, Samuel McColloch was commissioned major, in 1775.

In the month of August, 1777, information was received, from some friendly Moravian Indians, that a large army of Indians—composed chiefly of warriors from the great North-western Confederacy—were making vigorous preparations to strike an effective and terrible blow upon some of the settlements on the upper Ohio. It

---

* Arranged from DeHass' History of Western Virginia.

was stated, too, that this chosen body of savages would be under the lead of Simon Girty, a renegade white man of most relentless and insatiable ferocity toward his renounced countrymen. It soon became manifest at what point the enemy designed to strike. With apprehensions of dread, the settlers at the mouth of Wheeling (numbering about thirty families) betook themselves to their fort, and with calm resolution awaited the issue.

Early in the evening of the thirty-first of August, Captain Joseph Ogle, who had been sent out some days before, at the head of ten or fifteen men, to scout along the different routes usually followed by the Indians, returned to Wheeling, and reported no immediate cause of danger. The Indians, with their accustomed sagacity, suspecting that their movements might be watched, abandoned all the paths usually trodden, and dividing, as they approached the river, into small distinct parties, struck out along new lines for the Ohio. Without discovery, they reached the vicinity of Boggs' Island (two miles below Wheeling Creek), and there consolidating their force, crossed the river and proceeded directly to the creek bottom, under cover of night, and completed their plans for movement in the morning. The Indian army consisted of over three hundred and fifty Mingoes, Shawnees, and Wyandotts. It was commanded by the notorious renegade, Simon Girty, and well furnished with arms, ammunition, etc., by the infamous Hamilton, governor of Canada. Girty disposed of his men in two lines across the bottom, which, at that time, was cleared and mostly in corn, and stretched from the river to the creek. They were arranged at convenient distances, and effectually concealed by the high weeds and corn.

Posted near the center of these lines, and close to a path leading from the fort (which they supposed some of the whites would pass along in the morning), were six Indians. Shortly after daybreak of the first of September, Dr. McMechen, who was about returning east of the mountains, sent out a white man named Boyd, and a negro, to catch the horses. The two men had not proceeded far before they discovered the six Indians. Hoping to escape, they made a hurried retreat, but Boyd was killed. The negro was permitted to return, doubtless to mislead the whites as to the actual number of the foe.

The commandant immediately ordered Captain Samuel Mason, who had brought his company to the fort on the previous evening, to go out and dislodge the enemy. With fourteen of his men, the gallant captain sallied forth, and, after proceeding partly across the bottom, discovered the six Indians and fired upon them. Almost simultaneously with this discharge, the entire Indian army arose, and, with horrid yells, rushed upon the little band of whites. Finding that to stand were madness, Mason ordered a retreat, and in person commenced cutting his way through the Indian line. This he succeeded in doing, but most of his gallant little party perished in the attempt. Out of the fourteen but two escaped, and they, like Captain Mason, eluded the pursuing savages by concealing themselves beneath brush and fallen timber. The names of those who escaped this general slaughter, were Hugh McConnell and Thomas Glenn. William Shepherd, son of Colonel David Shepherd, had gained the spring, near where the Wheeling market-house now stands, when one of his feet caught in a vine, and, falling, the pursuing savage was instantly upon him, and, with a war-club, dispatched him on the spot. A dense fog concealed this from the sight of those in the fort.

So soon as the disaster to Mason had been ascertained at the fort, Captain Joseph Ogle, with his dozen experienced scouts, advanced to his relief, but not without forebodings of imminent danger, as the yells of the savages, and shrieks of the whites, told too plainly that a terrible massacre was taking place. With fearless steps Captain Ogle moved on to the scene of conflict, determined to cover the retreat of his unfortunate countrymen, or perish in the attempt. An excited and bloody foe rushed upon them, with the fury of demons, and all but two or three shared the fate of the first detachment. Captain Ogle, Sergeant Jacob Ogle, Martin Wetzel, and perhaps one other, were all who escaped.

The loss of so many brave men, at such a time, was a sad blow to this part of the country. Those who fell were the pride of that little fortress. They were heroes in every sense of the word; men of iron nerve, indomitable courage, and devoted patriotism. The valor of either would have done honor to the victors of Marathon. Scarcely had the shrieks of the wounded and dying been quieted, than the army of savages, with reeking scalps, just torn from the heads of the ill-fated soldiery, presented themselves in front of the fort, and demanded a surrender. The appearance of the enemy, as they approached, was most formidable. They advanced in two separate columns, with drum, fife, and British colors. The morning was calm, warm, and bright; and the sun, just rising over the high hill which overlooked the fort, was gently dissipating the heavy fog which covered the bloody scene on the bottom.

As the Indians advanced, a few scattering shots were fired at them from the fort, without much execution. Girty, having brought up his forces, proceeded to dispose of them as follows: The right flank was brought around the base of the hill, and distributed among the several cabins convenient to the fort; the left was ordered to defile beneath the river bank, close under the fort. Thus disposed, Girty presented himself at the window of a cabin, holding forth a white flag, and offering conditions of peace. He read the proclamation of Hamilton, governor of Canada, and, in a stentorian voice, demanded the surrender of the fort, offering, in case they complied, protection; but if they refused, immediate and indiscriminate massacre. He referred, in a very boasting manner, to the great force at his command; and called upon them, as loyal subjects, to give up, in obedience to the demand of the king's agent, and that not one of them should be injured.

Although the whole number of men then in the fort, did not exceed ten or a dozen, still there was no disposition to yield; but, on the contrary, a fixed determination to defy the renegade, and all the power of King George.

Girty having finished his harangue, Colonel David

Shepherd, the commandant, promptly, and in the most gallant and effective manner, replied, "Sir, we have consulted our wives and children, and all have resolved—men, women, and children—sooner to perish at their posts than place themselves under the protection of a savage army, with *you* at the head; or abjure the cause of liberty and the colonies." The outlaw attempted to reply, but a shot from the fort put a stop to any further harangue.

A darker hour had scarcely ever obscured the hopes of the West. Death was all around that little fortress, and hopeless despair seemed to press upon its inmates; but still they could not and would not give up. Duty, patriotism, pride, independence, safety, all required they should not surrender and forswear the cause of freedom.

Unable to intimidate them, and finding the besieged proof against his vile promises, the chagrined and discomfited Girty disappeared from the cabin, but in a few minutes was seen approaching with a large body of Indians, and instantly a tremendous rush was made upon the fort. They attempted to force the gates, and test the strength of the pickets by muscular effort. Failing to make any impression, Girty drew off his men a few yards, and commenced a general fire upon the port-holes.

Thus continued the attack during most of the day, and part of the night, but without any sensible effect. About noon, a temporary withdrawal of the enemy took place. During the cessation, active preparations were carried on within the fort, to resist a further attack. Each person was assigned some particular duty. Of the women, some were required to run bullets, while others were to cool the guns, load and hand them to the men, etc. Some of them, indeed, insisted upon doing duty by the side of the men, and two actually took their position at the port-holes, dealing death to many a dusky warrior.

About three o'clock, the Indians returned to the attack with redoubled fury. They distributed themselves among the cabins, behind fallen trees, etc. The number thus disposed of, amounted to perhaps one-half the actual force of the enemy. The remainder advanced along the base of the hill south of the fort, and commenced a vigorous fire upon that part of the stockade. This was a cunningly devised scheme, as it drew most of the inmates to that quarter. Immediately a rush was made from the cabins, led on by Girty in person, and a most determined effort made to force the entrance. The attempt was made with heavy timber, but failed, with the loss of many of their boldest warriors.

Several similar attempts were made during the afternoon, but all alike failed. Maddened and chagrined by repeated disappointment and ill-success, the savages withdrew to their covert until night-fall. Day at length closed; darkness deepened over the waters, and almost the stillness of death reigned around. About nine o'clock, the savages re-appeared, making night hideous with their yells, and the heavens lurid with their discharge of musketry. The lights in the fort having been extinguished, the inmates had the advantage of those without, and many a stalwart savage fell before the steady aim of experienced frontiersmen. Repeated attempts were made, during the night, to storm the fort, and to fire it, but all failed, through the vigilance and activity of those within.

At length that night of horror passed, and the second of September dawned upon the scene, only to bring a renewal of the attack. This, however, did not last long, and despairing of success, the savages prepared to leave. They fired most of the buildings, killed the cattle, and were about departing, when a relief party of fourteen men, under Colonel Andrew Swearingen, from Holliday's Fort, twenty-four miles above, landed in a pirogue, and, undiscovered by the Indians, gained entrance to the fort. Shortly afterward, Major Samuel McColloch, at the head of forty mounted men from Short Creek, made their appearance in front of the fort, the gates of which were joyfully thrown open. Simultaneously with the appearance of McColloch's men re-appeared the enemy, and a rush was made, to cut off the entrance of some of the party. All, however, succeeded in getting in except the gallant major, who, anxious for the safety of his men, held back until his own chance was entirely cut off. Finding himself surrounded by savages, he rode, at full speed, in the direction of the lofty hill, which overhangs the present city of Wheeling. The enemy, with exulting yells, followed close in pursuit, not doubting they would capture one whom of all other men they preferred to wreak their vengeance upon. Knowing their relentless hostility toward himself, he strained every muscle of his noble steed to gain the summit, and then escape along the brow in direction of Van Metre's Fort. At length he attained the top, and galloping ahead of his pursuers, rejoiced at his lucky escape. As he gained a point on the hill, near where the Cumberland Road now crosses, what should he suddenly encounter but a considerable body of Indians, who were just returning from a plundering excursion among the settlements.

In an instant, he comprehended the full extent of his danger. Escape seemed out of the question, either in the direction of Short Creek or back to the bottom. A fierce and revengeful foe completely hemmed him in, cutting off every chance of successful retreat or escape. What was to be done? Fall into their hands, and share the most refined torture savage ingenuity could invent? That thought was agony; and, in an instant, the bold soldier—preferring death among the rocks and brambles, to the knife and faggot of the savage—determined to plunge over the precipice before him.*
Without a moment's hesitation, for the savages were pressing upon him, he firmly adjusted himself in his saddle, grasped securely the bridle with his left hand, and supporting his rifle in the right, pushed his unfaltering old horse over. A plunge, a crash—crackling timber and tumbling rocks were all that the wondering savages could see or hear. They looked chagrined, but bewildered, one at another; and while they inwardly

---

* The hill, at this point, is full three hundred feet in height, and, at that time, was in many places perpendicular. Since then the construction of the road has somewhat changed its features. The exact spot where the rider went over, is close to a small house standing near where the road crosses.

Fearful Leap of Major Samuel McColloch. [See page 368.]

regretted that the fire had been spared its duty, they could not but greatly rejoice that their most inveterate enemy was at length beyond the power of doing further injury. But, lo! ere a single savage had recovered from his amazement, what should they see but the invulnerable major, on his white steed, galloping across the peninsula. Such was the feat of Major McColloch, certainly one of the most daring and successful ever attempted. The place has become memorable as McColloch's Leap, and will remain so long as the hill stands, and the recollections of the past have a place in the hearts of the people. Our engraver has given a very effective and correct representation of this "leap."

It is a matter of great regret that more of the stirring incidents in this man's life have not been collected and preserved. Toward the latter end of July, 1782, indications of Indians having been noticed by some of the settlers, Major McColloch and his brother John mounted their horses, and left Van Metre's Fort, to ascertain the correctness of the report. They crossed Short Creek, and continued in the direction of Wheeling, but inclining toward the river. They scouted closely but cautiously, and not discovering any such "signs" as had been stated, descended to the bottom, at a point about two miles above Wheeling. They then passed up the river to the mouth of Short Creek, and thence up Girty's Point, in the direction of Van Metre's. Not discovering any indications of the enemy, the brothers were riding leisurely along (July 30, 1782), and when a short distance beyond the "point," a deadly discharge of rifles took place, killing Major McColloch instantly. His brother escaped, but his horse was killed. Immediately mounting that of his brother, he made off to give the alarm. As yet no enemy had been seen; but turning in his saddle, after riding fifty yards, the path was filled with Indians, and one fellow in the act of scalping the unfortunate major. Quick as thought the rifle of John was at his shoulder, and, in an instant more, the savage was rolling in the agonies of death. John McColloch escaped to the fort unhurt, with the exception of a slight wound on his hip.

On the following day a party of men, from Van Metre's, went out and gathered up the mutilated remains of Major McColloch. The savages had disemboweled him, but the viscera all remained, except the *heart.* Some years subsequent to this melancholy affair, an Indian, who had been one of the party on this occasion, told some whites that the heart of Major McColloch had been divided and *eaten by the party.* This was done, said he, that "we be bold, like Major McColloch." On another occasion, an Indian, in speaking of the incident, said, "The white (meaning John McColloch) had killed a great captain, but they (the Indians) had killed a greater one."

REMARKABLE ESCAPE.

ONE of the most remarkable escapes upon record, is that of Thomas Mills. The circumstances were these: On the thirtieth day of July, 1783, Mills and two other men, Henry Smith and Hambleton Kerr, started on a fishing excursion, up the river, from Wheeling. When near Glenn's Run, a party of Indians, who had watched the movements of the whites, fired upon them, killing Smith, and wounding Mills in fourteen places. He had that many distinct bullet-holes in him, and yet not one of them was mortal. Kerr escaped. Just before the attack, Mills and his companions had caught an enormous catfish (weighing 87 pounds); and when the men were taken from the canoe, at Wheeling, their appearance was truly frightful—they were literally covered with blood and sand. Mills recovered from his wounds, and, as late as 1850, was living on the Ohio, near Shade River. He was, in his time, a most useful man on the frontier, possessing great experience as a hunter and scout.

Kerr was one of the most efficient spies west of the

Ohio River. His father was killed near the mouth of Duck Creek, in the summer of 1791. Two of his neighbors who were passing down the river in a canoe, on the Virginia side of the island, hearing the report of a gun, landed and passed over the island, where they saw two Indians going from the canoe in which Kerr lay, with the struggles of death still upon him. This murder of his father greatly exasperated Hambleton, and, thenceforward, no Indian was safe who crossed his path, whether in time of war or peace. He settled at the mouth of a small stream, now known as Kerr's Run, at the upper end of the flourishing town of Pomeroy, Ohio.

CAPTIVITY OF TWO BOYS.

In the spring of 1785, the Indians early re-appeared in the neighborhood of Wheeling. One of their first acts, on Wheeling Creek, was the captivity of two boys, John Wetzel, jr., and Frederick Erlewyne, the former about sixteen years of age, and the latter a year or two younger. The boys had gone from the fort, at Shepherd's, for the purpose of catching horses. One of the stray animals was a mare, with a young colt, belonging to Wetzel's sister, and she had offered the foal to John, as a reward for finding the mare. While on this service, they were captured by a party of four Indians, who having come across the horses, had seized and secured them in a thicket, expecting the bells would attract the notice of their owners, so they could kill them. The horse was ever a favorite object of plunder with the savages; as not only facilitating his own escape from pursuit, but also assisting him in carrying off the spoil. The boys, hearing the well-known tinkle of the bells, approached the spot where the Indians lay concealed, congratulating themselves on their good luck in so readily finding the strays, when they were immediately seized by the savages. John, in attempting to escape, was shot through the wrist. His companion hesitating to go with the Indians, and beginning to cry, they dispatched him with the tomahawk. John, who had once before been taken prisoner, and escaped, made light of it, and went along cheerfully with his wounded arm.

The party struck the Ohio River early the following morning, at a point near the mouth of Grave Creek, and just below the clearing of Mr. Tomlinson, who with his family was at that time in the fort at Wheeling. Here they found some hogs, and killing one of them, put it into a canoe they had stolen. Three of the Indians took possession of the canoe, with their prisoner, while the other was busied in swimming the horses across the river. It so happened that Isaac Williams, Hambleton Kerr, and Jacob, a Dutchman, had come down that morning from Wheeling, to look after the cattle, etc., left at the deserted settlement. When near the mouth of Little Grave Creek, a mile above, they heard the report of a rifle. "Dod rot 'em," exclaimed Mr. Willlams, "a Kentuck' boat has landed at the creek, and they are shooting my hogs." Quickening their pace, in a few minutes they were within a short distance of the creek, when they heard the loud snort of a horse. Kerr, being in the prime of life, and younger than Mr. Williams, was several rods ahead, and reached the bank first. As he looked into the creek, he saw three Indians standing in a canoe; one was in the stern, one in the bow, and the other in the middle. At the feet of the latter lay four rifles and a dead hog; while a fourth Indian was swimming a horse, a few rods from shore. The one in the stern had his paddle in the edge of the water, in the act of turning and shoving the canoe from the mouth of the creek into the river. Before they were aware of his presence, Kerr drew up and shot the Indian in the stern, who instantly fell into the water. The crack of his rifle had scarcely ceased, when Mr. Williams came up and shot the one in the bow, who also fell overboard. Kerr dropped his own rifle, and seizing that of the Dutchman, shot the remaining Indian. He fell over into the water, but still held on to the side of the canoe with one hand. So amazed was the last Indian at the fall of his companions, that he never offered to lift one of the rifles, which lay at his feet, in self-defense, but acted like one bereft of his senses.

By this time the canoe, impelled by the impetus given to it by the first Indian, had reached the current of the river, and was some rods below the mouth of the creek. Kerr instantly reloaded his gun, and seeing another man lying in the bottom of the canoe, raised it to his face as in the act of firing, when he cried out, "Don't shoot, I am a white man!" Kerr told him to knock loose the Indian's hand from the side of the canoe, and paddle to the shore. In reply he said his arm was broken, and he could not. The current, however, set it near some rocks not far from land, on which he jumped and waded out. Kerr now aimed his rifle at the Indian on horse-back, who, by this time, had reached the middle of the river. The shot struck near him, splashing the water on his naked skin. The Indian, seeing the fate of his companions, with the utmost bravery slipped from the horse, and swam for the canoe in which were the rifles of the four warriors. This was an act of necessity as well as of daring, for he well knew he could not reach home without the means of killing game. He soon gained possession of the canoe, unmolested crossed with the arms to his own side of the Ohio, mounted the captive horse, which had swam to the Indian shore, and, with a yell of defiance, escaped into the woods. The canoe was turned adrift, to spite his enemies, and was taken up near Maysville, Kentucky, with the dead hog still in it—the cause of all their misfortunes.

THE TWO JOHNSON BOYS.

ANOTHER BRAVE BOY.

SINCE giving, on page 286, the remarkable story of the two Johnson boys, we have met with a detailed statement of the whole transaction, by Henry Johnson, the younger brother, who was still living, in 1851, in Monroe County, Ohio. We copy from De Hass' History of Western Virginia, page 300:

ANTIOCH, MONROE COUNTY, OHIO, }
January 18, 1851. }

DEAR SIR:—Yours of the eighth instant has just come to hand, and I, with pleasure, sit down to answer your request, which is a statement of my adventure with the Indians. I will give the narrative as found in my sketch book.

I was born in Westmoreland County, Pennsylvania, February 4th, 1777. When about eight years old, my father, James Johnson, having a large family to provide for, sold his farm, with the expectation of acquiring larger possessions farther west. Thus he was stimulated to encounter the perils of a pioneer life. He crossed the Ohio River, and bought some improvements on what was called Beach Bottom Flats, two and a half miles from the river, and three or four miles above the mouth of Short Creek, with the expectation of holding, by improvement-right, under the Virginia claim. Soon after we reached there, the Indians became troublesome; they stole horses, and killed a number of persons in our neighborhood. When I was between eleven and twelve years old, in the month of October, 1788, I was taken prisoner by the Indians, with my brother John, who was about eighteen months older than I. The circumstances were as follows:

On Saturday evening we were out with an older brother, and came home late in the evening. The next morning one of us had lost a hat, and, about the middle of the day, we thought that perhaps he had left it where we had been at work, about three-fourths of a mile from the house. We went to the place and found the hat, and sat down on a log by the road-side, and commenced cracking nuts. In a short time we saw two men coming toward us from the house. By their dress, we supposed they were two of our neighbors, James Perdue and J. Russell. We paid but little attention to them, until they came quite near us, when we saw our mistake—they were black. To escape by flight was impossible, had we been disposed to try. We sat still until they came up. One of them said, "How do, brodder?" My brother asked them if they were Indians, and they answered in the affirmative, and said we must go with them. One of them had a blue buckskin pouch, which he gave my brother to carry, and, without farther ceremony, we took up the line of march for the wilderness, not knowing whether we should ever return to our cheerful home; and, not having much love for our commanding officers, of course we obeyed orders very tardily. The mode of march was thus, one of the Indians walked about ten steps before, the other about ten behind us.

After traveling some distance, we halted in a deep hollow, and sat down. They took out their knives and whet them, and talked some time in the Indian tongue, which we could not understand. My brother and I sat eight or ten steps from them, and talked about killing them that night, and making our escape. I thought, from their looks and actions, that they were going to kill us; and, strange to say, felt no alarm. I thought I would rather die than go with them. The most of my trouble was, that my father and mother would be fretting after us—not knowing what had become of us. I expressed my thoughts to John, who went and began to talk with them. He said that father was cross to him, and made him work hard, and that he did not like hard work; that he would rather be a hunter, and live in the woods. This seemed to please them; for they put up their knives, and talked more lively and pleasantly. We became very familiar, and many questions passed between us; all parties were very inquisitive.

They asked my brother which way home was several times, and he would tell them the contrary way every time, although he knew the way very well. This would make them laugh; they thought we were lost, and that we knew no better.

They conducted us over the Short Creek Hills in search of horses, but found none; so we continued on foot until night, when we halted in a hollow, about three miles from Carpenter's Fort, and about four miles from the place where they first took us. Our route being somewhat circuitous, we made but slow progress. As night began to close in, I became fretful. My brother encouraged me, by whispering that he would kill them that night. After they had selected the place of our encampment, one of them scouted round, whilst the other struck fire, which was done by stopping the touch-hole of his gun, and flashing powder in the pan. After the Indian got the fire kindled, he re-primed the gun, and went to an old stump to get some tinder wood; and, while he was thus employed, my brother John took the gun, cocked it, and was about to shoot the Indian. Alarmed, lest the other might be close by, I remonstrated, and, taking hold of the gun, prevented him shooting; at the same time I begged him to wait till night, and I would help him kill them both. The other Indian came back about dark, when we took our supper, such as it was—some corn parched on the coals, and some roasted pork. We then sat down and talked for some time. They seemed to be acquainted with the whole border settlement, from Marietta to Beaver, and could number every fort and block-house, and asked my brother how many fighting men there were in each place, and how many guns. In some places, my brother said, there were a good many more guns than there were fighting men. They asked what use were these guns. He said that the women could load while the men fired. But how did these guns get there? My brother said, when the war was over with Great Britain, the soldiers that were enlisted during the war were discharged, and they left a great many of their guns at the stations. They asked my brother who owned that black horse that wore a bell. He answered, father. They then said the Indians could never catch that horse.

We then went to bed on the naked ground, to rest and study out the best mode of attack. They put us between them, that they might be the better able to guard us. After a while, one of the Indians, supposing we were asleep, got up and stretched himself on the other side of the fire, and soon began to snore. John, who had been watching every motion, found they were sound asleep. He whispered to me to get up, which we did as carefully as possible. John took the gun with which the Indian had struck fire, cocked it, and placed it in the direction of the head of one of the Indians. He then took a tomahawk, and drew it over the head of the other Indian. I pulled the trigger, and he struck at the same instant; the blow, falling too far back on the neck, only stunned the Indian. He attempted to spring to his feet, uttering most hideous yells, but my brother repeated the blows with such effect that the conflict became terrible, and somewhat doubtful. The Indian, however, was forced to yield to the blows he received on his head, and, in a short time, he lay quiet at our feet. The one that was shot never moved; and, fearing there were others close by, we hurried off, and took nothing with us but the gun I shot with. They had told us we would see Indians about to-morrow, so we thought that there was a camp of Indians close by; and fearing the report of the gun, the Indian hallooing, and I calling to John, might bring them upon us, we took our course toward the river, and, on going about three-fourths of a mile, came to a path which led to Carpenter's Fort. My brother here hung up his hat, that he might know where to take off to find the camp.

We got to the fort a little before day-break. We related our adventure, and, the next day, a small party went out with my brother, and found the Indian that was tomahawked on the ground; the other had crawled off, and was not found till some time after. He was shot through, close by the ear.

Having concluded this narrative, I will give a description of the two Indians. They were of the Delaware tribe, and one of them a chief. He wore the badges of his office—the wampum belt, three half-moons, and a silver plate on his breast; bands of silver on both arms, and his ears cut round and ornamented with silver; the hair, on the top of his head, was done up with silver wire. The other Indian seemed to be a kind of waiter. He was rather under size, a plain man. He wore a fine beaver-hat, with a hole shot through the crown. My brother asked him about the hat. He said he killed a captain, and got his hat. My brother asked him if he had killed many of the whites, and he answered, a good many. He then asked him if the big Indian had killed many of the whites, and he answered, a great many, and that he was a great captain—a chief. . . . .
[Signed] HENRY JOHNSON.

In connection with the above, and to still farther show of what material the boys were made in the great heroic age of the West, we give the following, which we find in a recent communication from Major Nye, of Ohio. The scene of adventure was within the present limits of Wood County, Virginia:

"I have heard, from Mr. Guthrie and others, that, at Bellville, a man had a son, quite a youth, say twelve or fourteen years of age, who had been used to firing his father's gun, as most boys did in those days. He heard, he supposed, turkeys on or near the bank of the Ohio, opposite that place, and asked his father to let him take the gun and kill one. His father, knowing that the Indians frequently decoyed people by such noises, refused, saying it was probably an Indian. When he had gone to work, the boy took the gun and paddled his canoe over the river, but had the precaution to land some distance from where he had heard the turkey all the morning, probably for fear of scaring the game, and perhaps a little afraid of Indians. The banks were steep, and the boy cautiously advanced to where he could see without being seen. Watching awhile for his game, he happened to see an Indian cautiously looking over a log, to notice where the boy had landed. The lad fixed his gun at a rest, watching the place where he had seen the Indian's head, and when it appeared again, fired, and the Indian disappeared. The boy dropped the gun and ran for his canoe, which he paddled over the river as soon as possible. When he reached home, he said, 'Mother, I have killed an Indian!' and the mother replied, "No, you have not.' 'Yes, I have,' said the boy. The father coming in, he made the same report to him, and received the same reply; but he constantly affirmed it was even so; and, as the gun was left, a party took the boy over the river to find it, and show the place where he shot the Indian, and, behold, his words were found verified. The ball had entered the head, where the boy had affirmed he shot, between the eye and ear."

Such "boys" made the men of the Republic in after years—men whom neither tyranny nor oppression could subdue.

CAPTAIN SAMUEL BRADY.

OF the many brave spirits who started into existence at the first drum-tap of the Revolution, but few have become better known or more respected, in the West, than the gallant Brady, captain of the spies. At a very early age, this devoted partisan gave indications of future usefulness; exhibiting, in all his movements, a spirit and a purpose to do and dare which marked him as a man of no ordinary character, and proved him fit for almost any emergency.

Brady was emphatically the Marion of the West. Like the Chevalier Bayard, he was "without fear and without reproach." A bolder or braver man never drew a sword or fired a rifle; and these marked elements of his nature rendered him the terror of the Indian warrior, whether on the scout or in the wigwam, for he felt himself alike insecure from the noiseless vengeance of the "leader of the spies." No man stood higher in the esteem of the hardy settlers, and no name could inspire more of confidence and of safety than that of *Samuel Brady*. During the whole of the fierce, protracted, and sanguinary war, which ravaged the frontier settlements of Virginia and Pennsylvania, from 1785 to 1794, no man could so quiet the trembling and fear-stricken settlers as Captain Brady. His presence, backed by the band of devoted followers who always stepped in his foot-prints, was felt as security every-where. The fond mother, who, in after years, related to her children the many thrilling incidents of frontier life which she witnessed and passed through, never failed, as she thanked her Heavenly Father for having protected her little innocents from the scalping-knife and tomahawk, to express her heartfelt gratitude to him who had been the instrumentality of saving her all from savage barbarity.

Samuel Brady was born at Shippensburgh, Pennsylvania, in 1756. His father, John Brady, was made a captain in the Colonial army, for his services in the old French and Indian wars. The family, at an early day, moved to the Susquehanna. On the breaking out of the Revolution, Samuel joined a volunteer company, and marched to Boston. The patriotic fervor of the youth, prompted the commander to offer young Brady a commission; but his father objected, thinking he was too young, saying, "First let him learn the duties of a soldier, and then he will better know how to act as an officer."

"In 1776, Samuel Brady was appointed a first lieutenant. He continued with the army, and was in all the principal engagements, until after the battle of Monmouth, when he was promoted to a captaincy, and ordered to the West, under Colonel Brodhead. On their march, he had leave to visit his friends in Northumberland County. His father, in 1776, had accepted a captaincy in the twelfth Pennsylvania regiment, been badly wounded at the battle of Brandywine, and was then at home. Whilst there, he heard of his brother's death, who had been murdered by the Indians, on the ninth of August, 1778. He remained at home until 1779, and then rejoined his regiment at Pittsburgh. During the same year, his father was murdered by the Indians; and then it was that our hero swore vengeance against the whole race. Terribly, too, did he keep that vow."

In 1781, the Indians became very troublesome in the settlements above Pittsburgh. Washington, as we have elsewhere noticed, knew very well that the only guaranty of safety was to strike the enemy at home. With this view, he directed Colonel Brodhead to send some suitable person to their towns, who could ascertain their strength, resources, etc. Colonel Brodhead's keen military eye saw in Brady the very man for the service, and giving him the necessary instructions, the gallant soldier started on his perilous mission, accompanied by John Williamson and one of the Wetzels. These men were so completely disguised as Indians, that it would almost have defied the skill and cunning of a genuine chief to detect the deception.

After a hurried march, they reached the Indian town at Upper Sandusky, shortly after dark. Brady posted his men, then entered the town, and after a thorough reconnoiter, rejoined his companions, and commenced a rapid retreat. His keen eye had caught a lurking suspicion in some of those whom he met, and it was deemed important to get beyond their reach as rapidly as possible.

With scarcely a moment's intermission, the three traveled all night, and stopping a few minutes in the morning, discovered the Indians were in pursuit. Increasing their movements, and adopting the precaution of traveling upon logs, and avoiding direct routes, the trio were soon beyond immediate danger. The remainder of that day, all of that night, and part of the third day, passed without any cause of apprehension. Fatigued and hungry (their sole diet since leaving home having been parched corn and jerked venison), the party concluded to take a rest. Williamson stood guard while the others slept. Brady, at all times a great snorer, on this occasion gave vent to sounds that, in the language of Williamson, "were enough to alarm all the Indians between here and Sandusky." Thinking a change of position might stop the nasal artillery, Williamson turned Brady, and then resumed his seat by the fire. Scarcely had he seated himself, when he detected the stealthy tread of a savage. Looking attentatively in the direction of the sound, he saw an Indian cautiously approach, and waiting until he came nearly up, the guard took steady aim and fired. One convulsive spring, a heavy fall, and deep groan, were all that could be seen or heard. His companions sprang to their feet and moved rapidly off, to avoid an attack; but this was the only Indian, and the three traveled on without further attempt at molestation. According to the account furnished by one of the family, of which we shall have occasion frequently to avail ourselves during this notice—

"The map furnished by General Brodhead was found to be defective. The distance was represented to be much less than it really was. The provisions and ammunition of the men were exhausted by the time they had reached the Big Beaver, on their return. Brady shot an otter, but could not eat it. The last load was in his rifle. They arrived at an old encampment, and found plenty of strawberries, which they stopped to appease their hunger with. Having discovered a deer-track, Brady followed it, telling the men he would perhaps get a shot at it. He had gone but a few rods, when he saw the deer standing broadside to him. He raised his rifle and attempted to fire, but it flashed in the pan. He sat down, picked the touch-hole, and then started on. After going a short distance, the path made a bend, and he saw before him a large Indian on horse-back, with a child before, and its mother behind, and a number of warriors marching in the rear. His first impulse was to shoot the Indian on horseback; but, as he raised the rifle, he observed the child's head to roll with the motion of the horse. It was fast asleep, and tied to the Indian. He stepped behind the root of a tree, and waited until he could shoot the Indian, without out danger to the child or its mother.

"When he considered the chance certain, he fired, and the Indian, child, and mother, all fell from the horse. Brady called to his men, with a voice that made the forest ring, to surround the Indians, and give them a general fire. He sprang to the fallen Indian's powder-horn, but could not pull it off. Being dressed like an Indian, the woman thought he was one, and said, 'Why did you shoot your brother?' He caught up the child, saying, 'Jenny Stoop, I am Captain Brady; follow me, and I will secure you and your child.' He caught her hand in his, carrying the child under the other arm, and dashed into the brush. Many guns were fired at him, but no ball touched, and the Indians, dreading an ambuscade, were glad to make off. The next day he arrived at Fort M'Intosh, with the woman and her child. His men had got there before him. They had heard his war-whoop, and knew they were Indians he had encountered, but having no ammunition, had taken to their heels and run off."

"The incursions of the Indians had become so frequent, and their outrages so alarming, that it was thought advisable to retaliate upon them the injuries of war, and to carry into the country occupied by them the same system with which they had visited the settlements. For this purpose an adequate force was provided, under the immediate command of General Brodhead, the command of the advance guard of which was confided to Captain Brady.

"The troops proceeded up the Alleghany River, and had arrived near the mouth of Redbank Creek, now known by the name of Brady's Bend, without encountering an enemy. Brady and his rangers were some distance in front of the main body, as their duty required, when they suddenly discovered a war-party of Indians approaching them. Relying on the strength of the main body, and its ability to force the Indians to retreat, and anticipating, as Napoleon did in the battle with the Mamelukes, that, when driven back, they would return by the same route they had advanced on, Brady permitted them to proceed without hinderance, and hastened to seize a narrow pass, higher up the river, where the rocks, nearly perpendicular, approached the river, and a few determined men might successfully combat superior numbers."

In a short time the Indians encountered the main body under Brodhead, and were driven back. In full and swift retreat they pressed on to gain the pass between the rocks and the river, but it was occupied by Brady and his rangers, who failed not to pour into their flying columns a most destructive fire. Many were killed on the bank, and many more in the stream. Cornplanter, afterward the distinguished chief of the Senecas, but then a young man, saved himself by swimming. The celebrated war-chief of this tribe, Bald-Eagle, was of the number slain on this occasion.

"The army moved onward, and after destroying all the Indians' corn, and ravaging the Kenjua Flats, returned to Pittsburgh.

"Shortly after Captain Brady's return from Sandusky, he was observed one evening, by a man of the name of Phouts, sitting in a solitary part of the fort, apparently absorbed in thought. Phouts approached him, pained, to the bottom of his honest heart, to perceive that the countenance of Brady bore traces of care and melancholy. He accosted him, however, in the best English he had, and soothingly said, 'Gabtain, was ails you?' Brady looked at him a short time without speaking; then, resuming his usual equanimity, replied, 'I have been thinking about the red-skins, and it is my opinion there are some above us on the river. I have a mind to pay them a visit. Now, if I get permission to do so, will you go along?' Phouts was a stout, thick Dutchman, of uncommon strength and activity. He was also well acquainted with the woods. When Brady had ceased speaking, Phouts raised himself on tiptoe, and bringing his heels hard down on the ground, by way of emphasis, his eyes full of fire, said, 'By dunder und lightnin, I would rader go mit you, Gabtain, as to any of te finest weddins in this guntry.' Brady told him to keep quiet, and say nothing about it, as no man in the fort must know any thing of the expedition but General Brodhead. Bidding Phouts to call at his tent in an hour, he then went to the general's quarters, whom he found reading. After the usual topics were discussed, Brady proposed, for consideration, his project of ascending the Alleghany, with but one man in company; stating his reasons for apprehending a descent, from that quarter, by the Indians. The general gave his consent; at parting took him by the hand in a friendly manner, advising him how to proceed, and charging him particularly to be careful of his own life, and that of the men or man whom he might select to accompany him. So affectionate were the general's admonitions, and so great the emotion he displayed, that Brady left him *with tears in his eyes*, and repaired to his tent, where he found Phouts deep in conversation with one of his *pet* Indians.

"He told Phouts of his success with the general, and that, as it was early in the light of the moon, they must get ready and be off betimes.

"They immediately set about cleaning their guns, preparing their ammunition, and, having secured a small quantity of salt, lay down together and slept soundly until about two hours before daybreak. Brady awoke first, and stirring Phouts, each took down the 'deadly rifle,' and whilst all but the sentinels were wrapped in sleep, they left the little fort, and, in a short time, found themselves deep buried in the forest. That day they marched through woods never traversed by either of them before; following the general course of the river, they reached a small creek* that put in from the Pittsburgh side; it was near night when they got there, and having no provision, they concluded to remain there all night.

"Next morning they started early, and traveled all day; in the evening they espied a number of crows hovering over the tops of the trees, near the bank of the river. Brady told Phouts that there were Indians in the neighborhood, or else the men who were expected from Susquehanna at Pittsburgh were there encamped, or had been some time before.

---

* Probably Puckety Creek, which empties into the Alleghany at Logan's Ferry.

"Phouts was anxious to go down and see, but Brady forbade him; telling him at the same time, 'We must secrete ourselves till after night, when fires will be made by them, whoever they may be.' Accordingly, they hid themselves among fallen timber, and remained so till about ten o'clock at night. But even then they could still see no fire. Brady concluded there must be a hill or thick woods between him and where the crows were seen, and decided on leaving his hiding-place to ascertain the fact. Phouts accompanied him. They walked, with the utmost caution, down toward the river bank, and had gone about two hundred yards, when they observed the twinkling of a fire, at some distance on their right. They at first thought the river made a very short bend, but, on proceeding further, discovered that it was a fork or branch of the river, probably the Kiskeminetas. Brady desired Phouts to stay where he was, intending to go himself to the fire, and see who was there; but Phouts refused, saying, 'No, by George, I vill see too.' They approached the fire together, but with the utmost caution; supposing it to be an Indian encampment, much too large to be attacked by them.

"Resolved to ascertain the number of the enemy, Captain Brady and his brave comrade went close up to the fire, and discovered an old Indian sitting beside a tree near the fire, either mending or making a pair of moccasins.

"Phouts, who never thought of danger, was for shooting the Indian immediately; but Brady prevented him. After examining carefully around the camp, he was of opinion that the number by which it was made had been large, but that they were principally absent. He determined on knowing more in the morning; and, forcing Phouts away, retired a short distance to await the approach of day. As soon as it appeared they returned to the camp, but saw nothing, except the old Indian, a dog, and a horse.

"Brady wished to see the country around the camp, and understand its features better; for this purpose he kept at some distance from it, and examined about, till he got on the river above it. Here he found a large *trail* of Indians, who had gone up the Alleghany; to his judgment it appeared to have been made one or two days before. Upon seeing this, he concluded to go back to the camp and take the old Indian prisoner.

"Supposing the old savage to have arms about him, and not wishing to run the risk of the alarm the report of a rifle might create, if Indians were in the neighborhood, Brady determined to seize the old fellow singlehanded, without doing him further 'scath,' and carry him off to Pittsburgh. With this view, both crept toward the camp again, very cautiously. When they came so near as to perceive him, the Indian was lying on his back, with his head toward them.

"Brady ordered Phouts to remain where he was, and not to fire, unless the dog should attempt to assist his master. In that case he was to shoot the dog, but by no means to hurt the Indian. The plan being arranged, Brady dropped his rifle, and, tomahawk in hand, silently crept toward the old man, until within a few feet; then raising himself up, he made a spring like a panther, and with a yell that awakened the echoes round, seized the Indian hard and fast by the throat. The old man struggled a little at first, but Brady's was the grip of a lion; holding his tomahawk over the head of his prisoner, he bade him surrender, as he valued his life. The dog behaved very civilly; he merely growled a little. Phouts came up, and they tied their prisoner. On examining the camp they found nothing of value, except some powder and lead, which they threw into the river. When the Indian learned that he was to be taken to Pittsburgh, and would be kindly treated, he showed them a canoe, which they stepped into with their prisoner and his dog, and were soon afloat on the Alleghany. They paddled swiftly along, for the purpose of reaching the mouth of the run on which they had encamped coming up, for Brady had left his wiping-rod there. It was late when they got to the creek's mouth. They landed, made a fire, and all laid down.

"As soon as daylight appeared, the captain started to where they left some jerk hanging on the evening before, leaving Phouts in charge of the prisoner and his canoe. He had not left the camp long, till the Indian complained to Phouts that the cords upon his wrists hurt him. He had probably discovered that in Phouts' composition there was a much larger proportion of *kindness* than of *fear*. The Dutchman at once took off the cords, and the Indian was, or pretended to be, very grateful. Phouts was busied with something else in a minute, and had left his gun standing by a tree. The moment the Indian saw that the eye of the other was not upon him, he sprang to the tree, seized the gun, and the first Phouts knew was that it was cocked and at his breast. The trigger was pulled, but the bullet whistled harmless past him, taking with it a part of his shot-pouch belt. One stroke of the Dutchman's tomahawk settled the Indian forever, and nearly severed the head from his body.

"Brady heard the report of the rifle, and the yell of Phouts; and supposing all was not right, ran instantly to the spot, where he found the latter sitting on the body of the Indian, examining the rent in his shot-pouch belt. 'In the name of Heaven,' said Brady, 'what have you done?' 'Yust look, Gabtain,' said the fearless Dutchman, 'vat dis d—d black b—h vas apout;' holding up to view the hole in his belt. He then related what has been stated with respect to his untying the Indian, and the attempt of the latter to kill him. They then took off the scalp of the Indian, got their canoe, took in the Indian's dog, and returned to Pittsburgh the fourth day after their departure."

Beaver Valley was the scene of many of Captain Brady's stirring adventures. We have recently visited some of the interesting localities, celebrated as Brady's theater of action, and heard from many of the older citizens their accounts of his thrilling exploits. They speak in unbounded terms of admiration of his daring and success; his many hair-breath escapes by "field and flood;" and always concluded by declaring that he was a greater man than Daniel Boone or Lewis Wetzel, either of whom, in the eyes of the old pioneers, was the very embodiment of dare-devilism.

The following, illustrating one of Brady's adventures in the region referred to, we give from a published source. In one of his trapping and hunting excursions, he was surprised and taken prisoner by a party of Indians who had closely watched his movements.

"To have shot or tomahawked him would have been but a small gratification to that of satiating their revenge by burning him at a slow fire, in the presence of all the Indians of their village. He was therefore taken alive to their encampment, on the west bank of the Beaver River, about a mile and a half from its mouth. After the usual exultations and rejoicings at the capture of a noted enemy, and causing him to run the gauntlet, a fire was prepared, near which Brady was placed after being stripped, and with his arms unbound. Previous to tying him to the stake, a large circle was formed around, of Indian men, women, and children, dancing and yelling, and uttering all manner of threats and abuses that their small knowledge of the English language could afford. The prisoner looked on these preparations for death and on his savage foe with a firm countenance and a steady eye, meeting all their threats with truly savage fortitude. In the midst of their dancing and rejoicing, a squaw of one of their chiefs came near him with a child in her arms. Quick as thought, and with intuitive prescience, he snatched it from her and threw it into the midst of the flames. Horror stricken at the sudden outrage, the Indians simultaneously rushed to rescue the infant from the fire. In the midst of this confusion, Brady darted from the circle, overturning all that came in his way, and rushed into the adjacent thicket, with the Indians yelling at his heels. He ascended the steep side of a hill amidst a shower of bullets, and darting down the opposite declivity, secreted himself in the deep ravines and laurel thickets that abound for several miles to the west. His knowledge of the country, and wonderful activity, enabled him to elude his enemies, and reach the settlements in safety."

From one of Brady's old soldiers—one of the noble spies, who, in 1851, had not answered to the roll-call of death—one who served with him three years, during the most trying and eventful period of his life, we have gathered the facts of the following incident. On one of their scouting expeditions into the Indian country, the spies, consisting at that time of sixteen men, encamped for the night at a place called "Big Shell Camp." Toward morning, one of the guard heard the report of a gun, and immediately communicating the fact to his commander, a change of position was ordered. Leading his men to an elevated point, the Indian camp was discovered almost beneath them. Cautiously advancing in the direction of the camp, six Indians were discovered standing around the fire, while several others lay upon the ground, apparently asleep. Brady ordered his men to wrap themselves in their blankets and lie down, while he kept watch. Two hours thus passed without any thing materially occurring. As day began to appear, Brady roused his men and posted them side by side, himself at the end of the line. When all were in readiness, the commander was to touch, with his elbow, the man who stood next to him, and the communication was to pass successively to the farthest end. The orders then were, the moment the last man was touched, he should fire, which was to be the signal for a general discharge. With the first faint ray of light rose six Indians, and stood around the fire. With breathless expectation the whites waited for the remainder to rise, but failing, and apprehending a discovery, the captain moved his elbow, and the next instant the wild wood rang with the shrill report of the rifles of the spies. Five of the six Indians fell dead, but the sixth, screened by a tree, escaped. The camp being large, it was deemed unsafe to attack it further, and a retreat was immediately ordered.

Soon after the above occurence, in returning from a similar expedition, and when about two miles from the mouth of Yellow Creek, at a place admirably adapted for an ambuscade, a solitary Indian stepped forward and fired upon the advancing company. Instantly, on firing, he retreated toward a deep ravine, into which the savage hoped to lead his pursuers. But Brady detected the trick, and, in a voice of thunder, ordered his men to tree. No sooner had this been done, than the concealed foe rushed forth in great numbers, and opened upon the whites a perfect storm of leaden hail. The brave spies returned the fire with spirit and effect; but as they were likely to be overpowered by superior numbers, a retreat was ordered to the top of the hill, and thence continued until out of danger.

The whites lost one man in this engagement, and two wounded. The Indian loss is supposed to have been about twenty, in killed and wounded.

Captain Brady possessed all the elements of a brave and successful soldier. Like Marion, "he consulted with his men respectfully, heard them patiently, weighed their suggestions, and silently approached his own conclusions. They knew his determination only by his actions." Brady had but few superiors as a woodman: he would strike out into the heart of the wilderness, and, with no guide but the sun by day, and the stars by night, or in their absence, then by such natural marks as the bark and tops of trees, he would move on steadily in a direct line toward his point of destination. He always avoided beaten paths and the borders of streams, and never was known to leave his track behind him. In this manner he eluded pursuit, and defied detection. He was often vainly hunted by his own men, and was more likely to find them than they him.

Such was Brady, the leader of the spies.

THE END.

INDEX.

	PAGE
Adoption, manner of Indian...	19
Adventures of—	
Col. Jas. Smith...	13
Daniel Boone...	45
Simon Kenton...	87
Gen. Benjamin Logan...	118
Col. Wm. Crawford...	128
Dr. Knight...	128
John Slover...	145
Capt. Robert Benham...	159
Alexander McConnel...	161
Rob't and Sam'l McAfee...	164
Bryant and Hogan...	167
McKinley...	169
David Morgan...	171
Andrew Poe...	174
Mrs. Woods...	180
Davis, Caffree and McClure...	181
Capt. James Ward...	185
Francis Downing...	187
The Widow Shanks...	189
A Wild White Man...	193
Mrs. John Merril...	197
Charles Ward, Calvin and Kenton...	199
James Ward, Baker and Kenton...	205
May, Johnston, Flinn and Skyles...	207
Capt. William Hubbell...	243
Jackson Johonnet...	255
William Kennan...	270
Lieut. Col. Darke...	276
Private Miller...	281
Two Johnson boys...	286, 374
Robinson...	293
Lewis Wetzel...	335
Jacob Wetzel...	337
John Wetzel...	355
Kinzie Dickerson...	357
Maj. Sam. McColloch...	362
John McColloch...	369
Boys Wetzel and Erlewyne.	371
Capt. Sam. Brady...	379

	PAGE
Aiken, death of...	256
Arbuckle, Capt...	301
Armstrong, Capt., sent against the Indians...	253
Baker...	205
Baker's Station...	337
Bald Eagle, murder of...	292
Bear, Indian fight with...	189
entrapped...	315
Bell, used by Indians as a decoy...	371
Benham, Robert, adventure of...	159
Big Foot, death of the Indian..	178
Biggs, Thomas, death of...	357
Blackfish, Indian chief...	103
Blue Licks, battle of...	76
capture of salt party at...	54
Boats attacked...	211, 216, 217, 245, 246
Boone, Daniel, adventures of..	45
starts for Kentucky...	46
captured by Indians...	47
family start for Kentucky..	50
death of eldest son...	50
capture of daughter...	53
captured at Blue Licks...	54
ransom refused for...	55
escape of...	56
Paint Creek expedition...	59
death of his brother...	61
memoirs of himself...	85
moves to Louisiana...	85
Boonesborough, first attack on.	52
again attacked...	53, 54, 57
nine days' siege of...	60
Bowman, Col., arrival of...	54
expedition...	121
Boys, captivity of two...	371
bravery of...	248, 286, 371, 374
Braddock's defeat, incidents of...	17
army, slaughter of...	296
Brady, John...	380, 381

(393)

Brady, Capt. Samuel............379
 stratagem 383
 and Phouts' expedition.....384
 captures an Indian...........387
 capture and escape............389
Breckinridge, Dr. Robert J...xxiii
Briscoe, Dr., exploring party of 91
British regulars burned......... 18
Brodhead, Col., ordered West..380
Brooks, William, aids Hubbell.249
Bryant's station, attack on.66, 70
Bryant, Wm., settles a station......................166, 168
Bullitt, Capt..................... 92
Butler, Clarke, Patterson, Majors.....................264, 303
Butler, Major-General under St. Clair................264, 306

Cabin built by Kenton.......... 93
Calloway, Misses, capture of.. 53
Calvin, Spencer.................199
Calvin, Luther, Capt............199
Campaigns compared............309
Campbell, Capt., British commandant,......................284
Camp Union.....................295
Catawba Indians, cunning of.. 22
Catfish, large, caught............370
Chickatommo, chief, fate of....241
Chillicothe, Indian town of.55, 56
Christian, Col......................295
Clark, Col. George Rogers, expedition of............83, 353
Clark, Major......................305
Collins, Judge Lewis.............xxi
Coon-hunt, incidents of......... 32
Cornplanter.......................384
Cornstalk's resignation..........302
Courtship, Indian................. 21
Cowardly actions.....199, 200, 203
Crawford, Col. William, adventures........................128
Cresap, Capt., murders Logan's family........................... 92

Dances, Indian....................315
Darke, Lieut. Col..........265, 303
Delzel, Capt......................331
Denton, Mrs...................... 52
Devine.............................213
Dickerson, Kinzie, escape of...357
Dickerson, Veach................345

Downing, Francis, adventure..187
Dream and its cause.............225
 of McIntyre...............203, 204
Duchouquet ransoms Johnston 228
Dunlap, Mrs., escape............164
Dunmore's expedition............295
Du Quesne, Fort, erected........ 13
Du Quesne, Capt.................. 58
Dutchman, named Jacob........372
Dutchman, named Phouts......384

Edwards, Col......................192
Emigrants being decoyed.......208
Erlewyne, Fred'k, capture of..371
Estill's station.................... 62
Estill, Capt., defeat.............. 64
Expedition of
 Col. Bowman...................121
 Col. George Rogers Clark... 83
 Crawford..........................128

Female, captive, released.......353
 courage,........67, 180, 191, 198
Ferguson, Maj........306, 264, 304
Fields, Col. John.................295
Findley, little known of......... 45
First explorer of Kentucky..... 14
 white woman in Kentucky 52
 house in interior of Ky..... 52
Fitzpatrick, found by Kenton. 94
Fleming, Misses, two sisters...207
                                211, 240
 Col. William..................295
Flinn..........................207, 230
Forbes, Gen., advance of........ 31
Ford, Capt........................305
Fort, British, destruction of...284
 Defiance 285
 at Detroit................327, 331
 Harmer...........................345
 Holliday 367
 McIntosh.........................383
 Pitt.............................. 90
 at Point Pleasant..............301
 Recovery 279
 Van Metre.......................368
 Washington..285, 278, 252, 263
Fowler, Major....................350

Gaither, Bedinger, Majors.265,303
Gilmore killed....................302
Girty, James, advice of...107, 184
 Simon..................62, 71, 363

INDEX.

Girty, Simon, pleads for Kenton 109
Gladwyn, Major 327
Glenn, Thomas, escape of 364
Graham, Lieut 332
Grant, companion of Bryant ... 168
and Lewis, quarrel 297
Greathouse, Jacob 89
Capt., whipped to death 246, 250
Greaton, Capt 305

Habeas Corpus, Wetzel released by 351
Hartshorn, Lieut., escape 253
Hamilton, Gov. of Canada 363
Hardin, Col., and militia 253
Harland, Major 76
Harmer, Gen., sent against Indian villages 252, 344
expedition, result of 255
Harrison, Col., death of 150
Harrod, Jas., settles Harrodsburgh 52
Harrodsburgh, attack on 53
Hart and Clark, Majors 306
Heart of Maj. McColloch eaten 370
Hedges, Joseph, death of 357
Hendricks, found by Kenton 94, 95
Herochche's address 324
Hog, killed by Indians 372
causes death of 3 Indians.. 372
Hogan, Mrs 52
James 167
Holder, Capt., defeat of 65
Horses, race after wild 26
Hough, John, escape of ... 357, 358
Hoy's station 65
Hubbell, Capt. Wm 243, 245
Human sacrifices common 35

Indian town, Tallihas 18
adoption, manner of 19
courtship 21
custom, to invite visitors to eat 21
pastimes 24
hospitality of 25
endurance of 25
discipline with children 27
punishment of children 27
deserted by squaw 28
superstition of 28
conjuror 29

Indian medicine man 29
military principles of 30
sagacity of 30
contempt for book-learning 31
woodcraft with 31
fondness for rum 34
drunken revels of 34
religion of 35
theology, beautiful 35
sweating house of 41
mining by 58
destruction of villages 84
Chief Blackfish 103
fight with a bear 189
humane action of 213
booty captured by 218
war-dance 225
manners (the chase) 310
shot in time of peace 345
capture of, by Brady 387
Indian race, destiny of xiii
Indians, preparations for an encounter 215
noble conduct of 240
incident of three brothers .. 286
eat heart of McColloch 370

Johnson boys, capture of the two 374
Henry, letter of 374
companion of Kenton 89
Johnston, Charles 207, 212, 230
Johonnet, Jackson, adventure. 255

Kennan, Wm., escape 270
heroic act of 274
Kennedy, Mrs. Mary, a prisoner 107
Kenton, Simon ... 87, 199, 205, 360
adventure with his rival ... 87
changes name to Butler 89
travels with Johnson 89
at Big Bone in 1774 92
cabin built by 93
on a secret mission 97
capture of 101
tortured 104
runs the gauntlet 104
attempted escape 106
finds a friend 108
rescued by Drewyer 113
taken to Detroit 114
escapes, with others 115
death of 117

396 INDEX.

Kentucky, tribute to............. xii
  bravery of...................... xii
  Colonization society.........xiii
  first explorer of................ 14
Kerr, Hamilton, escape of......370
  shoots Indians..................372
Kilpatrick killed.............243, 248
Kirkwood, Capt.....................275
Knight,Dr.,captured 128, 135, 141

Leap of Major McColloch......368
Lee, Hancock....................... 92
  Gen. Henry, of Virginia....277
Leitchman, adventures of...... 87
Lewis, Col. Charles..........295, 297
Lewis, Gen., with Dunmore...295
  personal appearance.........298
  battle with Indians...........299
Lewis, companion of Clark.....355
Lexington, house built in...... 61
Light, Daniel........................243
Linn, Mr., death of...............357
Little Turtle.........................275
Logan, murder of family of.... 92
  benevolence toward Kenton 113
  death 300
Logan's Station, attack on..53, 54
Logan, Gen. Benj., adventures 118
  moves to Kentucky............118
  settles Logan's Station.......119
  noble deed of 119
  expedition of.....................121

Madison, John, death of........355
Mahon, John....................... 89
Marshall, Col. Thomas..........183
Marshall,Capt.Thos.,attacked 216
Marshall, Dr. Louis, as a
  teacher v
Marshall's school................. v
Mason, Capt. Samuel, defeat
  of 364
Masquerade before DuQuesne.. 30
Master of life, Indian trust in
  the 321
May, John, surveys lands......207
McAfee, James.....................165
  Robert, adventure............165
  Samuel, adventure............164
  Station, attack on.............166
McBride, Major.................... 76
McCleland, Colonel, supposed
  death 150

McClung, John A..................
  birth and parentage......... v
  early education................ v
  studies theology............... vi
  marriage vi
  licensed to preach............ vi
  scholarship...................... vii
  remarkable memory......... vii
  popularity as a preacher... vii
  wavers in his faith........... vii
  writes "Sketches of West-
    ern Adventure.".......... vii
  writes " Camden," a novel.viii
  how he wrote...................viii
  retires from the ministry...viii
  studies law......................viii
  as a lawyer..................... ix
  in the Kentucky Legisla-
    ture............................ x
  speech on railroad bill....... x
  Railroad bank at Charles-
    ton xi
  withdraws from public life. xii
  speech on Colonization......xiii
  seeks to prove the Scrip-
    tures untrue.................xvii
  and then seeks light.......xviii
  again joins the church......xix
  at the water-cure............. xx
  re-licensed and ordained... xx
  synopsis of labors of.........xxi
  remarkable congregations.xxii
  is made a D. D...............xxii
  speech in General Assem-
    bly xxii
  striking effect of............xxiii
  accepts a call to Mays-
    ville...........................xxiii
  domestic habits of...........xxiv
  his daughter's tribute to..xxiv
  familiar with the poets...xxiv
  success of his ministry.....xxv
  teacher of the Scriptures..xxvi
  character of expositions...xxvi
  touching incident...........xxvii
  death of........................xxviii
  family of......................xxviii
  personal appearance of..xxviii
  personal attributes.........xxix
  Mrs. Susan, sketch of....... v
  Miss Anna Maria............xxv
  Miss Sue.......................xxiv
  Mrs., death of...............xxviii

INDEX. 397

McColloch, Abraham............362
McColloch, John.................362
  adventure of....................369
McColloch, Major Samuel......362
  adventure of..............367, 369
  fearful leap of..................368
  heart eaten by savages......370
McCullough, Wm., escape.357, 358
McConnell, Alex., adventure..161
  Hugh, escape of................364
McGary, at Blue Licks........75, 80
  murders Indian chief........127
  fight with Indians.............166
McGary, Mrs........................ 52
McIntyre as spy...................200
McIntyre, David..................355
McKee, Col., Indian agent.....284
McKinley, death of Capt.......137
McKinney, fight with wild cat 169
McMahan, Maj., expedition of 339
  prevents massacre............346
Memminger, Colonel, of South
  Carolina.....................x, xii
Merrill, John, attack on house
  of.................................197
Messhawa....................215, 241
  kindness to Johnston........221
  saves lives of children........226
Michillimackinac, massacre of.333
Miller, Lieut., at Estill's defeat 63
Mills, Thomas, escape of........370
Mills, Thomas, death of.........338
Moluntha, murdered.............127
Montgomery, accompanies Kenton........................97, 102
Morgan, David, combat with
  Indians..........................171

Netherland, bravery of.......... 77
Night attack upon Indians.....201
Nungany, Indian boy........... 35

Oaths picked up by Indians...102
O'Fallon, Major...................315
Ogle, Serg. Jacob, escape........364
  Capt. Joseph....................362
Oldham, Lieut. Col...............306

Paint Creek, defeat of Indians 57
Patterson, Capt., escape of...... 78
Phouts, narrow escape of.......388
Plascut, William...........243, 248

Poe, Adam..........................174
  Andrew, fight with Big Foot174
Pontiac's conspiracy.............330

Railroad from Charleston to
  Cincinnati....................... x
Reynolds, Aaron, speech........ 72
  noble conduct of............... 78
Rodgers, Major, attacked......158
Rogers, Major.....................332
Robinson and Hellen, capture.293
  life saved by Logan...........294

Sackville, adventure......257, 261
Schooner attacked by Pontiac.............................332
Shelby, Capt. Isaac..............300
Shepherd, Wm., death of........364
Sheppard, Col. David...........364
Skyles, Jac., starts for Ky.207, 232
  at Indian village..............234
Slover, John, narrative of......145
  captive with the Indians...145
  in Crawford's defeat..........145
  is captured.....................149
  saved by rain..................154
Smith, Col. James, adventures 13
  his head "picked"............ 17
  ears and nose bored.......... 17
  ducked by squaws............ 18
  narrative of.................... 44
Smith, Henry, death of.........370
Station, Baker's...................337
  Boonesborough or Boone's. 52
  Bryant's....................66, 166
  Estill's........................... 62
  Harrodsburgh or Harrod's. 52
  Hoy's............................. 65
  Kelly's, on Kenawha........207
  Logan's......................53, 54
  McAfee, attack on............166
St. Clair's, Gen. A., expedition 263
  censure of................269, 308
  treatment by Congress......270
  official letter...................303
Stoner, John................243, 248
Strader.........................89, 91
Stuart, John, captured by Indians..........................47, 48
Swearingen, Col. Andrew......367
Sweating-house of Indian...... 41
Symmes, Judge, grants *habeas
  corpus*............................351

Tecaughnetanego, chief.30, 32, 35
Theology, example of Indian. 35
Thomas 213, 214
Tobacco, Indian prayer for..... 42
Todd, Levy, death of............ 76
Todd, Rev. John.................. vii
Tomlinson, clearing of..........372
Thompson, Wm. R. as a teacher v
Tontileaugo, Indian warrior... 23
Trigg, Col........................ 76
Tucker......................243, 248
Turkey-call, used as decoy.....342

Van Metre's Fort.................368

Washington, Gen., censured...277
Washington, George, death of Indian 345
Ward, Capt. Charles..............199
Ward, Capt. James................185
  boat of, attacked 185
  attack on Indians............205
Ward, John............107, 204, 206
Warrior,Chickasaw,activity of 274
Wayne, An., incidents of..277, 278
Wetzel, Jacob, capture of........337
Wetzel, John, father of Lewis.337
  adventures of............355, 359
  escape of..................357, 358
Wetzel, John, Jr., capture of and escape.....................371
Wetzel, Lewis, adventures of................335, 340, 351

Wetzel, Lewis, character of....335
  Indian dread of................337
  capture of......................337
  kills three Indians.339,343,351
  kills a turkey-caller 342
  custom of........................342
  kills another Indian...344, 345
  captured by Harmer's men.347
  escape of 348
  released 349
  captured by Lawler..........350
  petition for release............351
  imprisoned in New Orleans 353
  reply of to Mrs. Cookis......354
  fools an Indian.................354
  death of......................... ..354
Wetzel, Martin, escape of......365
Wheeling, first siege of..........362
White woman & child rescued..383
Whittaker.....................238, 241
Wild cat, adventure with........169
Wild white man, account of...193
Williams, Isaac....................372
Wilson, Ensign, shot.............276
Worrall, Rev. John M.......xxviii
Wood, Dr........................ 92
Wood, Mrs., defense of..........180
Woods, Mrs. Hamilton.........343
Wyllys, Major, battle with Indians..........................254

Yager........................ 89
Yates, adventure of..............187

www.ingramcontent.com/pod-product-compliance
Lightning Source LLC
Chambersburg PA
CBHW051734300426
44115CB00007B/553